INSIGHT GUIDE

PORTUGAL

DISCOVERY
CHANNEL

APA PUBLICATIONS

Part of the Langenscheidt Publishing Group

ABOUT THIS BOOK

Editorial

Project Editor
Pam Barrett
Managing Editor
Emily Hatchwell
Editorial Director
Brian Bell

Distribution

UK & Ireland
GeoCenter International Ltd
The Viables Centre , Harrow Way
Basingstoke, Hants RG22 4BJ
Fax: (44) 1256-817988

United States
Langenscheidt Publishers, Inc.
46–35 54th Road, Maspeth, NY 11378
Fax: (718) 784-0640

Australia & New Zealand
Hema Maps Pty. Ltd.
24 Allgas Street, Slacks Creek 4127
Brisbane, Australia
Tel: (61) 7 3290 0322
Fax: (61) 7 3290 0478

Worldwide
APA Publications GmbH & Co.
Verlag KG (Singapore branch)
38 Joo Koon Road, Singapore 628990
Tel: (65) 865-1600
Fax: (65) 861-6438

Printing

Insight Print Services (Pte) Ltd
38 Joo Koon Road, Singapore 628990
Tel: (65) 865-1600
Fax: (65) 861-6438

©1999 APA Publications GmbH & Co.
Verlag KG (Singapore branch)
All Rights Reserved
First Edition 1992
Fourth Edition 1999

CONTACTING THE EDITORS
Although every effort is made to
provide accurate information in
this publication, we live in a
fast-changing world and would
appreciate it if readers would
call our attention to any errors or
outdated information that may
occur by writing to us at:
**Insight Guides, P.O. Box 7910,
London SE1 8WE, England.
Fax: (44 171) 403 0290.**
e-mail:
insight@apaguide.demon.co.uk

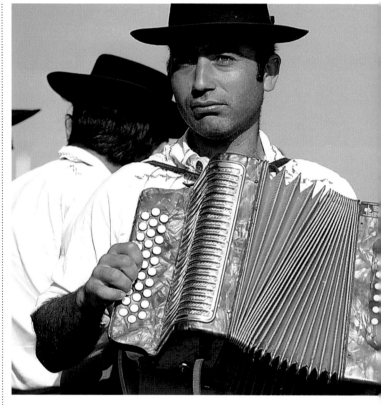

This guidebook combines the
interests and enthusiasms of
two of the world's best known
information providers: Insight
Guides, whose titles have set the
standard for visual travel guides
since 1970, and Discovery Channel, the world's premier source
of non-fiction television pro-
gramming.

The editors of Insight
Guides provide practical
advice and general under-
standing of a destination's
history, culture, institu-
tions and people. Discov-
ery Channel and its Web
site, www.discovery.com,
help millions of viewers explore
their world from the comfort of
their own home and also encour-
age them to explore it first-hand.

How to use this book

The book is carefully structured
to convey an understanding
of Portugal and its culture
and to guide readers
through its sights and
attractions:

◆ The **Features** section,
identified by a yellow bar,
covers Portugal's history
and culture in lively, auth-
oritative essays written by
specialists.

◆ The **Places** section, with a blue bar, provides full details of all the sights and areas worth seeing. The chief places of interest are coordinated by number with specially drawn maps.

◆ The **Travel Tips** listings section provides information on travel, accommodation, restaurants and other practical aspects of the country. Information may be located quickly using the index on the back cover flap, which also serves as a bookmark.

The contributors

This new edition was edited by **Pam Barrett**, building on the original book put together by **Alison Friesinger Hill**.

The history chapters were written by Harvard graduate **Thomas Hill**, while **Ruth Rosengarten** described Art and Architecture. The cuisine section was the work of **Jean Anderson**, author of *The Food of Portugal*, and **Scott Carney**, a New York wine expert contributed the chapter on wine. **Katherine Barrett Swett** wrote about travellers' accounts of their journeys to Portugal.

Sharon Behn contributed the chapters on *pousada* accommodation and on the Algarve, and **Martin Symington** wrote about the lure of Portuguese boats. Other regional chapters were written by: **Marvine Howe** (Lisbon and area); **Deborah Brammer** (Alentejo); **Jeremy Boultbee** (Trás-os-Montes; the Beiras); **Jenny Wittner** (Coimbra and surroundings); **Nigel Tisdall** (Madeira).

This edition was updated by **Brian and Eileen Anderson**, authors of several books on Portugal. They wrote a new chapter on *Natural Portugal*, and also contributed the features on *Port, Azulejos, Crafts* and *Festivals*. **Pat Underwood** updated the chapter on Madeira, and **Andreas Stieglitz** updated the Azores.

They were aided by **Paul and Denise Burton**, based in Lisbon, who took on the task of updating Travel Tips and dealt with innumerable other queries.

Many of the photographs are by **Tony Arruza** and **Bill Wassman**, who are both regular contributors to Insight Guides.

Penny Phenix proofread and indexed the book.

Map Legend

Symbol	
—— ·· —	International Boundary
— — —	Province Boundary
— · — · —	National Park/Reserve
— — — —	Ferry Route
Ⓜ	Metro
✈ ✈	Airport: International/ Regional
🚌	Bus Station
Ⓟ	Parking
❶	Tourist Information
✉	Post Office
† ⍭	Church/Ruins
†	Monastery
☪	Mosque
✡	Synagogue
🏰 ⌂	Castle/Ruins
∴	Archaeological Site
∩	Cave
𝟙	Statue/Monument
★	Place of Interest

The main places of interest in the Places section are coordinated by number with a full-colour map (e.g. ❶), and a symbol at the top of every right-hand page tells you where to find the map.

CONTENTS

Maps

Portugal **146**

Central Lisbon **154**

Lisbon **164**

Cascais, Sintra & Setúbal **176**

Sintra Vila **182**

Algarve **198**

Evora & Alentejo **216**

Evora **219**

Estremadura & Ribatejo **242**

Coimbra **256**

Side Trips from Coimbra **266**

Porto **276**

The Douro Valley **286**

Costa Verde & the Minho **300**

Trás-os-Montes **312**

Beira Alta & Beira Baixa **324**

Madeira **334**

The Azores **346**

A map of Portugal is on the inside front flap, and a map of Lisbon Transport is on the inside back flap

Introduction

Diverse, Delightful Portugal **15**

History

Decisive Dates **18**

Ancient Lusitania **21**

A Nation is Born **29**

The English Connection **34**

Empire Building **37**

The Conquerors are Conquered **47**

Revolution and Evolution **55**

Features

The Portuguese **67**

Saints, Miracles & Shrines **75**

Travellers' Tales **80**

Traditional Boats **85**

Portuguese Food **91**

Wines of Portugal **103**

The History of Architecture .. **115**

Art Through the Ages........... **123**

Pousadas and Manor Houses **128**

Natural Portugal **133**

A quiet
afternoon in
the Algarve

Insight on ...

Festivals 110
The Art of Azulejos 170
Arts and Crafts 236
The Story of Port 294

Information panels

Castles in the Air 33
Luís de Camões 45
António Salazar 61
Port Dynasties 109

Getting Acquainted **354**
Planning the Trip **355**
Practical Tips **358**
Getting Around **361**
Where to Stay **362**
Where to Eat **370**
Nightlife **373**
Great Outdoors **375**
Sport **376**
Shopping **377**
Language **378**
Further Reading **381**

◆ **Full Travel Tips index
is on page 353**

Places

Introduction 145
Lisbon 151
Estoril and Cascais 175
Sintra 181
Setúbal and the Arrábida
    Peninsula 189
Algarve 197
Evora and Alentejo 215
Estremadura and Ribatejo .. 241
Coimbra 255
Side Trips from Coimbra 265
Porto 275
The Douro Valley 285
Costa Verde and the Minho .. 299
Trás-os-Montes 311
Beira Alta and Beira Baixa 323
Madeira 333
The Azores 345

MARIA EULALIA

BARCO RABELO

FABRICA ALELUIA
=AVEIRO=

WHERE LAND ENDS AND SEA BEGINS

Portugal's diverse landscapes as well as its history and culture set it apart from the rest of Europe

Portugal is a land on the edge, "where land ends and sea begins" as the 16th-century epic poet Luís Vaz de Camões put it. At the western periphery of Europe, it is also caught between traditional living – fishing and farming – and the technology that has made the world smaller, more integrated, more complex.

It is a cosy country, encompassing an area of 92,072 sq. km (33,549 sq. miles – a bit bigger than Austria), but has a stunning diversity of lovely landscapes: long white beaches and pretty coves; ranges of rolling hills and mountains – the central Serra da Estrela ("Mountains of the Stars") being the highest; numerous rivers and, in the southern central area, Alentejo's broad plain which is patched with cork oaks and olive plantations.

Crowning Portugal's natural beauty for much of the year are blue skies and a glowing light: an agreeable climate of hot summers and chilly but never freezing winters. It's a temperate country, in mood as in weather, and its people (numbering about 10½ million) are for the most part gentle, courteous, hospitable to visitors, fatalistic and immensely tolerant.

The traveller is welcome in every corner, from the discos and *boîtes* in Lisbon, open for dancing until the early hours, to the most obscure village in Trás-os-Montes, with its simple ways of baking, spinning and farming. Sample whatever is to your taste, perhaps try a little of everything.

This guide will start you off with a lesson in Portugal's long and fascinating history, followed by a brief introduction to its people – insofar as it is possible to sum up any nation of individuals. Next, the book's features section will familiarise you with Portugal's foods and wines, its wonderful *pousada* inns and manor house accommodation, and with its glorious art and architecture. Finally, the Places section will take you on a tour of the entire country. It's a trip well worth making. ❏

PRECEDING PAGES: Porto, seen from the south bank of the Douro; the cavalry parades in Belém, Lisbon; a reluctant worker; Cup Final day.
LEFT: Portugal is famous for its tiles (*azulejos*) and its port boats (*barcos rabelos*).

1147

1227

1385

Decisive Dates

EARLY DAYS

9th–6th century BC Phoenician and Greek traders establish settlements.

5th century BC Carthaginians in control of the Iberian peninsula.

130 BC Roman conquest. Bitter fighting between them and the Lusitani, strongest indigent group, which gave the country its early name, Lusitania.

60 BC Julius Caesar makes Olisipo the western capital of the Roman Empire.

4th century AD Christianity spreads throughout the

Roman Empire. Bishoprics are established at Braga and Evora.

AD 419 The Germanic Suevi spread into Lusitania, but during the next half century are vanquished by the Visigoths.

711 Moors from Africa occupy Iberia.

718 A victory by the Christians over the Moors at Covadonga starts the reconquest.

868 Porto reconquered; Coimbra 10 years later.

883 Area between the Douro and the Minho is recognised as Portucale. Remains under Spanish control but with increasing power and autonomy.

11th–12th century A complex round of civil wars occurs as Henri of Burgundy and his cousin Raymond battle for supremacy.

RECONQUEST AND NATIONHOOD

1143 Afonso Henriques is declared first king of Portugal, but is not recognised by Pope Lucius II.

1147 Aided by Crusaders, Henri's son Afonso Henriques captures Lisbon.

1179 At the age of 70, Afonso Henriques is finally recognised by Pope Alexander III as king.

1189 Silves in Algarve is captured by Sancho I but lost again to the Moors.

1249 The Moors are finally expelled from Algarve.

1260 Afonso III is transferred capital from Coimbra to Lisbon.

1279–1325 Reign of King Dinis, great reforming king and castle builder; married Isabel of Aragón.

1297 Treaty of Alcañices with Castile establishes borders of Portugal.

1348 Plague – the Black Death – ravages Lisbon.

1355 Inês de Castro is murdered.

1373 First Anglo-Portuguese Alliance signed with John of Gaunt who had married a Spanish princess.

1385 Defeat of the Castilians at the Battle of Ajubarrota. João I becomes king and founder of the second dynasty, the House of Avis.

1386 Treaty of Windsor is signed (and remains unbroken to this day).

1387 João I marries Philippa of Lancaster, daughter of John of Gaunt.

THE AGE OF DISCOVERIES

1415 Ceuta, on north African coast, is taken by a Portuguese force including Henry the Navigator. Madeira discovered.

1427 Azores discovered.

1434 Gil Eanes discovered West African lands beyond Cape Bojador.

1460 Death of Henry the Navigator.

1481 João II comes to the throne.

1487 Bartolomeu Dias rounds the Cape of Good Hope.

1492 Around 60,000 Jews are expelled from Spain take refuge in Portugal.

1494 Treaty of Tordesillas: Portugal and Spain divide up the world.

1497–98 Explorer Vasco de Gama opens a sea route to India.

1500 Pedro Alvares Cabral discovers Brazil.

1510 Conquest of Goa establishes Asian empire.

1519–22 Ferdinand Magellan circumnavigates the globe.

1536 Holy Inquisition is introduced.

1557 Trading post is established in Macau.

1580 Portugal falls under Spanish rule. The third dynasty, the Habsburgs, commences.

WARS AND REVOLUTIONS

1640 The Spanish are overthrown; the Duke of Bragança becomes João IV, commencing the fourth dynasty, the House of Bragança.

1662 Catherine of Bragança marries England's King Charles II.

1668 Treaty of Lisbon, under which Spain recognises Portugal's independence.

1703 Methuen Treaty signed, giving England dominance in the wine industry.

early 1700s Gold is discovered in Brazil and boosts Portuguese economy.

1755 The Great Earthquake devastates Lisbon. The Marqês de Pombal, granted emergency powers by the king, sets about rebuilding Lisbon.

1777 Maria I becomes queen, Pombal dismissed.

1807 Portugal invaded by the French; royal family leave for Brazil.

1808 The Peninsular War. Portugal invokes the British Alliance. Sir Arthur Wellesley (later Duke of Wellington) leads British forces.

1820 Liberal revolution.

1822 New liberal constitution lasts only two years, but ends the Inquisition. Brazil proclaims itself independence.

1829–34 Miguelist Wars between factions led by the brothers Miguel and Pedro. The latter wins and becomes Pedro IV in 1834.

1834 Religious orders expelled from Portugal.

1834–1908 Rise of political parties, Septembrists (liberals) and Chartists (conservatives). Power alternates between them through the reigns of successive monarchs

1908 King Carlos and the Crown Prince are shot dead in Lisbon. Manuel II ascends the throne.

1910 Portugal becomes a republic; Manuel II exiled.

1910–26 A period of political turmoil, military coups and assassination.

SALAZAR AND AFTER

1926 Military coup overthrows Democratic government and brings General Carmona to power.

1928 Carmona appoints Dr António de Oliveira Salazar finance minister.

1932 Salazar becomes prime minister and rules Portugal as a dictator until 1968.

1936–39 Salazar defies League of Nations and secretly aids Franco in the Spanish Civil War.

PRECEDING PAGES: the evolution of Portugal's flag.
LEFT: Fernando, the Duke of Bragança.
RIGHT: As the venue for Expo '98, Lisbon received a boost to its ego as well as its coffers.

1939–1945 World War II: Portugal is neutral.

1955 Portugal allowed to join the UN.

1961 Angolan uprising brutally crushed.

1960s Wars in Africa continue; at home, support for them dwindles.

1966 Suspension bridge over the Rio Tejo opens.

1968 Salazar suffers a stroke.

1970 Death of Salazar. Marcelo Caetano becomes prime minister.

1974 Young Captains Revolution restores democracy to Portugal. Armed Forces Movement, founded in 1973, governs until 1976.

1975 Private banks and insurance companies nationalised; monopolies and estates taken over.

1976 Mario Soares, the leader of the socialist party, becomes prime minister. Minimum salary instituted; new constitution upholds socialism and democracy.

1979 Coalition of the right takes power.

1986 Portugal, together with Spain, becomes a member of the European Community (EC).

1987 Aníbal Cavaco Silva wins election.

1989 Revised constitution opens way to privatisation and free market.

1994 Lisbon becomes Europe's Capital of Culture.

1995 Socialist António Guterres becomes prime minister.

1998 Lisbon hosts Expo '98.

1999 Portugal joins the EU single currency. ❏

ANCIENT LUSITANIA

For centuries, successive waves of invaders swept over the peninsula. The Moors
held on longest, even after Afonso Henriques became Portugal's first king

Portugal is something of an anomaly on the map of Western Europe. It is separated from Spain, a neighbour five times its size, not so much by natural frontiers but rather by the dictates of historical destiny. Geographically, almost every region of Portugal corresponds closely to a region across the border. The northern Minho district is similar to Spanish Galicia; the southern Algarve and Alentejo districts bear a resemblance to Andalusia. The Tejo and Douro rivers and the mountains of the Beiras extend from Spain. In fact, the natural division of the Iberian peninsula would not be east from west, but north from south, separating the Atlantic culture and climate from that of the Mediterranean.

Yet Portugal, with borders already established by the 13th century, is one of the oldest nations in Europe. It has discovered and lost an empire, relinquished and regained its cherished autonomy and, since the 1974 revolution that ended decades of dictatorship, has formed new ties with former possessions.

Cultural diffusion

A rich prehistoric culture has left its traces throughout Portugal. There is evidence of the earliest stages of human evolution and a large number of megalithic sites. The variety and quantity of these finds have led many scholars to a theory that cultural diffusion came primarily from overseas. Opponents of this notion point out that most of the megalithic sites are far from the coastline. They think the population grew via natural land routes of settlement which, unsurprisingly, correspond to the paths invaders have taken throughout Portugal's history: across the Rio Minho from the north and over the Alentejo flatlands from the south.

In any case, by the 2nd millennium BC, social organisation consisted of scattered *castros* – garrisoned hilltop villages that suggest warfare between tribes. The people subsisted on goatherding and primitive agriculture, and clad themselves in woollen cloaks. Some of their constructions are still standing, for example, at the Citânia de Briteiros near Guimarães.

In the south, tribes came under the influence of Phoenician trade settlements in the 9th-

century BC, and Greek ones in the 6th-century BC, both on the coast and inland, where metals were mined. Interestingly, it is only at this late point that there is evidence of a significant fishing economy among the indigenous people. Perhaps before then the rough-hewn and storm-beaten Atlantic coast was too intimidating for their small boats. During the 5th century BC, the Carthaginians wrested control of the Iberian peninsula from these earlier traders, but lost it to the Roman Empire in the Second Punic War.

Wars of conquests

The Romans called the peninsula Hispania Ulterior. Here, as elsewhere in the empire, they

---

LEFT: Roman milestones in north Portugal.
RIGHT: prehistoric settlement at Citânia de Briteiros in the Minho region of northern Portugal.

combined their economic exploitation with cultural upheaval. They were not traders, after all, but conquerors, who set about the business of founding cities, building roads, and reorganising territories. They also implemented governmental and judicial systems.

The locals resisted. The largest and most intransigent group were the Lusitani, who lived north of the Rio Tejo (Tagus), and after whom the region was called Lusitania. Bitter guerrilla fighting was intermittent for two centuries. The most renowned rebel was a shepherd named Viriathus, who led uprisings until he was assassinated in 139 BC by three treacherous com-

linked the north and south. Lisbon became an important administrative centre, at the hub of the Romans' road network, linking all the major population centres. These centres and routes have waned in importance, but many today – most notably Lisbon – are still geographic focal points. Before their empire eventually fell, the Romans had infused the area with their language, legal systems, currency, agriculture and, eventually, with Christianity. The organisation of *latifundios* – great, landed estates – was particularly significant as it brought large-scale farming to the area for the first time.

With the conversion of the late Roman

rades who had been bribed by the Romans. It was during these wars of conquest that Roman troops are said to have refused to cross the Rio Lima, believing it to be the *Lethe*, the mythical River of Forgetfulness. Their commander, the story goes, had to cross the river alone, then call each soldier by name to prove that the dip had not affected his memory. The death of Viriathus took the heart out of the revolt, although the Lusitanian uprisings were not finally quelled until 72 BC.

From 61 BC, Julius Caesar governed the province from the capital established at Olisipo (Lisbon). Cities were established and colonised at Evora, Beja, Santarém, and elsewhere. Roads

emperors (Constantine, who issued an Edict of Tolerance in AD 331 was the first of the Christian emperors), the tenets and organisation of Christianity spread throughout the fading empire. Bishoprics were established in a number of cities, Braga and Evora among them. As the church expanded it usurped the administrative power that had been developed by the empire at the height of its strength.

Heretical Christian doctrines held sway in Portugal during the 3rd and 4th centuries. In the early 5th century various groups of barbarians occupied the land. The Alani and Vandals each settled for a short time, but by 419 the Suevi were in sole, if not steady, possession of

Galicia, and from there they conquered Lusitania and most of the Iberian peninsula. The Suevi apparently assimilated easily with the existing Hispano-Roman population, but the tide turned on them with the arrival of the Visigoths.

For the next half century, military conquest meant religious conversion. In 448, Rechiarius, the king of a diminished Suevi empire, converted to Catholicism, perhaps hoping to elicit aid from Rome in battling against the Visigoths who were nominally Christian but clung to vestiges of heretical beliefs. When Rechiarius was killed in 457, the Suevi kingdom survived, led by Masdra. In 465, Masdra's son Remismund renounced Christianity, probably hoping to appease the Visigoths. But by 550, the growing power of the Catholic Church had produced a new round of conversions, led by St Martin of Dume. The remnants of the Suevi were politically extinguished in 585.

Invaders from the south

Visigoth rule, an elective monarchy that soon bred internal dissent, was not seriously challenged until the Moors, who had arrived on the southern coast in 711, began their expansion northwards. The Moors were following the instructions of their leader, the Prophet Mohammed (who died in 632), to wage a holy war (*jihad*) against non-believers. However, like the Christian Crusades which followed (*see pages 25–26*) their advances were increasingly concerned with empire building.

The Visigoths were defeated at the Battle of Jerez, and Lisbon soon fell into Muslim hands. Southern Portugal became part of Muslim Spain, loosely organised under the Córdoba caliph – caliphs were successors of the Prophet, regional rulers created under the Umayyad dynasty (650–749).

To the Moors, this land was known as Al-Gharb (the West), from which was derived the modern name Algarve. The Moors soon ruled all Portugal, and Christianity was forced north of the Minho where it lay gathering strength for the reconquest – the *Reconquista*.

OMAR KHAYYÁM

The most famous Sufi poet was Omar Khayyám (1048–1120), whose *Rubaiyat*, in which women and wine are given mystical significance, was translated into English by the Victorian poet Edward Fitzgerald.

A nation in prospect

Stirrings of the *Reconquista* were believed to have started as early as 718 at Covadonga. Here in Asturias, the Christians defeated a small force of Moors. Galicia became a battle-ground over the next century and a half. The kings of Asturias-León made ever-increasing excursions into Galicia. Slowly, towns fell before the Christian armies: Porto in 868, Coimbra in 878, and by 955 the king of León, Ordona III, had engineered a raid on Lis-

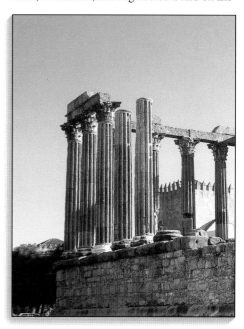

bon. Most of the victories below the Douro, however, were transient ones, amounting to nothing more than successful raids, as the territory was seldom held for more than a season or two.

Over the next decade, the overarching authority of the caliph decayed, and small kingdoms, *taifas*, took over. Decentralisation naturally led to internal dissent, partly caused by the rise of the Sufi religious sect. Sufism was considered a subversive and heretical brand of mysticism, which gained popularity in reaction to the rationalism of conventional Islamic beliefs. The significance of internal divisions was that they allowed Christian forces to push

LEFT: a sculpture found in Lisbon's Roman theatre.
RIGHT: the Temple of Diana at Evora.

the frontier lines down from the north, and also permitted radical Muslim military groups like the Almoravids and the Almohads to rise rapidly to power.

The Almoravids, who had built an empire in Africa, spread northwards. After helping the Islamic rulers to force the Christians back, they decided to take over, unifying the *taifas* under their own rule. By 1095 they had succeeded, installing an austere military system and harsh government. Worse still, they were soon followed by the still more fanatical Almohads. The simmering *Reconquista* took on the aspect of a Holy War for both Christians and Muslims.

The split with Spain

Portugal's independence from Spain has been attributed to various causes, including the indigenous megalithic groups whose borders were accepted by Rome, and the resistance that the Suevi offered to the Visigoth hordes. However, it was during the Christian reconquest of Iberia that Portugal first truly asserted its independent stance and its leaders gained their sense of national destiny.

Late in the 9th century, the area between the Lima and Douro rivers, a territory which became known as Portucale, was variously divided under the unstable feudal states. Stability came only when the province was held by one family for a century, beginning in 950. It was still under the supreme control of the Kingdom of León, but differed from León's other provinces in that the power and autonomy of Portucale were on the rise.

Fernando I of León was the great consolidating force in northern Spain during the 11th century. As part of his policy of centralising authority, he tried to dismantle Portugal, dividing it into different provinces under separate governors. When Fernando's successor Alfonso VI took the title of emperor, he ruled over the kingdoms of León, Castile, Galicia and Portugal. The title of "emperor" was a pronounced exaggeration, given the unstable ties of vassalage between the various players of the period, but it was an important claim, if only because an emperor rules over kings. Yet it may have been the lure of the title "king" that inspired Afonso Henriques, in the 12th century, to battle, deal and connive for the autonomy of his particular *terra*, Portugal.

Feuding cousins

Afonso Henriques was the son of Henri of Burgundy and his wife Teresa. Henri was among a number of French knights who had arrived in the late 11th century to fight the infidels. They were mostly second and third sons, who, under the prevailing system of male primogeniture – which meant that the eldest son inherited property and titles – were left with no real inheritance. If they wanted land and riches, they usually had to travel abroad to win them.

Henri's cousin Raymond, who, like Henri, was a fourth son, also came south. After proving his heroism in battle, Raymond married Alfonso VI's daughter Urraca, and was granted the territories of Galicia and Coimbra. When Henri married Teresa, who was Alfonso's favourite (although illegitimate) daughter, he was given the territory of Portugal. With the death of Raymond and Alfonso VI, Urraca inherited that crown, but her second marriage, to another Alfonso – this one known as Alfonso I of Aragon – also set off a complex round of civil wars. (The complexity is not made easier for the reader by the fact that most of the leading figures seem to have been called either Afonso or Alfonso.)

During this period, Henri made significant strides towards gaining autonomy for the state of Portugal. The most important of these was the support he offered to the archbishops of Braga in a dispute with those of Toledo.

In 1126 Urraca died and her son, Alfonso Raimundez, became the Emperor Alfonso VII. Henri had also died and Teresa ruled Portugal as regent for her son, Afonso Henriques. Without wasting much time in mourning, she took a Galician count, Fernão Peres, as a lover, displeasing some of the nobility and her son. Continuing Henri's policies, Teresa schemed successfully to maintain Portugal's independence, but in 1127 she submitted to Alfonso VII's dominion after her army was defeated. In 1128 the 18-year-old Afonso

cousins, wherein Alfonso VII gave Afonso Henriques the title of King of Portugal in exchange for the usual feudal ties of military aid and loyalty.

Yet Afonso Henriques sought to fix the title more firmly by seeking recognition from Rome. Pope Lucius II refused, keeping to a policy of supporting Iberian union in the hope of stemming the tide of Islam. It was only in 1179 that Pope Alexander III, in exchange for a yearly tribute and various other privileges, finally granted recognition of the Portuguese kingdom. By that late date, papal acceptance served only to formalise an entity that was not

Henriques led his first rebellion, ending his mother's rule at the battle of São Mamede, near their castle in Guimarães.

A king is crowned

Over the next decade, Afonso Henriques vied with his emperor cousin for ultimate control of Portugal. After a brilliant military victory over the Moors in the Battle of Ourique in 1139, he began to refer to himself as king. In 1143, the Treaty of Zamora was signed between the two

LEFT: Afonso Henriques, first king of Portugal.
ABOVE: an 18th-century engraving showing Afonso rallying his troops at the conquest of Lisbon in 1147.

MILITARY ORDERS

The crusades produced an unusual kind of soldier – that is, those belonging to the military orders created by St Bernard of Clairvaux in 1128. The Knights Templar was the first such order, based in Jerusalem, which had been captured in the First Crusade (1096–99). They were followed by the Knights of St John (the Hospitallers), established in Rhodes, and by the Teutonic Order and the Spanish Knights of Calatrava. Originally, their role was to fight for the true faith while obeying monastic rules of poverty, chastity and obedience. Soon, however, the spoils of war became more important for many of the knights than the spread of Christianity.

only well-established but growing. Afonso Henriques had enlisted the aid of crusaders and beaten back the Moors, adding his conquests to the emerging nation. Santarém and Lisbon were both taken in 1147; the first by surprise attack, the second in a siege that was supported by French, English, Flemish and German crusaders who were passing through Portugal on their way to the Holy Land, to fight what we now know as the Second Crusade.

The inestimable assistance of these 164 shiploads of men was extremely fortuitous; it very nearly fell through when Afonso Henriques pronounced that he expected them to

fight only for Christianity and not for earthly rewards. This was not the way the crusaders believed holy wars should be fought. The English and Germans walked out, and the king quickly compromised, offering loot and land in exchange for military service.

The western crusade

The bishop of Braga also offered aid in recruiting foreign crusaders, providing theological assurance that the enemies would be heathens, and therefore no different from those they would be fighting in the Holy Land. However, Afonso Henriques's confessor questioned the diversion of troops from the crusade, and the

story is told that on the way to Santarém – with crusaders in tow – the king, believing his confessor to be right, was besieged by guilt. He was also, understandably, anxious because of the Moorish stronghold's reputation for impregnability. To soothe his torment, he vowed that he would build an abbey at Alcobaça (some 90km/55 miles southwest of Coimbra) in the Virgin's honour if the attack was successful. The battle was won, and Afonso Henriques laid the foundation stone of the promised building the following year. The abbey still stands (*see page 247*).

Convincing crusaders that one batch of infidels was as good as another was crucial to the *Reconquista*. One result of the crusades (which began in 1096 and lasted for more than 150 years) was the founding of military-religious organisations such as the Knights Templar and the Hospitallers (*see previous page*). These orders were rewarded with land grants in exchange for chasing out the Moors, and grew wealthy and powerful – the Templars, in fact, became prestigious bankers.

In 1170, Afonso Henriques fought his last battle, at Badajoz. The powerful Almohads had enlisted the aid of Fernando II of León, who felt that the Portuguese were recapturing not only the Moorish-held land, but territory that was by right a part of León. The most renowned of Afonso Henriques's military cohorts was Geraldo Geraldes, a local adventurer dubbed O Sem Pavor ("The Fearless") for his brilliant raids into Muslim territory.

This popular hero had won a string of epic victories, but at Badajoz the combination of Moorish and Leonese forces was too much for both Geraldes and his king. The aging Afonso Henriques broke his leg and was captured. His release came only after he had surrendered hard-won castles and territories to enemy parties. His retreat allowed the Moors to entrench their forces along the battle zone.

The founding king of Portugal's days of victory were over, with the *Reconquista* still a century away. Yet, with Henriques' monarchy, a country was born. Whether it was through an act of political will or not, the independence and individuality of the Portuguese nation was forever determined. ❑

LEFT: the early crusaders, out to subdue the infidel.
RIGHT: an ancient royal coat of arms.

DOM IOAO IIIR
DE PORTVGAL

A NATION IS BORN

With the final expulsion of the Moors, Portugal steadily established
a kingdom under the House of Burgundy

For a century after the death of Afonso Henriques in 1185, the first order of business was the slow riddance of the remaining, and still feisty, Moors. The *Reconquista*, now virtually sanctioned by the Church with various papal bulls and indulgences as a "western crusade", was still very much under way.

The Knights Templar had arrived in Portugal when they stopped on their way to Palestine in 1128. They were soon followed by other military-religious orders, the Hospitallers, and the Knights of Calatrava and Santiago, who all clung to the religious justification for their warmongering and for their massive accumulation of land and loot. However, the western crusade remained controversial. In Palestine the dividing line between Christians and infidels was clearly drawn, but southern Iberia had intermingled Muslim, Christian, and Jewish people in economic, cultural and political spheres. In 1197, papal indulgences were even promised in a war against Alfonso IX of León, a Christian, though at that time an ally of the Muslims.

The war proceeded steadily, if slowly. The first kings of the Burgundian line after Afonso Henriques continued to press the borders southwards. Under Sancho II, the eastern Algarve and Alentejo were incorporated in the burgeoning nation. By 1249, during the reign of Afonso III, the western Algarve and Faro fell. By 1260 Afonso had moved the capital south from Coimbra to Lisbon. These boundaries – much like today's – were finally recognised by Castile in the Treaty of Alcañices in 1297.

Social transformation

The *Reconquista* brought Portugal fundamental social transformation. The lands of the south, having been reclaimed, now had to be populated. In order to do this, the Burgundian kings needed to balance their centralised, essentially military power with popular and financial support. The need for such support forced successive kings

to consult the *cortes*, local assemblies of nobles, clergy, and, later, mercantile classes. At the *cortes* of Leiria (1254), Afonso III conceded the right of municipal representation in taxation and other economic issues. For the most part, the *cortes* were gathered whenever the king needed to raise money. When later monarchs used trade

and their own military orders to reap great and independent profits, the *cortes* fell into disuse.

Another result of the *Reconquista*, with the expansion of properties and the need for labourers who were willing to resettle, was an increase in social mobility among the lower classes. Distinctions fell away among the various levels of serfs as farm workers became a scarcer and so more valuable commodity. Another, more general, effect was the early amalgamation of the divergent cultures of north and south. The south was a culture of tolerance, marked by refinement and urbanity, while in contrast, the northern culture had a rough arrogance, the attitude of invaders. Differences remain even today.

LEFT: King Dinis, depicted in a 17th-century screen.
RIGHT: the 13th-century cross of Sancho I.

The church rode the *Reconquista* to riches. The various military-monastic orders were granted vast areas of land in return for military assistance. Furthermore, the church and clergy were free from taxation, and were granted the right to collect their own tithes from the population. Their power was such that it soon threatened the monarchy. Afonso II was the first ruler of Portugal to defy the church by attempting to curb its voracious acquisition of property. His efforts generally failed, as did those of his successor, Sancho II, who was finally excommunicated and dethroned in 1245 for his insistence on royal prerogatives.

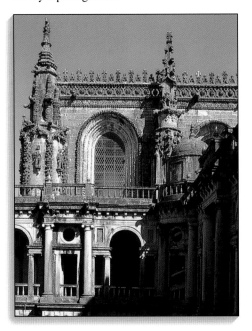

The poet king

It was the reign of Dinis, who was known both as "the farmer king" and "the poet king", that truly cemented Portuguese independence and the power of the monarchy. After briefly joining Aragon in war against Castile, Dinis ushered in a long period of peace and progress. He encouraged learning and literature, establishing the first university in 1288; initially in Lisbon, this was transferred to Coimbra. Portuguese, having distinguished itself from its Latin roots and from Castilian (which would become Spanish), was established as the language of the troubadour culture, and the official language of law and state.

The troubadour culture – poetry and music spread by peripatetic minstrels – was greatly influential. Drawing upon the French tradition and Moorish influences, the Portuguese troubadours created a native literature. These song-poems of love and satire were often written by nobles, among them, of course, Dinis the poet king, as well as Sancho I. Other forms of literary expression lagged far behind poetry.

Dinis's rule also brought political progress. Landmark agreements were made to seal peace with Castile (the Treaty of Alcañices, 1297) and the clergy (the Concordat of 1289). The latter agreement was a major victory for royal jurisdiction in matters of property. Dinis also fortified the frontier with the construction of some 50 castles.

Economic advances

By now a monetary economy was well established, internally as well as for international trade. Agricultural production was more and

THE STORY OF PEDRO AND INÊS

Betrothed to Constanza, a Spanish princess, Pedro, son of Afonso IV, fell in love with her lady-in-waiting, Inês de Castro, a member of a powerful Castilian family. She was banished in 1340, but returned upon the death of the princess in 1345. The threat of a Castilian heir was intolerable to Afonso, and, under pressure from three of his noblemen, he agreed to her assassination, then immediately withdrew consent. In 1355, taking matters into their own hands, the nobles murdered Inês in the grounds of what is now Quinta da Lágrimas (House of Tears) in Coimbra (*see page 260*).

Pedro was inconsolable. Two years later, when he assumed the throne on his father's death, he tracked down his lover's assassins, caught two of them, and had their hearts torn out. He then ordered the exhumation of Inês, who was dressed in royal robes, and placed next to him on the throne. Each member of the court was forced to pay homage by kissing her decomposed hand. She was finally entombed in Alcobaça Monastery along with Pedro, who insisted their tombs were placed foot to foot so that, on the Day of Judgment, the first thing they would see would be each other. Both tombs carry the same inscription *Até o Fim do Mundo* – "Until the End of the World".

This dramatic story of love and revenge has been an inspiration to generations of writers and poets.

more geared towards markets, although self-sufficient farming did not disappear. Dinis encouraged the expansion of the economic system with large fairs, trading centres that encouraged internal trade. Dinis was responsible for chartering 48 such fairs, more than all the other Portuguese kings combined. This concentration of trade also, not coincidentally, allowed for more systematic taxation.

FARM REFORM

In his role of "farmer king" Dinis reformed the agricultural system, and initiated programmes that encouraged the export of olive oil, grain, wine and other foodstuffs.

The only section of the economy to lag during this period was industrial production. Dinis,

wealth within the country and prevent the Church from appropriating it. In 1317 he founded the Order of Our Lord Jesus Christ, which was granted all the former possessions of the Knights Templar, under royal control.

Plagues and crises

Afonso IV succeeded Dinis. His administration was less secure, and hostilities with Castile waxed and waned. More significantly, his reign was burdened with the Black Death. The first bout devastated the country, particu-

and later kings, were counter-productive in their resistance to the idea of corporations. Craftsmen tended to work on their own, and thus confined themselves to local markets and limited quantities. Some goldsmithing, shipbuilding, and pottery was done in commercial quantities.

Perhaps the most significant of Dinis's accomplishments was the disbanding of the Knights Templar in 1312. The order was under fire throughout Europe, and its demise was imminent. Dinis's triumph was to retain its

larly the urban centres, in 1348–49. Throughout the next century the pestilence returned again and again, causing depopulation and despondency. Concurrently, various demographic and economic crises were undermining the nation. The attraction of the urban centres left the interior underpopulated, causing inflation in food prices. Monarchs tried to regulate population movements but were ineffectual. Economic stagnation, whose dreary influence extended to literature, religion, and every element of daily life, dragged on until the coming of the maritime empire.

Politics of this period were motivated largely by fear of Castilian domination. In fact, con-

LEFT: the Convento do Cristo, in Tomar.
ABOVE: the tomb of Pedro I in the monastery at Alcobaça.

tinual intermarriage between the two royal families did keep the possibility of unification open. But the Portuguese were committed to maintaining total independence, and this, coupled with general social unrest, caused turbulence for Pedro I and his son Fernando, and finally brought down the House of Burgundy.

The reign of Pedro I was marked by peaceful coexistence with Castile. Social and political growth flourished as the country recovered from the convulsions of the Black Death. But the increasing power of the nobles, the clergy and the emergent bourgeoisie, all represented in the *cortes,* would later break loose in active

social discontent during the reign of his son, Fernando I.

Fernando tried to unite Portugal and Castile under his rule, engaging the country in a series of unpopular and unsuccessful wars. France and England joined the turmoil, using the Iberian peninsula as a theatre for the Hundred Years' War. In 1373, Fernando signed an Anglo-Portuguese alliance with John of Gaunt, who had married a Spanish princess. The same year, Enrique II of Castile attacked Lisbon, burning and pillaging the city. To add to the confusion, the "Great Schism" divided the Catholic Church under opposing popes from 1378 onwards, and Fernando changed loyalties frequently. Wars ravaged the entire country, leaving the populace tired and angry.

Fernando further alienated his subjects with his unpopular marriage to Leonor Teles, who was perceived to represent the landed gentry. Riots broke out at the wedding and again in 1383 when Fernando died, leaving his widow (aided by her lover, the Galician count, João Fernandez Andeiro) to rule as Queen Mother.

Andeiro was assassinated within weeks by João, illegitimate son of Pedro I. In the ensuing civil war, Leonor had the support of most of the nobles and clergy, while João relied upon that of the middle class. He depended upon the deepening resentment the people felt towards Castile – where Leonor had fled after Andeiro's death – and rode this growing wave to victory. The final military conflict was the Battle of Aljubarrota (1385), a decisive victory for João's troops, despite being outnumbered.

The subsequent rule of João I, founder of the House of Avis, one of the military-religious orders, represented a new political beginning. The disputes with Castile continued, but they were winding down. The unsteady Anglo-Portuguese alliance was cemented by the Treaty of Windsor in 1386, a document cited as recently as World War II, when Britain invoked it to gain fuelling stations in the Azores.

João I brought stability, but the change of order was not a social revolution. New political representation was established by the mercantile class, but in time it became clear that only the names had changed. The landed aristocracy still held the real power, and the new dynasty was much like the old. ❑

THE BATTLE OF ALJUBARROTA

A number of stories surround the Battle of Aljubarrota. Nuno Alvares Pereira, captain of João's army, was ravaged by thirst when leading his forces into battle, and swore that no traveller would ever go thirsty there again. Since 1385 a pitcher of water has been placed daily in a niche of the Aljubarrota chapel of São Jorge. João, too, made a vow: to build a church in the Virgin's honour if his vastly outnumbered army was victorious. As the enemy turned tail and fled, João hurled his lance into the air to pick the spot where the monastery of Batalha would be built. He must have had a very strong arm, because the battlefield is 16 km (10 miles) from the monastery.

LEFT: a portal in João I's monastery at Batalha.

Castles in the Air

It is said that there are 101 castles in Portugal. In fact there are more, many of them either built or rebuilt between the 12th and 14th centuries. King Dinis (1279–1325) alone began the construction or expansion of more than 50 fortresses during his reign. Perhaps he should have been called "the king of the castle" along with his other titles: "the poet king" and "the farmer king". Dinis's labours can be seen throughout Portugal, but he concentrated his efforts along the eastern boundary. He strengthened the towns of Guarda, Penedo, Penamacor, Castelo Mendo, Pinhel and others, attempting to secure the area from the threat posed by Castile. He was well rewarded: the Treaty of Alcañices, signed in 1297, initiated a period of peace and stability between the neighbouring countries.

Dinis provided the money for the castles, and even specified the exact measurements of the walls and towers. Those initiated by him were of a particularly fine construction, with decorations and designs not found on other buildings. Some of the towers were slender and elegant; many balconies were elaborate, with detailed machicolations. Dinis often gave a specific character and grandeur to the structures, as in the 15 towers he had built at Numão, or the Torre do Galo ("Rooster Tower"), at Freixo de Espada à Cinta, with its beautiful and unusual seven faces.

Many castles – built by Dinis and others – were on the sites of earlier forts: Moorish, Visigothic, Roman, or even earlier. It is interesting to note the developments in warfare as they are reflected in physical features of Portugal's castles. Long wooden verandahs, for example, were attached to the castles' walls in early days. Later these verandahs were covered with animal hides to prevent, or at least inhibit, them being burned by flaming arrows, but these too were abandoned at the end of the 13th century.

By this time, the carved stone balconies were being used for defensive purposes, with machicolations which allowed the defending forces to repel attackers as they attempted to scale the castle walls. (Machicolation is the name given to a space between corbels, or in the floor of a balcony, from which boiling oil or other substances could be poured or dropped onto the enemy.)

RIGHT: the romantic island castle at Almourol.

The most significant change came with the advent of gunpowder and artillery. The heavy cannons required thicker walls, sloped to resist the more powerful projectiles. Thicker walls also meant that the ramparts, running along the tops of the walls, could be wider, and enabled the castles' heavy artillery to be perched on top. Arrow slits, a common feature in castles, were rounded to accommodate the new artillery, then abandoned as impractical.

All Portugal's castles – many still sound, some in semi-ruin – are dramatically sited. Among them are Lamego, in the Douro Valley (*see page 288*); Almourol, perhaps the most romantic of all, set on

its own tiny island in the Rio Tejo (Tagus) and the subject of many myths (*see page 242*); and, of course, Guimarães, the birthplace (*circa* 1110) of Portugal's first king, Afonso Henriques. Guimarães is one of Portugal's oldest castles, having been built in the 10th century, and restored many times since. Early in the 19th century the castle was used as a debtors' prison. It underwent extensive renovation in the 1940s (*see page 304*).

Most castles are open to visitors; some have been converted to hotels, while others stand ignored in empty fields. Solid though their construction may have been, do be careful when visiting the semi-ruined ones; it wouldn't do to end your visit under a piece of falling masonry. ❏

THE ENGLISH CONNECTION

An English queen for Portugal, military alliances, and mutually beneficial trade have all helped cement the Anglo-Portuguese relationship

I n 1147 a band of crusaders – English, German, French and Flemish – broke their Atlantic journey in Porto en route to the Holy Land (some by choice, while others may have been shipwrecked) They were persuaded by the new king of Portugal, Afonso Henriques, to join him in an expedition to seize Lisbon

from the Moors. Chronicles of the time praised the beauties of Lisbon as first seen by the British crusaders. Its fertile countryside, lush with figs and vines, epitomised the seductive pleasures of the south, and encouraged many Englishmen to settle there. The first Bishop of Lisbon, Gilbert of Hastings, was English.

The 17-week siege of the city ended in victory for the Christian forces, but this was neither the first nor last of such stopovers for the crusaders, although it was the most celebrated. Much later it became the subject of a poem by William Mickle, the 18th-century translator of Luís de Camões (*see page 45*), who is now considered Portugal's greatest poet:

The hills and lawns to English valour given
What time the Arab Moors from Spain were
*   driven,*
Before the banners of the cross subdued,
When Lisboa's towers were bathed in
*   Moorish blood*
By Gloster's Lance – Romantic days that
*   yield*
Of gallant deeds a wide luxuriant field
Dear to the Muse that loves the fairy plains
Where ancient honour wild and ardent
*   reigns.*

The Portuguese themselves had less happy memories of the crusaders from the north, whom they generally considered a loud and drunken lot, given more to piracy than to piety. But the British, with their superior numbers and martial skills, would long feel a condescending pride in their Portuguese achievement, expecting gratitude and more than a little deference from their allies to the south.

Treaties and alliances

Kingdoms were there for the taking. In 1371, John of Gaunt, Duke of Lancaster, hoped to ensure one of his own by marrying the ex-Infanta Constance, the elder of two surviving daughters of the murdered King Pedro the Cruel of Castile. Gaunt then firmly believed himself to be the rightful king of Castile. To double the family's claim to the crown, his brother married Constance's younger sister. There remained one problem, however: the incumbent king of Castile needed to be convinced. John of Gaunt enlisted the help of King Ferdinand of Portugal, and after rounds of courtship, lavish entertaining and the bestowal of favours, an alliance was signed in 1373 by which these two allies agreed to help one another against all enemies.

In 1386, with the new and youthful Dom João ascending the Portuguese throne, John of Gaunt felt the time was right to go to Castile to invoke the alliance and collect his crown. Along with his wife Constance and two daughters – 26-year-old Philippa from his first marriage, and the younger Katherine – a couple of his illegitimate children and an army, he set up court in Santiago de Compostela. The duke eventually met the king and the earlier alliance was formalised as the Treaty of Windsor. In return King João was offered the hand of the devout and virtuous Philippa. They married in Porto and the city celebrated lavishly.

The English queen

Philippa was a remarkable queen judged by any standards. By surrounding herself in court with an essentially English retinue, she encouraged merchants from England to come in pursuit of trade. Admired by the Portuguese, generous, kind, high-minded Philippa brought a virtue to the marriage which slowly transformed the king himself. João, a notorious womaniser, strayed no more and his only bastard children remained the two born before his marriage. He ended his days translating religious books.

Children were born of the marriage at regular intervals, six in all, alternately given English and Portuguese names. All five princes were highly gifted and excelled during their lifetimes. Henry, known later as Henry the Navigator, became the most famous of them all through his contribution to Portuguese exploration of the world. Philippa died of the plague in 1415, at the age of 51, and was mourned throughout the country.

Wellington rides in

Contact between these two Atlantic nations remained close. Following the period of Spanish domination of Portugal, the old alliance with England was restated, with Charles I (1642), Oliver Cromwell (1654) and finally by the Treaty of 1661, by which Charles II married Catherine of Bragança. Combined Anglo-Portuguese armies were not unusual: they were in action on a number of occasions, fighting each other's battles. The most heavily recorded is the Peninsular War in the Napoleonic era. Sir Arthur Wellesley, who became the Duke of Wellington, commanded the British troops and built the famous defensive Lines of Torres Vedras which effectively repelled the French and won the war for Portugal.

LEFT: the tomb of João I and his English queen.
RIGHT: *barcos rabelos* still bear the names of British port wine dynasties, such as Sandeman.

The wine trade

Throughout the long history of trade between these two countries, cotton and woven cloth made its way to Lisbon and Porto, but there was usually wine in the hold on the return trip. During the second half of the 17th century, more and more factors of British firms settled in Viana do Castelo, Monção and Porto, and selected the wines for shipping home. Porto soon became the main centre of the wine trade and British firms increased in number (*see page 109*). Names like Taylor, Croft, Cockburn, Symington, Sandeman and Graham became established and by the 19th century these fam-

ilies were busy buying their own *quintas* (manor houses) along the banks of the Douro.

The trade in port wine flourished through wars, civil dissent, and fierce regulation, and the British made a valuable contribution, especially through people like Baron Joseph James Forrester, who helped improve safety standards in the port, and also mapped every twist and turn of the Rio Douro, in which he eventually drowned in 1862.

Born out of mutual need, the Anglo-Portuguese friendship has been touched by romance, passion, piety, greed, hope and despair, and yet has endured more or less intact for almost a millennium. ❑

EMPIRE BUILDING

Under the House of Avis, Portugal matured as a nation. The golden age

of discoveries began, bringing untold wealth to the church and the king

João I ruled from 1385 to 1433, fending off the demands of a resurgent nobility by installing his legitimate sons Duarte, Pedro, Henry, Fernão, and João in powerful positions as the leaders of military-religious orders. (Henry the Navigator, for example, headed the wealthy Order of Christ.) It was under João I that Portugal first began to look across the seas for solutions to internal economic and political problems. Trade and exploration, it was thought, would serve both to occupy the nobility and to boost commerce.

João's successor, his eldest son, Duarte, initially continued with overseas expansion, but drew back after a disastrous failed attack on Tangiers in 1437. The following year Duarte died, precipitating a brief civil war to determine who would act as regent to his young son, who became Afonso V.

Two of Afonso's uncles were particularly trusted advisers: Henry the Navigator, who was in the forefront of exploration and conquest, and yet another Afonso, the Duke of Bragança, leader of the newly strengthened nobility. Each was granted a large share of independent power. King Afonso himself remained above the administrative fray. He was not particularly inept, but he was a chivalric leader in an era where politics had been sullied by the growing power of mercantilists and low nobility, and he was out of tune with the times. Afonso concerned himself largely with martial glory, which he found crusading in North Africa. In 1471 he took Tangiers. Another of his accomplishments was the minting of the first *cruzado,* the gold coin that became a symbol of the wealth flowing in from the voyages.

In 1475 dispute over the crown of Castile led to civil discord. Afonso decided to marry his niece, Joana, one of the claimants, and thus unite Portugal and Castile under his monarchy. He invaded in support of his wife's claims, and

occupied León, but failed to hold his ground. Defeated by the forces of Ferdinand of Aragon and Isabella of Castile, he tried to enlist the aid of King Louis XI of France in support of his claims to the Castilian throne, travelling to France to make a personal plea. He arrived in the midst of Louis XI's tumultuous rivalry with the Duke of Burgundy and proved to be a hapless diplomat, quickly alienating both sides.

Frustrated, he announced his intention of abdicating his throne to go on a pilgrimage to the Holy Land, but even this quixotic voyage was thwarted. Louis prevented him from embarking, and the despondent Afonso was sent back to his homeland. His son, the future João II, allowed Afonso to resume his nominal position, and rule was shared until the older man's death in 1481.

Overseas expansion

The 15th century was the era when overseas expansion began in earnest, but no one had any

LEFT: a Japanese screen commemorates the arrival of Portuguese traders.

RIGHT: a statue of Henry the Navigator in Lagos.

idea of the empire that was to come. The existing policy was a strange mixture of crusading ideals, romantic curiosity, and, of course, the profit motive. Charting the world was a secondary matter to João II – less important, for example, than the acquisition of spices, or the search for the odd figure who was known as Prester John.

A mythical priest and king, Prester John was supposed to have been the leader of a vast and powerful Christian empire located somewhere in the African interior. His legend was elaborated with tales of a kingdom that was an earthly paradise peopled with a bizarre

lims wherever they could be found gave the voyages all the benefits of a crusade: the effort was legitimised, and the church lent its financial resources along with spiritual support. The sanctions of Rome, like the papal bull of 1455, would become an important factor when maritime competition intensified.

Economic and social needs undoubtedly motivated the voyages. There was a shortage of gold all over Europe, and without it, coinage was severely debased and the growth of commerce retarded. Gold from Africa, America, and India eventually did find its way into the coffers of Lisbon, but it also proved to be a

menagerie of chimeras and mythical characters. Strange as it seems, this tale had an enormous influence on early exploration of Africa. In fact, in 1455, after the Portuguese had established their dominance all along the northern coast, a papal bull granted them the sole right to discovery and conquest of all Africa except those parts ruled by Prester John. It was only later, by the early 16th century, that Portugal's explorers began to realise that spice and gold were more tangible goals, and the voyages in and around Ethiopia were replaced by more profitable itineraries.

Another goal of the seafarers was the still-popular slaughter of the infidel. Attacking Mus-

debilitating obsession, diverting attention from surer if less spectacular sources of profit. These lesser goals were nevertheless an impetus for exploration from the start. Fishing ships had circled further and further out in search of more richly-stocked waters. Moroccan grain, sugar, dye-stuffs, and slaves were all highly prized. These commodities were eventually joined by the pungent spices and rare woods of India and the Orient.

Henry the Navigator

Before any exploration could begin, of course, the technical aspects of navigation had to be mastered and improved. Navigators familiar with the Pole star, dead reckoning and the compass, began to establish their position with the quadrant, the astrolabe adapted for sea use, and a simple cross-staff from which they calculated latitude. Celestial tables and so-called *portolano* charts, basic maps, became ever more detailed. Ships, too, radically changed – neatest of all was the nimble caravel, derived from the heftier cargo-carrying *caravela* of the Rio Douro. Prince Henry, who was born in Porto, would have known it well.

Henry the Navigator (as he became known) is credited with masterminding the discoveries from his school of navigation in Sagres (at Cabo de São Vicente in the Algarve) where he surrounded himself with expert astronomers and shipbuilders. His financial sponsorship and enthusiasm made him a profound influence, and the research material he assembled was unrivalled at the time (much of it contributed by his brother, Pedro, a true wanderer who sent Henry every relevant map and book he could find). But discovering the world – the Portuguese were the first Europeans to find two-thirds of it – was beyond the scope of any one man, and there must be other, unsung heroes.

With many hands at the tillers, the enterprise was not always well-coordinated. The main goal was to press the crusade forward and eventually to reconquer Jerusalem. Maps were accurate enough to suggest that there were islands in the unknown Sea of Darkness, and land beyond it, but it needed courage and determination to sail into oceans that legend had filled with fearsome monsters.

Prince Henry's primary goal was the taming of the North African coast, which meant the banishment of the Moors. He never travelled further than Morocco himself, where he had taken Ceuta in battle 1415, and gained his lifelong interest in discovery and conquest. The chronicles portray Henry devoting most of his time to squeezing profits out of his various tithes, monopolies and privileges. Only later in life, they suggest, with increasing reports of wondrous and far-off places to inspire him, did he give the discoveries his full attention. Yet he ploughed much of his profits back into the enterprises, which were a costly business, and died in debt.

LEFT: Pedro Alvares Cabral lands in Brazil.
RIGHT: the Monument of the Discoveries in Lisbon.

Epic voyages

It is easy to see why popular history might accord undue credit to an individual like Henry. The Age of Discoveries was a time for heroes and adventurers, and also a time for the rebirth of chivalric ideals. Fearless mariners sailed off into unknown realms. Their voyages were imbued with noble intentions: the greater glory of the church, the advancement of knowledge, and the benefit of their nation.

Popular history also makes unverifiable, but plausible, claims that Portuguese mariners were the first Europeans in America. Among explorers who sailed from the Azores were members

ISLAND OUTPOSTS

It was expeditions initiated by Henry the Navigator which, quite accidentally, discovered Madeira and the Azores. In 1415, two ships were blown off course, and landed on the uninhabited island which they named Madeira (meaning "wood") because it was thickly forested. The first of the nine Azores (Açores) islands was discovered a dozen years later, the others over a period of 25 years. Henry proved to be an efficient and able coloniser, introducing wheat, vines and sugar cane to Madeira, and organising the settlement of the Azores, which later became recognised ports of call for sailors en route to and from the New World.

of the Corte Real family who explored the North American coast in the 1470s. One of them, Miguel, may have been marooned there.

Perhaps the first indisputable hero of the discoveries was Gil Eanes. Madeira and the Azores, along with the north of Africa, had been charted. The islands had begun to be colonised. The fabulous tales of the edge of the world and the various horrors of the southern seas were soon connected with the stormy promontory of Cape Bojador, on the west coast of Africa. It became the boundary.

FISH FROM AFAR

The Portuguese began fishing for cod (*bacalhau*) in Newfoundland's Grand Banks shortly after Columbus's voyage of discovery. It soon became a very popular dish.

Finally, in 1434, Gil Eanes, a pilot commissioned by Henry the Navigator, broke the barrier. He found more coastline and safe waters, and returned to Portugal triumphant, bringing wild plants plucked from the land beyond. The next year he led voyages further down Africa's coast, and the way was opened for the many who followed. They searched primarily for the legendary Rio do Ouro (River of Gold). Eventually some of the precious ore was found.

In 1482, Portuguese ships explored the mouth of the Congo. Five years later, Bartolomeu Dias rounded the Cape of Good Hope. So intense did the competition between Spain and Portugal become that in 1494 papal intervention resulted in the famous Treaty of Tordesillas, which divided the newly discovered and the still unknown lands between the two countries. It granted Portugal the lands east of a line of demarcation 592 km (370 miles) west of the Azores, which put Brazil (discovered by Pedro Alvares Cabral in 1500) within Portugal's sphere. In 1497–99, Vasco da Gama sailed to Calicut (Calcutta) in India and back (with great loss of life), immediately throwing Portugal into competition with Muslim and Venetian spice traders. In 1519–22, Fernão de Magalhães (anglicised to Ferdinand Magellan), a Portuguese in the service of Spain, led the first voyage to circumnavigate the globe, although he died before it was completed.

The expeditions opened the seaways, but there were battles to be fought to establish trading posts in Africa and the Indies. Arabs, protecting their own trade interests, fought the Portuguese wherever they could. The Portuguese, of course, were still intent on eradicating such infidels from the face of the earth. So although Portugal originally had no intentions of land conquest, by simply striving to establish and maintain a monopoly of the high seas, they were constantly at war.

Colonies

The great leader of these campaigns of discovery was Governor Afonso de Albuquerque, a brilliant strategist and, in essence, the founding father of the empire in Asia. His victories allowed garrisoned ports and fortresses to be built in key locations. Goa, in India, conquered in 1510, became the centre for all operations. Malacca (now in Malaysia) fell in 1511 and served as the East Indies hub, while Ormuz came under Portuguese control in 1515, proving the ideal seat from which to dominate the Persian Gulf. Later, in 1557, Macau was established on a kind of permanent lease with China, extending Portugal's reach to the Far East.

Albuquerque administered these new holdings under a basic policy of colonisation rather than exploitation. All the major cities, Goa in particular, were converted by architecture and government into European towns. Inter-racial marriages were encouraged and Catholic missions established.

The growth of Goa was extraordinary. By 1540, there were 10,000 households of European descent and the town was the seat of a bishopric. However, these few much-changed cities and the battles of the Indies were in marked contrast to the general policy of peaceful coexistence that Portugal adopted wherever it could. In Africa, Brazil, and the various islands and archipelagos, they tried to set up trading stations without interfering with local customs or politics.

It is, however, the exceptions that proved the most interesting. In the Congo, for example, where a number of missions were established,

His son took the name Afonso, and from that point until the 17th century the land was ruled by a succession of native Henriques, Pedros, and Franciscos.

The Congo, although it provided both ivory and slaves, was not of central economic importance. The Portuguese ships were too busy reaping bounty elsewhere to pay much attention to cultural matters: spices were carried from the Indies, gold was found in the Sudan and other parts of Africa, sugar and wine were brought from Madeira, while sugar and dyestuffs came from Brazil.

The wealth reaped overseas made for a stable

the people were quite taken with their European visitors, though they could provide little of interest to the traders. The Portuguese had begun by overestimating the political and cultural sophistication of these people, and once the Congolese were exposed to certain Western practices, they embraced them rapidly. They took to Christianity, and imitated the manners and fashions of the Portuguese. Their first Christian monarch dropped the unwieldy title "Nzinga a Nkuwu" and renamed himself João I.

LEFT: Vasco da Gama stands tall in Sines.
ABOVE: Afonso de Albuquerque, painted by an unknown artist, *circa* 1509.

economy, but it did not make Portugal rich. Enterprising individuals and the monarchy – taking its royal fifth of all trade revenues – flourished, but even they eventually found it difficult to build or hold on to their fortunes.

At its beginning, the "empire" demanded little from its diminutive fatherland. Like other small trading centres in Italy and the later Dutch empire, organisation and central authority were more important than mere size. Furthermore, the early expeditions required little manpower. It was only later, when they found themselves trying to enforce the worldwide trade monopoly, that the sparseness of Portugal's population began to tell. It has also been suggested that a crucial deficiency was Portugal's lack of a middle class – quashed by royal and noble dominance of commerce – a group that might have provided qualified and educated planners, pilots and administrators.

In explaining the empire's failure, some have pointed to widespread corruption or to the foreign control of profits garnered from Portuguese expeditions. How great an effect they had is arguable. Certainly the religious efforts that went hand in hand with Portuguese voyages did not make the wheels of commerce spin any more freely. Whether fighting Muslims, or trying to force Christianity down the throats of local populations, the Portuguese wasted time and diverted their focus from the business at hand. Whatever the causes, potential benefits of the burgeoning overseas trade were not being reaped. Deflation in Europe stifled trade. Domestic agricultural production, hampered by a lack of manpower, lagged, occasionally causing serious shortages of meat and grain. Even the Crown was in debt, as the cost of the trading empire rose higher than its revenues. It was, of course, many years before these flaws and inadequacies truly sank the empire. Trade was to continue for several centuries, although it steadily deteriorated.

Domestic life

Before the slide began, the lucrative age of empire did bring sufficient peace and prosperity for Portugal to sustain truly great eras of artistic and humanist achievement. João II had taken over from his father, the unreliable Afonso V, in 1481. Revitalising the throne, he managed to take up where Henry the Navigator, who died in 1460, had left off. João turned away from the nobility, minimising their rights and calling upon the *cortes* for support. A conspiracy soon gathered against the king, but he learned of the central traitors soon enough to strike back. In 1484, the Duke of Bragança was briefly tried and beheaded. When other members of the nobility fled the country, their titles and holdings reverted to the Crown.

The Duke of Viseu, who was both cousin and brother-in-law to the king, unwisely mounted a second plot, and was stabbed by the king himself. Another group fled the country, and João II was left in full command.

THE JEWS IN PORTUGAL

As money-lenders, tax collectors, bankers, physicians and astronomers, the Jews had lived peaceably in Portugal for a thousand years or more. In 1492, when Spain had rid itself of the Moors, it was equally determined to expel the Jews. Some 60,000 were allowed to settle in Portugal.

The contribution of the Jews to the economy and progress of the country was already invaluable, and their influence was increasing. It was the Jews who opened Portugal's first printing presses, and the first 11 books published were all in Hebrew. Abraham Zacuto, astronomer and mathematician, published the *Almanach Perpetuum*, which contained tables enabling mariners to determine latitude by declination of the sun. The *Almanach* was translated into Latin and became the basis of a system used by the Portuguese for many years.

When King Manuel married Princess Isabella of Spain in 1497, he was forced as a condition of marriage to act against the Jews. Realising their value to the country, he was reluctant to expel them so he offered the option of baptism as "New Christians", with a 20-year period of grace before their faith would be tested. Many refused, and those who accepted soon found that they were not treated as equals. Prejudice and intolerance was soon to burgeon into full-scale repression as the Inquisition took hold.

The prestige and authority that these tactics bestowed on the monarchy would stand undiminished for centuries. However, João's successor, Manuel I, who came to the throne in 1495, had to find a balance between the ferocity of his predecessor and the confused idealism of Afonso V. This was accomplished through diplomatic and far-sighted administration. The estates of the noble families were largely restored, though this did not restore their political power. Judicial and tax reforms worked to bring authority to government on both the national and local levels. The postal system was instituted. Public services such as hospitals were centralised. Essentially, Manuel lifted the power of the monarchy above both the nobles and the *cortes,* launching the first era of enlightened absolutism.

The importance of education

Manuel also fostered contacts with proponents of Renaissance humanism, which was then spreading throughout Europe. There were many trading, religious and cultural contacts with Italy, in particular, and young Portuguese men began to seek education abroad, at universities in France or Spain. Manuel actually tried to buy Paris's renowned Saint Barbara College, and although he failed it became a centre for Portuguese students. By 1487 a printing press had been established in Lisbon. Portugal entered the 16th century with a rush of new cultural currents and ideas.

New colleges and educational reforms were basic elements of the new century's progress. Teaching methods were modernised and the curriculum expanded. The students were drawn from a larger pool, including aristocrats and members of the wealthy bourgeoisie, in addition to young men from the religious orders.

These changes were not without crises. The University of Lisbon had a cultural and political influence that threatened the Crown. It was difficult to impinge on its traditional autonomy, but Manuel, as part of his process of centralisation, tried to force change through economic and legal pressure.

Finding great resistance, he turned to the idea of founding a new university elsewhere, without success. João III, who came to the throne in 1521, on his father's death, continued these efforts, later giving control of national education to the Jesuits and moving the university to Coimbra, where it established its permanent home. It was a victory for the monarchy. There would be no university in Lisbon until 1911.

Nonetheless, the century inspired a broad-ranging intellectual vigour. Some of the works produced were directly attributable to the expeditions of discovery. Travel books, with both scientific and cultural themes, were a rich vein: Tomé Pires, for example, wrote *Suma Oriental* in 1550, describing his voyages to the East.

Portugal's main contributions to the intellec-

tual ferment of the Renaissance were in science, particularly in navigation, astronomy, mathematics, and geography. This was not the mere accumulation of facts from foreign places: they amounted to a kind of sceptical empiricism, a science based on experience. Having disproved a dozen theories about the shape, limits, and contours of the earth, Portuguese intellectuals felt free to question the other dogmas of antiquity.

Yet even as new writers and new sciences were emerging, a Counter-Reformation was casting a pall of religious conformism over learning and creativity (even though there had been no real Reformation in Portugal, since the

LEFT: the library at Coimbra University.
RIGHT: João III, in a portrait by Cristovão Lopes.

Portuguese Catholics felt an essential antipathy to the Germanic philosophies). In addition, the political threat to Portuguese autonomy – the future union with Spain was already an undercurrent – hung over all these academic achievements. In fact, Luís de Camões, Gil Vicente (the 16th-century father of Portuguese theatre) and many others wrote about half of their works in Castilian.

Portuguese Inquisition

João III ruled from 1521 to 1557. He continued Manuel's expansion of the trading empire and of royal authority, but his most significant

act was the establishment of the Inquisition in Portugal. The papacy knew there was no real need for it, no menaces to the unity of faith, so resisted its introduction. But João III used every diplomatic intrigue at his disposal and finally, in 1536, won approval for a greatly limited version. Eleven years later, those limitations were lifted and the power of the Inquisitors increased.

The rule of João III turned, too – away from the humanist influences of Europe and towards religious fanaticism. The power and the bureaucracy of the Inquisition expanded rapidly, its main target being the converted Jews known as New Christians. What had been intended as a

tool of the monarchy soon took on a direction and authority of its own. The Inquisitor-Generals, who took their orders from Rome, had the right of excommunication and, utilising the spectacular *autos-da-fé*, soon wielded an influence far beyond their legal authority.

The influence of the Inquisition, with its rigid orthodoxy, vengeful judiciary, and general intolerance, was equally deadening to both culture and commerce. Many of the bourgeois leaders of trade were targets. Later, the Inquisition would virtually govern Portugal, usurping the authority of the monarchy during the union with Spain.

The accession of King Sebastião in 1568, when he was 14 years old, only exacerbated the problem. His regency, from 1557–68, was a period of stability, although marked by signs of trouble to come. The Inquisition grew more powerful. The Casa da India, the national trade corporation, went into bankruptcy in 1560.

An unstable and idealistic king, with a dangerous streak of misplaced chivalry, Sebastião took upon himself a crusade against the Moors of North Africa. A lack of funds prevented him from undertaking the task for many years. In the meantime he surrounded himself with cohorts no older and no more sensible than himself, dismissing the warnings of older, more prudent statesmen. Finally sensing that the time was right, he spent every *cruzado* he could raise on mercenaries and outfitting his troops. He set sail for Morocco in 1578.

Sebastião was as bad a military leader as he was an administrator, dismissing stratagem and planning as cowardice. He refused to consider the possibility of retreat, and therefore had no plan for it. Outnumbered and outmanoeuvred at the Battle of Alcácer-Quibir, his army of 18,000 men was destroyed. Some 8,000, including Sebastião and most of Portugal's young nobility, were slaughtered. Only 100 or so escaped.

With this debilitating disaster, the way was open for Spain to step in. From 1578 to 1580, Cardinal Henrique ruled the country, occupied primarily with raising the ruinous ransoms for the captured soldiers of Alcácer-Quibir. In 1580, Philip II of Spain invaded and within a year was installed as Philip I of Portugal. ❑

Left: heretics are led to their death in an *auto-da-fé* procession.

Luís de Camões

Luís Vaz de Camões (1524–80), Portugal's greatest poet, never reaped fame or riches during his lifetime. He was born poor, and he died poor, but the life he led – of passion and adventure – enthrals the Portuguese almost as much as the epic, eloquent phrases in his works, which many people can quote at length even today.

After attending the University at Coimbra, the young poet's prospects were good. But many twists of fate lay ahead. An affair with one of the queen's ladies-in-waiting caused his banishment to North Africa, where he lost an eye in military service. Returning to Lisbon, Camões was involved in a skirmish that wounded a magistrate. He ended up in prison and then was banished again, in 1553, this time to the colony of Goa in India.

It was 1570 before he returned to Lisbon. Having written poetry and plays for many years with some success, he published *Os Lusíadas* in 1572. The poem's worth was recognised immediately, and Camões received a small royal pension. His final illness, however, was spent in a public hospital, and he was buried in a common grave.

The title *Os Lusíadas* means "The Sons of Lusus", the mythical founder of Portugal: symbolically, then, it means "the Portuguese". Echoing classical models, the poem chronicled the voyages of Vasco da Gama, before a panorama of strangely mixed Christian and pagan images.

Os Lusíadas has been hailed throughout Europe (Lope de Vega and Montesquieu were among early admirers), sometimes to the detriment of the rest of Portugal's extensive literature. Under Salazar (*see page 61*),*Os Lusíadas* became an icon of Portuguese nationalism. Speeches and propaganda were peppered with quotes from it, providing a mythos for imperialism, with no reflection on the differences between the 16th and 20th centuries.

The 18th-century verse translation by W.J. Mickle, and quoted below, though tinged with the lyrical romanticism of that era, captures the proud spirit of the poem from the opening lines:

Arms and the heroes, who from Lisbon's shore,/Thro' seas where sail was never spread before,/Beyond where Ceylon lifts her spicy breast,/And waves her woods above the watery waste,/With prowess more than human forc'd their way/To the fair kingdoms of the rising day.

In the second canto the Muslims - the "faithless race" – prepare to attack:

On shore the truthless monarch arms his bands,/And for the fleet's approach impatient stands:/That soon as anchor'd in the port they rode/Brave Gama's decks might reek with Lusian blood:/Thus weening to revenge Mozambique's fate,/And give full surfeit to the Moorish hate...

In the world of the great Portuguese discoverers, the enemy forces take their strength from the netherworld:

As when the whirlwinds, sudden bursting, bear/Th' autumnal leaves high floating through the air;/So rose the legions of th' infernal state,/Dark

Fraud, base Art, fierce Rage, and burning Hate:/Wing'd by the Furies to the Indian strand/They bend; the Demon leads the dreadful band,/And in the bosoms of the raging Moors/All their collected living strength he pours.

At Vasco da Gama's request, the chronicler aboard his ship retells Portugal's history, and, in this section, recounts the "glad assistance" brought by the crusaders who helped take Lisbon from the Moors. *Their vows were holy, and the cause the same,/To blot from Europe's shores the Moorish name./In Sancho's cause the gallant navy joins,/And royal Sylves to their force resigns./Thus sent by heaven a foreign naval band/Gave Lisboa's ramparts to the Sire's command.* ❏

RIGHT: Luís de Camões.

O DIABO COXO   O DIABO CORSO

O Gato Frances destruindo a Religião   emblemas   a Serpente e a Hyena

Como o Leaõ rugindo, e o Urso grunhindo afim o perverso Mandarim trata o pobre povo Prov. Cap. 28

...aõ das Armas de Napoleaõ q por si se fes Imperador agora o açoute d'a Europa cortando o bar.... da tranquilid. o Globo abr...

...de Inglaterra e Suecia a maõ e a daga p.ª Espanha dá a entender os seus designios por entre o fumo e devisaõ seus Estandartes

...lho o seu nacimento o Cocodrilho, a maõ sanguinolenta, o Coraçaõ negro e a Golotina, mostraõ as suas traiçoẽs e tirania

...e q mandou fazer perto de Jaffa a 800 indefezos Turcos prizioneiros.

...r envenenado os seus proprios Soldados doentes no Hospital de Jaffa.

...cutaõ do Duque Enghien.

...adre a vir á sua coroaçaõ e pondo na sua propria cabeça a coroa de ferro com huma maõ e com a outra

...reja Catholica a sua Cabeça.|| 6. a morte do Capitaõ Wright por naõ querer ser traidor á s... eu R...

THE CONQUERORS ARE CONQUERED

Portugal was under Spanish rule for 60 years, until a popular uprising against the Habsburgs put the country back in charge of its own destiny

Throughout their rule over Portugal, the Spanish Habsburg kings faced many challenges to their authority. Not the least of their problems was that King Sebastião kept rising from the grave. After the massacre at Alcácer-Quibir in 1578, a devastating blow to national pride, there arose a popular belief, known as *sebastianismo*, that the lost Portuguese king would rise again. Consequently, a number of false Sebastiãos tried and failed to reclaim the throne.

At the root of the continuation of the Iberian Union was the support provided by merchants and traders. The Netherlands and other countries were strongly challenging Portuguese shipping, slicing into vital profits. It was supposed by the bourgeoisie that by combining Spanish and Portuguese interests, the maritime empire could be reclaimed. The "alliance" with Spain would also open up inland trade. In any case, there were few options: Portugal's treasury was empty.

The three Philips

Politically, the union was accomplished by Philip II of Spain. After Alcácer-Quibir, a number of candidates had aspirations to the Portuguese throne. Though his genealogical claim was more tenuous than those of his competitors, he was the grandson of Manuel I, and a far more viable ruler than any of the others. The majority of the populace was opposed to the Spanish king, but the relatively impoverished nobles, clergy, and upper bourgeoisie saw that Philip could provide fiscal and military stability. Ironically, the most powerful group to resist the union were the Spanish ruling classes, who saw the danger of untrammelled Portuguese trading within their traditional markets.

Part of Philip's appeal was that he promised to maintain Portugal's autonomy: no Spanish representation in Portuguese legislative and judicial bodies; no change in the official language; the overseas empire would still be ruled by Portugal; no grants of Portuguese assets to non-Portuguese; and so forth. Philip took up residence in Lisbon. In 1581 he summoned the *cortes* to declare him King Philip I.

After the years of mismanaged government,

the efficient bureaucracy of the union was a relief. However, with the succession of Philip II (Philip III of Spain), the Spanish began to press their powers too far. Philip I's diplomatic savvy was lacking, relations between the two countries were bungled, and the Spanish tried to correct their mistakes through force. Resistance grew. Philip III succeeded to the throne in 1619, but the union continued to erode. Spain was weakened by its involvement in the Thirty Years' War with France. Portuguese troops were forced into battle and taxes increased.

The 60 years of union with Spain did nothing to protect Portugal's empire. Between 1620 and 1640, Ormuz, Baia, São Jorge da Mina and

LEFT: a 19th-century cartoon satirising Napoleon.
RIGHT: Antão de Almada, one of the movers and shakers of the Restoration.

many more trade centres fell. In 1630 the Dutch established themselves in Brazil; in 1638 they took Ceylon. There were still ports and territories controlled by the Portuguese traders, but the monopoly of the seas was an era quickly fading from memory. What's more, to a country that had once been intent upon ridding the earth of the last vestige of the infidels, it was devastating to surrender their missions to the Dutch, purveyors of the heretical Protestantism.

For the Portuguese, each of the three Philips

RESTORATION DAY

Restoration Day on 1 December is still celebrated in Portugal as a national holiday to commemorate the 1640 coup in Lisbon.

was worse than is predecessor. Philip II did not even deign to visit the country for years after his coronation. Philip III systematically breached all the guarantees put in place by his grandfather. The incipient revolution was aided by secret diplomatic agents sent by the French, who were still embroiled with Spain in the Thirty Years' War.

The Bragança regime

On 1 December 1640, a coup in Lisbon reflected the growing revolutionary fervour. The palace was attacked, and the reigning Spanish governor, the Duchess of Mantua, was deposed and arrested, while her strongman,

Miguel de Vasconcelos, was defenestrated. The Duke of Bragança, though he had been reluctant to lead the revolt, was declared King João IV. So began Portugal's final royal period: the House of Bragança would hold power until the 20th century.

Most of João IV's 16-year reign was occupied in hapless efforts to form diplomatic ties in Europe. France, England, Holland, and the Pope all refused to confirm Portuguese independence. Only Spain's preoccupation with other battles, some heroic Portuguese military stands along the frontier, and a well-organised national administration enabled the country to retain its restored independence.

When he ascended the throne in 1656, Afonso VI (João's son), who suffered both physical and mental handicaps, was still a minor. Later, married off to a French princess, he associated with criminal elements and, worst of all, proved to be impotent, a fact elicited from the public inquiry needed to annul his marriage. He was eventually usurped by his brother, who ruled as Pedro II.

War with Spain waxed and waned from 1640 until 1665. In 1654, a treaty of friendship and cooperation was signed with England, a useful link, but also the first step down a path that guaranteed Portugal's economic subservience to Britain for centuries to come. The alliance was sealed by the marriage of Princess Catherine to the English king, Charles II, in 1662. Included in her dowry gifts were Tangiers and Bombay. In 1661 a treaty was signed with Holland. These moves sparked a new round of battles with Spain. In 1665 a decisive Portuguese victory at Montes Claros ended the fighting and three years later, in the Treaty of Lisbon, Spain offically recognised Portugal's independence.

Pedro II became prince-regent to his brother in 1668, was officially crowned king 15 years later, and ruled until 1706. His long reign, although stable, was deeply marked by an unrelenting economic depression. The spice trade was almost entirely out of Portuguese hands, while trade in sugar and slaves went through periods of competition and crisis at a time when Portugal could ill afford such instability.

On the mainland, olive groves and vineyards offered good profits, but they were largely controlled by British interests. The Treaty of

Methuen (1703) established British dominance of the wine industry and served to stifle industrialisation in Portugal. Grain shortages were common throughout the era – perhaps because investment went into vines instead of wheat.

Two of Pedro's finance ministers, the Count of Ericeira and the Marquês of Fronteira, helped plan numerous factories. Glass, textile, iron, tile and pottery industries were all supported by the state in an effort to balance national trade deficits.

Going for gold

The mercantilist approach made some headway, but what finally dispelled the economic gloom was the discovery of gold in Brazil. But the constant stream pouring in from across the Atlantic was not invested in the infant industries, which spluttered and halted. The Count of Ericeira committed suicide, while Fronteira renounced his previous economic philosophy.

Even before gold, Brazil had offered a number of valuable commodities: sugar, cotton, and tobacco, as well as some spices and dyestuffs. The husbandry of cattle started slowly, but by the end of the 17th century was providing lucrative exports of meat and leather.

The Jesuit missionaries were extremely influential in Brazil, as both explorers and settlers. Among other things they held the brazilwood monopoly for over two decades (1625–49). More importantly, they were successful in winning over the native populace to Christianity, and in large part preventing their enslavement. But the abundant colonial economy naturally had a great need for native labour, and the Jesuits were pressured to step aside, even though they had the clear support of Rome in the form of a Papal Bull (1639) that threatened excommunication for the trading of natives.

In 1706, João V succeeded Pedro II, and began to spend the Brazilian gold with a vengeance. Taking his cue from the French court of Louis XIV, he quickly earned the nickname "The Magnanimous". Palaces, churches and monasteries were erected, and support was granted to the arts and to education. Along with this extravagance came a moral profligacy. Convents around Lisbon were converted from religious houses into aristocratic brothels. Among the royal constructions were palaces to house João's numerous bastard sons, born of various nuns.

When João died in 1750 his son José succeeded him, but he proved to be more interested in opera than in matters of state. The full power of the crown was entrusted to a diplomat, Sebastião José de Carvalho e Melo, who eventually earned the title by which he is better known: the Marquês de Pombal.

Enlightened absolutism, as typified by the ministry of Pombal, represented both a beginning and an end. The Enlightenment ideal of

rationalism meant a leap towards modernity, while the concomitant republican ideal of social equality meant royal absolutism was on its last legs. Pombal's insistence on exercising royal prerogative sounded a death knell for the political power of nobles and clergy alike, and, quite unintentionally, allowed the bourgeoisie to take over administrative and economic control. His was an oppressive, dictatorial rule, though he was careful never to claim any personal power.

The great earthquake

In 1755, on All Saints' Day – just as Mass was beginning – Lisbon was destroyed by a massive earthquake. Estimates vary, but at least

---

LEFT: Pedro II, a more effective king than his brother.
RIGHT: a scene in Lisbon harbour during the Great Earthquake of 1755.

5,000 people were killed in the initial impact, many while attending morning services. Many more died later. Fallen church candles quickly ignited the wreckage around them. Survivors rushed toward the safety of the Tejo, only to be met by a huge tidal wave.

In the subsequent weeks infected wounds, epidemics and famine increased the death toll, which may have been as high as 40,000. The Jesuits tried to fix the blame for what they saw as divine retribution upon Pombal's wayward and "atheistic" policies. He weathered both their criticism and their plot to assassinate him. The Jesuits' power throughout Europe was dis-

solving, and in 1759 they were officially disbanded and exiled from Portugal.

The catastrophe that shook the country's faith allowed Pombal's policies of secularisation and rational government to take firm hold. He took absolute control, and with the order to "close the ports, bury the dead, feed the living", began reconstruction. José granted his minister emergency powers (which were not rescinded for some 20 years) and Pombal used them to rebuild Lisbon according to a neo-classical plan, both neatly geometric and functionally sound. The social and legal distinction between "Old" and "New" Christians (the latter being Jews who had converted at the end of the 15th

century) was abolished. Pombal's economic reforms helped Portugal remain stable when Brazilian gold production waned in the middle of the century and he managed to rebuild Lisbon without depleting the treasury.

As Pombal's sponsor-king José neared the end of his reign, the Marquês plotted to force the crown-princess Maria to renounce her rights so that her son, another José, and a disciple of Pombal, could continue the policy of despotism. These efforts failed and Maria, a pious but unbalanced woman with no sympathy for Pombal's methods or rule, took over in 1777. She immediately had Pombal tried for various crimes against the state and, when convicted, confined him to his estate rather than to prison, out of deference to his age.

Though she revived religious elements in a government and culture that had become increasingly secular, Maria allowed most of Pombal's essential economic and administrative reforms to stay in place. Her reign was a conservative one, with steady, if slow, economic progress.

Both Maria's political and personal health were badly shaken by news of the French Revolution. In 1798, long after her behaviour had become an embarrassment, she was declared insane. Her son João, an awkward, nervous man, took over as regent, officially becoming king after Maria died in 1816.

The Peninsular War

The Portuguese monarchy and nobility feared that the fervour behind the French Revolution of 1789, and to a lesser extent, the American one the previous decade, might be contagious.

POMBAL'S LEGACY

Anyone visiting Lisbon should know a little about the Marquês de Pombal, in order to better appreciate the city. Under his direction, the whole of the devastated Baixa area was rebuilt in neo-classical style, laid out in an orderly grid system. The upper part of the city – the Bairro Alta and Alfama – had been spared the worst effects of the tremors. In the centre of the great Praça do Comercio he erected a statue of his king, José, astride his horse. Pombal's own statue was erected much later, high on a column in the square that bears his name, and looking out over the new city which, under his guidance, rose like a phoenix from the ashes.

They were particularly wary about possible insurgency in Brazil. In 1793, Portugal sent troops to fight revolutionary France, further aligning itself with Britain and against French-controlled Spain. In 1801, Spain invaded in the War of the Oranges. Portugal ceded various political concessions, and lost forever the town of Olivença.

In 1807, Napoleon delivered an ultimatum to Portugal, in which he demanded that Portugal declare war on Britain, and close its ports to British shipping. But Portugal could not turn on its long-term allies, and Napoleon was defied. While the royal family speedily sailed to the safety of Brazil, the French General Junot marched into Lisbon. Initially, the Portuguese government offered no resistance.

In July 1808, Britain came galloping to the rescue under the leadership of the master military tactician, Sir Arthur Wellesley (1769–1852), who became the Duke of Wellington. The Peninsular War, sometimes called the War of National Liberation, lasted two years, expelling the French, but devastating the country. Three waves of attacks were halted by Portuguese victories at Roliça, Vimeiro, Buçaco, and the famous Lines at Torres Vedras. The wars left the country in a rocky state. Since the flight of the royal family, Portugal's capital was effectively located across the ocean in Rio de Janeiro and the nation's general weakness fostered Brazil's claims for autonomy. In 1822 Brazil was declared a kingdom on an equal footing with Portugal.

The regency in Lisbon showed very little political intelligence or common sense, governing with uncoordinated despotism and completely ignoring the burgeoning democratic groundswell. The monarchy's blindness to contemporary political ideas fostered the revolution that would break out in 1820.

The British military occupation, under the leadership of Marshal William Carr Beresford (1768–1854), although necessary and sometimes appreciated, further undermined Portuguese self-determination. British control had been growing throughout the 18th century. In the 19th, it became stronger. In 1810, Portugal was forced to cede to Britain the right to trade directly with Brazil, eliminating its own role as middle-man. Portugal was taking on the aspects of a British protectorate, with William Beresford wielding virtually dictatorial control.

The liberal revolution

The roots of the liberal uprising of 1820 lay in the French Revolution, its influences disseminated by military and secret societies, especially a Masonic lodge called Sinédrio. A plot against British rule by one of these clandestine groups proved to be a catalyst. A dozen conspirators accused of plotting to assassinate Marshal Beresford in 1817 were summarily tried

and executed, a brutal reprisal which heated Portuguese resentment and fostered support for the liberal movement.

In 1820, the Spanish liberal movement won control of their government, providing further inspiration, as well as political support, for Portuguese liberal forces. When Beresford left for Brazil on a diplomatic mission to discuss the growing problem his absence sparked the Portuguese military into revolt. The uprising began in Porto, and eventually forced João VI to return from Brazil. By the time he arrived, the new constitutional ideology had gained ground. A constitution was adopted in 1822. The document was ahead of its time, with broad guar-

LEFT: the Marquês de Pombal, an enlightened despot.
RIGHT: the Duke of Wellington, who led the British troops into battle against Napoleon.

antees of individual liberties and no special prerogatives for nobles or clergy. It lasted only two years, but succeeded in ending the Inquisition.

Conspiracy and confusion

Portugal's profoundly conservative streak made the revolution a simple split between republicans and absolutists. New charters and new efforts to restore full-bodied monarchy kept the country unsettled throughout the first half of the century. In 1824, João VI resisted a conspiracy of royalist extremists led by his own wife Carlotta and his son Miguel.

João's queen was the Spanish princess Car-

chose to stay in Brazil, abdicating the Portuguese throne to his seven-year-old daughter, Maria. Pedro intended her to marry her uncle, the exiled Miguel, who would rule as regent under a moderate constitution.

Miguel had other ideas. Upon his return he abolished the constitution and invoked a counter-revolutionary *cortes* to name him king. There was considerable popular support for these moves, but enough sympathy for constitutional ideas remained for Pedro, who had abdicated power in Brazil, to return and eventually defeat his brother in the Miguelist Wars.

Pedro IV reigned until his death in 1834,

lotta Joaquina, who epitomised the old regime. She tried her best to make a Versailles of her palace at Queluz, surrounding herself with absolutists and engaging in outrageous decadence, producing children by various lovers. Her flamboyant leadership of the absolutist cause made her popular, but the failure of her conspiracy to dethrone her husband in favour of her son Miguel – who was then banished to Brazil – marked the end of her influence.

The politics of the next 50 years were endlessly complex. In 1826 João VI died, leaving the throne to Pedro, his eldest son, who was still in Brazil. After failing to unite the two kingdoms through political manoeuvres, Pedro

when his daughter, then 15, finally took the throne as Maria II. She reigned until 1853, during which time the first political parties developed. The liberals, victorious over absolutism, divided into conservatives and progressives. The Septembrists, named after their revolutionary victory in September 1836, came into power first. They initially restored the constitution of 1822, but then adopted a more moderate one. They were opposed by Chartists who took their stand, and name, from the conservative charter of 1826.

The Chartists came to the fore in 1839, when, supported by the queen and led by António da Costa Cabral, they took power. Costa Cabral's government was authoritarian, and, though it provided stability, became more and more corrupt and autocratic. In 1846 a popular uprising demanded his downfall. Maria II tried to replace him with the equally conservative Duke of Saldanha, a grandson of Pombal, and the country stood on the brink of civil war. English and Spanish intervention prevented mass violence, but resulted in Costa Cabral being returned to power. In 1851 he was (peacefully) ousted for good and Saldanha took his place.

The early period of Saldanha's rule was a period of transformation out of which came the political divisions that would exist throughout the century. Saldanha introduced a compromise that allowed his new party, Regeneração, to encompass both the old Chartists and the moderate progressives. The amendments to the constitution allowed for direct elections and an expanded electorate. A still more radical faction, initially a small group, became known first as the Históricos, and then the Progressistas.

In 1853 Maria II died in childbirth. Her husband, the German Duke Ferdinand of Saxe-Coburg-Gotha, ruled as regent until their son Pedro V, came of age in 1855. Pedro died only six years later and was succeeded by his brother, who became Luís I.

Literary Luís

The best constitutional monarchs are those who avoid politics, and the change from the meddling Maria to the literary Luís was a clear victory for the republican government. Among his other accomplishments, King Luís translated Shakespeare into Portuguese.

Arts and literature were greatly influenced by politics during this period. The energies of both liberal and conservative intellectuals were focused on rebuilding their nation. The best Portuguese prose was in essay form, the best poetry and drama was in satire, and historical writing flourished. Among the celebrated literati of the era were Alexandre Herculano (1810–77), who wrote historical fiction and a monumental history of Portugal; and the brilliantly versatile Almeida Garrett (1799–1854), best known for his drama, but also the author of poetry, novels, and essays.

The reign of Luís lasted until 1889 and was a period of relative peace. Conservatives and liberals alternated in controlling the legislature. Portugal's external affairs were more or less dictated by England, their protector under the Congress of Vienna's partitioning of small countries under major powers, in 1814–15. But Portugal was tenacious in holding on to many of its colonial claims and territories in Africa. The high expense of maintaining those colonies was a burden on the rickety national economy, but it would stand the country in good stead when the holdings finally did pay off during the 20th century. ❑

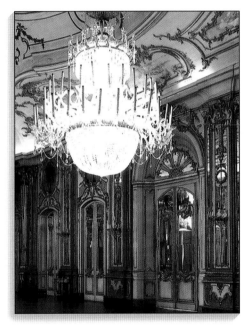

The influence of the rest of Europe on Portugal's cultural development in the 19th century was strongly felt. Intellectual conflicts were encapsulated in the "Coimbra question". Two groups of university scholars stood divided: the older group advocated the virtues of the status quo, while the "Generation of 1870", as they became known, called for revision of intellectual and spiritual values. Like their counterparts in other European countries, they were rationalist, anti-clerical, and anti-monarchist. In their writing could be heard the first strains of emerging socialism. Their daring critiques, however, were suppressed by the government in 1871.

LEFT: citizens rallied in the streets for the liberal revolution of 1820.
RIGHT: the throne room at Queluz, Carlotta's Versailles.

REVOLUTION AND EVOLUTION

Republicanism failed to restore Portugal's former glory. Political turmoil followed by dictatorship hindered growth and modernisation until the 1980s

The end of the 19th century saw Portugal's finances in complete disarray. The havoc wrought by the Peninsular and Miguelist wars, on top of the loss of Brazil, was insurmountable. In 1889, Carlos I became king, setting African expansion as his primary goal, but his efforts were unsuccessful. In 1892, Portugal declared bankruptcy.

Still dreaming of restoring the empire, Carlos could do little to defuse the growing anti-monarchical sentiment. Socialism and trade unionism were growing influences. The legislative *cortes* had degenerated into a powerless assembly that became full of obstructive and self-promoting debate. Corruption and inefficiency were rampant.

In 1906, struggling to maintain some form of control, Carlos appointed João Franco as prime minister, endowing him with dictatorial powers. He quickly dissolved the useless legislature. In 1908 unknown parties, either members of a republican secret society or isolated anti-monarchical fanatics, assassinated Carlos and his son, Luís Filipe, heir to the throne. In the assault on the royal carriage, Manuel, the king's second son, was wounded but survived.

Over the next two years Manuel II tried to save the monarchy, offering various concessions, but the assassination had fortified the republican movement. The long-decrepit House of Bragança finally crumbled to dust.

The rising tide

The rising tide of republicanism could not be stopped. The democratic ideal was combined with a nationalistic vision, a shift it was hoped would return Portugal to its long-lost glory. The national anthem adopted in 1910 echoed the theme: "Oh sea heroes, oh noble people... raise again the splendour of Portugal... may Europe claim to all the world that Portugal is not dead!"

The assassination of Carlos sealed the victory of republicanism, but it took time for the

various parties and coalitions to sort themselves into a workable government – practically speaking, they never did. Between 1910 and 1926 there were 45 different governments, with most of the changes being brought about by military intervention rather than parliamentary procedures. The early leadership pressed their radical anti-Church and social reforms too hard, causing a reaction that revived the influence of the Catholic Church. Labour movements sprang up with the best intentions, but often paralysed industry. First and foremost, the republicans were unable to deliver promised financial reforms and stability, both through their own ineptitude and, later, because of the international depression of 1920s. It was their economic failure that most significantly eroded their popular support.

Afonso Costa rose to leadership of the republican factions, but the hard stance of his anti-clericalism caused too much ill feeling to allow stability. Coups became standard. General

LEFT: the first republic was proclaimed in 1910.
RIGHT: an allegory of the 1908 elections.

Pimenta de Castro grabbed control briefly, but democratic forces deposed him. Sidónio Pais formed a dictatorial government in 1917, but was assassinated the following year.

Portugal, initially neutral, joined the Allies under Britain's influence in 1916. The motivations behind World War I meant little to the nation but cost thousands of lives, in Europe and Africa, and brought further financial upheaval and political unrest. In 1918 President Sidónio Pais was assassinated in Lisbon. Three years later, António Machado Santos suffered the same fate. In 1926, the democratic government of Bernardino Machado was overthrown

by military forces and the constitution suspended. Leadership passed through various hands and finally to General Oscar Carmona. He would remain as president until 1951, but it was not his leadership but that of his most influential appointee that made stability possible. In 1928, Carmona appointed António de Oliveira Salazar to the post of finance minister, with wide-ranging powers. By 1932, Salazar was effectively prime minister.

Salazar's New State

Salazar immediately set about reorganising the country's disastrous financial morass, mostly through the narrow-minded austerity which reflected his own character. Having achieved what no leader had been able to do for a century, Salazar used his political capital to form a dictatorship, taking Mussolini's Italy as his model for national order and discipline.

The "New State", though nominally a corporative economic system under a republican government, was a fascist regime, with the National Union its only political party. It was authoritarian, pro-Catholic, and imperialist. A state police organisation, the PIDE, was notorious in its suppression of subversion. A rigid and effective censorship settled like a thick fog over art, literature and journalism. Nothing negative or critical could find its way into print. A formerly lively journalism withered away. In blatant doublespeak, the government often referred to itself as a dictatorship without a dictator.

There was some resistance. In reaction to the powerful militaristic control of the country there were numerous attempted coups and an underground communist party that grew in power, leading the clandestine opposition. However, Salazar's leadership was never strongly challenged.

Putting self-preservation ahead of ideology, Salazar pretended to adhere to the League of Nations' non-intervention policy during the Spanish Civil War (1936–39) because he could not afford international censure, but actually sent a legion of some 20,000 soldiers to aid Franco's Nationalist forces. Franco's victory served to validate the authority of Salazar's own regime.

The republican era had seen a minor cultural resurgence, when democratic ideals encouraged efforts at mass education, a proliferation of journalism, and a few writers of modern fiction and poetry. But this was slowed by political upheavals, and effectively quelled with the advent of the New State. The greatest writer of the period, the poet Fernando Pessoa (1888–1935), had one major work, *Mensagem*, published in 1934, but it was not until after World War II that most of his works were published posthumously.

Few others transcended the romantic nationalism of the era, as formidable barriers to the larger currents of European culture were created. The censorship of the New State slowed original thinking to a trickle, and most of that was devoted to political subversion rather than artistic endeavour.

After World War II

During World War II, the New State concentrated on self-preservation. Though Salazar admired Hitler, Portugal's traditional political and economic ties with Britain demanded neutrality, at least. However, Portugal did supply the Axis with much needed wolfram (the ingredient necessary to alloy tungsten steel), almost until the end of the war. On the other hand, the Allies were granted strategic bases in the Azores. In fact, the war's main effect – though it was not widely advertised – was to replenish Portugal's coffers as the government did business with both sides.

The defeat of the fascists should have given a signal to Salazar, a warning to mute his totalitarianism, but he was by now firmly entrenched. The changes over the next decade served primarily to protect the dictatorship still further from democratic insurgency.

In the 1950s, opposition to the New State solidified into two blocs. The legal bloc took advantage of the relaxed censorship in the month preceding the 1951 elections (the state's way of giving the impression of some democratic freedom), to run independent candidates. Members of the other, furtive, bloc organised various protest actions and engaged in what propaganda they could. These means kept resistance alive, forcing Salazar's hand. Their actions provoked new rounds of repression, deceit, and constitutional changes which eroded both Salazar's authority and popularity.

In 1958, General Humberto Delgado, a disenchanted member of the regime, stood for president, announcing among other things that he would use the constitutional power of that position to dismiss Prime Minister Salazar. Despite the mass demonstrations in his support, the official count declared that Admiral Américo Tomás, a Salazar loyalist, had been elected instead. Afterwards, constitutional decrees were enacted to prevent the repetition of such an event. The president was to be elected not by popular vote, but by an electoral college of the National Assembly, which was

OPPRESSIVE TRADITION
Censorship was nothing new to a country dominated for so long by the Inquisition. In the 500-year history of publishing in Portugal, little more than 80 years have been free of censorship.

Salazar-controlled. Delgado was assassinated in 1965 by state police, while attempting to cross the Spanish border into Portugal.

The empire strikes back

Portugal's entry into the United Nations was prevented by the Soviet bloc and by opponents of Salazar's imperial colonialism, until 1955. Membership was finally granted not because of any real change, but by a successful diplomatic effort to whitewash his despotism. Salazar would not change his poli-

cies because, despite the increasing cost of maintaining military rule in the colonies, they were very profitable for the homeland. Subsistence crops were increasingly neglected in favour of products like cotton, which fed the mills of Portugal while the Africans went hungry. The policy of *assimilado* – claiming that the goal was to assimilate the ethnic culture into the Portuguese one – allowed Portugal to exploit these "citizens" as virtually free labour.

Salazar's imperial intransigence led to serious consequences in the post-war world, where the old empires were rapidly crumbling. An explosion of African nationalism was set off by the violent 1961 Angolan uprising, which was

LEFT: Salazar addresses the faithful.
RIGHT: parading military pomp in Belém at the annual anniversary of the 1974 Revolution.

brutally crushed by the Portuguese. Throughout the 1960s, the government became more and more involved in maintaining the colonies, which had been renamed "provinces" in a 1951 decree that semantically underscored the insistence on a permanent Portuguese settlement.

Meanwhile, the stagnation of Portugal's home economy grew more oppressive. Hydroelectric power projects were successful, but industry and agriculture fell farther and farther behind international standards. Emigration, a national issue for more than a century, once again began to take a serious toll on the country's demographic resources.

As many young men were conscripted for the wars in Africa, popular support waned rapidly. Angola continued to be an economic boon, but the other colonies were a drain. Salazar increasingly trusted fewer members of his regime, taking on more direct responsibilities himself for continuing the wars. He also relaxed his policy of fiscal austerity, and increasingly relied on foreign credit to finance the overseas operations.

The end of an era

In 1968, the 79-year-old dictator suffered an incapacitating stroke, and the long awaited suc-

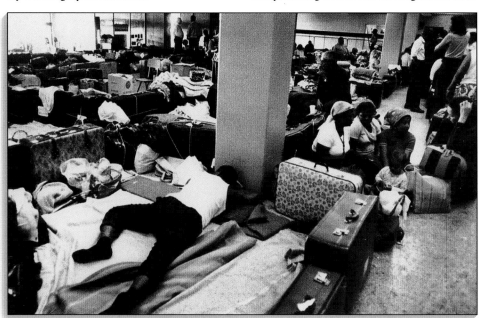

AN UNWILLING RETREAT

Despite international pressure, and increasing agitation within the colonies, Salazar's regime fiercely resisted any incursions on its colonial outposts, taking this resistance to ridiculous lengths. In 1961, the territory of São João da Ajuda, a tiny enclave surrounded by the country of Dahomey, consisted only of a decrepit fortress and the governor's estate. When Dahomey became independent from France, and delivered an ultimatum to Lisbon to return Ajuda, the Portuguese governor was forced to comply, but he waited until the last possible moment to surrender this tiny and useless sliver of territory, then spitefully burned down the buildings before departing.

cession had arrived. Because Salazar – who was unwilling to face his own mortality – had made no provision for a successor, major upheavals were expected. But the transition to power of "Acting Prime Minister" Marcelo Caetano was relatively smooth. Salazar lived his final years in seclusion and died in 1970.

Caetano, once a protégé of Salazar, had resigned seven years earlier over conflicts with his superior. Now called upon to resolve the national crisis, he saw the need for balanced change and stability, but he was not bold enough. Though many of the gravest injustices of the old regime were righted, other changes were superficial, and the colonial issue was not confronted. When his early efforts at liberalisation failed to appease opposition unrest, Caetano returned to oppressive hostility.

Discontent among all ranks of the military over the continued ineffective colonial wars led to the formation of the Armed Forces Movement (MFA) in 1973. The following year, General António de Spínola published *Portugal and the Future*, a stinging and comprehensive critique of the current situation, which recommended a military takeover to save the country. The book's messages had been voiced before, but never by so powerful a source. Many factors built towards the revolution, but this pub-

less coup began in Lisbon. Involving General Spínola and his fellow General Costa Gomes, it was conducted by angry "young captains" who commanded the 27 rebel units that seized key points throughout the city.

Caetano and other government officials took refuge in the barracks of the National Republican Guard. The formal surrender came after a young officer threatened to crash a tank through the gates. The rebel takeover was quickly accepted throughout the country. The revolution, taking the red carnation as its symbol, sparked nationwide celebration culminating in joyful demonstrations on 1 May.

lication lit the fuse. Caetano himself felt its importance, saying later that he began reading it in the late evening and "did not stop until the last page, which I read in the small hours of the morning. And when I closed the book I understood that the military coup, which I could sense had been coming, was now inevitable".

Bloodless coup

Two months later, on 25 April 1974, after a handful of premature uprisings, a near-blood-

The initial government was a National Salvation group of military men, designed to give way to a constituent assembly as soon as it was practical. A provisional government was soon in place, and negotiations with African liberation movements went ahead. There were divisions about overseas policies, and an odd coup-within-a-coup developed, with Spínola attempting to wrest control from his opponents. It was unsuccessful and liberal forces continued to divest Portugal of its colonies. Guinea-Bissau, Mozambique, the Cape Verde Islands, São Tomé and finally Angola were granted independence. One result of decolonialisation was a mass return of Portuguese nationals to

LEFT: *retornados* pour into Lisbon as the colonial wars come to an end. **ABOVE:** Prime Minister Mario Soares signs Portugal into the EC in 1988.

their homeland. As many as 500,000 people flowed into Lisbon and other urban centres.

In 1976, with the economy in dire straits, a socialist-influenced constitution was adopted, and Mário Soares, leader of the Socialist Party, was appointed prime minister. The next decade brought little stabilisation. The socialists fell in 1977, then rose again as part of a coalition government, with the Social Democratic Central Party. That too fell the next year, replaced by a government of technocrats that lasted just 17

> ### CALL TO ARMS
> One of the signals used to coordinate the coup's launch was the playing on the radio of a song called *Grândola, Vila Morena*, which became the unofficial anthem of the movement.

days. Small, powerful groups ranged the political gamut, keeping the government in turmoil. Among various short-lived governments was an interim period led by the first woman prime minister, Maria de Lurdes Pintassilgo. At the end of 1979, a coalition of the right took power.

In 1982, the long-awaited revision of the constitution arrived. The democratic alliance and the far right were determined to rid the document of its Marxist taint. They were partially successful, but only after a period of nationwide demonstrations, strikes, and resignations. The Council of the Revolution was eliminated, but the hope for a truly classless society remained an unrealised goal.

In the next few years, the country witnessed a shift away from socialism towards capitalism. Although the veteran socialist leader Mário Soares was elected president in 1986 (the first civilian to hold the post in over 60 years) and re-elected by a landslide in 1991, the capitalistic social democrats under youthful economist Aníbal Cavaco Silva, won an overall majority in July 1987. In 1991, after a campaign based largely on his own forceful personality and on his claims that his government had wrought nothing less than an economic miracle, he won another resounding electoral victory.

Joining the European club

Such stability allowed Portugal to emerge from being the most backward economy in Europe to becoming, by the early 1990s, one of the most buoyant. In 1986, it joined the European Community and in 1992 proudly took its turn at assuming the presidency of the EC.

Among Cavaco Silva's most successful programmes was the reprivatisation of many companies and industries nationalised by the communists after the revolution. These poorly managed national resources slowly began to regain vitality as private enterprises. By 1995, however, the Portuguese Socialist Party (PSP) was back, with the 46-year-old Antonio Guterres taking over as prime minister and Jorge Sampaio returned as president. But this time their policies, imposed by Guterres on an often reluctant party, put a notable emphasis on free market economics.

In 1997, the Portuguese economy met the requirements for the country to join the single currency, along with 10 other qualifying European Union states, an event which took place in January 1999. Major public works projects such as the new bridge over the Tejo in Lisbon, and the continued expansion of new roads, had already culminated in the successful hosting of Expo '98, and this, even more than monetary union, was seen by many Portuguese as the final confirmation of their country's arrival as a modern, thriving European economy, poised to meet the challenges of the new millennium. ❑

LEFT: Socialist Party leader António Guterres was elected prime minister in 1995.

Salazar

António de Oliveira Salazar (born in 1889) was a country boy who took the strict conservative values of his father far beyond the small rural world that formed them, ultimately transforming the whole nation of Portugal into his image of what it should be.

As a professor of economics at Coimbra, Salazar was an active polemicist for the right. He made his first political impact as the youthful leader of the Centro Académico da Democracia Cristã (Academic Centre for Christian Democracy), a Catholic intellectual group that opposed the anti-clerical and individualistic philosophy of the republic. He made a brief foray into national politics but only accepted a political position when he could be assured of complete control.

This came in 1928, when the prime minister, General Carmona, offered Salazar the role of finance minister with absolute power over national finance. In 1932, he was appointed President of the Council of Ministers – which was another name for prime minister. Although there was opposition, dissent, and various plots against his life, Salazar's pervasive influence on Portugal would not truly lift until the April revolution of 1974, six years after a disabling stroke, and four years after his death.

Salazar's imposed his own character upon the nation. He was austere, introverted, and he seldom travelled outside Portugal, perhaps taking pride in this as a mark of cultural purity. He steered his country through international affairs with as much neutrality as possible.

Portugal accepted Salazar's fascism as a kind of defensive posture in the face of the worldwide technological explosion of the 20th century. His conservative and at times reactionary attitudes toward industrialisation, agricultural reform, education and religion kept Portugal apart from the turbulence of the age. His attitude that Portugal was a naturally poor country – good for living in but not for producing anything – was widely held. Catholic cults, like that of Our Lady of Fátima, were encouraged and turned into propaganda for the regime.

Salazar also drew upon the romanticised history of Portuguese exploration and trade, inculcating a

---

RIGHT: at the end of his regime, Salazar's portrait adorns the cover of a biography.

generation of schoolchildren with the self-aggrandising idea of Portugal's manifest destiny as an "empire". The country turned inwards, though still holding on to its colonies for as long as possible, and tried to ignore the changing face of world politics. It was a comforting but debilitating attitude. Portugal, in the end, would be obliged to catch up.

Salazar lived quietly, taking modest vacations by the sea or in his beloved Beira countryside. He remained unmarried, though he had a close but apparently celibate relationship with his lifelong housekeeper, Dona Maria de Jesus Caetano.

On 3 August 1968, in his fortress sanctuary in Estoril, Salazar suffered from a stroke that left him

an invalid. He left no designated heir, but with surprisingly little turmoil, Marcelo Caetano, a brilliant lecturer but a rather weak politician, was made prime minister.

For the remaining two years of Salazar's life, he received few visitors and was given very little public attention. Those close to him chose not to tell him the truth about the succession of Caetano. Instead, they fabricated an image of Portugal still led by the old dictator.

When Dona Maria tried to convince him to retire, he refused and, in a last pathetic boast, claimed that he had no choice but to remain, because there was no one else. He died, aged 81, believing that he was still in control. ❑

THE PORTUGUESE

A rare passion for coffee and cakes is a national characteristic to which visitors can instantly relate. Other traits are a little more complex

Defining a national character is never easy. The Portuguese are often portrayed as easy-going, smiling, patient, good-natured but imbued with an inner *saudade*, a feeling variously defined as nostalgia or melancholy. Certainly the Portuguese offer a relaxed welcome to foreigners seeking sunny beaches, medieval architecture, the beauties of the countryside, and the local food and wines.

For the visitor in a hurry, the worst Portuguese character flaw seems to be a lack of awareness of time, although no discourtesy is intended when appointments are not kept. But the Portuguese have faced more serious criticism. Writing in the 1930s, the great modern poet Fernando Pessoa criticised their "provincialism", meaning their naively uncritical appreciation of all things "modern": big cities, new fashions, and so on.

Paul Descamps, a Frenchman writing earlier this century, isolated permissive child-rearing as a key to understanding national characteristics. This may seem a specious argument, but its conclusions make sense. Portugal is a matriarchal and child-centred society, and people who have been spoiled by their mothers learn to operate by cajolery rather than diligence, to favour patience over perseverance. Raised with a lot of personal freedom, they grow up without great self-discipline, with only a vague sense of time constraints, and with a streak of independence and an unsinkable self-esteem.

Internal differences

Generalities are great liars, however. Ten and a half million individuals live in this country, from whose ancient roots (its national boundaries are the oldest in Europe) has emerged, since the 1974 revolution, a new-born fervour. Even the tempo is changing: Portugal has been

PRECEDING PAGES: at work in the Quinta da Eira Velha, in the port wine district of Pinhão; children out for a walk in Grandola.
LEFT: a leaping dancer in the Douro valley.
RIGHT: a couple on a working day in Aldeia Solveira.

listed as having the fastest expanding economy in the European Union, growing by 2.8 percent between 1994 and 1997. Faster growth than in its European Union neighbours is, understandably, a source of pride. Perhaps more interesting to travellers is the fact that Portugal has the lowest pollution in the industrial world.

In the bucolic backways of Trás-os-Montes and the Beiras, however, among the windmills, the cobbled roads, and horse-drawn farmers' carts, you may well feel that you have stepped back in time. Rural people generally distrust Lisbon and all that it stands for: social turmoil, taxes, bureaucracy, centralised education. They would rather keep their distance. Able to sustain themselves by their harvests, they are fully aware of EU grants but have little interest in inflation or trade deficits. They are self-reliant.

In both city and country, there are ingrained social classes, but there is also a broad sense of equality. All men expect to be treated with dignity. Manners tend to be elaborate, especially in forms of address. Handshakes are exchanged at every encounter.

Women, however, are on a separate footing. Feminist ideas are only now beginning to be heard. Some urban women hold important jobs, and the lifestyle of many younger ones in the cities is similar to that of their counterparts in other European countries, but despite legal equality, attitudes are slow to change, particularly in rural areas, where most people live.

If in many ways the rhythm of Portuguese life is slow and habits cautious, this is less to do with Latin temperament or the sunny climate than with the effects of the Salazar era, which

paeans to the discoveries and to national pride. In fact, this aspect of Portuguese identity – as explorers, colonisers, a world power – lent itself to dangerous illusions during Salazar's regime. The tendency to look overseas for answers to internal woes is only now being overcome.

Work

The control of many industries was usurped by the state in 1974, and though the policies of Aníbal Cavaco Silva's social democrats (1987–95) established reprivatisation, a few remain state-owned. Unemployment, rampant in the 1970s, is relatively low, except among young

persist after some 25 years of democratic government – although this, too, is a simplification.

Helped by EC (now EU) funding, the country took a big leap forward in social commercial, industrial and communication terms in the 1980s. But stability also saw the return of a familiar indifference to the shifts and turns of policy and to sharp-suited, self-seeking politicians whose doings helped fill the daily papers and, by 1993, four television channels.

Beneath the face of contemporary life lie the proud contours that comprise Portugal's history. Camões's *Os Lusíadas* (*see page 45*) is hailed as the seminal Portuguese work not only for its beauty and literary influence, but for its

COMING HOME

Long-term emigration caused strange demographics for many years, as the very young and the old were left behind while wage-earners went abroad to work and send home wages. But about half the estimated 800,000 who worked in France, Germany and other industrialised countries have now returned. And as EU capital brought new life to the country, many professional workers – doctors, lawyers and so on – arrived from Brazil and elsewhere, bringing with them their different tastes and lifestyles. With the return of Macau to Chinese rule in 1999, many more may follow, but Portugal is a tolerant country and will no doubt assimilate its new residents.

people seeking first jobs, and the strikes which characterised the 1980s are now rare.

Well over half the population, around 65 percent, lives a rural life. In industry and commerce there are a few conglomerates; the large majority of companies are small- and medium-sized businesses employing, for the most part, fewer than 10 people; textiles and shoes are the top manufactured products.

With a long coastline, fishing remains strong. Agriculture has never been more than basically productive, despite the country's rustic image. Portugal's olive oil production, for example, just meets its own needs. Forestry is profitable

70 percent of the population living in poverty. The gross national product in 1994 was $92 billion, but had risen to $112 billion by 1997.

Family ties

Home and family life is a strong, stable framework of all Portuguese society. At the top everyone knows everyone, even across political boundaries. Families, especially in the north, tend to be large. The extended family is common, as grandparents help care for the children, and young adults – without any other housing option – often live at home until they marry.

Portugal is predominantly a Roman Catholic

(the spread of eucalyptus an ecological issue), with cork still a major harvest. Port wine from the Douro valley is among Portugal's most famous products, but table wines from many newly designated areas are reaching new peaks of quality. Tourism now contributes a high proportion of foreign earnings.

Salaries, although rising, are about a third of the European average, and despite recent growth Portugal remains near the bottom of the list of Europe's poorest countries with nearly

FAR LEFT: a carrier in Caria.
LEFT: time out for the latest gossip.
ABOVE: graduation day at the University of Coimbra.

country, with a few Protestant communities, and a few Jews and Muslims, too. One interesting group is the so-called *Marranos*, Jews who converted during the 16th- and 17th-century prosecutions, and who retain some Jewish rituals, sometimes in combination with a nominal Catholicism.

The Portuguese are sympathetic to unmarried couples living together. They adore babies and small children. They can be deeply superstitious: wax images in churches and herbalist witchery in villages are commonplace. They love a rude joke and earthy gossip. With books, cinema and the arts in general accessible only to a small minority, television is the common cultural experience. More homes in Portugal, the 1991 census revealed, have television (94.8 percent) than a refrigerator (94.2 percent). Computers are commonplace in business, and 8.4 percent of all homes had a personal computer. As there has not been a more recent census, many of these figures may have changed.

A changing society

Tolerance might be considered Portugal's prime virtue – capital punishment for civil crimes was abolished as long ago as 1867, and violent crime is rare. But behind the wheel of a car the easygoing nature turns too often to dangerous

bravado. The urge to overtake has given the Portuguese the dismal distinction of having one of the highest accident rates in Europe.

Statistics in 1991 stated that there was one car for every 6½ people in Portugal (compared with one for every 2½ people in the European Union, and one to 1½ in the United States), but this number has more than doubled since then. You will also see – and certainly hear – numerous motorbikes and under-powered, overladen scooters. Laws, in theory, forbid high levels of noise or small children on bikes. These laws are frequently ignored by traffic police, but they may well charge you steeply for not wearing the mandatory seat belt.

Traffic or judiciary police, the GNR – the National Republican Guard – continue to have a role in a peaceful society. Uniforms that are disappearing are those of the military, but in 1996 there were still nearly 50,000 members of the armed forces. Compulsory service, still applicable, is being reduced, in many cases to periods of only four months. Women have for some time been welcomed in all three forces, including the air force, whose pilots have publicly yearned for the better pay of civil airlines.

Education has been thoroughly modernised. Pre-school is an option for 3- to 6-year-olds, while there is free compulsory education for children between the ages of 6 to 15. Competition to enter university has become intense as secondary school graduates have increased in recent years. A major issue in this volatile generation is a qualifying entry exam that many consider unrelated to their years of study. Adult literacy stands at about 85 percent, but is much lower in remote inland areas.

Infinite variety

To the Portuguese, their nation is an entity calling for a proper patriotism. Their *terra*, or homeland, is the place they truly love. A Lisboeta cannot believe there is a city more beautiful than lovely, hilly Lisbon. The citizens of Porto dote on their own granite city on the banks of the Douro.

The country displays surprising variations from region to region and quite distinctly between north and south. There are also some physical differences in the people: in the north the basic Iberian strain – dark, thick-set – has been leavened with Celtic blood, while in the south, Jewish, Moorish and African ancestors are evident. The north is generally more conservative, both politically and culturally, and is the bastion of Portuguese Catholicism. The south has a tradition of liberalism and adaptation. The two temperaments – the warm Mediterranean and cool Atlantic – wash over each other. The people are as varied as their land. There is a saying that "Coimbra studies while Braga prays, Porto works while Lisbon plays". Nothing is that simple, but it is true that travelling here unveils not only a beautiful landscape but a rich panorama of humanity. ❏

LEFT: Portuguese children have a lot of freedom.
RIGHT: all dressed up for a Viana do Castelo festival.

SAINTS, MIRACLES AND SHRINES

Religion in Portugal touches all aspects of life. Every town and village has its own saint, which is a cause for celebration at least once a year

In the middle of the 6th century a young monk named Martin arrived in Mondoñedo, in northwest Spain, where he founded the abbey of Dume. His mission then took him to Braga, the former Roman city that had become the political and religious stronghold of the Suevi, a barbarian tribe that had adopted Arianism, a heretical form of Christianity. Martin, who had been inspired at the shrine of St Martin at Tours, was determined to convert their leaders to true Christianity.

In 559, he succeeded in converting the Suevi king, Theodomirus. Within the next decade, Martin was appointed archbishop of Braga. He found a further challenge, however, among the general population. Although they had been Catholics since their conversion under the Roman Empire, the people had incorporated many local beliefs and customs into their religion. To Martin, this amalgam was unacceptable, and in a written sermon entitled *De Correctione Rusticorum* (*On the Correction of Peasants*), he called for an end to the use of charms, auguries and divination, of the invocation of the devil, and of the cults of the dead, of fountains and stars.

In this St Martin did not succeed, nor have 14 centuries of similarly inclined zealots and reformers. All these unorthodox elements are present to this day as an obstinate strain within Catholic traditions.

Naturally, there is still much wrestling over these issues between the church hierarchy and the parishes. The bishops have banned a certain Padre Miguel, a priest from an isolated northern mountain parish who was supposed to have healing powers. Yet, though frowned upon by the orthodox church, spontaneous, independent Catholicism should not be seen as a form of superstition or magic; rather, it is evidence of a vigorous religious tradition.

PRECEDING PAGES: the shrine of Fátima draws thousands of pilgrims and worshippers.
LEFT: a Good Friday procession in Braga.
RIGHT: kissing the crucifix on Easter Sunday.

What are some of these still-current beliefs? When a newborn child proves healthy, it is said that it was conceived when the moon was waxing. The states of the moon are believed to be very influential in the way all living things grow – vegetables, animals and human beings. Similarly, certain fountains are reputed to have

particular healing powers. And under many of these, Moorish princesses are said to be hiding, watching over treasures.

A variety of beliefs function to reassure people during the most frightening moments of the human life cycle. For instance, many practices have evolved that are meant to protect children as they gestate in their mothers' wombs, or just after they are born. Thus, to protect it against the "evil air" a newborn should not be taken out of the house during certain hours; its father's trousers should be placed over the cot to frighten away witches; and the mother should not eat at the same time as she is breast-feeding, or the child may grow up to be greedy.

Around midnight

One of the more dramatic folk practices is the Midnight Baptism. This happens when a pregnant woman is prone to miscarriages or when her previous child was stillborn. The "baptism" takes place at midnight in the middle of a bridge that divides two municipalities – a powerful spot that is neither one place nor another, at the moment that is neither one day nor the next. Certain bridges, such as the Ponte da Barca in the Minho, are famous for this.

When everything is ready, the child's father and a friend, armed with sticks, stand guard at the ends of the bridge. They are there to ward returned to the church, it is a symbol of the new life shared by the whole community.

Similarly, on All Saints' Day and All Souls' Day (1 and 2 November), the celebrations at the parish cemetery are attended by everyone. Lamps are lit, tombs are cleaned and decorated with flowers. The whole parish celebrates this strongly felt sense of continuity with the past, praying together for their dead.

Perhaps the strongest evidence that the feeling of community extends beyond this life is the common belief in the "procession of the dead". Certain people claim that they have the power to hear or see a procession of the ghosts

off cats and dogs – which may be witches or the devil in disguise. The first person who passes after the church bells strike midnight must perform the rite. He or she pours river water over the expectant mother's belly and baptises the child "in the name of the Father, the Son and the Holy Ghost..." but the final "Amen" must not be uttered. This must wait until the child is born and properly baptised by a priest in church.

The church is the central meeting place of the whole parish. At Easter, the cross that represents the resurrection of Christ is taken from the church and carried to all the households. It is kissed as it enters each house, and when it is of those parishioners who have recently died. This procession is seen leaving the cemetery, with a coffin in its centre. When it returns, the ghost of the parishioner who will be the next to die will be in the coffin. Thus these seers predict how many people are going to die imminently – but they cannot reveal the names if they themselves want to remain alive.

Patron saints

The use of religion to establish a communal identity is most clearly shown by the celebrations for the local patron saint. An organising committee busies itself all year collecting money, planning decorations, arranging events.

The importance of these celebrations is immense. They represent and solidify local pride. The *festa* is a joyful occasion heralded by firecrackers and by music blaring from loudspeakers placed on the church tower. The pivotal event is the procession after Mass, when the image of the patron saint is carried with great pomp on a brightly decorated stand in a traditional, roughly circular path.

After that, the secular celebrations begin. These usually involve dancing to traditional brass bands, folk-dance groups and, nowadays, rock and pop bands. A great deal of wine is consumed and the festivities are a focus for young people, who use these opportunities as social mixers. Not surprisingly, it is this aspect of the celebration that some priests oppose.

Popular attitudes to saints differ from church doctrine not so much in content as in emphasis. The people place great importance on material benefits and personal, reciprocal relationships with saints. They pray to specific saints for specific problems – St Lawrence if they have a toothache, St Brás if suffering from a sore throat, St Christopher when going on a journey. Our Lady of the Conception, naturally, helps with problems of infertility, and the Holy Family is asked to intervene in family problems, and so on. People will also address personal prayers to particular saints. If the believer's prayer is answered, this proves that the particular image is a singularly sacred one, a favoured line of communication. In this way shrines develop, whether individual, family, or even national, with images famous for their miraculous powers.

The notion of the miracle in popular religion is also more loosely interpreted than in the church. Essentially, a miracle is considered to have taken place every time a specific prayer is answered. The believer must then "pay" the saint whatever he or she had promised.

Wax offerings

When a prayer to St Anthony asks for a specific favour – that a loved one, or even a pig or sheep, recover from a bout of ill health, or an offer of marriage be accepted – a promise is made to give the saint something in return. A wax heart might be given for a successful engagement, or a wax pig if the animal has fully recovered. If the promise is not fulfilled, punishment may follow.

If you visit churches in northern Portugal, you will often see these *ex voto* offerings hanging on the walls alongside other gifts such as bridal dresses, photographs, written testimonies or braids of women's hair. Shrines of great importance such as Bom Jesus and Sameiro, near Braga, have large displays. At Fátima, the best known shrine in the country, wax gifts accumulate so quickly that special furnaces have been installed to burn them.

OUR LADY OF FATIMA

Fátima, near the town of Leiria, is one of the largest shrines in Western Europe (*see page 244*). On 13 May 1917, the Virgin is supposed to have appeared to three children (two of them died young; the third, a Carmelite nun, was still re-affirming her vision in the 1990s). The event is said to have been repeated on the 13th of the subsequent five months, and each time the Virgin spoke about peace in the world. Fátima soon became a rallying point for the revival of Catholicism in the 1930s and 1940s. Today, from May to October the roads around Leiria are lined with pilgrims, many of whom have come great distances on foot to "pay" the Virgin for her favours.

LEFT: lighting candles for the dead, All Saints' Day.
RIGHT: St Anthony, Lisbon's unofficial patron saint, is celebrated in the streets of the capital in June.

There is also another kind of gift: a personal sacrifice. Recently, the church has been strongly critical of this, but until the late 1960s, it was strongly encouraged. If you visit the shrine of São Bento da Porta Aberta (St Benedict of the Open Door), in the beautiful mountain landscape of Gerês near the dam of Caniçada on 13 August, you will find men and women laboriously circumambulating the church on their knees.

This scene is even more striking because these people are surrounded by others celebrating the day with singing, dancing, eating and drinking. But those on their knees are cel-

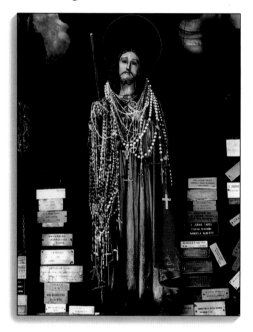

ebrating, too – because the saint has answered their prayers.

Another kind of payment to patron saints has all but disappeared due to strong church opposition. In the parish of Senhora da Aparecida in Lousada, for example, before the main procession leaves the church there is another one in which 20 or more open coffins – containing living people, their faces covered with white handkerchiefs – are carried through the streets. Those who ride in the coffins are offering a false burial to the saint who saved them from having to participate in a real one. The occasion, therefore, is a joyful one, although it sounds macabre. There is plenty of light-hearted banter, and the

participants mingle with the other parishioners afterwards, drinking and dancing.

Cults and compromises

The cult of the dead, another morbid religious tradition, and one of the targets of St Martin during the 6th century, remains an object of popular fascination today in northern Portugal. Very occasionally, a body is buried but does not undergo the normal process of decay. Such people are often considered to be saints. There are a number of such grim shrines where the corpses are exposed. The Church nearly always opposes these cults at first, but eventually tolerates them as they grow in popularity – three such are the Infanta Santa Mafalda in Arouca, the São Torcato near Guimarães, or the Santinha de Arcozelo near Porto. Even in an unlikely spot like the small urban cemetery of the elegant neighbourhood of Foz in Porto, a shrine to one of these "saints" can be found.

Along rural roads one will frequently find pretty little shrines, but these are intended to protect travellers, and are not connected with the cult of the dead. They contain images of Christ or the Virgin or a popular saint. At the base, little moulded flames surround figures which represent the souls of sinners suspended in Purgatory.

Portuguese history is full of examples of the continuing conflict between the spontaneous and all-embracing religiosity of the less educated classes, and the more restrictive attitudes of the theologically-minded – and the ways in which the two have learned to coexist. From the early days of the Western Crusade in the 12th century, and the power of military-religious orders like the Knights Templar and the Hospitallers, to the dark days of the Inquisition, religious and secular authorities have vied with each other for power, and used each other to the best advantage. Imperialism, like the early exploration and discoveries, was seen as a form of religious crusade: each victory along the way was considered a miracle. And Salazar's regime actively encouraged the cult of Our Lady of Fátima, even managing to present its policy of neutrality during World War II as being based on the soothsayings of the Virgin. ❑

LEFT: plaques affixed by grateful supplicants.
RIGHT: a floral offering to the Virgin in Lamego's Cathedral.

TRAVELLERS' TALES

There were some distinguished names among early visitors to Portugal,

and they left with some strong impressions

English visitors to Portugal have long believed themselves to be discoverers of the one exotic land left in well-visited, well-described Europe. In 1845, Dorothy Quillinan, daughter of William Wordsworth, wrote, "There is, I believe, no country in Europe that is less thoroughly familiar to me". A century

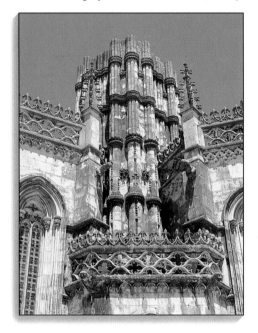

later, Evelyn Waugh thought it was still a well-kept secret, and wrote: "There is no European capital of antiquity about which one hears so little". But English travellers have been going to Portugal, and writing about it, for some time.

Eighteenth-century opinions

The most flamboyant of the 18th-century visitors to Portugal was William Beckford, who set up a sumptuous house in Ramalhoa near Sintra in 1787. He inspired Byron's *Childe Harold*, whose first stop on his pilgrimage to Portugal was to wander through Sintra conjuring Beckford's ghost and meditating on the brevity of life and pleasure.

Beckford first visited the peninsula in 1787, shortly after the publication of his Gothic novel *Vathek*. The unorthodox Englishman, who had left England in the wake of a homosexual scandal, caught the fancy of the pious Marquis of Marialva, who hoped to convert Beckford to Catholicism. But Beckford, as we learn from his diary, was desperate not for the salvation of his soul but for an introduction to the court of Queen Maria. England's ambassador Sir Hugh Walpole refused to perform this service for his disgraced countryman. The Marquis guaranteed an introduction if Beckford would convert, but the writer had no such intention and he left, petulant and thwarted. By the time he was finally presented at court in 1794, poor Maria had long been insane.

Beckford's *Sketches of Spain and Portugal* give an idiosyncratic, slighty bitchy but sensitive view of Portugal's art, music, nature and society. Beckford's is a land of the senses: he describes the *modinha*, a haunting, erotic song, and the luxuriant beauty of the vegetation. His journals provide a brilliant, if haphazard guide to Portugal's art and climate.

On his first visit to Portugal in 1796, Robert Southey, a Romantic and the future English Poet Laureate, expressed disapproval of the filth of Lisbon, the discomfort of the country inns, and the corruption and superstition of the priests. But on a subsequent visit, four years later, although he still mourned the lack of "genial company", he fell in love with the country, and delighted in the sensual orange groves, long lazy days and lush, fertile fields.

William Mickle, the 18th-century poet and translator of Luís Camões' works, was an unqualified admirer of Portugal's "genial clime" and contrasted the "gloomy mists" of England to the "sun-basked scenes... where orange bowers invite".

Lord Byron

These writers offer a pleasant alternative to the vitriolic portrait of Portugal left by the 19th century's great promoter of European travel,

George Gordon, Lord Byron. The poet left two accounts of Portugal, neither favourable: one in his letters home during his visit there in 1809, the other in Childe Harold's pilgrimage, *Canto I*. His hatred for the Portuguese has mystified and disturbed scholars and admirers of Portugal since the latter work first appeared in print in 1812. There is no record of any encounter during his brief stay there that would have led to such dislike. The most likely explanation for his anger is that the Portuguese felt resentful rather than grateful to the British for their help in expelling the French invader, "Gaul's locust host", from their country during Napoleon's Iberian campaign. Byron, like many of his countrymen, may also have been ashamed that at the Congress of Sintra, Arthur Wellesley (later the Duke of Wellington) allowed the defeated French to carry off their booty, including many of Portugal's treasures.

Some of Byron's criticisms reveal a typical Anglo-Saxon ambivalence toward the south, but while he admired the southern spirit in Italy, Spain or southern France, his image of Lisbon is of a faithless harlot of a town, a siren who glitters beautifully from the water but who reveals, on closer contact, only filth and treachery:

> But whoso entereth within this town,
> That, sheening far, celestial seems to be,
> Disconsolate will wander up and down,
> Mid many things unsightly to strange see;
> For hut and palace show like filthily...
> Poor paltry slaves! yet born midst noblest
>   scenes.

Borrow's travels

That ingratitude of the Portuguese towards their northern liberators is testified to by another Englishman, George Borrow. Travelling in 1835, on a mission for the Bible Society, he complains that the English "who have never been at war with Portugal, who have fought for its independence on land and sea, and always with success, who have forced themselves by a treaty of commerce to drink its coarse and filthy wines... are the most unpopular people who visit Portugal." But, unlike Byron, Borrow attributed this not to the Portuguese nature but to "corrupt and unregenerate man".

LEFT: Batalha Monastery, which inspired William Beckford in the 18th century.
RIGHT: Lord Byron, no great admirer of Portugal.

Borrow's account of Portugal, less famous than Byron's stanzas, is an original, entertaining and evocative description. He is a great reporter of human eccentricity, and is also enthusiastic about the beauties of Portugal. Lisbon, he claims, "is quite as much deserving the attention of the artist as even Rome itself". Sintra, which captivated all travellers and was praised lavishly even by Byron, is "a mingled scene of fairy beauty, artificial elegance, savage grandeur, domes, turrets, enormous trees, flowers, and waterfalls, such as is met with nowhere else under the sun". It is truly, Borrow writes, "Portuguese Paradise". ❑

SPEAKING TO THE NATIVES

George Borrow is a wonderfully comic traveller, erratic and egoistical, and nothing like as pious as one would expect of a Bible Society missionary. His self-confidence is typified by his belief that after just two weeks he could speak fluent Portuguese. He refused to accept that much of the time people could not understand what he was saying, and his advice to novices speaking a foreign language offers the sort of wrong-headed lesson that some tourists seem to take to heart even today.

"Those who wish to make themselves understood by a foreigner in his own language should speak with much noise and vociferation, opening their mouths wide."

TRADITIONAL BOATS

Portugal's colourful boats used to be vital to the country's wine, weed and fishing industries, but most are now used for sport and pleasure

On his return to Lisbon after discovering the sea route to India in 1498, Vasco da Gama proclaimed "*Somos a gente do mar*" ("We are the people of the sea"). Using small, light, high-prowed caravel sailing ships based on an ancient Mediterranean design, 15th-and 16th-century Portuguese explorers voyaged the world and Portugal became the greatest maritime nation on earth.

A generation later Portugal lost its superior position and driftwood was all that was left of the caravels. Nevertheless, the numerous seafaring traditions which history had thrust on the country were still in place. And as Portugal retreated into centuries of introspection, some of the boat-building techniques and traditions left by ancient mariners were absorbed in the rivers and inland waterways.

Port boats

Best known are the flat-bottomed, square-rigged *barcos rabelos*, familiar to anybody who has ever visited Porto. A flotilla of them lines the quayside of the Rio Douro at Vila Nova de Gaia opposite the city, their sails emblazoned with the motifs of the port-wine firms whose warehouses are scattered around the wharfs. The boats have become a symbol of the product with whose destiny they have been entwined for hundreds of years.

Not always appreciated are the similarities in design with Viking longships which sailed along the Portuguese coast from the 9th to the 11th century on their way to the Mediterranean. In traditional *barco rabelo* building the hull's shell is laid first, then the ribs are placed. This is the Nordic "clinker building" method which may be a direct Viking legacy. A comparison between the bare hull of a *rabelo*, and that of a reconstructed longboat in Oslo's Viking Museum, shows striking similarities.

PRECEDING PAGES: sailing boats in a realistic mural. **LEFT:** the port of Lisbon painted in the 1940s by José Almada Negreiros, one of Portugal's greatest 20th-century artists. **RIGHT:** racing *moliceiros*.

Other features of the *rabelo*'s design evolved in the early 17th century, the nascent period of the trade in port wine. Ever since then the grapes for the fortified wine have been grown in the upper reaches of the Douro valley from where it is transported to Vila Nova de Gaia for shipment abroad. The adapted indigenous boats

of the Douro were constructed in large numbers and put to this use on the treacherous river, stacked with casks or "pipes" of wine. Flat bottoms were needed to shoot the rapids, negotiate the shallows, and also to achieve high loading ratios. A tall platform at the stern gave the helmsman a clear view over the rows of pipes and a huge steering oar, or *espadela* – effectively a rudder – was needed to change course rapidly. The rudder also had to be capable of being levered out of the water to avoid smashing in the rapids and rocky shallows. Intrepid boatmen slept and ate on board, suspending cauldrons from a beam and boiling their traditional dishes of pungent *bacalhau* (dried cod).

Racing *rabelos*

The damming of the Douro for hydroelectric power brought to an end the era of the *rabelo's* interdependence with the port trade. Or so it seemed. Although for nearly 30 years port has made the journey down from the Upper Douro by road, the *rabelo* has proved to be an irrepressible symbol of the product. Boats are still constructed, at great expense, to compete in the annual race of *rabelos* owned by the various port-shipping firms. The regatta, enthusiastically contested but without much store set by winning or losing, is held on 24 June – the festival of São João (St John the Baptist and

sq. ft) of sail billowing in the wind, and need at least a dozen crew members. Payloads are up to 65 pipes, each one holding 522 litres of port.

The São João regatta provides proof that the boats are more than simply advertisements for the wares of their owners.

Weed boats

Fewer visitors to Portugal come across the *moliceiro*, another craft of ancient ancestry which has been adapted for specific commercial use. *Moliceiros* are the seaweed-gathering boats of the Ria de Aveiro, a great lagoon which is linked to the Atlantic by a narrow breach in

Porto's patron saint) when the city erupts in revelry. The boats set off from the mouth of the Douro, with the race climaxing at the double-decker Dom Luís I bridge.

What *is* taken absolutely seriously is the set of rules ensuring that the *rabelos* are constructed precisely according to the specifications evolved during their heyday. The craft have to be built in boatyards along the banks of the Douro, with the hull constructed from maritime pine, forests of which cloak the north coast of Portugal, and laid down by the shell-first "clinker building" technique. The largest *rabelos* are around 24 metres (80 ft) long by 5.5 metres (18 ft) wide with 80 sq. metres (860

the dunes and spreads over the misty, marshy wetlands of the Beira Litoral province.

The seaweed, or *moliço*, which grows in profusion along the shallow bed of the Ria, is used as fertiliser on the fields of the Beiras. The high curling "swan-neck" prows of the *moliceiros* emerge soundlessly from the marshes, where the stillness is broken only by the splash of a flock of waterfowl, or by a boatman's cry.

Moliceiros are 10–15 metres (33–50 ft) long, and usually crewed by two men. At the stern is a vast rudder operated by means of ropes, and at the centre a mast on which a white, trapezoidal sail of about 24 sq. metres (260 sq. ft) is rigged. Hefty oars are also kept on board, but when the boat is becalmed or in reeds, a punting pole is preferred. Boatmen stand on the prow, which is painted with motifs of flowers, saints, bulls, or mythical heroes, and thrust the wooden pole into the mud which is never far from the surface, deftly propelling the boat through the reeds. The weed is scraped from the floor of the lagoon by multi-pronged rakes known as *ancinhos*, and deposited on the bottom of the boat. The harvest is then taken ashore to be dried and sold to farmers.

have arch-shaped hulls built to ride the Atlantic swell. Designs vary, but typically the boats are about 5 metres (16 ft) long with their prows tapering up to a peak. A common motif is the pair of eyes painted on to the bows to ward off evil spirits, similar to those found on fishing boats in Malta.

Traineiras, the wooden trawlers based in Portugal's major fishing ports, also have a long pedigree. These are deep-sea fishing boats which for centuries have voyaged to distant waters in search of cod which, dried,

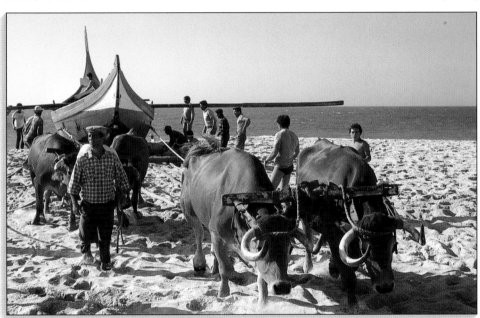

The number of *moliceiros* has dwindled. In the first half of the century over 1,000 worked the Ria, but artificial fertilisers have largely replaced *moliço*, leaving only enough demand to sustain a handful of working *moliceiros*.

Off-shore

More high-prowed boats are found on the beaches of Praia da Mira west of Ria, and along the coast of the Beira Litoral and Estremadura. Instead of having flat bottoms and sails, these off-shore fishing boats are driven by oars, and

becomes *bacalhau*. Some believe that *traineiras* from Cascais reached America in 1482, and that it was thanks to the ensuing rumours that Christopher Columbus made his discovery a decade later. Today's *traineiras* are 10–25 metres (32–80 ft) long and are fitted with diesel engines. Those going great distances have radios and radar, too, but most stick to Portugal's coastal waters.

You may see the lights of the *traineiras* on the horizon at dusk, or you might be on the quayside as a boat returns with its catch. Pull out a 50-escudo coin, minted with the emblem of a caravel, and you might notice the similarity between the two vessels. ❏

LEFT: the gaily painted boats are a source of pride.
ABOVE: hauling a *traineira* home.

PORTUGUESE FOOD

If you like fresh fish, succulent pork and hearty soups, laced with plenty of garlic, you'll find Portuguese food to your taste

To dine in Portugal is to taste the presence of other countries, other cuisines. It is to conjure up images of empire: Brazil, Angola, Mozambique, Goa – these and others all belonged to Portugal once. In a manner of speaking, each helped to stir the pot.

The period of Portuguese empire, when this small nation reached out across the terrifying "Green Sea of Darkness", as the Atlantic was called, has long passed. Yet Portugal, left with only the Azores and Madeira (Macau became independent in 1999), has preserved the flavours of other cultures in its cooking.

Prince Henry the Navigator, less than 30 years old when he began to promote exploration, was a true scientist in an age of superstition. He ordered his explorers to bring back from new lands not only riches and wild tales, but also fruits, nuts and plants. In 1420 he sent settlers to colonise the newly discovered island of Madeira. With them went plants he believed would thrive in Madeira's volcanic soil and subtropical climate, including grapevines from Crete and sugar cane from Sicily. Even more significant for Portuguese cooking was Vasco da Gama's discovery of the sea route to the east in 1497–98, only five years after Christopher Columbus's discovery of the West Indies.

Spices of the orient

Black pepper was what Vasco da Gama sought, but cinnamon, which he also found in Calcutta, would soon become equally precious to Portuguese cooks. Indeed, one boatload of cinnamon sticks fetched enough money to pay for an entire expedition to India. Cinnamon is perhaps the most beloved spice in Portugal today, certainly for the famous egg sweets (*doces de ovos*). Spaniards, on the other hand, prefer vanilla for their puddings and flans. There's good reason for this: it was the Spaniards who

found Montezuma sipping vanilla-spiked hot chocolate in Mexico and learned the trick of curing vanilla beans, the seed pods of a wild orchid. Perhaps this is why chocolate, too, is more popular in Spain than in Portugal.

The Portuguese fondness for curry powder is another legacy of Vasco da Gama's voyages.

In the beginning, only the rich and the royal could afford the precious yellow powder, which pepped up even the blandest dish, and also retarded spoilage.

Today, curry powder can be found in *supermercados* everywhere. Its function, rather than to set food afire, is to mellow and marry the other ingredients, and add a muskiness to a large repertoire of soups and stews. The spiciest Portuguese dishes, incidentally, are not found on the mainland but in the Azores and Madeira. These islands were ports-of-call for the early navigators, who would barter with the natives – offering spices in exchange for fresh fruits, vegetables, meat, and the local brew.

PRECEDING PAGES: an elegant place to eat – at the Hotel Palace Buçaco, near Coimbra.
LEFT: the colourful market in Funchal, Madeira.
RIGHT: Portuguese sardines are plump and succulent.

New food for old

During Portugal's lavish Age of Empire, its navigators became couriers, bringing New World foods to the Old and vice-versa. Mediterranean sugar cane, for example, was cultivated in Brazil. Brazilian pineapples were introduced to the Azores, a colony established under Prince Henry. They still flourish there in hothouses, ripening under wafting wood-smoke. Azorean pineapples, chunky, honey-sweet and tender to the core, are teamed today with rosettes of Por-

> ### A CUP OF CHAR
>
> The Portuguese word for tea – *chá* – is almost identical to the Cantonese one – *ch'a* – from which comes the colloquial English term "char".

were African coffee, transplanted to Brazil, which today produces about half of the world's supply; Brazilian cashews, which landed in both Africa and India; and Oriental tea plants, which were taken to the Azores.

All this fetching and carrying of seeds, leaves, barks, roots, stems, stalks and cuttings by Portuguese explorers across oceans and continents dramatically affected Portuguese cooking. New World tomatoes and potatoes came to Portugal about the same time as they did to Spain, in the 16th

tugal's mahogany-hued, air-cured *presunto* (prosciutto-like ham) and served as an elegant appetiser in fashionable Lisbon restaurants.

Tiny, incendiary Brazilian chili peppers took root in Angola, another important Portuguese colony, early on, and became so essential to cooks there that today they're known by their African name, *piri-piri*. Since Angola ceased to be a Portuguese colony in the mid-1970s and the subsequent influx to Lisbon of thousands of Angolan refugees, *piri-piri* sauce (an oil and vinegar mixture strewn with minced chilies) is as popular a table condiment in mainland Portugal as salt and pepper.

Other exchanges, thanks to the Portuguese,

century. Portuguese cooks might drop a few garlic cloves into the soup or stew along with the tomatoes and potatoes, or tuck in a stick of cinnamon.

A la Portugaise

It's unlikely that anyone grows nuttier, earthier potatoes today than the Portuguese. Indeed, along the New England coast in the United States, where so many Portuguese families have settled, there's an old saying: "If you want your potatoes to grow, you must speak to them in Portuguese." Tomatoes respond to the Portuguese touch, too, and those harvested in the vast Alentejo province, east of Lisbon, are as juicy, red and tasty as any on earth. Not for nothing does the phrase found on French menus, *"à la Portugaise"*, mean a dish that is richly sauced with tomatoes.

Onions and garlic, indispensable to any respectable Portuguese cook, were probably introduced by the Romans, who established colonies in Portugal. The Romans are believed to have brought wheat here, too. They aimed to make the Iberian peninsula the granary of Rome. They also probably introduced olives (a major source of income today), and grapes. From shards found in Alentejo, it is known that the Romans were making wine there as early as the 2nd century AD.

The Moors, who occupied a large chunk of Portugal from the early 8th to the mid-13th centuries, enriched the pot even more than the Romans. The southern provinces were the Moorish stronghold – the Algarve and Alentejo, in particular – and many traces of North Africa can still be seen.

It was the Arabs who dug irrigation ditches, who first planted rice (it now grows up and down the west coast), and who also covered the Algarve slopes with almond trees. The Algarve's almonds were ground into paste, sweetened, and shaped into delicate miniature fruits, birds and flowers displaying intricate detail, which are still produced today.

The Moors also introduced figs and apricots to the Algarve, together with the trick of drying them in the sun. They planted groves of lemons and oranges and, as was their custom, they combined fish with fruit and fruit with meat.

It was the Arabs who invented the *cataplana*, a hinged metal pan, a sort of primitive pressure-cooker shaped like an oversize clam shell that can be clamped shut and set on a quick fire. The food inside – fish, shellfish, chicken, vegetables or a medley of them all – steam to supreme succulence. What goes into a *cataplana* depends on the whim of the cook (and on what's available), but the most famous recipe is *amêijoas na cataplana,* clams tossed with rounds of sausage and cubes of ham in an intensely garlicky tomato sauce. This unlikely pork and shellfish combination was supposedly created at the time of the Inquisition as a test of

true Christianity. Pork and shellfish, of course, were forbidden to Jews and Muslims alike.

There is no shortage of examples of Portugal's culinary ingenuity. Thrifty Portuguese cooks with an eye on their *escudos* made bread a main course by layering yeast dough into a pan with snippets of chicken and sausage and two kinds of ham – a classic from the remote northern Trás-os-Montes which is called *folar.* And when times were hard they would crumble yesterday's bread into shrimp cooking water and come up with the Estremadura favourite, known as *açorda de mariscos.* Less economical but equally inventive is the Serra da Estrela

recipe which involves braising duck with bacon and rice; or smothering red mullet, the Setúbal way, with tiny tart oranges; or scrambling flakes of salt cod with eggs and shoestring potatoes, as is done all over the country.

Cod country

Dried salt cod, or *bacalhau* (pronounced buckle-yow), is a purely Portuguese invention. António M. Bello, first president of Portugal's gastronomic society, wrote in his *Culinária Portuguesa,* published in Lisbon in 1936, that the Portuguese were fishing Newfoundland's Grand Banks for cod within just a few years of Columbus's discovery of America.

FAR LEFT: sausages spice up many soups and stews.
LEFT: chilis and garlic are essential ingredients.
ABOVE: *bacalhau à Gomes de sá,* a classic dish.

The cod-fishing continues today, with the men putting to sea in spring and not returning until autumn. Sometimes, of course, they do not return; to see their widows dressed in black, some of them barely 20 years old, is to understand why so many of Portugal's poems, stories, folk sayings, and *fado* songs focus on the nation's bittersweet seafaring tradition:

> *O waves from the salty sea,*
> *From whence comes your salt?*
> *From the tears shed on the*
> *Beaches of Portugal.*

It was in the 16th century that Portuguese fishermen learned to salt cod at sea to last the long voyage home, and to sun-dry it into board-stiff slabs that could be kept for months then soaked in cool water before cooking.

Cod is still sun-dried on racks in the old way on the beach at Nazaré, although much less of it is available now. The Grand Banks have become so over-fished that the Portuguese have taken to importing *bacalhau* from Norway just to be able to meet their annual demands. This of course prices salt cod – once an inexpensive staple of the national diet – beyond the reach of the very people it sustained for centuries.

Someone once said that the Portuguese live on dreams and subsist on salt cod. They do

SARDINE SEASON

Nearly as popular as salt cod are the sardines netted off the Atlantic coast. These are what the fishermen of Nazaré go out looking for day after day – although the men are less likely now to wear their traditional tartan, and the flat-bottomed boats have mostly given way to motorised craft. Portuguese sardines are considered the sweetest and fattest in the world, and local women grill them right on the streets in every town and village, using little terracotta braziers. But you will only see this going on in spring, summer and early autumn, the "sardine season". As every right-minded Portuguese knows, sardines are too bony to eat from November to April.

claim to know 365 ways to prepare it, one for each day of the year. The best and most famous dishes are *bacalhau à Gomes de sá* (cod cooked in a casserole with thinly sliced potatoes and onions, garnished with hard-boiled eggs and black olives), *bacalhau à brás* and *bacalhau dourado* (two similar recipes composed of scrambled eggs, onions and shoestring potatoes), *bacalhau à Conde de Guarda* (salt cod creamed with mashed potatoes) and *bolinhos de bacalhau* (cod fish balls, a very popular hors d'oeuvre). All these once-humble recipes are served today in the most expensive restaurants. Prepared properly they are delicious but if too little care is taken they can be very salty.

King carne

If salt cod and sardines share top billing as the favourite fish, pork reigns supreme as the king of *carne* (meat). Portuguese pork is incomparably sweet and tender because of the pigs' agreeable diet and life of leisure. In the northerly Trás-os-Montes province, they say that if you want good pork in the autumn you must feed your pigs twice a day in August. Some farm women even go so far as to cook potatoes for their animals.

Small wonder the hams *(presunto* and *fiambre)* and sausages *(salsichas)* are so highly prized here (the best of all are said to come

with baby clams, still in the shell. The clams open slowly under the gentle heat, spilling their briny juices into the ambrosial red mixture. The secret behind achieving the distinctive nut-like flavour of Alentejo pork is that the pigs are turned loose each autumn to forage in the cork orchards. Here they are able to nibble on acorns and wild herbs, as well as the occasional truffle.

Sausage-making is also highly-prized in the Alentejo, and this region's garlicky *chouriços, linguiças, farinheiras* (sausages plumped up with cereal) and chunky, smoky *paios* are without peers. As one of Portugal's food authorities, Maria de Lourdes Modesto, writes in

from Chaves). Small wonder, too, that *charcuterie* figures so prominently in the regional soups and stews. Cooks here will wrap freshly-caught brook trout in slices of *presunto,* then bounce them in and out of a skillet so hot the ham is transformed to a crisp, deeply smoky sort of pastry.

But Portugal's most famous pork dish comes from the Alentejo. It's *porco à alentejana* for which cubes of pork are marinated in a paste of sweet red peppers and garlic, browned in the fruity local olive oil, then covered and braised

LEFT: the fish market in Setúbal.
ABOVE: *carne de porco à alentejana.*

Cozinha Tradicional Portuguesa, "The grand destiny of the pig in the Alentejo is to become sausage".

Here, every part of the pig is used – ears, snout, tail, feet – even, it would seem, the squeal. At carnival time, for example, the centrepiece of each banquet festa is *pezinhos de porco de coentrada,* dainty pigs' feet braised with onions, garlic and fresh coriander.

Another province famous for its pork is the coastal Beira Litoral, particularly the little town of Mealhada, which is not much more than a wide place in the road about 20 km (12 miles) north of Coimbra. Here both sides of the highway are lined with restaurants that make suckling pig *(leitão assado)* a speciality. The piglets are rubbed with secret blends of oil and herbs, skewered from head to tail, then spit-roasted over white-hot hardwood coals until their skin is as crisply brittle as an onion's and their milk-white flesh so meltingly tender it falls from the bones at the touch of a fork.

Cabbage patch

The Portuguese national dish, ironically, is built neither upon salt cod nor pork. Its key ingredient is cabbage, specifically a richly emerald, tender-leafed variety *(couve galega)*. The dish itself is called *caldo verde,* a bracing, jade-green soup which is brimming with potatoes, onion, garlic and filament-thin shreds of green cabbage. Sometimes the soup may be fortified with slices of *chouriço* or *linguiça,* although in the humblest Minho versions (it's here that the recipe originated), it often contains nothing more than water, potatoes, onion, garlic, cabbage (of course) and perhaps a tablespoon or two of robust olive oil.

To some people, "robust" may seem a bit of a euphemism. Portuguese olive oil, *azeite,* is richly aromatic – and far too strong for some unaccustomed palates. The distinctive flavour comes from the harvesting methods. The festive

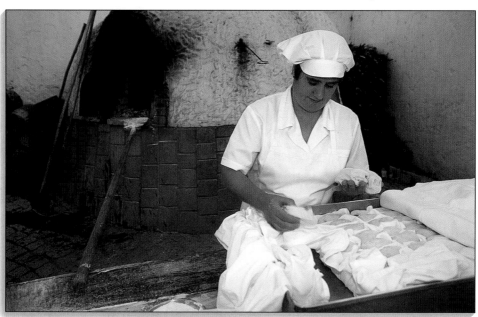

BALANCING ACT

An common sight in rural Portugal is that of a small, ramrod-straight woman balancing cabbages on her head, sometimes six or eight of them at a time, as she goes about her shopping or chats with friends, seeming completely oblivious to the burden she carries. Anyone who drives around the back roads of Portugal will be awed by the inventory of items that Portuguese women manage to balance atop their heads: crates of squawking chickens, baskets of laundry, terracotta water jugs, tables, chairs, even sewing machines and gas bottles. It must be very good for their posture but it's hard to imagine many European women emulating them.

December olive harvest is a casual event. The olives, once beaten down from their branches, are left to age lying on the ground, only gathered after a week or so. That, in addition to the hot-water pressing methods, accounts for their intense flavour.

Every Portuguese province now calls *caldo verde* its own, and it's not unusual to find kettles of it steaming in every kitchen. Indeed, *caldo verde* is such a staple of the Portuguese diet that plastic bags of minutely shredded *couve gallego,* ready to drop into the pots of potato broth bubbling at home, can be bought at Lisbon's Mercado da Ribeira and other markets – the ultimate in convenience food.

The preparation of *couve galega* is something every country girl learns, by the time she's grown head-high to the kitchen table. The trick is to shred it with the speed of light: the leaves are stacked, perhaps five or six deep, rolled into a fat cigar, then literally shaved as a razor-sharp knife is whisked back and forth across the end of the cabbage roll so fast the movements are scarcely visible. The fineness of the cut is what makes a bowl of *caldo verde* resemble molten jade; also the cabbage is tossed into the pot just minutes before serving so that its colour intensifies but does not turn to a paler shade.

Soups and stews

The food of Portugal has often been referred to as the food of farmers and fishermen. Fishermen brew giant drums of *caldeirada* (literally, "kettle of fish") on the beaches at Sesimbra, Nazaré, Albufeira and Sagres, beginning with water (sometimes sea water), adding tomatoes, onions and garlic, then white and oily fish in roughly equal proportions, and if their catch has been especially good, squid or octopus, too. No two *caldeiradas* are ever alike. One of the pleasures of visiting a deserted beach in Portugal is the chance of running into a group of fishermen cooking their latest catch. They're nearly always willing to share.

Farmers' soups and stews are ever-changing, too, as country women improvise with odds and ends – a bit of chicken from the Sunday dinner, a few *favas* (beans) left over from lunch, a handful of carrots, a sprinkle of rice, some crumbs of yesterday's bread, and maybe some freshly minced coriander. This is the way many of Portugal's great recipes were created.

Next to *caldo verde,* Portugal's most famous soup is probably *açorda à alentejana,* a coriander-strewn, bread-thickened, egg-drop soup seasoned, as someone once remarked, "with enough garlic to blow a safe". The soups and stews of Portugal – whether they're made of chick-peas and spinach (another Alentejo classic), of tomatoes and eggs (a Madeira speciality), of pumpkins and onions (a Trás-os-Montes staple), or of dried white beans and sausages (the universally beloved *feijoadas)* – are frugal and filling, nourishing and soul-satisfying. All

LEFT: making bread the traditional way in the Algarve.
RIGHT: sweet fried dough is sold on street corners.

they need for accompaniment are a glass of wine, a chunk of cheese and a crust of bread.

Bread and cheese

Does any country bake better bread than Portugal? The simple country breads usually contain only the usual four ingredients – flour milled from hard wheat, water, yeast and salt – but they're kneaded until their dough fairly springs to life. And because they're baked in wood-stoked brick or stone ovens, they have a faintly smoky flavour. There are fancier breads, to be sure, notably the sweet festival breads, the *pão doce* of Easter and the fruit-studded

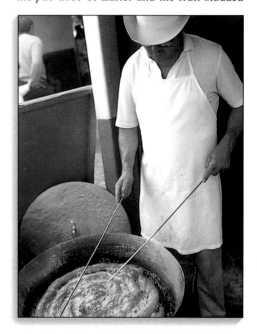

bolo rei of Christmas. There are huskier breads, too, the rough round barley breads and, most famous of all, the *broas* – yeast-raised cornbreads of the Minho that are sold by the truckload at the market in the river town of Barcelos.

Barcelos' country market is Portugal's biggest and best. Held every Thursday in a vast tree-shaded square, it's divided into quadrants: one for breads, cakes and other baked goods; one for fresh produce (everything from potatoes to poultry); one for farm and wine-making equipment; and the fourth for the lace tablecloths, fancifully painted brown pottery and exuberantly decorated ceramic roosters of the region.

Cheeses can be bought at country markets everywhere. The queen of them all is the ivory-hued *queijo da serra,* a cheese so strictly demarcated it can be made only from the milk of sheep grazing on the wild mountain herbs of the Serra da Estrela. At the peak of its season – winter – a properly ripened *serra* is as biting, buttery and runny as the finest Brie.

Portugal also produces a number of other cheeses that are a match for the world's best: the nutty, semi-dry *serpa* from the Alentejo town of the same name, which connoisseurs rank as the nation's second best (it's cured in caves and brushed regularly with paprika-laced

olive oil); *beja,* a buttery semi-hard cheese from Beja, near Serpa; *azeitão,* lovely little rounds of gold, tangy and creamy, that come from the village of Azeitão on the Arrábida Peninsula just across the Tejo from Lisbon. Finally, there are the *queijos frescos,* snowy, uncured cheese much like cottage cheese, which calorie-conscious Portuguese sprinkle with cinnamon.

Egg sweets

The Moors are thought to have introduced egg sweets to Portugal during their 500-year occupation. But it was the 17th- and 18th-century nuns of Portugal who glorified them – one reason, no doubt, why so many egg sweets bear such names as "bacon from heaven" *(toucinho do céu),* "nuns' tummies" *(barriga-da-freira)* and "angel's cheeks" *(papos d'anjo).*

Regardless of their names, what the dozens of different egg sweets have in common is a prodigious use of egg yolk and sugar. Many are flavoured with cinnamon, others with lemon or orange or almonds, and each is shaped in its own traditional way: like little bundles of straw, for example, miniature haystacks, or even lamprey eel. The Portuguese so love this ugly river fish they make golden egg effigies of it for festive occasions. A ritual practised at nearly every Portuguese restaurant, whether simple or sophisticated, is the pastry cart, a glittering double-decker trolley laden with *doces de ovos* brought round at the meal's end.

Usually there are half a dozen choices – sunny little hillocks bathed in clear sugar syrup, flans decorated with cinnamon, individual goblets of rice pudding *(arroz doce)* as radiant as molten gold, flat yellow sponge cakes twirled around orange or lemon custard fillings, tiny translucent tarts *(queijadas)* and a snowy poached meringue ring known as *pudim molotov* (one of the few egg sweets made out of the whites). All are beautifully presented.

The egg sweets look irresistible but most of them are excruciatingly sweet and far too rich for contemporary non-Portuguese palates. The Portuguese, on the other hand, find that nothing complements – or follows – an egg sweet so well as a silky, syrupy wine – a vintage port, or a madeira.

But if you do choose a *doce* from the cart, you can bypass the wine, because you'll always be assured of a good cup of coffee to cut the sweetness. Coffee houses are a national institution, a gathering place morning, noon and night, which is not surprising in a country whose former colonies – Brazil and Angola – still produce some of the finest coffee beans in the world. The choice may be a *bica,* a powerful espresso-type brew, or a *café,* which is closer to standard percolated or filter coffee. Or you can order *carioca,* which is half-*café,* half-hot water; it will still be pretty strong and very good. Be aware, though, of regional variations: there are different ways of ordering coffee, depending on where you are. ❑

LEFT: Café Brasileira in Lisbon.
RIGHT: preparing the ubiquitous *caldo verde.*

WINES OF PORTUGAL

Wine-making is moving into an exciting phase. New favourites are supplementing old reliables, and many smaller quintas *are producing quality wines*

ort wine is virtually a national emblem, and for many years the only wine (except Madeira) that many people associated with Portugal. But things are changing fast: the country's scintillating *vinhos verdes* have gained a well-deserved reputation, and there is an expanding range of excellent wines available. Under European Union (EU) regulations, closely supervised by the Instituto da Vinha e do Vinho (Vineyards and Wines), wine areas are "determined" or "demarcated" under the initials VQPRD (Quality Wines Produced in Demarcated Regions). Twenty-eight newly determined areas mean that fanciers familiar with classic Bairrada or Dão wines can look with fresh interest to *zonas vinícolas* like the exhilarating Douro, to Tomar in the Ribatejo, or the always popular Alentejo. The scene is an exciting one, but port still leads the field.

Port wine

Port wine begins life in the Upper Douro, a demarcated region whose boundaries cling to the banks of the Douro and its tributaries. A wide variety of grapes grow here: preferred reds include Tinta Roriz, Tinta Francesa (a descendant of the French Pinot Noir), Touriga Nacional and Bastardo; among the whites are Malvasia, Esgana Cão and Rabigato.

Come October, the silence on the great terraced slopes is broken when the harvest – *vindima* – begins. Groups of grape pickers, mainly women and girls, are specks in a vast landscape. Men stride the terraces carrying 50-kilo (112-lb) baskets of grapes to waiting containers. At night, in some wineries, platoons of barelegged treaders reduce the grapes to a purple must, accompanied by an accordion and encouraged by watching, dancing girls. In other wineries, rows of shining auto-vinificators silently perform the same function.

PRECEDING PAGE: *barcos rabelos*, the clinker-built port wine boats, are still raced on the Douro.
LEFT: casks must be tended with skill and care.
RIGHT: tawny port is aged in wood for seven years.

As new vineyards are planted, modern techniques – bulldozing and dynamiting – have made expansion economically feasible. Virtually all the new area has been forged upriver, in the valleys of the Douro tributaries: the Pinhão, Tua, Torto and Távora. The regions producing the finest ports presently centre around Pinhão,

some 20 km (14 miles) east of Régua, and extend to the Spanish border.

The famous shipping firms all have their *quintas* (manor houses) in the hills of the Douro. It is here that the fermentation process takes place in autumn, interrupted by the addition of grape brandy, to create the raw, fortified wine. Young port then spends the winter at the *quinta.* In springtime, it is transported to the port lodges in Vila Nova de Gaia by truck, where it is blended and matured into a variety of styles.

In times past, the port was shipped to the lodges in the lovely *barcos rabelos,* flatbottomed, clinker-built boats with large square sails, very similar in construction to the Viking longboats (*see page 85*). Restored versions adorn the Douro's southern bank at Vila Nova de Gaia. During the São João *festas* in June they are raced in a lively regatta.

Vila Nova de Gaia, facing Porto, has more than 80 port lodges; many of them are open to the public. It is here that you can learn the basic differences of port styles, aided, delightfully, by sampling the product itself.

Vintage port

The most famous and most expensive of the ports is the vintage variety. Representing only

two percent of the entire annual port production, it is the jewel of Portuguese wines. It is produced from the grapes of a single harvest and is "declared" only in years when the quality is deemed extraordinary. Vintage port is bottled after just two or three years in wood. This is what distinguishes vintage from all other ports: the majority of its ageing takes place in glass, rather than wood. From a legal standpoint, vintage port must identify itself as such – stating the name of its producer and the year of the vintage – and must carry the governmental seal. For example, the great 1963 vintage must, by law, have been bottled between 1 July 1965 and 30 June 1966.

As bottle ageing progresses, vintage port "throws" a heavy sediment as heavier particles in the wine succumb to gravity. So it is important that the wine is stored correctly: horizontally, yet at a slight incline, wine in contact with the cork. When vintage port – or any ageing red wine, for that matter – is then opened, its contents will be decanted, a simple procedure whereby the clear wine is poured away from the accumulated dregs. A properly stored bottle will facilitate this procedure.

Vintage port may be drunk as soon as 10 years after its vintage date, but most wines hit their stride after about 15 to 20 years. Classic wines were produced in 1985, 1983, 1980, 1977, 1966 and 1963; and 1991 was a year when several shippers "declared". Taylor, Graham, Croft, Noval and Ferreira are some of the best-known names among a host of eminent port wine makers.

Crusted port

Crusted port differs from vintage port in that its grapes need not come from a single year, or vintage, but is mostly created from two or three different harvests. Crusted port spends extra time in wood, accelerating the maturation process. This extended ageing makes for a lighter-bodied wine. Like vintage port, however, it throws a sediment and needs to be decanted.

Late bottled port

Late bottled vintage (LBV) sees even more time in wood – from four to six years. As its name implies, the wine comes from a single year's harvest, but is much lighter in colour than vin-

---

CONFUSING *COLHEITAS*

There is a confusing offshoot of the vintage-dated wines, called "Port of the Vintage" or "Port with Date of Vintage". These wines come from a single year, but will have been aged in wood for no less than seven years. The bottle will often say *Colheitas* (which means "vintage") and give the year; it will show the date of bottling and some indication that the wine has been aged in wood.

The house of Nierport has a wonderful stock of these *Colheitas*. They are the first step into tawny ports, but the fact that they are from a single vintage prevents them legally being so titled under the strict regulations which control all aspects of port making and marketing.

tage port and need not be decanted. Both the date of the vintage and the date of bottling must appear on the label. When buying, it is worth remembering that shippers generally do not offer late bottled vintage in the same years as they offer real vintage port.

Wood ports

Wood ports are the bread and butter of the port trade. They are blended wines – using grapes from several harvests – that are matured in cask until they are ready for drinking. Because they are

TASTING AND TESTING

One good place to sample various port wines is at the Solar do Vinho do Porto (near Palácio Cristal). Here you can taste port wine of almost any age and type.

usually older, and certainly more expensive.

White ports are also matured in wood. They can come from either red or white grapes: a clear wine can be obtained from red grapes by separating the juice from the skins during fermentation before the colour has been extracted. Wine-makers have tried to popularise whites by fermenting out the sugar, adding brandy, and marketing them as dry aperitif wines.

Last, but by no means least, there is tawny port, a special blend of port wine from different

blended, it is the goal of the shipper to define his style through this wine so that year after year the customer can confidently expect a consistent product. The three main types are ruby, white and tawny.

Ruby is young and hearty, not complex and not expensive. To a port drinker, it is the staple wine, attractive for its full, overt flavour. It is aged for two or three years in cask before bottling. One offshoot of ruby port is called "Vintage Character" port. It will have the same general features but will be of a higher quality,

vintages which sees many years in cask. Through the more rapid oxidisation process within the barrel, this wine matures rather more quickly. Tawny port is thus more mellow in style than the "vintage-dated" ports, but it is refined, with a rich tawny colour and fabulously scented bouquet.

Old tawnies are rather expensive, priced in correlation to the long years the wine has spent ageing in barrel. They should not be confused with the cheap tawny port available abroad, which owes its existence to the strong world demand for a less concentrated but drinkable port wine. The port shippers have handled this demand by concocting a blend of ruby and

LEFT: traditional wicker baskets are used at harvest time. **ABOVE:** treading grapes to make white port.

white port. The product is a simple wine of pinkish hue, in contrast to the fading russet of a true tawny. It will have none of the complexity that real tawny port gains through long ageing. Since the name "tawny" can apply to either wine, the consumer must rely on colour and price to distinguish between the two. Real tawny is not cheap; cheap tawny should never be expensive.

Among a wide choice, Ferreira, Noval and Taylor 10-, 20- and 30-year-olds are fine examples of tawny port. Only the "real thing" will reveal why this is the wine which many port houses most prize and which many blenders

Light and refreshing with an alcohol content of only 8 to 11 percent, *Vinho verde* is made from fully matured grapes from varieties that include Azal, Trajadura, Alvarinho and Loureiro for the whites, and Brancelho, Pedral and Tinto Cão for the reds. The taste is dry, with many subtle shadings. The fizz – known as *pétillance* to wine connoisseurs, *agulha* to the Portuguese – is not added, but appears naturally during the making.

First, the grapes are fermented to convert their natural sugars into alcohol. Then a secondary fermentation, called the malolactic, takes place. Induced by naturally occurring bac-

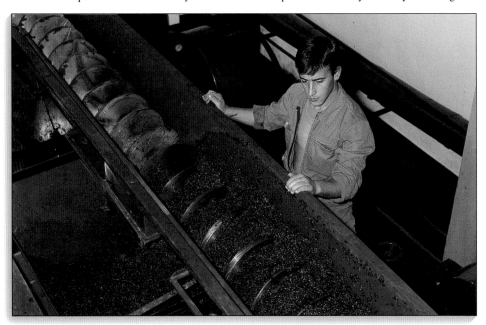

enjoy as an all-day drink (and have even been seen to add ice cubes to).

Vinho verde country

The lush, green Minho is the country's oldest and most intensively cultivated wine area, the region of *vinho verde*. The vine seems to be everywhere – along narrow roads, framing houses with pretty bowers called *ramadas,* across new, neat plantations of *cruzetas,* crosses with wire supports a tractor can reach, and still, in places, clinging to tall trees – though *vinho verde* does not, as a cheerful promotion had it, grow on trees. Nor, as its name suggests, is *vinho verde* a green wine.

teria, this converts malic acid to lactic; a harsher, rather unpleasant acid into a milder, more palatable one.

While this secondary fermentation is common to wines made in many countries, the *vinhos verdes* are distinguished by their retention of the fermentation's by-product: carbon dioxide. From this comes that characteristic sparkle in the wine, which can vary, depending upon age, technique and storage, from a light tingle on the tongue to a spritely carbonation, the hallmark of *vinhos verdes*.

The *vinho verde* region was demarcated in 1908, and has six sub-zones. The differences

Much admired among single-estate wines is the Palácio da Brejoeira *vinho verde* produced from a single grape variety, Alvarinho, in Monção. It is also the most expensive. You can, though, taste a good, and cheaper Alvarinho made by the Adega Cooperativa of Monção.

Wine regions

Truly superb wines, a few eccentric and many sublime, are to be found in Portugal. From the once-cherished Dão area, which in recent years has tumbled from its pedestal, comes Caves São João's good red Porto dos Cavaleiros (its Reserva among the very best Dão wines) or the

in the wine's taste from grower to grower reflect location and climate, as well as the grape itself, but also result from the increasing number of single-estate producers in recent years.

Notable estate-made *vinhos verdes* come from over 50 members of the Association of Producers and Bottlers of Vinho Verde who must produce wine only from their own grapes (not buy them, as bulk producers do). The result is a range of wines produced in small quantities but with individual characteristics.

LEFT: grape pulp from an auto-vinificator in Pinhão.
ABOVE: a rich harvest of grapes on their way to becoming *vinho verde*.

Sogrape Dão Reserva; and, from Sogrape's technologically advanced winery, the old favourites Grão Vasco and Terras Altas.

Bairrada, a small area north of Coimbra, has held its reputation for classic wines, more than 80 percent red, mainly from the Baga grape. The whites include a pleasant espumante, or sparkling wine. Good Bairrada wines are made by Sogrape, Messias and Caves Aliança.

For something really special, though, you might head for the bizarre and extravagant neo-Manueline Palace Hotel do Buçaco, whose cellar of its own Buçaco wines, dating from the 1920s, is virtually a national treasure. Reasons to visit this unusual palace are numerous – the forest is enchanting, historical aspects intriguing, and you can stay in the suite occupied by the last king of Portugal. But if wine is your pleasure, and you have the resources, you can luxuriate for days eating classy food and sampling 30-year-old whites and 40-year-old reds.

You can also taste perfectly good Bairrada wines at the cluster of down-to-earth roadside restaurants that can be found in nearby Mealhada, all offering the local speciality, *leitão*, suckling pig.

The Douro is the source of many of Portugal's finest table wines (even in the port region only 40 percent of the grapes go into port). Ferreira, a distinguished port wine producer, also makes the renowned Barca Velha, probably the finest of all Portugal's red wines. Other Ferreira reds include their Reserva Especial or the more accessible Esteva. Top-ranking Douro wines also include those under the Quinta do Cotto label – Grande Escolha is one. As in other areas, Sogrape are conspicuous – Planalto is just one of their good Douro wines. Adriano Ramos Pinto produce the really excellent Duas Quintas red.

Closer to the capital

From nearer to Lisbon comes a variety of good wines – the white from Bucelas is a consistent favourite. Pleasant wines, too, come from the Colares area, just beyond Sintra, which is particularly interesting as its rootstocks are among the few survivors of the phylloxera plague which struck Europe in the late 19th century.

To the south of Lisbon two major wineries, confusingly with very similar names, are in Azeitão, near Setúbal (both are open to the public). One, José Maria da Fonseca, makes a very popular red Periquita and the excellent dry Branco Seco. If you care for sweet muscatel dessert wines, you might like to try the Moscatel de Setúbal.

The second and more modern winery is J.M. Fonseca International, widely known for its very successful Lancer's red, white and rosé, sold in their distinctive clay jars. Two eminent wines from the Setúbal area are João Pires, and the deep red from the Quinta de Bacalhoa, both developed by the skills of Australian oenologist, Peter Bright.

Wines from Portugal's southernmost province, the Algarve, have never won much respect overseas (they are largely consumed on the spot by local residents and tourists, who seem quite happy with them) but the range of good wines made in the eastern Alentejo is another thing altogether. The quality of wines made in such towns as Borba, Reguengos and Vidigueira (from where comes a very good white *reserva*) has been higher than ever in recent years.

Look, too, for the deep red and distinctive Esporão. In good Lisbon restaurants you will very likely be recommended an Alentejo red, rather than the more usual white, if you choose any variety of *bacalhau* (salt cod). ❏

PHYLLOXERA

Phylloxera was a devastating disease which hit European vineyards in the last quarter of the 19th century. It was caused by an unpleasant louse, which found its way to Europe from America, where it bred and fed, unseen at first, on the roots of the vines, which gradually withered and died. The disease wiped out many vineyards and caused severe hardship to growers. Eventually, it was found that grafting indigenous vines onto imported American stock – which was resistant to the louse – would ensure healthy plants, and the industry began to recover. Today's rootstocks are the American ones, and there has been no recurrence of the disease.

LEFT: wine-producer's logo, in the Douro valley.

Port Dynasties

In a technological age there are few trades where heritage and family ties are a matter of pride. Port is one of them, a commerce with its roots in the wild upper reaches of northern Portugal's Douro valley, a wine region that has had virtually the same frontiers since the Marquês de Pombal defined them in 1756.

At the time, the reforming Pombal, who felt a hearty dislike for the British and their leading role in Portuguese trade, was determined to restrict the hold they had had on the area ever since the Methuen Treaty of 1703 had established their dominance of the industry. In subsequent centuries, port has improved immeasurably in quality and the profits are more evenly spread. But although snobbish exclusivity is long gone, the British are still very much part of the port scene.

The British association with port is long and eventful – although these days the French buy more. British buyers enthusiastically explored the Douro valley in the 17th century. One of the pioneers, cartographer Joseph James Forrester, a Scot, fought tirelessly for high standards and mapped every inch of the river. He was made a baron in 1855 for his efforts.

It was regarded as a national tragedy when, in May 1862, Forrester's boat overturned and he drowned in the Douro. He was travelling between various wine-growing *quintas*, paying the farmers in gold coins, and it is said that it was his money-belt, heavy with gold, which helped to drag him down. A survivor of the tragedy was another outstanding personality in the saga of port: Dona Antónia Adelaide Ferreira, whose vineyards covered huge areas of the Douro.

These and other colourful characters are familiar to everyone in the business. The founders of the port wine trade are ever-present, their faces and names on port wine labels. Many rival companies have family links. Their names, however, can be deceptive: for all its English ring, Cockburn Smithes has had a Portuguese managing director for years.

But at Taylor, Fladgate & Yeatman (founded in 1692), managing director Alistair Robertson is descended from a Yeatman, and the company's characterful taster, Bruce Guimaraens, has Fladgate ancestors.

RIGHT: Bruce Guimaraens, who tastes for Taylor, Fladgate & Yeatman.

In 1983, 18-year-old Nicholas Delaforce, a seventh-generation Delaforce, was experiencing his first *vindima* or harvest; and in 1993 he was actively involved in the company run by his father, David, in which grandfather John had been an eminent personality.

At Ferreira, too, the sense of dynasty remains strong. In the firm founded by the remarkable Dona Antónia Adelaide Ferreira, eighth-generation Francisco ("Vito") de Olazabal is the managing director. In the early 1990s, his son, Francisco, was completing a degree in oenology (the science of wines). Even as a boy Francisco knew what he wanted to be – and he didn't even like wine at the time.

Inescapable since the 1800s is the name of Symington. The family owns and manages a distinguished list of companies: Warre's (founded in the 1670s), Silva & Cosens (whose brand is Dow), Quarles Harris, Smith Woodhouse, and Graham's. In the 1990s two generations and eight members of the Symington family are involved in management, production, sales and marketing of the fine ports made by these independent companies.

Efficient modern methods are used in the wine industry these days but technology blends smoothly with tradition. Even the Symingtons' Gaia offices hold echoes of port's memorable past: they are in Travessa do Barão Forrester, in the very house where Baron Forrester once lived. ❏

FESTIVALS FOR ALL SEASONS

You can't go far in Portugal without stumbling across a festival – colourful occasions which demonstrate a national talent for celebration

On almost every weekend throughout the year there will be a festival taking place somewhere in Portugal. Saints' days are the biggest single stimulus for holding a *festa*, and every village and town in the country enjoys the protection of a patron saint. *Romarios* are generally more sober affairs with a greater religious dimension. Plenty of these take place too, especially at Easter time.

There are other causes for celebration, some of them distinctly pagan, but there will invariably be a strong religious element, even if this is lightened, as it usually is, with feasting and decidedly secular revelry.

All these events involve a vast amount of work and planning. Committees must be formed, fundraising events held, and local authorities involved. Routes must be planned, traffic diverted, and streets colourfully decorated. When the big day arrives, it all seems worthwhile. Crowds gather to watch the parades starting out from the local church. Flower-decorated religious tableaux, saints, virgins and icons are carried in solemn procession with music provided by local bands. With the procession over, celebrations starts in earnest, with eating and drinking, music and dancing and general merrymaking. A fitting climax, bringing everything to a close, is usually provided by a spectacular and very noisy firework display.

◁ **ALTE, ALGARVE**
This May Day folk festival in Alte features processions and dancers in regional costumes.

△ **VILA FRANCA DO LIMA**
At the Festas da Senhora das Rosas, richly costumed women carry huge constructions of rose petals and flowers on their heads.

◁ STREET DISPLAYS
Lavish street decorations raise the profile of any good *festa*. These, in Serpa, Alentejo, are in honour of Nuestra Senhora da Guadaloupe.

△ AUGUST CELEBRATIONS
Nossa Senhora da Agonia in Viana do Castelo, one of Portugal's biggest festivals, celebrates the Virgin Mary with a colourful display of national costumes.

REGIONAL CELEBRATIONS

It is not a question of see one festival and you've seen them all. Many are unusual and unique to a particular region. At Miranda do Douro, Trás-os-Montes, stick dances are performed to the music of bagpipes, cymbals and drums (15 August); and in Amarante (early June) young men offer phallus-shaped cakes as tokens of love to the young ladies in celebration of São Gonçalo, the patron saint of love and marriage. Others are simpler affairs, where the fringe activities, such as biscuit-eating competitions (*above*) are as popular as the main attraction.

Lisbon hosts several lively festivals: one of the biggest is Festas dos Santos Populares in June, which celebrates Saints Anthony, John and Peter, and takes place in Alfama. The liveliest night is 12 June, when thousands gather to eat sardines, drink vast amounts of wine and join in the singing and dancing until late.

▷ FESTAS DAS CRUZES
The Festas das Cruzes in Barcelos commemorates the Miracle of the Cross each May, with much pomp and ceremony.

▽ FIREMEN ON PARADE
The whole community takes part in local *festas*, especially in smaller villages. In Almoçageme the *bombeiros*, the voluntary fire brigade, parade in full dress uniform.

▷ MONÇAO
Corpus Cristi celebrations in Monçao in mid-June start with a procession led by a "blessed ox" and finish with a lively skirmish between good and evil which is reminiscent of the battle of St George and the dragon.

THE HISTORY OF ARCHITECTURE

*Some of Portugal's finest architecture is found in its religious buildings,
but the wealth from the Age of Discoveries also left a legacy of fine palaces*

Portugal's unusual geographical position, cut off from Europe by Spain on one side, facing the New World on the other, is reflected in its architecture. The country's architects have always looked outside for influence and affirmation, and local traditions have blended harmoniously with imported ideas.

Romanesque

The story of Portuguese architecture really begins in the Romanesque period of the 12th century, when nearly all buildings of any importance were religious ones. This was the time when the kingdom was founded, when Portugal was (largely) reconquered from the Moors, and Christianity was strongly felt. The construction of cathedrals followed the path of reconquest from Braga to Porto, southwards to Coimbra, Lamego, Lisbon and Evora.

In the north, Romanesque-style churches continued to be built well into the 14th century, when the Gothic style was already spreading throughout the rest of the country. Portuguese Romanesque is an architecture of simple, often dramatically stark forms, whose sturdiness is frequently explained by the need for fortification against the continued threat of Moorish or Castilian invasion. This fortified appearance is enhanced in the cathedrals of Lisbon and Coimbra by the crenellated façade towers.

Most of these buildings are of granite. The hardness of this material renders detailed carving impossible, thus favouring a simplicity of form. In areas where the softer limestone abounds, such as the central belt of the country (including Coimbra, Tomar and Lisbon), carved decorations are more common.

These Romanesque churches share a certain robustness; a method of construction based on semi-circular arches and barrel vaults; a cruciform plan; and a solid, almost sculptural sense

PRECEDING PAGES: exquisite ceiling in the Igreja dos Paulistas, the Bairro Alto, Lisbon.
LEFT: the Unfinished Chapel at Batalha.
RIGHT: the Romanesque Old Cathedral in Coimbra.

of form in the interior which allows for a play of light and shade. This sobriety is accentuated by the paucity of decoration, which is frequently reduced to the capitals of columns and the archivolts surrounding the portals. When the tympana are not bare, the simplified carvings are usually stylised depictions of Christ in Majesty, or the *Agnus Dei* (Lamb of God), or simply of a cross. In some cases, animals and serpents climb up the granite columns, as in the *Sé Velha* (Old Cathedral) of Coimbra or in the unusually richly decorated principal portal of the early 13th-century church of São Salvador in Bravães in the Minho.

Gothic

In France, new methods of construction involving pointed arches and ribbed vaults allowed for lighter, taller architectural forms. As the main weight of the building was now borne outside at fixed points by flying buttresses, the walls could be pierced at frequent intervals. The light filtering into these Gothic interiors became a metaphor for Divine Light, replacing the Romanesque emphasis on Mystery.

The first building in Portugal to use these new construction methods was the majestic church of the abbey of Alcobaça, commissioned by Afonso Henriques. With its great height and elegant, unadorned white interior bathed in a milky light, Alcobaça is one of the most serene and beautiful churches in Portugal. Begun in 1178 and consecrated in 1222, it is almost purely French in inspiration: its plan echoes that of Clairvaux, the seat of the Cistercian Order in Burgundy – a nave and two side aisles of almost the same height, a two-aisled transept, and an apse whose ambulatory fans out into chapels.

The apogee of the national Gothic style came after the Portuguese armies defeated the invading Castilians at the Battle of Aljubarrota. In fulfilment of a religious vow made prior to the battle, King João I commissioned the construction in 1388 of the Dominican Monastery of Santa Maria da Vitória (St Mary of the Victory), better known as Batalha, which simply means battle.

The stylistic influence of Batalha is seen in various churches throughout the country, such

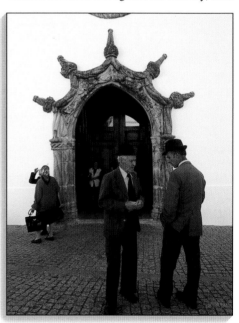

BUILDING BATALHA

Batalha's construction can be divided into three stages. ❶ The first phase ran from 1388 to 1438, when the central nave, with simple ribbing supporting the vault, was built. The Founder's Chapel and the chapterhouse vault have a greater refinement and elegance, influenced by English Gothic. Contact with England was close at this time as João I's wife, Philippa of Lancaster, was the daughter of John of Gaunt. ❷ During the second stage, which lasted until 1481, a second cloister was built. ❸ The third, Manueline, phase culminated in the Arcade of the Unfinished Chapels and the Royal Cloister.

as the cathedral at Guarda and the now-ruined Carmo church in Lisbon, which were both begun at the end of the 14th century.

Generally speaking, Portuguese Gothic leaned towards temperance rather than flamboyance, a reflection of the austerity imposed by the mendicant orders and, perhaps, the sombre streak in the national character.

The Manueline style

The exhilaration of Portugal's overseas discoveries had a marked effect on art, architecture and literature. The term "Manueline" was first used in the 19th century to refer to the reign of Manuel I (1495–1521), during which Vasco da

Gama reached the coast of India (1498), and Afonso de Albuquerque conquered the Indian city of Goa (1510). The term is now used more often to refer to certain stylistic features predominant during the Avis dynasty (1383–1580), especially in architecture.

Manueline architecture does not have major innovative structural features – the twisted columns, such as those at the Church of Jesus in Setúbal, perform the same function as do plain ones. Rather, Manueline can be seen as heterogeneous late Gothic, its real innovation lying in its stone decoration, the exuberance of which reflects the optimism and wealth of the period.

nave. Perhaps the most notable feature of Manueline architecture is the copious carving that surrounds portals and semi-circular windows. The imposing southern portal of Jerónimos, together with the window of the chapterhouse at the Convent of Christ in Tomar, well deserve the acclaim that they both receive. Construction on the Tomar window began much earlier, in the 12th century, along with the Templar Charola – a chapel with a circular floor plan. During the 16th century, the convent buildings, including four cloisters, were added. The lavish Manueline decoration of the church culminates in the famous window,

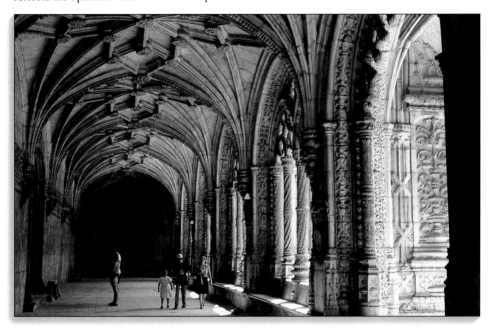

Inspired by the voyages to the New World, it is ornate and imposing, uniting naturalistic maritime themes with Moorish elements and heraldic motifs: during the reign of Manuel I, the king's own emblems are usually included – as they were in the churches built in the newly discovered overseas territories.

The Monastery of Santa Maria de Belém in Lisbon, which is better known as Jerónimos, is one of the great *hallenkirchen* of the period – that is, a church whose aisles are as high as its

which is designed with two great ship's masts on either side, covered with carvings, topped, like the southern portal at Jerónimos, by the cross of the Order of Christ.

Manueline architecture also adopted and modified certain Moorish (*morisco*) features. At the Palácio Nacional at Sintra, for example, restored during Manuel's reign, *morisco* features include the use of tiles, merlons, and windows divided in two by columns. Another important *morisco* feature is the horseshoe arch, which can be seen in the chapterhouse of the Convent of Lóios in Evora. In Alentejo, numerous provincial palaces have *morisco* decoration, including lattice-work ceilings.

Far left: a portal in the lovely Gothic abbey at Alcobaça. **Left:** Manueline archway at Monchique. **Above:** the graceful cloister of Jerónimos Monastery.

Renaissance and Mannerism

The Renaissance has been described as a narrow bridge crossed the moment it was reached. This was certainly the case in Portugal. In their art and architecture, the Portuguese shied away from Renaissance rationalism, instead inclining towards naturalism or towards the drama of the baroque.

The Renaissance in Portugal, then, was best represented by foreign artists. Foreign sculptors were frequently invited to decorate the portals and façades of Manueline buildings, introducing elements of Renaissance harmony and order within the general flamboyance of

the Manueline decorative scheme. The coincidence of Manueline and Renaissance influences, and later of Renaissance and Mannerist forms, explains the hybrid style prevalent during this period. Mannerism uses elements of Renaissance classicism but the sense of an ordered, harmonious whole gives way to an exaggeration of these elements.

The Spaniard Diogo de Torralva is thought to have been responsible for one of the finest examples of Renaissance design in the Iberian peninsula – the Chapel of Nossa Senhora da Conceição (Our Lady of the Conception) in Tomar (*circa* 1530–40), with its simple exterior and diffusely lit, barrel-vaulted interior. Also

in Tomar, Torralva's Great Cloister at the Convent of Christ evokes the balance and harmony of Palladian classicism. Many years after Torralva's death in 1566, this majestic cloister was completed by the prestigious Italian architect Filippo Terzi, a specialist in military architecture who had been invited by Philip II of Spain (who became king of Portugal in 1581).

Azulejos

Azulejos, the painted ceramic tiles so familiar to visitors to Portugal, were one of the major features of the 17th century. First used in the 15th century, they gained ground during the next 100 years, and by the 17th century, when economic conditions permitted extensive restoration and reconstruction, they were virtually indispensable. Vast decorative schemes of tiles panels filled churches and palaces, but the *azulejos* were put to good use in humbler settings, such as kitchens and stairways, as well.

In addition to murals (for which *azulejos* were most commonly used), there were small floral panels, or single tiles adorned – in the Dutch style – with birds, flowers and human figures. The Palácio of Queluz (*see page 181*) is a fine example of the use of *azulejos* in garden design. (*See pages 170–71 for a special feature on* azulejos.)

Baroque

The baroque is considered to be the stylistic range which, although it uses a basic classical vocabulary, strives for dissolution of form rather than definition. Emphasis is given to motion, to the state of becoming rather than being. This obliteration of clear contours – whether by brushstrokes in painting or as an optical illusion in sculpture and architecture – is further enhanced by a preference for depth over plane. These features all stress the grand, the dynamic and the dramatic.

The first truly baroque Portuguese church is Santa Engrácia in Lisbon, with its dome and undulating interior walls. This building, begun in 1682, was not completed until 1966. The richness of the coloured marble lining the walls and floor, the dynamic interior space, and the general sumptuousness of the edifice are typical of construction during the reign of João V (1706–50), known as João o Magnânimo.

The wealth from Brazil and the extravagance of João V made the early 18th century a period of great opulence. He was the king who commissioned the Chapel of St John the Baptist at the Church of São Roque in Lisbon. The entire chapel was built in Rome, blessed by the Pope, shipped to Lisbon and reassembled in the church, where it shines with bronzes, mosaics, rare marble and precious stones.

In the north of the country the major centres for the development of the baroque were Porto and Braga. Here, the influence of the Tuscan architect-decorator Nicolau Nasoni, who came to Portugal in 1725, predominated. He introduced a greater buoyancy and elegance, and rich contrasts of light and shade. He incorporated local characteristics as well: his elliptical-naved Church of Clérigos in Porto had no successor. But his secular buildings, such as the Freixo Palace in the same city, with their interplay of whitewash and granite, established a large following.

The gleaming Basilica da Estrêla in Lisbon, dating from the 1780s and commissioned by Maria I, was the last church to be built in the baroque Grand Style. By then, architectural styles had moved on and, with the dissolution of the monastic orders in 1834, religious architecture lost its privileged position in Portugal.

Rococo

In the rococo style, drama was replaced by fantasy, and an emphasis on flourish, sensuality and ornament. The chapel of Santa Madalena in Falperra is a good early example of the style. Rococo was also marked by a growing interest in landscaping. The type of church represented by Bom Jesus in Braga became popular: surrounded by gardens it sits atop a hill and is reached by a sweeping succession of stairways which at a distance seem to cascade downward.

POMBAL'S PROJECT

The reconstruction of Baixa, the lower city of Lisbon, which the Marquês de Pombal embarked on after the devastating earthquake of 1775, was the most ambitious urban planning scheme ever seen in Europe, and serves as the statesman's lasting memorial. "Pombaline Lisbon", as it is known, is built on a grid system, with clean, uncluttered lines. The area is epitomised by the Praça do Comércio, the huge square bounded on three sides by neo-classical pink-hued arcades. In the centre stands a large equestrian statue to José I, erected in 1755. The majestic triumphal arch, however, was not completed until the 1870s, long after Pombal's death.

FAR LEFT: the baroque church of Nossa Senhora dos Remédios in Lamego (1750–60).
LEFT: *azulejos* adorn a façade in Alfama, Lisbon.
RIGHT: Rua D'Oura Totta, part of "Pombaline Lisbon".

In Lisbon the rococo was more sober than in the north. After the earthquake of 1755 Carlos Mardel designed many of the city's public fountains in a toned-down version of rococo, including those of Rua do Século and Largo da Esperança. Mardel was also responsible for part of the Aguas Livres Aqueduct, which withstood the earthquake, and is still a familiar landmark.

Neo-classicism

Although it took place at much the same time, the Pombaline style of the reconstruction of Lisbon – named after Marquês de Pombal, who masterminded the project – is closer in many

respects to classical models than to the rococo constructions in the north. The neo-classical style proper, with its emphasis on Greco-Roman colonnades and porticoes, was introduced to Lisbon in the last decade of the 18th century. It received court approval when used for the Royal Palace of Ajuda (begun in 1802 and never completed) after a fire destroyed the wooden building that had been the temporary royal residence since the earthquake.

After the construction of this palace, perhaps the only noteworthy public building to be built in Lisbon the first half of the 19th century was the Theatre of Dona Maria II (1843), with its white Greco-Roman façade. The dissolution of the monasteries had a negative effect on the development of large-scale public buildings, as well as on religious architecture.

The middle-class ambience of Porto proved fertile ground for conservative neo-classicism to take root. It was favoured by the English community connected with the port industry, perhaps because of its affinities with the work of Scottish architect Robert Adam (1728–92). The British consul, Sir John Whitehead, commissioned the Feitoria Inglesa in Porto, and the Hospital of Santo António, perhaps the finest neo-classical buildings in the country.

Romanticisim

If neo-classical art and architecture represented an escape from the turmoils of the present into a restrained, harmonious classical ideal, another form of escapism was an important ingredient of Romanticism. It was typified by flights into medievalism and orientalism, or into altered-states of dreams and madness.

The most extraordinary architectural manifestation of this was the Pena Palace in Sintra (commissioned by Prince Ferdinand of Saxe-Coburg-Gotha, consort of Maria II, in around 1840). The building is a strange mix of medieval and oriental forms, including Manueline, Moorish, Renaissance, and baroque, and incorporating parts of the site's original structure – a 16th-century monastery. The result is a pastiche of English Gothic revivalism.

Modern styles

One of the best examples of Portuguese architecture from the first half of this century is the art deco Casa Serralves in Porto (now a museum); while a distinctive post-war style commenced with the construction of the Gulbenkian Museum in the 1950s. More recently, Porto architects such as Fernando Távora and Alvaro Siza have established solid reputations: the rebuilding of the Chiado district after Lisbon's 1988 fire was entrusted to the latter. The post-modernist work of Tomás Taveira is also notable in Lisbon, particularly his office towers at the Amoreiras. And Expo '98 produced some stunning modern pavilions, many of which will remain in use as government offices.   ❏

LEFT: Portugal has major modern landmarks, too, such as the new mosque in Lisbon's Avenidas Novas. **RIGHT:** the flamboyant Pena Palace, Sintra.

PORTUGUESE ART
THROUGH THE AGES

*From 15th-century altarpieces to modernist masterpieces, the
country's museums, galleries and churches cover the artistic spectrum*

The 15th century was the first great age of Portuguese painting. Almost no paintings from the 12th to 14th centuries have survived, although frescoes were certainly painted in churches. One interesting, rare example of an early 15th-century fresco is a surviving fragment from a secular painting – the allegory of justice entitled *O Bom e o Mau Juiz* ("The Good and the Bad Judge") in a Gothic house in the town of Monsaráz.

The most notable surviving religious fresco of the same period is the *Senhora da Rosa* in the sumptuous Church of São Francisco in Porto. It has been attributed to an Italian painter, António Florentino, who, it is thought, may also have painted the portrait of João I now at the Museu Nacional de Arte Antiga in Lisbon

By far the most brilliant contribution to painting during this period was the introduction of Flemish-influenced painted altarpieces called retables (*retábulos* in Portuguese). In 1428, the Flemish master Jan van Eyck was invited to the court of João I to paint a portrait of the Infanta Dona Isabel, future wife of Philip the Good (1396–1467), Duke of Burgundy. The Netherlands were, at the time, under the control of the dukes of Burgundy who were renowned for their excellent taste in art. When the Flemish artists turned from illumination to the painting of altarpieces, they added to their own love of realistic detail the Burgundian passion for gem-like decoration.

The polyptych of St Vincent

The most outstanding *retábulo* of the 15th-century Portuguese School is the polyptych of St Vincent attributed to Nuno Gonçalves, in Lisbon's Museu Nacional de Arte Antiga. The mystery that enshrouds this work has increased

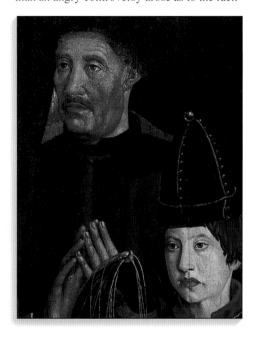

its aura. The panels were lost for centuries, and there are conflicting accounts of their reappearance at the end of the 19th century. No sooner were they cleaned and hung publicly than an angry controversy arose as to the iden-tity of their author as well as of the figures depicted. A touch of drama was added when one eminent scholar committed suicide after a dispute concerning two documents which radically altered the direction of the research. The documents were later proved false.

The theme of the polyptych has also given rise to dispute. Some see in it the veneration of the Infante Santo Fernando, the uncle of Afonso V, who died at the hands of the Moors. But nowadays it is generally thought to represent the adoration of St Vincent, the patron saint of the kingdom and of the city of Lisbon. The important point of departure was the identification of the Infante Henrique (Prince Henry

---

LEFT: detail from Nuno Gonçalves' *The Adoration of St Vincent* polyptych, a 15th-century masterpiece.
RIGHT: detail from the same altarpiece (*retábulo*), showing Henry the Navigator and the future João II.

the Navigator) to the left of the saint in the third panel from the left.

The panels, from left to right, are known as the Panel of the Monks (of the Cistercian Order), the Fishermen, the Infante, the Archbishop, the Calvary and finally, the Relic Panel.

The work's real genius and originality lie in the exquisiteness of the portraiture: its masterful attention to realistic detail as well as its psychological dimension. It appears to be the visual representation of King Afonso's dreams of conquest and of the magical world of Prince Henry's navigations, blessed by the patron saint of the kingdom

The Flemish influence

During the reign of João II (1481–95), when voyages of discovery occupied the energies of the nation, there was a lull in painting activity. However, with the discovery of the sea route to India and the consequent prosperity, painted *retábulos* again became a dominant form of expression. At the end of the 15th century, Portugal was one of the largest importers of Flemish paintings. Many of the altarpieces in Portuguese churches were Flemish, and some can still be seen today, such as the *Fons Vitae* at the Misericórdia church in Porto.

Nevertheless, Portuguese painting main-

THE TOMBS OF PEDRO AND INES

While little surviving painting predates the 15th century, some lovely pieces of sculpture do. The crowning glory of 14th-century funerary sculpture are the tombs of King Pedro and his lover, Inês de Castro at Alcobaça (*see page 30 for the dramatic story of love, murder and revenge*).

The sarcophagi do justice to the tale: the sculptor is unknown and the influences are hybrid, but the naturalistic detail and rich symbolism are unsurpassed. Inês, surrounded by angels, is crowned queen in death as she never was in life. Pedro's tomb, displays a magnificent rosette, believed to symbolise a wheel of fortune, representing life's vicissitudes.

tained local features, giving rise to the "Luso-Flemish" style. Manueline painting evolved during the reign of Manuel I (1495–1521), although the style is more closely associated with architecture (*see page 116*). It has been characterised by features such as monumentality, a fine sense of portraiture, brilliant gem-like colours, a growing interest in the naturalistic depiction of both architectural and landscape backgrounds, and an increasing preoccupation with expressive detail.

During this period painting was not the expression of an individual sensibility, but more often the collaborative effort of a master and his assistants. Attribution, then, is extremely difficult, and often paintings are known as the products of particular workshops. The two principal workshops were those of Jorge Afonso in Lisbon, and of Vasco Fernandes in Viseu. Afonso was appointed royal painter in 1508: documents identify various projects with which he and his workshop were involved, but none show his direct responsibility, although he is believed to have painted some of the panels in the rotunda of the Convento de Cristo in Tomar.

Grão Vasco

Vasco Fernandes, better known as Grão (the "Great") Vasco, is undoubtedly the most cele-

housed in the Museu Grão Vasco, Viseu) of a slightly earlier date. The stylistic differences between the two works confused scholars for some time, but it is now assumed that Flemish assistants at Lamego account for the differences. The panels for the chapels of the Viseu Cathedral (Museu also in the Grão Vasco), of which those of the Calvary and St Peter are the most renowned, are also attributed to him, but these date from his mature phase (1530–42).

Noteworthy for their emotional strength and drama, these works are also characterised by a denser application of paint than that used by the Flemish masters. Furthermore, the faces of

brated regional Manueline painter. For many years, the myth of Grão Vasco obscured his real work in a plethora of attributions – he was thought to be the author of Gothic and Renaissance paintings, although a single lifetime would not have sufficed for so large an output. But he was responsible for the altarpiece originally in the Lamego cathedral (now in the Museu Regional in that town), dating 1506–11, as well as the one for the Viseu Cathedral (now

the Portuguese works tend to be less stylised, more expressive, and, it would seem, often drawn from specific local models, just as the landscape backgrounds are drawn from the Beja region rather than being imaginary or purely symbolic.

The 16th and 17th centuries

As in architecture, the Renaissance, the "rebirth" of art based on classical models, was resisted by Portuguese artists and mainly represented by those from abroad. Mannerism employed many elements of Renaissance classicism but the sense of an ordered, harmonious whole gives way to an exaggeration of those

FAR LEFT: detail from the sepulchre of Inês de Castro.
LEFT: Grão Vasco's depiction of Calvary.
ABOVE: a detail from *Calvário* by Gregório Lopes.
RIGHT: King Sebastian, by Cristovão de Morais.

defining elements. The most characteristic feature of this style is a certain elongation, together with unexpected highlighting of seemingly incidental sections of a work.

The 17th century saw the flourishing of portrait painting in Portugal as elsewhere in Europe. Perhaps the most celebrated portraitist of the period was Domingos Vieira (1600–78), known as "the Dark" to distinguish him from his contemporary Domingos Vieira Serrão. His nickname stemmed from his predilection, in works such as the portrait of Isabel de Moura (in the Museu de Arte Antiga in Lisbon), to make dramatic contrasts between the deep, vel-

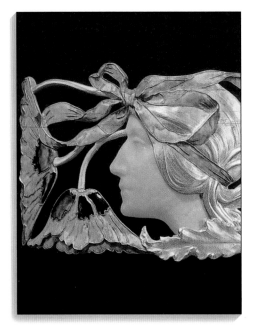

vety backgrounds and the rich, creamy whites of ruffs and headgear.

Neo-classicism

During the 18th century, two outstanding painters emerged: Francisco Vieira, known as Vieira Portuense (1765–1805), and Domingos António Sequeira (1768–1837). The two met in Rome, which was the essential venue for any serious artist. Vieira Portuense also spent some time in London, where the classicising Roman influence was tempered by that of Sir Joshua Reynolds (1723–92).

The work of Sequeira is a study in the transition from neo-classicism to Romanticism, a rare example of a single life encapsulating two eras. He was nominated court painter in 1802 by João VI, and was commissioned to provide paintings for the rebuilt Ajuda Palace. Political turbulence forced Sequeira to emigrate to France, and then to Italy, where he died.

His work can be divided into three stages: the first, largely academic and neo-classical in inspiration, corresponds to the first period he spent in Rome, and to his work as a court painter. The second stage (1807–23) which includes the *Alegoria de Junot* (in the Soares dos Reis Museum, Porto), is stylistically freer and more individualistic, with Goyaesque contrasts of dark and light, rapid brushstrokes and sudden bursts of luminous white.

The final phase of Sequeira's work corresponds to his visits to Paris and Rome. These late works show great painterliness and luminosity. The four cartoons for paintings in the Palmela collections, now in the Museu Nacional de Arte Antiga in Lisbon, are some of his most inspired, mystical works.

Romanticism and Naturalism

Romanticism was a form of escapism into medieval, oriental and mystical realms. Heroic, religious and ceremonial works gave way to more intimate and personal pieces. The mid-19th century also corresponded to the rise of the middle class. Courtly art had breathed its last. The liberal revolutions questioned the long upheld notion of history as the unfolding of a predetermined order, in favour of a relativism which heralded modern times. Similarly, the idea that art expresses timelessly valid principles gradually gave way to the subjectivist and individualist notions which continue to hold sway in art today.

Sequeira represented the mystical, religious side of early Romanticism. With his death, the movement in Portugal underwent a change: nature became the new religion. The humbling of man before the larger, inscrutable forces of nature was already a contemporaneous theme elsewhere. Tomás da Anunciação became the foremost romantic landscapist of his generation, along with Cristino da Silva.

Not surprisingly, portraiture not only became the art form of the bourgeoisie *par excellence*, but it also gave increasing emphasis to the sitter's inner life. In Miguel Luipi's *Sousa Martins' Mother*, now in the Museu de Arte

Contemporânea, the illumination of the hands and face, the most expressive parts of the body, conveys a sense of pensive dignity.

At the end of the 19th century, Romanticism began to give way to Naturalism in both landscapes and portraits – although the difference between the two styles was largely one of emphasis. Silva Porto, José Malhoa, and Henrique Posão were the foremost Naturalist painters. But in stark contrast to their luminous outdoor scenes, Columbano Bordalo Pinheiro (1857–1929) continued in the tradition of studio painting. Columbano, as he is known, is considered the Grand Master of Portuguese 19th-century art. He studied under Miguel Lupi at the Academy of Fine Arts (founded in 1836), and then spent three years in Paris.

His brother, Rafael Bordalo Pinheiro, was perhaps even more popular in his day. A celebrated ceramicist, he was also known for his biting political caricatures.

Modernism

The artistic ferment that gripped Europe and America in the first decades of the 20th century arrived late, or in diluted form, in Portugal. The political turmoil that ended the monarchy in 1910 did not provide a propitious context for an artistic revolution, and there was then a window of only some 15 years before Salazar's authoritarian regime closed the door to external cultural influences.

But some ideas took root. In 1911, the Museu Nacional de Arte Contemporânea was founded in Lisbon, and the first Salon of Humorists represented a move away from conventional salon painting. One of the most daring and interesting of this generation of painters was the Cubist Amadeo Souza-Cardoso, whose premature death in 1918 was a great loss. Many of his works are now in the Centro de Arte Moderno at the Fundação Calouste Gulbenkian in Lisbon, and some can be seen in a museum in his home town of Amarante.

The military regime, initiated in 1926 and led by António de Oliveira Salazar from 1933–74, actively prevented contact with outside stimulus, so all the artistic and intellectual exchange

necessary to keep the arts alive had to be clandestine during these years. The return to democracy in 1974 breathed new energy into the arts and an outburst of fervent activity echoed the sense of exhilaration after long years of repression and censorship.

Portugal's artists now have free access to external ideas, and the age-old conflict between the imported and the indigenous still provokes lively debate. Among contemporary artists, Paula Rego is one of the brightest stars, although she no longer lives in her home country. A collection of her work can be seen at the Museu de Arte Contemporânea in Sintra. ❏

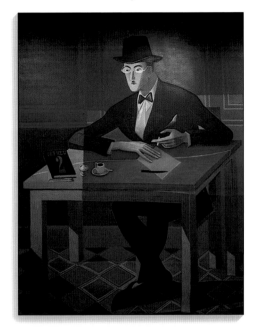

VOICE OF A GENERATION

One of the brightest lights among the generation represented in the 1911 Salon of Humorists was José Almada Negreiros (1893–1970), one of the most charismatic and energetic cultural figures in Portugal. His early cariactures drew the attention of the poet Fernando Pessoa who became his friend, and whose posthumously painted portrait now hangs in the poet's old home, with a replica in the Fundação Calouste Gulbenkian. One of Negreiros' most important commissions was for the frescoes at the port of Lisbon, in 1943–48 (see page 84). His last major project was the mural for the lobby of the Gulbenkian Foundation.

LEFT: René Lalique's art nouveau plaque in the Fundacão Calouste Gulbenkian, in Lisbon.
RIGHT: portrait of Fernando Pessoa by José Almada Negreiros, one of Portugal's 20th-century greats.

POUSADAS AND MANOR HOUSES

Pousadas and manor houses offer something different from ordinary hotels,

above all giving visitors a chance to experience local life and colour

Converted castles, palaces, monasteries, *quintas,* manor houses, water mills: there is no other country in Europe which offers good-quality accommodation in such variety. If taking a stroll around the castle walls before retiring to a grand bedroom once used by royalty, or waking to the tinkling sound of a stream

beneath a miller's cottage sounds appealing, Portugal could be just the right place.

Pousadas

Unlike some of the other accommodation available, *pousadas* have a clear identity. They are state-run establishments, usually historic buildings, national monuments or notable regional houses, and are found in both urban and rural areas throughout the country.

Architecturally and historically fascinating, *pousadas* have earned a reputation for quality and service. Lofty rooms and heavy stone walls do not always lend themselves to sumptuous luxury – in fact, some are extremely simple –

but the style of décor is always sympathetic to the character of the building. One constant concession to modernity is the provision of en-suite facilities, but some *pousadas* also provide air-conditioning and even a swimming pool. *Pousadas* pride themselves, too, on the high standard of their restaurants, which are also open to non-residents, and serve dishes based on local and regional recipes. A relaxed and distinctly Portuguese ambience is perhaps the one thing that they all have in common.

There is now a choice of over 40 *pousadas,* although many offer only a limited number of rooms, some as few as six.

For travellers in the lush green northwestern corner of Portugal, there is a good choice. To mention just a few: in the medieval town of Valença do Minho you will find the **Pousada de São Teotónio**. It sits on a high point inside the ancient walled city with a spectacular view of the Rio Minho across to Spain and the Galician mountains. It is also perfectly located for walks through the winding city streets.

Further to the east is the **Pousada de São Bento**, a chalet-style building on a hill just south of the Parque Nacional Peneda-Gerês. Its floor-to-ceiling windows overlook the Caniçada Dam and a forest. The *pousada* has its own swimming pool and tennis court.

Be the king of the castle

If castles hold a great fascination for you, the **Pousada do Castelo**, in the delightful old walled town of Obidos, north of Lisbon, is one which you might find most interesting. Built into a section of the 16th-century castle, the *pousada* is very small – with only nine rooms – and very popular. Advanced reservations are essential. **Palmela** is another castle *pousada* that is much in demand, and somewhat larger, with 26 rooms. Originally a fortress, it became a monastery in the 15th century and was severely damaged in the great earthquake of 1755. Now the old refectory has become the dining room and the cloisters are used on festive occasions for gala dinners.

Manor houses

The manor house scheme, to which numerous gracious old houses in Portugal belong, began in the north of the country. The scheme was created to conserve some of the country's most beautiful private manor houses and palaces. The owners of these magnificent homes can no longer afford the expensive maintenance and have opened them up to tourists, who are quite often treated as guests of the family.

The term "manor houses" has now broad-

> ### THE NITTY GRITTY
>
> For descriptions, addresses and telephone numbers, of *pousadas*, manor houses and other historic lodgings in Portugal, see the *Where to Stay* section of *Travel Tips*.

according to the period and are sometimes stuffed with antiques and valuable works of art.

● *Quintas and Herdades*: both of these are agricultural farms but a *quinta* differs in being a walled estate. Although mostly located in rural settings, some are handily situated for towns.

● *Casas Rústicas*: these are usually located in the heart of rural villages or on farms, and often quite isolated, they offer more simple architecture but still maintain a good level of comfort and amenities.   ❏

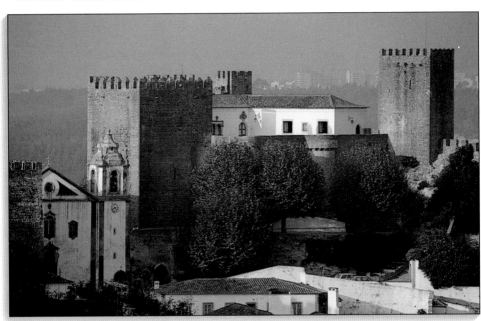

ened to encompass an extremely wide range of accommodation, which is available throughout the country. In the north of Portugal these houses are also known as *solares*. Stately manor houses, elegant country homes, farm houses and rustic cottages are all included in this one general description. They are often listed under three categories:

● *Casas Antigas*: elegant manor houses or country estates mostly originating from the 17th and 18th centuries. They are furnished

LEFT: an elegant corridor in the Pousada dos Lóios, in Evora. **ABOVE:** the Pousada do Castelo, in a prime spot in the walled town of Obidos.

> ### WHERE TO BOOK
>
> Although reservations can be made directly, there is a central agency in Lisbon which handles bookings for all *pousadas*. There is no minimum stay requirement. Contact **ENATUR**, Rua Santa Joana Princesa 10, 1700 Lisbon, tel: (01) 848 9078, fax: (01) 848 4349; web site: www.pousadas.pt. Several agencies handle bookings for Manor Houses. The chief ones are **PRIVATUR**, Central de Reservas, Manor Houses of Portugal, Apartado 596, 4900 Viana do Castelo, tel and fax: (058) 58 811491 (or visit on the Internet at www.manorhouses.com); and **TURIHAB**, Praça da República, 4990 Ponte de Lima tel: (058) 741 672, fax: (058) 741 444.

NATURAL PORTUGAL

*This is a land where complex forces of nature have created
diverse environments and opportunities for different lifestyles*

For a country no more than 565 km (350 miles) long and 220 km (137 miles) wide, at best, and edged by the Atlantic Ocean, Portugal enjoys a surprising diversity of topography, geography and climate. Half a day's journey in almost any direction leads through climatic zones, from wet to dry, hot to cool, through mountains to plains, from rich pastures to poor, from large estates to small farms, and from affluence to poverty. Adaptation, community by community and region by region, to the heterogeneous forces of nature has fashioned a country set apart from its neighbours and unique in Europe.

Climate

Portugal is the mixing pot of three powerful climatic regimes. It is attacked from the west by moist westerlies from the Atlantic, carrying rain deep into the country. These are arrested by a dry continental climate giving hot dry summers and cold dry winters in the interior. From the south a Mediterranean climate invades bringing hot dry summers and cooler, moist winters.

The high land mass of Serra da Estrela acts as a fulcrum point for all these climatic types. Descend from the mountain at any point and you will find a different country on the other side. The biggest contrast is from the wet northwest to the drier southeast.

Rain patterns vary from north to south, with the north receiving the highest rainfall, especially between November and March. Summer conditions are not too dissimilar, with all regions generally enjoying high temperatures tempered in coastal regions by Atlantic influences. Inland regions, particular in the port wine areas and Alentejo, suffer very high temperatures in summer.

One of the most useful indicators of a Mediterranean climate is the olive tree. This grows happily throughout most of Portugal with the exception of the mountainous regions and the most northerly part of Trás-os-Montes.

However, only Algarve enjoys anything approaching a truly Mediterranean-type climate and this has allowed its development as a year-round destination for holiday-makers. Even

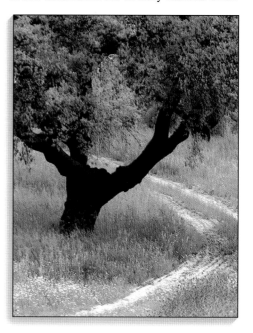

Algarve is not immune from Atlantic westerlies which sometimes bring spells of wet weather in winter.

Mountain life

Rolling granite mountains, safe refuges in ancient times, dominate the north. Many settlements from those early days remain even today. Here residents eke out an existence in a harsh environment using tools (adapted for their own needs) which have hardly changed over the centuries.

Although most of the mountain areas are lightly populated, there is an area of near-wilderness tucked away on the northern border

---

PRECEDING PAGES: hillside vineyards in the Douro valley.
LEFT: an isolated dwelling in the Alentejo plains.
RIGHT: a gnarled old cork tree.

of the country. Recognised as a sanctuary of wildlife and valued for the traditional way of life which persists in the villages on the fringes, the Parque Nacional Peneda-Gerês area, covering 720 sq. km (278 sq. miles) was opened in 1971. It is the country's only *national* park although other areas of natural beauty have been designated *natural* parks and are protected, but by less stringent regulations.

Most of the highest peaks in the northern mountains lie within the park. Many of these exceed 1,300 metres (4,265ft) with Nervosa reaching a height of 1,545 metres (5,069ft). But although this region is the most mountainous in the country, it is not the home of the highest peak of all. This distinction is reserved for the Serra da Estrela (Mountain of the Stars), an isolated, majestic mountain range in central Portugal which rises from the plains of Alentejo. Here, Torre, at 1,993 metres (6,539ft), marks the summit of Portugal. This area too enjoys protection but as a natural, not a national, park.

Geology

For its size, Portugal has remarkably diverse geology. Ancient crystalline rocks of granite and gneiss predominate in the mountainous regions, often presenting a landscape of grey

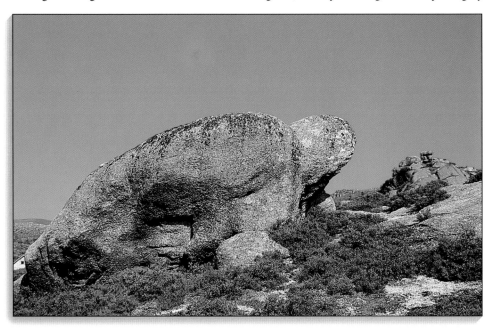

THE STORY OF MAIZE

The introduction of maize in the 16th century proved a lifeline for the people of the hill villages, for here was a crop they could adapt to their own situation. Land around the villages was pressed into use for maize and animals were moved to still higher pastures for the summer. More changes were demanded to meet the problems of storing the crop and grinding the corn. This resulted in granite-built stores perched on mushroom-shaped legs, *espigueiros*, as seen at Soajo. Water provided the power for grinding the corn. Water mills, again built of granite, were erected in profusion, often with the water of a single stream powering a succession of mills.

rounded hills and steep valleys. For many inhabitants, it is the only natural building material available and they have perfected the tools and ways to work this material to an art form. Granite is a hard material but it has just enough malleability to make it workable. The evidence is all around, especially in the north. Farms, churches, water mills and fencing posts for the vines are all solidly constructed from granite.

Limestone and marble are found in the central region, especially near Evora, where it is mined commercially, and near Coimbra. The Coimbra deposit is particularly valued by sculptors who have used it extensively. There is another significant limestone region, now protected as the Parque Natural de Serras de Aire e Candeeiros (*see page 245*). This area is riddled with deep caves, and three of them are open to the public.

River communities

Many of the rivers arising in the mountainous interior on the western side of the Iberian Peninsula flow to the Atlantic through Portugal. In fact, only one river, the Mondego, is truly Portuguese, rising in the region of Serra da Estrela and flowing into the sea at Coimbra. Some of these rivers were navigable in the past allowing boats access deep into the country-

see in Portugal, where productive farming has been practised for centuries.

In modern times, the Rio Douro has played a significant role in the development of the port wine trade. Good roads now penetrate the area but at the height of the port trade, all the wine had to be shipped down this difficult and dangerous river.

Perhaps the largest remaining river community is Lisbon itself, on the shores of the Rio Tejo (Tagus). The mouth of the Tejo proved to be a natural harbour offering safe anchorage to early traders. The prosperity of Lisbon has barely faltered throughout the ages.

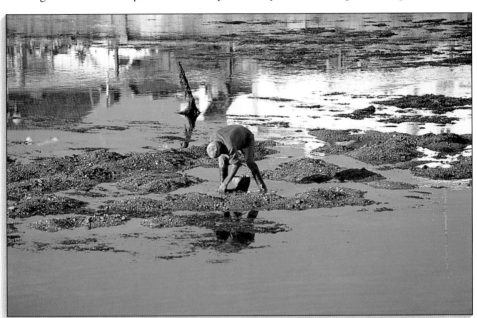

side. Early settlers were not slow to use the Rio Guadiana in this way to penetrate inland in search of metal ores. Mértola in Alentejo developed as a port under the Romans, to ship ores down the Guadiana from nearby São Domingos, and there are significant remains of the port area still to be seen.

The Romans were overwhelmed by the beauty of the Rio Lima in the north. This, for them, was the Lethe, the mythical River of Forgetfulness. This meandering river has created a fertile valley as beautiful as any you'll

Coastal life

With 832km (516 miles) of coastline, it is not surprising that the Portuguese are people of the sea. Fishing has sustained them over the centuries, providing an industry which has grown large on the one hand, especially through cod fishing, yet has also remained a small local activity. The coast is still littered with villages which rely heavily on reaping the harvest of the sea and especially on the sardine, which keeps many small fishermen in business.

Tuna fishing is another sector of this industry which grew to massive proportions. Shoals of tuna migrate along the southern shoreline towards spawning grounds in the Mediter-

LEFT: an ancient rock resembling a giant tortoise.
ABOVE: gathering shellfish on the Rio Gilao.

ranean. Floating traps were used to catch the fish and fishermen were on hand to complete the job. Regrettably, over-fishing led to a decline in numbers and the industry collapsed.

Fish, of which there is reckoned to be more than 200 species off these shores, is not the only commercial product. Algarve has produced salt from ancient times; the Romans salted fish here to export back to Rome, and there are still salt pans in operation. Seaweed for fertiliser is now less of an industry at Aveiro than it once was. Here, specially shaped boats, *moliceiros*, are used to collect seaweed from the extensive system of lagoons in the area.

found almost exclusively in the far west of the country. They can coexist with Mediterranean cistus species. Algarve offers the best display of Mediterranean flora including a rich array of wild orchids, like the bumblebee orchid (*Ophrys bombyliflora*) and the yellow bee orchid (*Ophrys lutea*).

Narcissus is especially associated with the Iberian peninsula and many are endemic, although some are found throughout the Mediterranean region. Portugal has its fair share, from the diminutive jonquil, *Narcissus gaditanus*, to more popular garden species like *N. bulbocodium* and *N. triandrus*.

The magnificent beaches adorning much of the coastline have themselves become an important commodity for tourism in this modern world. A lifelong dependence on the sea has yielded now to dependence on a transient industry subject to whim and fashion.

Flora

With so many different habitats, climates and micro-climates in this hugely diverse country, the flora responds with equal diversity. Many species simply reflect the climatic influence of the region. Certain erica heaths, green lavender (*Lavendula viridis*), and ulex species (gorse) typify Western Atlantic species and are

Fauna

Wild boars are one of the largest mammals roaming Portugal. Their foraging marks can be seen in many parts of the country, from the golf courses of Algarve – much to the fury of the green keepers – to the inland forests. Hunting for boar is a form of tourism which Alentejo is keen to develop. Rabbits and foxes are extremely common, genet (Egyptian mongoose) less so, but the best wildlife sanctuary is the Parque National Peneda-Gerês, in the north (*see page 134*). Brown bears have not been seen for centuries but there are still some wolves, and plenty of beech martens, deer, badgers and otters around.

Birdlife is particularly rich in some areas, especially around the old saltpans in Algarve, where some 300 species have been recorded. Around Lisbon, too, 200 sq. km (77 sq. miles) of the Tejo estuary are protected as one of the most important wetland areas in Europe. Apart from variety, the birds are often present in great numbers with, for example, as many as 10,000 avocet to be seen. The west coast estuaries and wetlands are situated on some of the major migratory routes, so spring and autumn can be particularly rewarding for ornithologists. Sadly, in some areas years of uncontrolled hunting have significantly reduced wildlife.

The Australian eucalyptus was introduced in 1856 for the paper industry, on account of its rapid growth, but its future is now in the balance. Environmentalists have thrown their weight behind farmers who oppose further plantations on the grounds of its destructive influence. Not only are eucalyptus rapacious in their demand for water, but they provide poor natural habitats and their litter is so slow to decompose that it further inhibits naturally occurring cycles within the soil.

The almond and the carob are indigenous to the Algarve, the latter bearing long wizened beans which yield a fine variety of oil. ❑

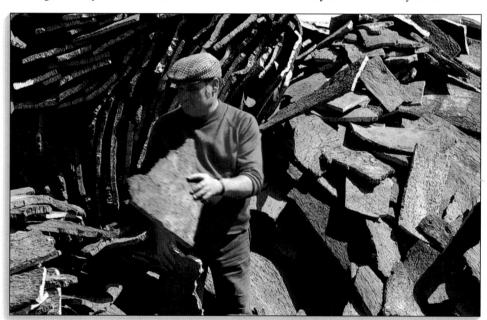

Trees of life

Forestry in Portugal is big business with around one-third of the country, some 3 million hectares (7.5 million acres), under forest. Pine, said in Portugal to be of use from cradle to grave, is used to produce timber for furniture and construction as well as resin for pitch and turpentine. Pine accounts for around 40 percent of the country's wooded land. Pulp, used to manufacture paper and cardboard, is economically the most important woodland product.

FAR LEFT: the *Narcissus bulbocodium*.
LEFT: thousands of avocet visit the Tejo estuary.
ABOVE: at work in a Portalegre cork factory.

THE CORK INDUSTRY

About half the cork in the world, from stoppers in champagne bottles to the linings of spacecraft, comes from Alentejo. The cultivation of cork is not for the impatient: there's a wait of 25 years before the first crop is stripped from the trunk and a further decade before the next harvest. Cork is a labour-intensive industry, as machines cannot duplicate the expertise of the men who strip bark from the trees, although the punching out of corks and stoppers is increasingly mechanised. Although plastic corks are becoming popular for wine bottling, it will be a long time before such artificial products make any significant impact on the Portuguese cork industry.

PLACES

*A detailed guide to the entire country, with principal sites
clearly cross-referenced by number to the maps*

There isn't a wrong way to explore Portugal – except to make too many plans in advance. A car is the handiest way to travel because, although the trains are good and the buses adequate, they won't allow you the freedom to go just over the next hill... and the next, and the next. Portugal is wonderfully seductive.

Roads have been enormously improved and extended in recent years. A motorway links Lisbon with Porto in the north, and goes on to Valença. The road south from Lisbon bypasses several towns which were once visited on a tortuous road. East–west expressways help you leap distances but north–south roads tend to be narrower, more winding, and less well maintained.

Lisbon and its environs are the best starting point for a first taste of Portugal. From there, if the weather is fine, you may want simply to head south, to the glorious beaches of Algarve. After relaxing for a few days, you might start meandering back through the Portuguese countryside. Begin by exploring the expanse of Alentejo, spectacular plains with the entrancing ancient town of Evora in their midst.

Cutting back towards the Atlantic, still heading north, you could visit the old university town of Coimbra and the surrounding sights. Look in on some of the traditional fishing communities along the coast: to the north is the Rio Douro and the wine districts of Douro and Minho. Here, world-famous port, delicious *vinhos verdes*, and other wines are produced.

The far interior north of Portugal is called Trás-os-Montes, a marvellous remote and hauntingly beautiful area. And below Trás-os-Montes, still ruggedly hilly, is the Beira Alta; below that, the plains of Alentejo creep up into the province of Beira Baixa. And if you have time to visit the islands of Madeira and the Azores, you'll discover a different world altogether.

Taste decides where you go, whether you prefer the north, rural and quiet, or the south, hot and crowded. You'll wander through towns with a rich and ancient architecture – and discos and smart shops. Accommodation ranges from luxury hotels, *pousadas* and private manor houses to simple rooms above village restaurants. Portugal is small, but almost everywhere you may have the sensation of being lost in a magical landscape – yet knowing that Lisbon, or wherever you next want to go, is handily close.

Once upon a time, fleets of bold explorers sailed from these shores. You might think discovery an out-dated notion – until you discover for yourself the pleasures of Portugal.   ❏

PRECEDING PAGES: rooftops of port bodegas in Vila Nova de Gaia, opposite Porto; a festival in Viana do Castelo; a shaggy traffic jam in the streets of Carviçais.
LEFT: proud prow of a painted boat.

Portugal

0   30 km
0   30 miles

Map on pages 164–5

LISBON

With cafés, culture and a castle, Lisbon is a vibrant city, mixing old-world charm, local colour and modern amenities. A good local transport system will help you discover the best of it

L isbon (Lisboa) offers a wealth of delights to indulge all tastes, from cultural forays to endless shopping opportunities and an abundance of places in which to sample the local gastronomy. There is no shortage of pleasant leafy retreats, and *miradours* (viewpoints) are liberally dotted around the city. By day, life centres around the cafés where delicious coffee and cakes will tempt even the most ardent dieter. The city really comes alive in the evening and can justifiably claim some of the best nightlife around, especially in the small wine bars and restaurants of Alfama and Bairro Alto. This is where you are most likely to chance upon impromptu *fado*, the soulful songs of lost loves and past glories.

A flavour of what Lisbon has to offer can be sampled in a crowded one-day visit, but that is barely enough even to scratch the surface of the city's complexities. Three days allow time to absorb some of the atmosphere, and city lovers will probably find a week too short. Lisbon's climate of hot summers and mild winters makes it an ideal place to visit for most of the year, although spring and autumn are good times to enjoy the city at its best.

Many of the highlights of a visit to Lisbon are conveniently concentrated in two main areas, the heart of the city centred around the Baixa, and a significant cluster out along the riverside at Belém. Baixa is the hub of the city centre, watched over by Castelo São Jorge, below which cling the narrow streets and alleys of Alfama. To the west lies Bairro Alto, entered through the Chiado area which has been restored after a disastrous fire all but destroyed it in 1988. North, beyond Rossio, lie Praça Marquês de Pombal and Parque Eduardo VII.

PRECEDING PAGES: a view of Castelo de São Jorge. **LEFT:** Monument of the Discoveries. **BELOW:** the Ponte 25 do Abril.

Building bridges

Most architecture in the city is post-1755, after the great earthquake, except for Alfama and Belém which escaped virtually unscathed. There has been an upsurge in the restoration of old buildings and many dilapidated palaces and mansions have been tastefully renovated. Many have become elegant restaurants, fashionable boutiques, art galleries and even discotheques. Crumbling houses in the old quarters are also being restored and in outlying neighbourhoods there are new hotels, vast and popular shopping malls, office complexes, cinemas and museums.

Visitors usually arrive by air and enter the city from the northeast but a spectacular entrance is over the Ponte 25 de Abril from the south. Completed in 1966, it was originally called the Salazar Bridge, after the dictator, but was renamed in 1974 when democracy was restored to Portugal. A new bridge, Ponte Vasco da Gama, further up the river, was built in time for Expo '98 to ease congestion but locals still prefer the convenience of the old bridge.

A touch of history

The mythical founding of the city on seven hills is attributed to Ulysses (Odysseus) and his encounter with the nymph Calypso. Left behind when he departed, the heartbroken nymph turned herself into a snake whose coils became the seven hills. In reality, there has been a settlement on the site at least since pre-historic times. Its advantageous geographical position caught the attention of Phoenician traders in search of safe anchorage who developed a port, Alis Ubbo (Serene Port), around 1200 BC. The Greeks then the Carthaginians subsequently laid claim to the site. In 205 BC Olisipo (as it was then known) was incorporated into the Roman province of Lusitani and became its capital 68 years later. Julius Caesar elevated the status of the city to a *municipium* in 60 BC and renamed it Felicitas Julia. What little remains of the Roman occupation today is from this period of relative prosperity and growth. As the Roman Empire crumbled, the city was left unprotected and vulnerable to attacks by a succession of barbaric Germanic tribes.

After the arrival of the Moors in the 8th century, the city enjoyed 400 years of stability and increasing prosperity, in spite of occasional attacks as the Christians pushed south in their attempts to expel the infidels. Moorish rule effectively came to an end in 1147, when the first king of the newly formed nation of Portugal, Dom (King) Afonso Henriques, captured Lisbon. It was to be over a century later, around 1260, before the Moors were finally vanquished and the capital moved from Coimbra to Lisbon.

The city continued to flourish and a university was established in 1290 by Dom Dinis but transferred to Coimbra in 1308. A power struggle between the Church and the Crown, over the next 200 years, saw the university shunted

BELOW: a 16th-century panorama of the city.

LISBONA.

between the two cities. In the end, Coimbra won that particular battle and Lisbon was left without a university until 1911.

Progress was cruelly interrupted by outbreaks of the Black Death during the 14th and 15th centuries, which destroyed a large percentage of the population. The dawn of the "Age of Discoveries" at the end of the 15th century saw Lisbon burgeon into an important trading centre. Wealth from the opening up of the sea route to India by Vasco da Gama, flowed into the country. Lisbon entered a golden age which lasted for a century before a 60-year period of Spanish rule saw a decline in fortunes.

For a while, after the Spanish were ousted, Lisbon suffered economically as maritime trade declined but the discovery of gold in Brazil ensured a return to former prosperity. Most of this fortune was squandered by Dom João V on lavish building projects, which were destroyed in the massive earthquake of 1755. Fortunately for Lisbon, the Marquês de Pombal was on hand to oversee the rebuilding of the city but the days of easy fortune were past.

Since then, Lisbon has witnessed the end of the monarchy and endured a period of dictatorship under Salazar. A return to democracy was achieved in 1974 after a peaceful revolution.

Baixa and the city centre

Baixa covers the level area in between the hills of Alfama and Bairro Alto. It slopes gently to the banks of the Rio Tejo (Tagus), from Rossio and down through the famous grid system of streets planned by the Marquês de Pombal after the 1755 earthquake. City life centres around the vast expanse of the **Praça do Comércio** ❶ by the riverside. The earlier name of the square, Terreiro do

Map on page 154

TIP

Walking is the best way to see the city, but there is a good transport system of trams (*eléctricos*), buses, taxis and lifts (*elevadors*). Avoid the inevitable traffic jams by using the efficient Metro system.

BELOW: the Praça do Comércio.

Central Lisbon

Map on page 154

Paço, is still used and dates back to the time before the earthquake when the 16th-century royal palace stood on the site. Behind the elegant Pombaline neo-classical arcades are housed Lisbon's Stock Exchange, or Bolsa, to the east and to the west the post office. In splendid isolation in the centre stands a bronze statue of the ruler at the time of the earthquake, Dom José I, which has given rise to the English name of Black Horse Square. The riverside serves as a quay for ferry boats along the Tagus and across to the *Outra Banda*, the communities on the southern shore of the river. Completely overshadowing the delicacy of the arcaded buildings is the impressive triumphal **Arco Rua Augusta**. The arch is a late 19th-century addition to Pombal's 18th-century layout.

A short walk along the road, from the northeast corner of the square, is the notable Manueline doorway of the church of **Nossa Senhora da Conceição Velha ❷**. Further along, the unusual pyramidal stone façade of the 16th-century **Casa dos Bicos ❸** ("House of the Pointed Stones") seems almost modernistic. There is a clear distinction between the lower storeys, which survived the 1755 earthquake, and the top two storeys which were faithfully reproduced from old engravings during the 1980s. A short distance further along the road lies the little noticed 13th-century fountain **Chafariz d'el Rei**, once the major source of the city's water supply.

Leaving the square from the northwest corner you pass the spot where, in 1908, Carlos I and his heir, Luís Felipe, were assassinated. Close by is the **Praça do Municipio ❹**, with an 18th-century *pelourinho* (pillory) and the **Câmara Municipal** (Town Hall), where Portugal was declared a republic in 1910. Further west, trains arrive from Estoril and Cascais at the Cais do Sodré railway station close to the city's main market, **Mercado da Ribeira ❺**. This is a colourful place selling an amazing array of fresh produce, including fish landed at the nearby Ribeira dock. There's a really lively atmosphere here, with plenty of bars, bistros and restaurants.

Back in the Praça do Comércio, make a grand entrance through the Arco Rua Augusta into the neat grid of streets which form the main area of Baixa, the lower town. Pedestrianised Rua Augusta provides plenty of diversions along the way as it sweeps up towards Rossio. Shops are definitely the main attraction but, at busy times, street entertainers and balloon sellers lend a carnival atmosphere and pavement cafés bring a Parisian feel to the scene. At one time, the streets of the grid represented various crafts, hence names such as Rua da Prata (silver), Rua do Ouro (gold) and Rua dos Franqueiros (habadashers). Today, many of these streets are home to banks and offices as well as shops.

Rua Augusta opens into **Praça Dom Pedro IV ❻**, better known by its common name of **Rossio**, and the focus of major city events for 500 years until the 18th century. This was where citizens gathered to enjoy carnivals and bullfights or to witness public executions, particularly the *autos-da-fé* of the Inquisition. Now, cafés, flower sellers, shops, kiosks and traffic create a swirl of activity and colour in a square much favoured by the locals, who spend the time of day at one of the many pavement cafés, such as **Café Nicola**.

Lottery tickets, on sale everywhere.

BELOW: the neo-Manueline Rossio Station.

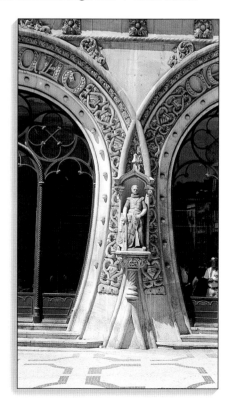

At the northern end of the square, the **Teatro Nacional** (Dona Maria II Theatre), built in the 1840s, overlooks the two fountains brought from Paris in 1890 which flank the statue of Dom Pedro IV. They are rather more authentic than the statue, which is really a cobbled version of an original statue of Emperor Maximilian of Mexico. This had arrived on a ship, carrying it from Marseilles to Mexico, just as news came of the Emperor's assassination. Obviously pressed for cash at the time, the city council snapped it up as the bargain of the day and attempted some remodelling in the hope no one would notice. **Paço dos Condes de Almada** (Palace of the Counts of Almada), just to the east of the theatre, is where the *Restauradores* conspired in 1640 to wrest power back from the Spaniards. The Igreja de São Domingos nearby oversaw the sentencing of victims of the Inquisition, who had been tried in the palace which once stood on the Teatro Nacional site. South of the church lies the quieter ambience of **Praça da Figueira** (Figtree Square) with its statue of João I.

To the northwest of Rossio is the **Estação do Rossio** (**Rossio Station**), with its lovely neo-Manueline façade. Trains from Sintra arrive on the fourth floor, at the level of Bairro Alto (the upper part of town), from where an escalator takes passengers down to Baixo level. They emerge not far from **Praça dos Restauradores ❼**, named in honour of the "Restorers", the conspirators who plotted to overthrow Spanish rule in the 17th century, and place King João IV on the throne. In this square stands the 18th-century **Palácio Foz**, now used by *Turismo* as a tourist information centre and a venue for cultural events. Until 1821, access to the square was closed off to keep out the rabble inhabiting Rossio Square and thereby create a peaceful haven for the gentry. It was then opened up to the general public and used for celebrations and dances.

BELOW: flowers for sale in the Rossio.

East to Alfama

Alfama is the oldest part of the city, and clings tenaciously around the feet of the Castelo de São Jorge. The steep narrow streets and alleys of this old Moorish quarter spill down to the riverside, and a succession of conquerors over millenniums have left vestiges of their occupation. A tapestry of life unfolds around every corner: drink it all in, but keep a tight hold on your valuables. The area really comes alive on 12 and 13 June for the feast of St Anthony of Padua (1195–1231), the unofficial patron saint of Lisbon who was born in the area (he acquired his title after a sojourn in Italy).

Head up from Baixa past the Igreja de Madalena, dating from the late 18th century but preserving a Manueline porch from an earlier church. On the left, as the Romanesque façade of the Sé comes into view, is the small church of **Santo António da Sé** (open Tues–Sun; closed 1–2pm; entrance charge). The church, built on the alleged site of St Anthony's birthplace, is now a museum, the **Museu Antóniano**, devoted to his life. It was rebuilt in 1767 and attracts many devotees.

Seeing the Sé

Dom Afonso Henriques, the first king of Portugal, ordered the **Sé (Cathedral)** ❽ (open Tues–Sun: closed 1–2pm) to be built soon after banishing the Moors from Lisbon in 1147. The first incumbent was an Englishman, Gilbert of Hastings, who fared rather better than the 14th-century Bishop Martinho Anes, who was flung from the north tower for harbouring Spanish sympathies. Today the cathedral's fortress-like façade stands testament to the turbulent times in which it was constructed: it was to be more than a century before the Moors

St Anthony is the unofficial patron saint of Lisbon.

LEFT: a colourful façade in Alfama.
BELOW: old cinema in Rossio.

The knife-grinder is a familiar figure in the streets of Lisbon, as in any Portuguese town.

BELOW: the ruined cloisters of the Cathedral.

were finally ousted from country. There has been much restoration over the centuries but the two original crenellated towers, softened by the large rose window in between, remain the most striking feature.

Inside, the barrel-vaulted ceiling leads to a low lantern and to the left, on entry, is the baptismal font where St Anthony was christened in 1195. Further along, in the first chapel on the left, is a beautifully detailed *crèche* – nativity scene – by the sculptor Joaquim Machado de Castro. The chancel is 18th century and the ambulatory was remodelled in the 14th century but the gloomy interior and cloisters are in desperate need of a complete overhaul. In the third chapel from the south side of the ambulatory are the tombs of Lopo Fernandes Pacheco and his wife. He was a companion in arms to Afonso IV (1325–57), and responsible for much remodelling during those years.

The ruined cloisters are well worth the modest entrance fee, if only to view the interesting excavations taking place in what were once the gardens. Remains of Moorish buildings overlay an obvious Roman street but there is still much speculation as to whether or not a mosque once stood on the site. Conclusive evidence, apparently, would lie under the existing building which the Church authorities are understandably loath to disturb. Long-term plans are for an underground museum, in which to view the remains, and the restoration of the cloister gardens above.

In the sacristy, off the south transept, is the cathedral treasury where numerous sacred objects are on view. Of most importance is the casket containing the remains of St Vincent, the official patron saint of Lisbon, which were brought here by the order of Afonso Henriques from Sagres in Algarve. Legend relates how ravens accompanied the boat that carried his remains from Spain and

Map
on page
154

again on the journey from Algarve to Lisbon. To this day, the raven is a feature of Lisbon's coat of arms.

Still heading uphill, you will reach the **Miradouro de Santa Luiza** which is a good vantage point to look down over Alfama. The church of the same name is decorated externally with some interesting *azulejo* panels, one showing the heroic soldier Martim Moniz, who died keeping the city gate open – an act which enabled Afonso Henriques to capture Lisbon. A little further up is **Largo das Portas do Sol** ➒ (Sun Gate), where one of the original city gates once stood. A statue of St Vincent looks out over the city from this popular viewpoint. Terrace cafés provide an excuse to linger, and the 17th-century palace of the counts of Azurara, now the **Museu Escola de Artes Decorativas (Museum of Decorative Art)** ➓, is certainly worth a visit (open Tues–Sun entrance charge). The museum is a showcase for the work of Portugal's master craftsmen.

The Spanish patron saint of Lisbon, St Vincent, has never enjoyed the same popularity as St Anthony, the city's unofficial patron saint.

The Castelo de São Jorge

Perhaps the most beautiful view of the city is from the ramparts of **Castelo de São Jorge** ⓫ (open daily; entrance free), which crowns the first hill east of the city centre. If you want to take the hard work out of the climb up to the castle, you could take a taxi or catch the Number 28 Graça tram to Portas do Sol, then visit the Sé and surrounding sites on the walk down. The castle can be seen from nearly anywhere in Lisbon, serving as an apt and romantic reminder of the capital's ancient roots. Many of the castle walls and towers are from the Moorish stronghold, although there were earlier fortifications on this site.

After the Portuguese drove out the Moors in 1147, the residence of the Moorish governor, Paço de Alcáçova, became the royal palace of Dom Dinis

BELOW: moonrise over Castelo do São Jorge.

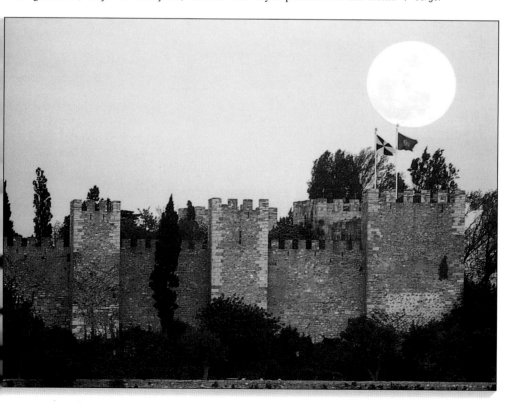

(1279–1325). It remained a royal residence until Dom Manuel (1495–1521) decided to build a more comfortable royal residence down by the river. Except for a short period, when Dom Sebastião preferred the military fortification of the castle to the graceful splendour of the palace, it served its time as a barracks and prison until 1939, when it was freed from any official duties.

All that is left now are walls, 10 towers and the remnants of the palace, but shaded gardens, fountains and a restaurant, presided over by a statue of Afonso Henriques, make it an ideal spot to escape the heat of summer. The *miradouro* (lookout spot) provides a marvellous panorama of the city, and from here it is possible to pick out many of the city's landmarks. Further good viewpoints lie to the north at the baroque **Igreja de Nossa Senhora da Graça** ⑫ and beyond that, the even higher Senhora do Monte.

The exiled King Carol of Romania, who died in 1953, is buried, with his wife, in the church of São Vicente de Fora.

Outside the city walls

A short walk from the castle leads to the **Igreja de São Vicente de Fora** ⑬ (open daily; entrance free): *de fora* describes the church's position outside the city walls. It was built on the site of a 12th-century monastery dedicated to St Vincent, which commemorated the battle fought by the crusaders to capture Lisbon. The white limestone building, with short twin towers, was designed by the Italian architect Filippo Terzi; construction began in 1582, and took more than 40 years.

Of more interest than the church interior are the cloisters (open daily; entrance charge), which are covered with 18th-century *azulejos* depicting La Fontaine's *Fables*. The former refectory, off the cloisters, has served as the Pantheon of the Royal House of Bragança since the mid-19th century. Portuguese kings and queens, princes and princesses, from João IV (who died in 1656), are entombed here.

BELOW: the Aqueduto das Aguas Livres.

A flea market, **Feira da Ladra** ⑭ – literally, the Thieves' Market – takes place twice a week in the Campo de Santa Clara. You must cross this square to reach the baroque **Igreja de Santa Engrácia** ⑮, now the National Pantheon containing monuments to many of Portugal's non-royal heroes. Work on this church started in 1682 but was not completed until 1966, giving rise to the Portuguese idiom for a project never finished: *"obras* [works] *de Santa Engrácia"*. Although the building is in the compact, satisfying shape of a Greek cross, with a central dome, the stamp of Salazar on its eventual completion has left it a somewhat sterile monument.

Back down towards the riverside, opposite **Estação Santa Apolónia**, the railway station for international arrivals, is the **Museu Militar** ⑯ (open Tues–Sun; entrance charge). This museum charts Portugal's military history in paintings and extensive collections of armour and weapons in a building which was, until 1851, the national arsenal.

Head eastward, along the coastal route, paralleling the railway lines, then turn left up Calçada dos Barbadinhos to the **Manuel da Maia Museu da Agua da EPAL** ⑰ (Museum of Water; open Tues–Sat, closed public holidays; entrance charge). Named after the engineer of the Aqueduto das Aguas Livres (*see* *page 162*), it was the first steam pumping station of its kind in Portugal. The building, in a surprisingly tranquil oasis, records the history of Lisbon's water supply from Roman times and includes the story of the aqueduct.

Further east stands the tile museum, the **Museu Nacional do Azulejo** (open Tues pm, Wed–Sun; closed 12.30–2pm; entrance charge). Again, the easiest route runs parallel to the railway track, but you may find it worth taking a taxi. The building was originally part of the Convento da Madre de Deus, founded in 1509 by the widow of João II, Dona Leonor of Lancaster. All that remains of the original exterior is the Manueline doorway, but the 18th-century interior of the main church provides the perfect foil for the national collection of *azulejos*, in a breathtaking combination of gilded woodwork, blue-and-white Dutch *azulejos* and superbly painted walls and ceilings. One of the most outstanding tile scenes is a 1730 panorama of Lisbon, some 37 metres (120 ft) long. Besides tiles and architecture, there are paintings to admire, a bookshop to browse in, and a very pleasant café/restaurant.

A long haul further up the Tejo, just past the Estação do Orient, is the Expo '98 site, now called Parque dos Nações where the Ocean Pavilion, one of the biggest oceanaria in Europe, remains as a permanent fixture, together with other pavilions which now house government offices and conference centres.

Through Bairro Alto

Bairro Alto rises just to the west of Baixa. This area is renowned for its choice shops and restaurants. Shoppers may prefer to stroll up past the delights of the fashionable **Chiado** district, stopping off for a drink in A Brasileira, a café favoured by artists and politicians. Alternatively, choose the easy way, the

The tram is the most pleasant way to get around in Lisbon – other than walking, of course.

BELOW: taking it easy in the Chiado.

Elevador de Santa Justa , designed by Raoul Mesnier de Ponsard, but often wrongly attributed to Gustave Eiffel. The restaurant on the very top of the Santa Justa lift offers excellent views down over the Baixa and across to the castle.

A walkway, alongside the roofless **Convento do Carmo** ⑳, connects the lift with the Largo do Carmo and entrance to the convent. This remarkable ruin is one of Lisbon's most poignant sights. It was built by Nuno Alvares Pereira, João I's young general at the Battle of Aljubarrota (1385), who spent the last eight years of his life here. Left unrestored after the 1755 earthquake, the remains of the nave give the most eloquent reminder of that tumultuous event. Gothic arches soar skywards over a grassy nave, a venue for occasional concerts, while the part which survived serves as an archaeological museum with some curious tombs, including that of Dom Fernando I, who died in 1383.

From the convent, turn right on Rua Garrett, then left on Rua Serpa Pinto, to reach Lisbon's opera house, the **Teatro de São Carlos** ㉑. La Scala in Milan and the San Carlos theatre in Naples were the inspiration behind its construction in 1792, and the Italian influence is obvious. A short walk to the northwest, along Rua Nova da Trindade, brings you to **Igreja São Roque** (St Rock Church) ㉒ (open Tues–Sun; closed 1–2pm). Behind an unremarkable post-1755 façade lies an opulent interior. The ceiling has been painted to give a beautiful *tromp l'oeil* effect, and the eight chapels are all individual works of art. There are notable *azulejos* by Francisco de Matos and an excellent canvas, *Vision of St Rock* painted by Gaspar Dias around 1584.

The main draw is the **Capela de São João Baptista**, said to be the costliest chapel in the world and commissioned in 1742 by João V. Luigi Vanvitelli and Niccol*o* Salvi designed and built it in Rome, where it was blessed by the Pope, then dismantled and transported to Lisbon. Gold, silver and bronze decorate the extravagant confection of lapis lazuli, alabaster, marble and ivory, central to which is a mosaic of St John.

Adjoining the church is the **Museu de Arte Sacra**, a small but impressive collection of vestments and ecclesiastical furnishings in rich baroque designs.

If you continue up Rua Dom Pedro V, you will reach the **Solar do Instituto do Vinho do Porto** ㉓, the Port Wine Institute. A vast selection of ports can be sampled in the cosy bar of this former 18th-century palace. Virtually opposite is the shady São Pedro de Alcântara *miradouro* (viewpoint) whihc offers a very admirable panorama of the city.

The Portuguese delight in gardens, so naturally Lisbon is laced with green spaces. Perhaps the finest of them all is the **Jardim Botânico** ㉔, to the right of the Praça do Príncipe Real, one of the richest such gardens in Europe. Created in 1873, it has a magnificent wall of 100-year-old palm trees, banana trees, bamboo and water lilies, and many tropical plants.

Northwest, up the Rua das Amoreiras beyond Largo do Rato, is a large, simple building, the **Mãe d'Agua das Amoreiras** ㉕, which once stored the city's water supply, brought in along the **Aqueduto das Aguas Livres** (enquire at *Turismo* about visits). Eager shoppers may be tempted to investigate the shops in the nearby **Centro Comercial Amoreiras**.

BELOW: the atmospheric ruins of the Convento do Carmo.

South from Amoreiras (head down Rua Ferreira Borges into Domingo Sequeira) are the attractive Jardim da Estréla and the splendid late 18th-century **Basílica da Estréla** ㉖, with its great dome and multi-hued marble interior. This neighbourhood is in some ways an Anglo-Saxon oasis. Close by is the British Hospital, the little English Church of St George, and the adjacent **Cemitério dos Ingleses** (English Cemetery) where Henry Fielding (1707–54), the author of *Tom Jones*, was buried, after a trip to the warmer climes of Lisbon failed to cure his gout or asthma. Special permission is required to visit the nearby **Palácio de São Bento** ㉗ (east along Calçada da Estréla), now the Portuguese Houses of Parliament. Originally built as a monastery, the palace was transformed into the parliament building at the end of the 19th century and was renovated in 1935.

From here, take the Avenida Dom Carlos I down to the river and turn right to reach the **Museu Nacional de Arte Antiga** ㉘ (Museum of Ancient Art; open Tues–Sun, Thur till 7pm; closed 1–2pm; entrance charge). This, one of Lisbon's most important museums, is located in a fine 17th-century palace (property of the Counts of Alvor), with a tasteful modern extension. The term "ancient" may be misleading, as most of the exhibits are only a few centuries old, but there are fine displays of 16th-century porcelain, brought back by Portuguese sailors from India, Japan and Macau, and displays of furniture, sculpture and glass. Perhaps of most interest, the museum's galleries also hold a wide selection of paintings by Nuno Gonçalves and other artists of the 15th–16th-century Portuguese School (*see page 123*), as well as works by Hieronymus Bosch, Brueghel the Younger, Hans Memling, Giambattista Tiepolo, José de Ribera and other great masters.

Maps on 154 & 164–5

The landmark Amoreiras Shopping Centre is a very popular destination for shoppers in Lisbon. It has over 300 shops.

BELOW LEFT: the Centro Comercial Amoreiras.
BELOW: interior of the Basílica da Estréla.

Lisbon

Belém

In a green spacious zone by the river, on the western side of town beyond the **Ponte 25 de Abril** and the broad Avenida da Ponte, a number of monumental buildings stand as testimony to Portugal's maritime past. Belém means Bethlehem, and reflects the country's involvement with the crusades.

A local speciality are sweet tarts, known as "Pastéis de Bélem". You can buy them from the Pastelaria Casa dos Pastéis de Bélem.

Lisbon's most glorious monument is the **Mosteiro dos Jerónimos** (open Tues–Sun; closed holidays; entrance charge to cloisters), built to honour Vasco da Gama and his successful journey to India in 1498, and now a UNESCO World Heritage Site. This vast opulent limestone building, a masterpiece of Manueline (or late Gothic) architecture (*see page 117*), took 70 years to complete. Entrance is through the west door into a low vaulted section, where effigies of Vasco da Gama and Luís de Camões lie. This contrasts sharply with the soaring elegance of the main body of the church. Ribbed vaulting, supported by polygonal columns, becomes an eye-catching star-shaped feature, where the transepts cross and elephant-supported tombs are a reminder of India. The delicacy of the sculpting make the double-storey cloisters well worth a visit.

Built on the western side of the monastery, in the latter part of the 19th century, is a wing which houses the **Museu Nacional de Arqueologia do Dr Leite Vasconcelos** (National Museum of Archaeology and Ethnology), which has an interesting collection of folk art dating to the Stone and Bronze Ages (open Tues pm, Wed–Sun; closed noon–2pm; entrance charge). Part of the same wing, the **Museu da Marinha** (Maritime Museum), tells the story of Portugal's seafaring discoveries with redundant royal barges and fishing vessels on display in a separate building (open Tues–Sun; closed Mon and holidays; entrance charge). The **Planetário Calouste Gulbenkian** (Planetarium) behind gives presentations every Saturday.

BELOW: the splendid portal of the Mosteiro dos Jerónimos.

Close by, the huge and highly controversial **Centro Cultural de Belém**, opened in 1992 when Portugal assumed the EC (now EU) presidency, impinges on the glorious architecture of an earlier age and continues to affront the sensibilities of the local people.

On the bank of the Rio Tejo, on the far side of the broad Avenida da India and a small park, stands the **Torre de Belém** (open Tues–Sun; entrance charge), on the site where Vasco da Gama and other navigators set out on their explorations. This exquisite little 16th-century fortress is another fine example of the Manueline style, with its richly carved niches, towers and shields bearing the Templar cross.

A short distance to the east is the **Museu de Arte Popular** (open Tues–Sun; closed 12.30–2pm; entrance charge), with regional displays of local folk art. On the waterfront close by, you can't miss the impressive **Padrão dos Descobrimentos**, the Monument of the Discoveries (open Tues–Sun; closed holidays; entrance charge). Erected in 1960, the monument is a stylised caravel, with Prince Henry the Navigator at the fore gazing seawards and other leading figures of the age behind him .

East of the monument, on the Calçada da Ajuda, rises the ornate rose-coloured **Palácio de Belém**, which once served as a royal retreat but is now the official residence of the President of the Republic.

Adjacent, in what was once the royal riding-school, is the **Museu Nacional dos Coches ㊳** (Coach Museum), which houses one of the finest collections of coaches in Europe (open Tues–Sun; closed 1–2pm; entrance charge). Up the hill to the side of the palace is the imposing **Palácio da Ajuda ㊴**, built after the earthquake as a royal palace but never completed. It is now used for exhibitions and concerts, and some rooms are open to the public (open Thur–Tues; entrance charge).

The northern hills

Travelling northeast and crossing the Avenida da Ponte again (all but the most hardy will do this by public transport or taxi), you will find that the **Parque Eduardo VII ㊵** provides an immediate escape from the clamour of the city and offers magnificent views back down to the Tejo. The park was named to mark the state visit of King Edward VII of England in 1903, which was the first he made to a foreign country after his coronation. In the top left-hand corner of the park, but reached from Rua Castilho, are two greenhouses, the **Estufa Quente** (hot-house), originally built to house exotic orchids, and the better known **Estufa Fria** (cold-house).

At the southeast corner of the park is the **Praça Marquês de Pombal ㊶**, or the Rotunda, as it is more commonly known. From his lofty perch in the centre, a statue of the Marquês looks out over the city he rebuilt. From here, the **Avenida da Liberdade** sweeps southwards, linking the Rotunda with the Baixa area. The Avenida was developed as a dual carriageway in 1879 and became the epitome of style, with palm trees and water features lining the route. Cafés and old façades still lend pockets of shaded elegance, despite modern-day intru-

Map on page 164–5

TIP

The Centro Comercial Colombo, one of the biggest shopping centres in the Iberian peninsula, is opposite the Benfica Football Stadium (Colegio Militar Metro) and opens daily from 10am–9pm.

LEFT: the Torre de Belém.
BELOW: tranquillity in the Parque Eduardo VII.

A colourful kiosk in the Avenida.

sions. The little **Parque Mayer**, about two-thirds of the way down, is an enclave of restaurants and theatres, the latter specialising in popular comedy known as *revistas*, satirical variety shows commenting on current political events.

Gulbenkian's legacy

Instead of returning to Baixa, leave the Parque Eduardo VII by the northern exit and walk northeast for a short way to a large landscaped complex containing the **Fundação Calouste Gulbenkian** ⓸ (open Tues–Sun; entrance charge). The Foundation was set up by the Turkish-Armenian oil magnate, who was born in Istanbul in 1869 and became very attached to Portugal after being exiled there during World War II. The Foundation is the most important funding source for the arts in Portugal, and there are Gulbenkian libraries and museums throughout the country . When Calouste Gulbenkian died in 1955 his collection, one of the richest private collections in the world, was bequeathed to the nation.

The museum's contents include displays of Middle Eastern and Islamic Art, Chinese porcelain, Japanese prints and gold and silver Greek coins. Among magnificent exhibits from the West, are paintings by 17th-century masters like Rubens and Rembrandt and by Impressionists such as Renoir, Manet and Monet. There are also rich Italian tapestries; and a whole room dedicated to the Art Nouveau creations of René Lalique. A pleasant walk through the park-like complex leads to the **Centro de Arte Moderna**, which displays the work of 20th-century Portuguese artists (open Tues–Sun; entrance charge).

For a rather diffrent form of entertainment, you can take the Metro one stop northwest to the zoo, or **Jardim Zoológico** ⓷ (open 9am daily; entrance charge), which is set in the Parque das Laranjeiras (Orange Tree Park). Just

BELOW: the Marquês de Pombal surveys his city.

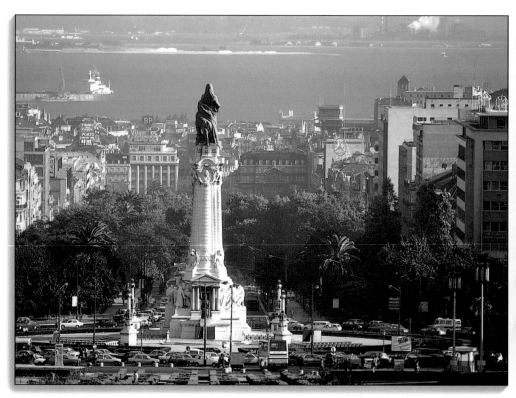

southwest of the zoo, on the edge of the Parque Florestal de Monsanto, you'll find an unexpected gem in the form of the walled, pink-washed 17th-century **Palácio dos Marquéses de Fronteira** ⑭ (one guided tour daily at 11am; closed Sun; entrance charge). The house and garden are decorated with some unusual and captivating *azulejos*.

Map on page 164–5

Campo Grande: north and south

On Campo Grande you'll find the group of pleasant modern buildings that make up the **Cidade Universitária** ⑮ (University) although the nearby **Arquivo Nacional da Torre do Tombo** ⑯, a fort-like building which holds the national archives, is architecturally more striking. In an 18th-century palace at the end of Campo Grande is the **Museu da Cidade** ⑰ (City Museum; open Tues–Sun; closed 1–2pm; entrance charge), with an interesting collection of archaeological pieces and engravings. Opposite, the Campo Grande becomes a shady promenade with a small lake.

Heading south along Avenida da República, the large 19th-century bull ring, **Campo Pequeno** ⑱ is hard to miss, and is not a bad place to witness one of Portugal's relatively animal-friendly bullfights. Across the street, the **Feira Popular** is a permanent, brightly-lit amusement park (open daily Mar–Sept; winter Fri 7pm–1am, weekends and holidays 1pm–1am).

If you head in the opposite direction, north from Campo Grande up Avenida Padre Cruz, you reach **Parque do Monteiro-Mór**. Located in old manor houses in these gardens are the Museu do Trajo (Costume Museum; open Tues–Sun; closed 1–2.30pm; entrance charge); and the Museu do Teatro (Theatre Museum; open Tues–Sun; closed 1–2.30pm; entrance charge). ❑

Sculpture in the park of the Gulbenkian complex.

BELOW: Palácio dos Marqueses de Fronteira, famous for its *azulejos*.

AZULEJOS: HOW TILES BECAME AN ART FORM

Featuring in everything from cathedral cupolas to beer houses, azulejos *are an integral part of Portugal's architectural heritage*

The Portuguese have had a lasting love affair with *azulejos* – painted ceramic tiles – ever since they first set eyes on those imported from Seville in the 15th century. *Azulejos* are not unique to Portugal, but they have become almost a national emblem.

Local production of tiles began soon after the arrival of the geometric Sevillian prototypes. Early ones, used mostly in church interiors, were mainly in shades of blue, with patterns established during the course of firing by separating the colours, using rivulets of linseed oil or ridges of clay. Quality improved with the introduction of the Italian majolica technique, in which the tile was covered with white enamel onto which paint could be applied directly. This greater freedom permitted more artistic expression. Tapestry designs, based on Moorish patterns, began to appear, founded on a module of four tiles, in blue, yellow, green and white.

The next leap was the introduction of Delft blue from Holland. The Portuguese took to it immediately and it dominated tile production for a period, but by the mid-18th century there was a return to high-quality polychrome tiles. During the rebuilding of Lisbon after the great earthquake of 1755, the demand for tiles escalated. They were used for internal and external decoration in every aspect of architecture: churches, private homes, public buildings and even on park benches. New factories opened to supply the demand but, inevitably, artistic standards fell and many tiles had to be imported.

The best place to trace the development of the tiles is in the Museu Nacional do Azulejo, in Lisbon.

◁ **HISTORY IN THE PARK**
Azulejos can be instructive as well as decorative: here a park bench in Portimão depicts scenes from Portuguese history.

△ **EXUBERANT DESIGN**
The god Bacchus, depicted in a 17th-century tile pattern, is a flamboyant early example of the use of *azulejos* for secular, as well as sacred, design.

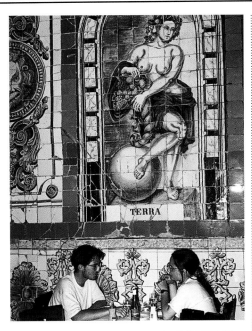

MASTERPIECES OF DECORATIVE ART

Towards the end of the 17th century, tile painting became a recognised art form in Portugal. One of the earliest masters to find fame in this field was António de Oliveira Bernardes. Together with his son, Policarpo, he set up a school of painters in Lisbon which rapidly became influential. Many beautiful works produced by this school in the first half of the 18th century found their way into churches, monasteries and palaces.

The interior of the Capela de São Lourenço in Algarve (*illustrated above*) is covered with *azulejos* depicting the life of the saint, many believed to be the work of Policarpo. Art historians have also identified the works of António Bernardes in Nossa Senhora da Cabaça at Evora.

△ CERVEJARIA, LISBON
Using tiles for internal decoration, as in this beer house, offers great opportunities for artistic expression.

▽ LISBON VERNACULAR
Azulejos became popular in vernacular architecture, lending distinction to facades such as this.

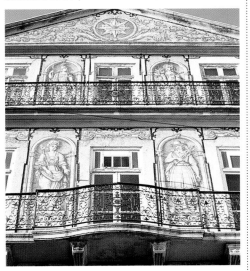

◁ FLORAL PATTERNS
A letter box set into a wall in Obidos is tiled with a floral motif. Once *azulejos* were no longer confined to churches and palaces, they cropped up everywhere.

▷ RESTORER AT WORK
Many of the earlier *azulejo* tiles are recognised as part of the country's heritage, and highly regarded. Restoring them is skilled and demanding work.

ESTORIL AND CASCAIS

Close to Lisbon, these neighbouring resorts are well connected to the city, convenient for exploring as far north as Sintra, and also a delight for windsurfers and golfers

Map on page 176

Handily located for **Lisbon ❶**, south-facing Estoril and Cascais are the most significant coastal resorts outside Algarve, although neither is especially large. They grew to prominence as a playground for Lisboetas, but modern times have witnessed a role reversal: these resorts and their environs are dormitories for wealthy Lisbon commuters, and are preferred places to stay for many visitors whose main intent is to explore the capital.

The electric train offers the quickest and most convenient way of travelling the 29-km (18-mile) distance into Lisbon. It arrives in Cais do Sodré station on the west side of town, close to the riverside. As part of the infrastructure improvements for Expo '98, Lisbon's Metro was extended to connect Cais do Sodré to central Lisbon. The mainline train also stops at Belém which is especially convenient for visiting one of the capital's most interesting areas.

A complexity of new motorways makes driving into Lisbon somewhat easier than in recent years although signposting is often confusing and accurate maps hard to obtain. Parking is considerably easier in the city now that metering is widespread – Portuguese motorists *hate* paying for parking. The *Marginal* route along the riverside, once regarded as a delightful drive, suffers from the modern contagion of congestion at busy times. Travelling this route out of Lisbon leads through Belém to the elegant hillside neighbourhood of Restelo, the location of many embassies and diplomatic residences. **Algés** is the first town outside the city limits, and it is here that taxi drivers turn off their meters and start calculating by kilometres.

A string of small riverside towns follow. **Dáfundo** has several splendid old mansions standing in rather sad contrast alongside dilapidated rent-controlled housing. It also has the **Aquário Vasco da Gama** (open Tues–Sun; closed holidays; entrance charge), with its fascinating world of sea turtles, eels, barnacles and all kinds of fish. **Cruz Quebrada** is the site of a stone-seated stadium built for soccer matches, while **Caxias** is known for its flowering villas, 18th-century gazebos and an infamous hillside prison-fort. In **Oeiras** you'll find a fine 18th-century baroque church, a lovely park, modern apartment blocks and an austere 16th-century fort.

Just beyond lies the 17th-century fortress of **São Julião da Barra**, marking the point where the Tejo meets the Atlantic. **Carcavelos** has several moderate hotels and a broad sandy beach.

Elegant Estoril

And so to **Estoril ❷**, the first point of what has often been called the Golden Triangle, and includes Cascais and Sintra. A flowering, palm-lined, pastel-coloured resort, it first gained fame at the turn of the

PRECEDING PAGES: Cascais is well geared to visitors. **LEFT:** windsurfing at Praia do Guincho. **BELOW:** Costa do Sol Hotel, Estoril.

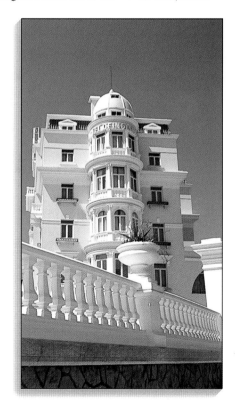

century for its therapeutic spring waters. During World War II, Estoril became known as the haunt of international spies. Later, this corner of the Atlantic, with its mild weather and gracious lifestyle, became a home-from-home for European royalty and other refugees fleeing the political upheavals after the war. Among the Triangle's illustrious residents were former kings Simeon of Bulgaria and Umberto of Italy, and Bolivia's ex-leader, Antenor Patiño.

With changing times, local aristocrats are selling or renting their villas. More and more Portuguese and foreigners come to the Triangle to live, retire or keep summer homes. Estoril has now become a cosmopolitan playground with its celebrated casino, first-rate hotels, restaurants and a range of popular international tennis and golf tournaments. There is no brashness here: the sophisticated image remains untarnished by rashes of modernity like fast-food outlets, trading posts, kiss-me-quick hats and the like. It is not that sort of resort.

Estoril's fine sandy **Tamariz** beach is attractively set with a touch of the picturesque added by a castellated private house surrounded by palms at the east-

TIP

The train service between Lisbon and Estoril and Cascais is frequent, and the journey takes only about half an hour.

Cascais, Sintra and Setúbal

ern end. Even this Atlantic location has suffered from water pollution in recent years, although the situation is improving, with continued investment in the infrastructure. Even so, beaches further west offer reliably safer waters.

Map on page 176

The **Casino** is a low white modern building with immaculately kept gardens. You need a passport or identity card to get in, and the minimum age limit is 18. Some people come to the Casino just to see the show, usually a colourful international extravaganza. There is also an elegant dining room, an art gallery, a cinema and a bar.

Festivals and rallies

The **Estoril Music Festival** takes place from mid-July to mid-August. Concerts and recitals are held in Estoril Cathedral, Cascais Cidadela (fort) and other impressive settings. The **Handicrafts Fair** has become a major production, lasting throughout the months of July and August. Located near the railway station, the fair features arts and crafts, food, wine and folk music from all over the country.

There is a lot to do in the way of sports in the Triangle. The **Autódromo do Estoril ❸**, the automobile race track located inland on the road to Sintra, used to draw large crowds for the Grand Prix Formula One races but, much to the dismay of local traders and hoteliers, the track fails to meet current safety requirements for Formula One racing and has been dropped from the list. There is no prompt movement to upgrade the track, and arguments revolve around funding. It is also the site for the start and finish of the annual international Port Wine Rally. A huge shopping development nearby with car parking for 3,000 vehicles has attracted some major stores such as Mothercare and C&A.

BELOW: faded elegance at Estoril.

GOLF IN THE GOLDEN TRIANGLE

The Estoril Golf Club's 9-hole course, on the outskirts of town, is one of the loveliest in Europe. It was laid out by McKenzie Ross on a hillside dotted with pine and eucalyptus groves. The smaller Estoril-Sol Golf Course is located in a pine wood at Linhó near Sintra. Overlooking the Atlantic coast just beyond Cascais is the Marinha Golf Club, with swimming pools, tennis and riding facilities and an 18-hole course designed by Robert Trent Jones. Quinta da Beloura, which was designed by William Roquemore and opened in 1993, lies beneath the hills of Serra de Sintra. Six lakes provide golfers with plenty of watery challenges.

Penha Longa, built with Japanese finance, is more than a golf course; it is a country club with a whole range of sporting activities, and includes a five-star hotel. The 18-hole course designed by Robert Trent Jones Jr embraces natural woodland and rocky outcrops. This is located between Serra de Sintra and the Atlantic. Finally, there is Quinta da Marina, which lies just west of Cascais. Also designed by Robert Trent Jones, this attractive course weaves through umbrella pines, water features and wind-blown sand dunes.(*See Travel Tips for telephone numbers and other details.*)

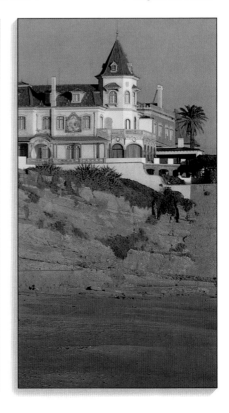

Mild winters and summers tempered by cool westerlies provide ideal conditions for golf all year around. There are six courses on the north side of the Tejo and four within easy reach on the south. **Penha Longa ❹** (*see box on page 177*) is one of the best.

Cascais: resort of kings

Estoril and Cascais are joined by a pedestrianised promenade which is a delight to walk. It passes by the beaches, and there are snack bars and restaurants along the way.

Although it was once a royal resort, **Cascais ❺** has all the glitter but none of the reputation of Estoril. In 1870, King Luís I established his summer residence in the 17th-century Citadel on the Bay of Cascais. Before that, it was known only as a fishing port. Locals claim that a fisherman from Cascais, Afonso Sanches, actually discovered America in 1482, and Christopher Columbus merely repeated the trip 10 years later and got all the glory. In 1580, the Duke of Alba attacked Cascais when Spain was laying claim to Portugal. And in 1589 the English arrived here to retaliate for the Spanish Armada's 1588 foray. The fishing port still remains, with the comings and goings of the colourful fishing boats in the bay, the noisy nightly auction at the central fish market, and good shopping and restaurants.

Around the port has grown a resort with all the vibrancy that Estoril lacks, and yet it has managed to avoid spilling beyond its original boundaries. Pedestrianised streets paved with traditional black and white *calçada* blocks recreating dynamic wave patterns may make seamen feel at home but can make landlubbers a little queasy. They are colourful for all that, especially where the street cafés spill out and the street traders set up stalls. A Wednesday market where you can buy fresh fruit and vegetables as well as handicrafts is repeated on a smaller scale on Saturday morning.

BELOW: Cascais is all about relaxing.

There are several lovely old churches and chapels in Cascais, including the 17th-century **Nossa Senhora da Assunção** with its plain façade, lovely tiles and marble nave. It contains several paintings by the 17th-century artist, Josefa de Obidos. On the outskirts of town, in an exotic garden, is the **Museu Castro Guimarães** (open Tues–Sun; closed 1–2.30pm and holidays; entrance charge). Housed in the former residence of the Conde de Castro Guimarães, this museum displays 17th-century Portuguese silver, tiles and furniture, and some good 19th-century paintings, as well as prehistoric finds.

Cascais also has its own bullring, although few fights are scheduled: it's usually too windy. There are also opportunities for horse riding at the Escola de Equitação de Birre on the road to Sintra, and at the Centro Hípico da Marinha, inland from the beach at Guincho (*see below*).

The main beaches lie between Cascais and Estoril; there is a small beach to the west, **Praia de Santa Marta**, but it's barely big enough for a game of volleyball. Take a short walk beyond, along the main road, and you will come to the **Boca do Inferno** ("Mouth of Hell"), a narrow inlet with arches and caverns. Waves crash into the inlet with some ferocity, especially when the Atlantic swell is running high. An informal flea market around the Boca do Inferno has been regularised with custom-built stalls selling colourful woven rugs, sheepskin carpets and craft work, which has taken over as the main attraction.

Beyond here lies the rocky Atlantic coast. Lisboetas flock here on weekends to enjoy seafood at several popular restaurants. Some also swim at the broad clean beach of **Praia do Guincho ❻**, where the waves can be wild and the undertow fierce. Windsurfers love it. Some people, however, simply like to take the road to Sintra, through the pines and along the open coast. ❑

Omnipresent Dom Pedro, immortalised in Cascais.

BELOW: the Boca do Inferno.

SINTRA

*Known by the Romans as the Mountains of the Moon, the
Serra da Sintra holds a delightful confection of palaces and
monuments along with some splendid beaches.*

Map
on page
176

With its lush forests and gentle surrounding plain, Sintra has long been a favourite summer resort for Portuguese and foreign visitors. People delight in the area because of its sheer natural beauty and it was declared a World Heritage site by UNESCO in 1995. Lord Byron, who could find little good to say about the Portuguese, was enamoured of Sintra and likened it to "Elysium's gates". In *Childe Harold*, he wrote: "Lo! Cintra's glorious Eden intervenes in variegated maze of mount and glen".

Some 32 km (20 miles) to the northwest of Lisbon, Sintra is another world with its own special climate – a clash of warm southerlies and moist westerlies over the Serra da Sintra – and an almost bucolic way of life. The most practical way to go is by train from Rossio. If you drive, rush hour traffic should be avoided if at all possible. It seems that most of the inhabitants of Sintra commute to Lisbon on weekdays and vice-versa at weekends. The road to Sintra from Lisbon starts at the Praça Marquês de Pombal and is well marked. Avenida Duarte Pacheco runs into the *auto-estrada* or super highway that leads out of town, past the Aqueduto das Aguas Livres, up the hill through Parque de Monsanto, turning right to join the highway to Sintra.

LEFT: the Swan
Ceiling in Sintra's
Palácio Nacional.
BELOW: the
splendid palace and
gardens at Queluz.

Queluz Palace

A slight detour to visit **Queluz ❼** is well worthwhile. The town has become a rather drab Lisbon dormitory, but its rose-coloured palace is anything but drab. The **Pálacio** (open Wed–Mon; closed 1–2pm and holidays; entrance charge) was built as a simple manor for King Pedro II in the mid-1600s and was enlarged when the court moved there. Most of the palace, including its magnificent façade, is baroque, but the courtyard and formal gardens were modelled after Versailles.

In summer, concerts are sometimes held in the Music Room. At other times, the public may visit the lavishly decorated Throne Room with its fine painted wood ceiling, the Hall of Mirrors, the Ambassador's Room, and others. The great kitchen, with stone chimney and copperware, has been turned into a luxury restaurant called **Cozinha Velha**. Palace and gardens are a spectacular stage during August and September for **Noites de Queluz** (Nights at Queluz), enchanting musical recreations of 18th-century court life.

Back on the main road continue along rolling hills, past modest whitewashed villages and rich *quintas,* or manors, to arrive at the Serra de Sintra. At the base of the mountain lies the village of **São Pedro de Sintra**, where on the second and fourth Sunday of each month, a wonderful country fair takes place. On display are all kinds of crafts from primitive wood carvings and ceramics to fine antique furniture, as well as the latest lines in plastic utensils and polyester tablecloths. São Pedro is also known for its popular tavernas, with spicy sausages, hearty codfish and heady wines.

Making use of the high winds.

Sintra Vila

The road now climbs slightly and curves around the mountain to reach **Sintra Vila ⓽**, the historic centre of Sintra. Here lies the *Turismo* office and, on the upper floor, the the municipal art gallery, the **Museu Regional ⓐ** (open Mon–Fri; closed noon–2.30pm; weekends and holidays 7pm only; entrance charge). The road to the left, Rua Gil Vicente, leads down to **Museu Ferreira de Castro ⓑ**, which is dedicated to the works of the great Portuguese novelist, Ferreira de Castro (1898–1974). A little further on is the **Hotel Lawrence ⓒ**, formerly Estalagem dos Cavaleiros, where Lord Byron stayed in 1809, and now restored as an inn under its original name.

The centrepiece of Sintra is the royal palace, the Paço Real, now called the **Palácio Nacional ⓓ**, parts of which date from the 14th century (open Thurs–Mon; closed 1–2pm and holidays; entrance charge). Broad stairs lead up to the stately building with Gothic arches, Moorish windows and two extraordinary chimney cones. Of special interest on the guided tour of the palace are: the Sala dos Brasões, with remarkable ceiling panels painted in 1515, which show the coat-of-arms of 71 Portuguese noble families (that of the Távoras was removed after the conspiracy against King José in 1758); the Sala dos Arabes, with marble fountain and 15th-century Moorish tiles; and the Sala dos Cisnes, an enormous reception hall with swans painted on the panelled ceiling; the Sala das Pegas, its ceiling covered with magpies brandishing banners reading "Por

BELOW: the Palácio Nacional at Sintra, with its distinctive chimney cones.

Sintra Vila

0   200 m
0   200 yds

Bem". It is said that when Queen Philippa caught João I dallying with a lady-in-waiting he claimed it was an innocent kiss. "Por Bem", he said, which loosely translated means: "It's all for the best". Philippa's response is not recorded.

Maps:
Area 176
City 182

The other Sintra

Estefânia, the third district of Sintra, is where you go to catch the train or a local bus to Lisbon. Walking in that direction from the historic centre, you pass the **Museu de Brinquedo** ❺ (Toy Museum; open Tues–Sun; entrance charge) and then the **Casa Museu Anjos Teixeira** ❻ (open Tues–Sun; closed 12–2pm; entrance charge), which houses an important collection of sculptures. Shortly after this, on the left and before the bus and railway stations, is Sintra's Town Hall, which is often overlooked amid so much fine architecture. It has a square castellated tower with a steeple in an exuberant Gothic style. Beyond the bus station, housed in a grand building, is the **Museu de Arte Moderna** ❼ (open Wed–Sun; entrance charge).

TIP

A bus service, in red open-topped London buses, runs from the bus station along the Colares road to Ribeira, to connect with the electric tram to the coast at Praia das Maçãs.

Mountain retreats

Sintra's other palace-museum, the **Palácio da Pena** ❽ (open Tues–Sun; closed 1–2pm and holidays; entrance charge), dominates the town from the top of the mountain . The road winds up steep rocky slopes through thick woods to the castle, built on the site of a 16th-century monastery: you can walk up, drive or take a bus. But some think Pena is better viewed from afar, from where the impression is of some medieval stronghold. Close at hand, the castle is an architectural monstrosity, a pot-pourri of various styles and influences: Arabic minarets, Gothic towers, Renaissance cupolas, Manueline windows. It was

BELOW:
architectural excess at the Palácio da Pena.

Tile detail on a wall outside at the Quinta de Monserrate..

commissioned by Prince Ferdinand of Saxe-Coburg-Gotha, husband of Queen Maria II, and built by German architect Baron von Eschwege around 1840.

At the entrance to the castle a tunnel leads to the ruins of the original monastery. The old chapel walls are decorated with fine 17th-century tiles and there is a splendid altar of alabaster and black marble by 16th-century French sculptor Nicolas Chanterène. But the best thing about the castle is the view. Below lies the **Parque da Pena**, with lakes and black swans, a wide variety of flora, tangled forest and tiled fountains.

Across the way are the ruins of another mountain-top castle, the **Castelo dos Mouros** , dating from about the 11th century. The fortifications visible along the mountain ridge were restored in the middle of the 19th century. To the southwest rises the highest peak, **Cruz Alta**, at 540 metres (1,772 ft) and marked by a stone cross. The mountainside is a luxuriant mass of vegetation – subtropical plants, boulders covered with moss, giant ferns, walnut, chestnut and pine trees, and rhododendron bushes. One of the strangest sights on the mountain is the **Convento dos Capuchos**, a 16th-century monastery built entirely of rocks and cork. Some say the monks lined their cells with cork to obtain absolute silence, but there is little noise here other than bird sounds. More likely, the cork helped insulate the monks from the long bitter winters.

On the outskirts of Sintra Vila (on the way to Colares) stands the **Palácio de Seteais**, an obscure name said to mean "the seven sighs". This was where the Convention of Sintra was signed in 1809, after the defeat of Napoleon by British and Portuguese forces. It is said that the terms of the treaty upset the Portuguese so much that the palace became known for their sighs of despair. Seteais was restored and turned into a luxury hotel and restaurant in 1955 and should be seen, if only for tea or a drink. The elegant rooms contain crystal chandeliers, wall-hangings, murals and antique furnishings. From the gardens you have a magnificent view of the surrounding countryside.

Almost opposite is the remarkable **Quinta da Regaleira** (open to visitors, enquire at the *Turismo* office), built at the close of the 19th century as an assembly of Gothic, Manueline and Renaissance styles that would be out of place anywhere but Sintra.

Nearby is the **Quinta de Monserrate**, a strange Moorish-type villa built in the 19th century. The villa is under renovation but the exotic garden and greenhouse are worth seeing for the trees and plants from all over the world: palms, bamboos, cedars, magnolias, cork-oaks, pines and giant ferns.

Once part of the Monserrate gardens, the **Quinta de São Tiago** is a 16th-century manor with a fine chapel, splendid kitchen, cell-like bedrooms, gardens, and its own swimming pool. The owners found taxes and other expenses prohibitive and, in 1979, opened the *quinta* to paying guests. You can also stay in the nearby **Quinta da Capela**.

For a delightful excursion, the road to Colares leads through vineyards, white-washed hamlets and stone walls to the sea. En route, it is possible to visit the **Adega Regional** ❾ a traditional winery. Colares grapes grow in sandy soil with humid maritime climate. The wines are dark ruby and very smooth.

Cabo da Roca ❿ is a wild desolate cape, the westernmost point of continental Europe, and visitors receive a certificate to mark their visit. Heading north, there are several beaches frequented mainly by the Portuguese: broad, sandy **Praia Grande** ⓫ and **Praia das Maçãs** ⓬. The attractive fishing village of **Azenhas do Mar** ⓭ has a natural rock seashore swimming pool.

Maps:
Area 176
City 182

Magnificent Mafra

Following the road north towards the coast from Sintra, you reach the beach resort and fishing village of **Ericeira** ⓮. From here it is an easy 10 km (6 miles) drive inland to **Mafra** ⓯, a name shared by both a modest village and a vast palace-convent (open Wed–Mon; closed holidays; entrance charge) nearby, which rises like a dark mirage across the plain. The complex of buildings almost as large as Spain's Escorial was erected by João V in fulfilment of a vow. Work began in 1717 and took 18 years, drawing so many artists from so many countries that João founded the School of Mafra, making these talented men masters to local apprentices. The most famous teacher was Joaquim Machado de Castro, who also worked on Lisbon's Basílica da Estrela (*see page 163*).

Mafra is the site of the church of Santo André. Pedro Hispano was priest here before he was elected Pope John XXI in 1276 – the only Portuguese pope in the history of the Vatican.

The limestone façade is 220 metres (720 ft) long. At its centre is the church, with two tall towers and an Italianate portico. The interior is decorated with the finest Portuguese marble, while the 14 large statues of saints in the vestibule were carved from Carrara marble by Italian sculptors. The church also contains six organs. Most impressive is the library, full of baroque magnificence and light. Among its 35,000 volumes are first editions of *Os Lusíadas* by Camões and the earliest edition of Homer in Greek. Other areas open to the public include the hospital, pharmacy, audience room, and the chapterhouse. ❑

FOLLOWING PAGES:
looking out to sea.
BELOW: the great
library at Mafra.

SETUBAL AND THE ARRABIDA PENINSULA

Map on page 176

A mixture of industrial sprawl, nature reserves, ancient sites and huge sandy beaches, the Arrábida Peninsula attracts few visitors but is the preferred place to live for many Lisboetas

isboetas call it *Outra Banda*, the other shore, meaning the southern bank of the Tejo, long neglected because of the inconvenience of getting there. This changed after 1966 with the completion of what was then Europe's longest suspension bridge, the Ponte 25 de Abril, and will change again with the opening of the rail link in 1999. A second, even longer bridge, the Vasco de Gama, opened in 1998 to relieve pressure on the first. The region, known as the Arrábida Peninsula, has developed rapidly and not always wisely.

Directly across the river is the unassuming ferry-boat port of **Cacilhas** ⑯. Its main charm is a string of riverfront fish restaurants with a grand view of Lisbon. About 5 km (3 miles) west of Ponte 25 de Abril is **Trafaria**; the whole town was burned to the ground on the orders of Pombal in 1777 as punishment for resisting press gangs, but was later rebuilt. Most visitors tend to drive through the neighbouring industrial town of Almada without stopping, except those who want to examine the **Cristo Rei** ⑰ (Christ the King monument) at close hand. You can go to the top of the pedestal – so high it seems to dwarf the figure on top – by elevator and stairs, for a magnificent view of Lisbon.

LEFT: the lighthouse at Cabo Espichel.
BELOW: the Cristo Rei monument.

Most people avoid the *Outra Banda* dormitory district by taking the super highway leading directly from the bridge. After a few kilometres, a turn-off leads to **Costa da Caparica** ⑱, a series of broad Atlantic beaches with moderately priced hotels and restaurants. This popular resort is cleaner than the Estoril/Cascais coast, and the currents are safer than those of the Atlantic north of the Tejo.

On to Palmela

Continuing south on the highway, you pass new factories. The road marked **Palmela** ⑲ leads to a small town with a great medieval castle. This has been restored and converted into a luxury *pousada*, with a lounge in the cloisters, and an elegant dining-room in the old refectory. The attached church is a beautiful Romanesque structure, its walls covered with 18th-century tiles.

Built by the Moors, the castle was reconstructed in 1147 as a monastery and the seat of the Knights of the Order of Saint James. In 1484, the bishop of Evora was imprisoned in the dungeon for his role in the conspiracy against João II. He died a few days later, probably poisoned. The castle was badly damaged by the 1755 earthquake, but was rebuilt and monks remained there until the abolition of religious orders in 1834.

Just outside Setúbal rises another great castle turned *pousada*, **São Filipe**, with a magnificent view of the

Setúbal may be an industrial town, but it is certainly not devoid of aesthetic sigthts, ranging from this relatively modest fountain to the fine Igreja de Jesus.

BELOW: the remarkable Igreja de Jesus, Setúbal.

Sado estuary. Philip II of Spain ordered its construction in 1590, to keep a watch over the area – Portugal was under Spanish rule at the time. The chapel is decorated with tiles that recount the life of Saint Philip (*not* Philip of Spain), signed by the master painter Policarpo de Oliveira Bernardes, and dated 1736.

Setúbal and the Tróia peninsula

According to local legend, **Setúbal** ❷⓿ was founded by Tubal, the son of Cain. It is said that Phoenicians and Greeks, finding the climate and soil of Arrábida similar to their Mediterranean homelands, started vineyards. Setúbal is known to have been an important fishing port since Roman times. Today it is an industrial town, a centre of ship-building, fish-canning, and the production of fertilisers, cement, salt and moscatel wine.

Setúbal's pride is the **Igreja de Jesus**, a spectacular monument dating back to 1491. The church was designed by Diogo Boytac, one of the founding fathers of the Manueline style of architecture. The narrow building has a high arched ceiling supported by six great stone pillars that look like coils of rope; its apse is etched with stone and lined with tiles. Arrábida marble was used, and the pebbled, multi-coloured stone gives it a distinct appearance. There are also lovely tiled panels along the walls. The cloister houses a museum, the **Museu de Cidade** (open Tues–Sun; closed 12.30–2pm; entrance charge).

Nearby is the **Praça do Bocage**, with palm trees and a statue honouring one of Setúbal's illustrious sons, 18th-century sonneteer, Manuel Barbosa du Bocage. Off the square stands the church of **São Julião** with a handsome Manueline doorway, built in 1513. The inside walls are decorated with 18th-century tiles showing fishing scenes and the life of the saint. Also of interest is the

Map on page 176

Museu Etnográfico with models depicting the main industries: fishing, farming and textiles (open Tues–Sun; closed noon–2pm; entrance charge).

Setúbal's harbour is fascinating, especially in the morning when brightly painted trawlers arrive, loaded with fish. There's a continual show, as fishermen mend nets and work on their boats. Best of all is the lively fish auction.

Setúbal is the main point of departure for the peninsula of **Tróia** ㉑, a long narrow spit jutting out into the Sado estuary. Ferry-boats make the 20-minute crossing frequently in season. On the northern end of the peninsula, there is a rather unattractive modern beach resort. The Tróia Golf Club has an 18-hole course designed by Robert Trent Jones. On the southern end of the peninsula, however, there are still miles of pine forest and glorious empty beaches and dunes. Tróia is said to be the site of the Roman town of **Cetóbriga** ㉒, destroyed by a tidal wave in the 5th century. Substantial ruins have been found but little has been excavated except for a temple and some tombs. Underwater, you may see remains of the walls of Roman houses.

Serra da Arrábida

A delightful excursion from Setúbal goes along the ridge of the **Serra da Arrábida** which rises to 600 metres (2,000 ft). As you leave the city, the only sight that mars the natural beauty of the coast is the cement factory, usually spitting out black smoke. A road descends to **Portinho da Arrábida** ㉓, a popular bathing beach with transparent waters, white sand and the splendid **Gruta da Santa Margarida**. Hans Christian Andersen, who visited the region in 1834, marvelled in his diaries at this cave with its imposing stalactites. Scuba diving is very popular here.

TIP

From Cetóbriga you could choose to return to Setúbal via Alcácar do Sal, a drive of some 120 km (75 miles), though of course it is much quicker to take the ferry from Tróia.

BELOW: the fine sandy beach of Tróia peninsula stretches as far as the eye can see.

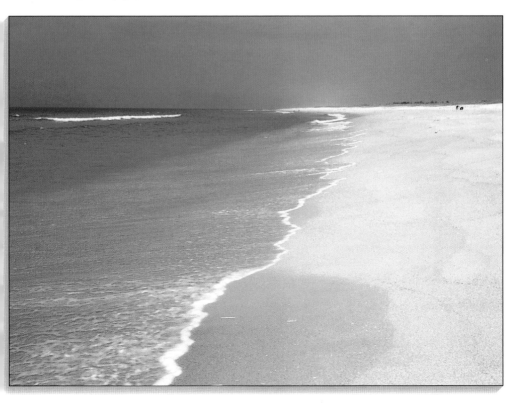

But it was the poet and historian of the Peninsular War, Robert Southey (1774–1843), who consecrated Arrábida for English readers, calling it "a glorious spot". He tells of going swimming at the base of the mountain and writes: "I have no idea of sublimity exceeding it".

Regaining the ridge, continue along the skyline drive. The next turn-off leads to **Sesimbra** ㉔, a lovely fishing village and resort with several notable sights. The castle above the village, although known as Moorish, has been entirely rebuilt since that time. Afonso Henriques captured it in 1165, but the Moors utterly razed the structure in 1191. King Dinis almost certainly helped with the rebuilding, and King João IV again added and repaired in the 17th century. Inside the walls are ruins of a Romanesque church, Santa Maria, and the old town hall. King João IV also ordered the fort of São Teodosio built, to protect the port from pirates. But the most fascinating sight is the port, which is always busy. There are several simple bistros nearby: swordfish is the local speciality.

Going westward about 11 km (7 miles), the road ends at **Cabo Espichel** ㉕. This promontory, and the shrine of **Nossa Senhora do Cabo**, used to be an important pilgrimage site, as shown by the long rows of dilapidated pilgrims' quarters on either side of the church. There is still a fishermen's festival here each October. On the edge of the high cliff is the small fishermen's chapel of Senhor de Bomfim, in a rather desolate state but with a breathtaking view.

Olive tree village

The road back to Lisbon goes through **Vila Nogueira de Azeitão** ㉖, sometimes simply called Azeitão, which means "large olive tree". In the centre of this charming village is the stately Palácio Távora, where the Duke of Aveiro and his

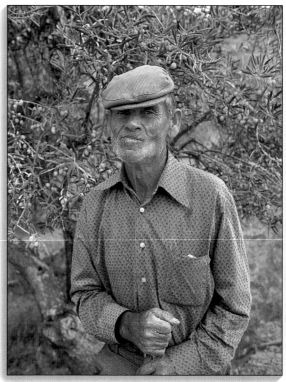

friends are said to have plotted to overthrow King José. They were burned at the stake in Belém in 1759. Lovely baroque fountains border the town's main street. The Igreja São Lourenço has been restored and has beautiful 18th-century altars, paintings and tile panels.

Map on page 176

The Azeitão fair, held in the central square on the first Sunday of the month, became so popular that it caused havoc and had to be moved to the outskirts of town. Less picturesque now, it is still a major attraction offering everything from shoes and pottery to furniture, plus a large section devoted to livestock.

In the village, is the original **José Maria da Fonseca Winery** ㉗, founded in 1834. The old family residence, which now houses a small museum, stands nearby. The winery still produces one of Portugal's best red table wines, the soft rich Periquita, as well as Setúbal's popular moscatel wines. Visitors are welcome to tour the factory and see its assembly-line production.

Not far from town stands one of the oldest inhabited manors in the country, the **Quinta da Bacalhoa**, built in 1480. It had fallen into ruins and was saved by an American woman from Connecticut, Mrs Herbert Scoville, who bought it in 1936. The gardens, open to the public, are admirable with their clipped boxwood in geometric design, orange and lemon groves, and pavilion with beautiful tile panels. One of these scenes, showing Susanna and the Elders, is dated 1565, and said to be the earliest known dated panel in Portugal.

Another attractive manor, the **Quinta das Torres**, stands just outside the neighbouring village of **Vila Fresca de Azeitão**. This 16th-century *quinta*, decorated with tile panels and set in a romantic garden, has been converted into a cosy inn and restaurant. In the village, there is yet another charming church, São Simão, with more ancient tile walls and polychrome panels. ❏

BELOW: Cabo Espichel sweeps into the Atlantic.

ALGARVE

Moorish arches drenched in sunshine and spectacular coves of golden sand: Algarve offers a touch of the exotic which attracts visitors by the million

Map on pages 198–9

I f one region of Portugal stands alone, it is Algarve. Its history under long Moorish control, its climate – more typically Mediterranean – and its abundance of fine sandy beaches endow Algarve with a character so different it could easily be taken as a separate country. In the minds of many visitors, it is.

Separated from the rest of Portugal by rolling hills, Algarve, the southernmost province, seduced the ancient Phoenicians with its abundance of sardines and tuna, which they salt-cured for export almost 3,000 years ago. Four centuries later, around 600 BC, the Carthaginians and Celts arrived, followed in turn by the Romans, who adopted the Phoenician practice of curing and exporting fish – the precursor of Portugal's large tinned sardine industry. They built roads, bridges and spas, such as that in Milreu.

But Algarve really blossomed under Moorish rule, which began in the early 8th century. The province's name comes from the Moorish *Al-Gharb* meaning "The West". The Moorish period was one of vivacious culture and great scientific advances. Moorish poets sang of the beauty of Silves, while the more practical settlers introduced orange crops, and perfected the technique of extracting olive oil, which is still an important Portuguese product. The blossoming almond trees in February are one of the most beautiful sights of Algarve thanks, according to folklore, to the passion a Moorish king once felt for a northern princess.

PRECEDING PAGES: the rocky coast near Lagos. **LEFT:** a languid lady at the palace in Estoi. **BELOW:** a typical Algarve chimney.

Legend has it that the princess, pining for the snows of her homeland, slowly began to waste away. Distraught, the king ordered thousands of almond trees to be planted across the region, then one February morning carried her to the window where she saw swirling white "snow flakes" carpeting the ground – the white almond blossoms. She quickly recuperated, and the two lived happily ever after.

Moorish legacy

King Afonso Henriques led the Portuguese conquest southward in the 12th century, and later his son Sancho I, with the help of a band of crusaders, was to spearhead the siege of Silves and its estimated population of 20,000 people. It took 49 days before the Moors of Silves surrendered. But in 1192 they reconquered the city and remained there for another 47 years. It was Sancho II, supported by military-religious orders under Paio Peres Correia, who finally crushed them. The last major city to fall was Faro in January 1249.

But the Arabic influence is visible even today: in many town names, in words beginning with the "al" prefix, in the so-called "North African blue" used in trimming the whitewashed houses, in the roof terraces used for the drying of fruit, and the white-domed

*Fashion accessories
for the beach.*

buildings still popular in many towns. The Algarvian sweets made of figs, almonds, eggs and sugar called *morgados* or *Dom Rodrigos* are yet another reminder of the area's ancient heritage.

For centuries almond, fig, olive and carob trees represented a major part of the Algarve's agriculture, as they are suited to dry inland areas. The carob, whose beans are now fed to cattle but also produce a variety of oil, are said to have sustained the British troops in Portugal during the Peninsular War. Thanks to the gentle climate Algarve also produces pears, apples, quinces, loquats, damask plums, pomegranates, tomatoes, melons, strawberries, avocados and grapes.

Regional specialities

Wine critics regard all Algarve wines as undistinguished, and even in quite modest restaurants the house wine is usually from the better Alentejo range, or perhaps from even further to the north. But many local wines are quite palatable and an agreeable way to decide for yourself the merits of a few worthy ones is to taste them – for free – in the **Artisans' Village** beside the main Estrada Nacional 125, about 5 km (3 miles) east of Lagoa. The proprietor, Klaus Schoon (despite the name he is an Englishman, and an enthusiastic collector of port) offers visitors two or three of the Lagoa wines, including a pleasant dry rosé *(rosado seco)* and a full-bodied dry red *(tinto)*.

You will find good beer, the preference of most young Algarvios, widely available. Older men passing the time in *tavernas* and *tascas* drink *medronho,* a clear firewater with the kick of a mule, distilled from the fruit of the strawberry tree, *Arbutus unedo.* Another individual drink in Algarve is *Brandymel*, a type of honey brandy.

The pleasant market town of Loulé (*see page 210*), with its central tree-shaded walkway, is the craft centre of Algarve, but local handicrafts are widely sold everywhere. Among them are esparto or straw baskets, hats, mats and hampers, which are made by women who pick and dry the esparto in spring, then shred it into thin strips before they weave and plait it. You will see mats of grass, and of cotton and wool (some of them come from Alentejo). Cane basketry is almost always the work of men in the eastern towns of Odeleite, Alcoutim and Castro Marim. Despite a modern prevalence of cardboard boxes, baskets are still used to carry eggs, to display golden smoked sardines, and as fish traps.

Lagos, Loulé and Tavira – as well as numerous stores along the main N125 highway – are good places to find pottery, from big pitchers, plant pots, hand-painted plates and tiles, to the distinctive, lace-like chimney tops that embellish Algarve's skyline. You'll find a considerable range of copper pots and bowls – one shop is on a street corner beside the market in Loulé. If you walk down the avenue you'll see – and hear – coppersmiths at work in tiny workshops.

Woodwork is also a regional craft, from spoons made in Aljezur to the brightly-coloured mule-drawn carts you'll still see on the roads. Hand-made lace is a skill that's being kept alive in such places as Azinhal. Up in the hills of Monchique (where a small craft shop has grown to an extensive display) you'll find wooden furniture and woollen weaves.

Key routes and places

The southern coastline, so richly endowed with golden sandy beaches in spectacular settings, is the region's prime asset. At the onset of mass tourism it attracted developers and much of the central region, around Albufeira, is now

Map below

BELOW: a leisurely ride in the country.

well developed. Those looking for smaller, quieter coastal resorts can still find them by travelling out to the west beyond Lagos and, to a lesser extent, east of Faro. Inland Algarve has its share of pretty villages and remains largely unspoilt countryside, although it is rapidly becoming the preferred dormitory for expatriate settlers.

Driving around Algarve has never been so easy, with new and improved roads appearing at a steady rate. The motorway, the Via do Infante, which covers eastern Algarve from Spain to Albufeira, where it connects with the Lisbon road, has reduced travelling times very appreciably. It is now possible to drive from Spain in the east to Sagres in the west in a little over two hours.

Faro: the hub of Algarve

The roots of **Faro ❶**, the capital of Algarve, are roots ancient but not well documented. Certainly it was used by Greeks and Romans as a trading post before it became a flourishing Moorish town. Largely devastated by the 1755 earthquake, the city now has an architectural hodge-podge of styles and eras.

To one side of the little harbour, through the 18th-century Arco da Vila, lies a peaceful and historic inner town dominated by the Renaissance **Sé (Cathedral)** (open weekdays till noon) with its 13th-century tower. Eighteenth-century polychrome tiles are an impressive feature in its chapels as well as in the body of the church. The red chinoiserie organ is also 18th-century, and the choir stalls a notable trophy from Silves Cathedral when the seat of the diocese was moved to Faro in the 16th century.

In the square behind the cathedral a former convent with strikingly beautiful Renaissance cloisters is now the **Museu Arqueológico** (Archaeological

BELOW:
cruising the coast.

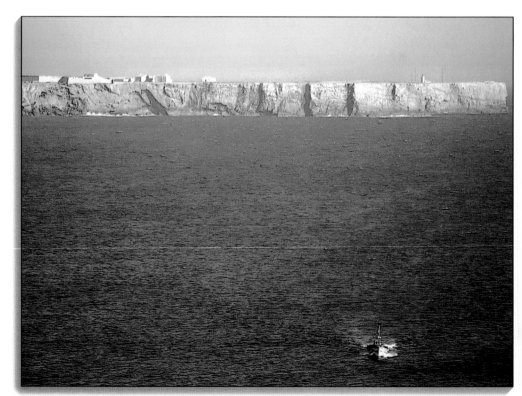

Museum; open Mon–Fri, closed 12.30–2pm; entrance charge), with a selection of Roman mosaics and stonework from Faro and the important Roman site at Milreu, 12 km (7 miles) to the north (*see page 210*). The **Museu Etnográfico** (Ethnographic Museum; open weekdays; closed 12.30–2pm; entrance charge), in the district assembly building in Praça Alexandre Herculano (at the top end of the main pedestrian street), has replicas of traditional Algarve homes, costumes and handicrafts.

Beside the harbour, in the Port Authority building, the **Museu Marítimo** (Maritime Museum; open Mon–Sat pm; closed public holidays; entrance charge) is worth a visit to see the broad range of Algarve fishing methods. Among the exhibits are model boats and a vivid depiction of the old way of trapping tuna in the bloody "bullfight of the sea".

Faro's most bizarre and macabre sight is a **Capela dos Ossos** (Chapel of Bones), reached through the baroque Igreja do Carmo with its impressive façade and twin towers. The little chapel was built in 1816, its walls entirely covered with bones and skulls (allegedly 1,245 of them) from the church cemetery. Some find this grim display of mortality less depressing than the high-rises that contrast with the church's fine façade.

The centre of Faro is walkable, its character changing as you wander through streets of tiny houses, 19th-century mansions, modern villas and shops. It's a bustling capital (with too much traffic), but it still has considerable charm.

Lighthouse and lagoon

Faro is protected on the seaward side by a huge lagoon dotted with sand banks with the airport on the western edge. Some of the sandbanks are huge, especially the outer barrier islands and the southern most point is marked by the Cabo de Santa Maria lighthouse (*faro* is "lighthouse" in Portuguese).

The sand spit which starts near the airport and extends out as a long crescent, Ilha de Faro, can be reached by car and is the location of **Praia de Faro ❷**, a sandy resort much loved by the locals. Ilha da Culatra is the only other inhabited sand spit and can only be reached by ferry from Olhão. The whole of this natural lagoon and the adjacent area, stretching some 50 km (30 miles) from Ançio in the west to Cacela in the east, is protected as the **Parque Natural da Ria Formosa ❸**. This lagoon system provides 90 percent of Portugal's harvest of clams and oysters. It is also an important bird sanctuary, especially for waders such as egrets and oyster catchers, and some rare species, including the purple gallinule.

East of Faro

Travelling eastwards out of Faro takes you to the busy 17th-century town of **Olhão ❹**, built in the Moorish style and with a big fish market. Get there early and be prepared to use your elbows to get to the slithery hills of fish which the women hawk at the top of their voices, poking them to prove their freshness. The best buys are gilt-head bream (*dourada*), bass (*robalo)* and sole (*linguado*). Nearby there is a fruit, vegetable and live fowl market.

Map on pages 198–9

The aerial view of Faro, seen by many visitors flying into the airport, is quite spectacular.

BELOW: the exterior of Faro's Igreja do Carmo.

Glistening white bell-tower in the architectural gem that is Tavira.

BELOW: the Rio Guadiana forms a natural border between Portugal and Spain.

If you are not catching the ferry out to Culatra, move on to **Fuzeta**, where a boat awaits to take you out to uninhabited **Ilha da Armona** for a spot of sunbathing. Almost next door to Fuzeta is Luz de Tavira, the starting point for an exciting little journey by train over to **Barril ❺** on the Tavira sandbank, the Ilha de Tavira. There is a footpath by the track, should the train be full.

A café or restaurant along the broad palm-lined promenade of **Santa Luzia,** a colourful fishing village overlooking the lagoon, is definitely the place to sit and watch the fishermen stacking up encrusted octopus pots (*alcatruzes*) after removing their catch.

Tempting Tavira

One of the larger towns on the eastern side, **Tavira ❻** has avoided the excesses of development and lost none of its grace. It elegantly borders both sides of the Rio Sequa, which becomes the Gilão as it slides under the seven-arched Roman-style bridge, the Ponte Romana, towards the sea. With its estuary and outlying island, Tavira flourished in the 16th century. But trade dwindled as the fish disappeared, and this lovely town composed of narrow streets, pastel-coloured patricians' houses, miniature towers, domes, unusual four-sided roofs and minarets today leads a quieter life.

There are more than two dozen churches and chapels in Tavira, of which the most interesting are the **Igreja da Misericórdia** (with some lovely *azulejo* decorations) and the church of **Santa Maria**, rebuilt on the site of the town's old mosque. Many of the churches are closed, but information about access to the major ones, as well as maps of the area, are available from the tourist office, to be found up the steps from the town hall in the main square.

Map on pages 198–9

Atmospheric fortified hamlets where time appears to have stood still are not what you expect to find along the southern coast of Algarve, but there is one at **Cacela Velha ❼**. It has a miniature 18th-century fortress and a gleaming white church. The whole village clings tightly to a perch looking over a lagoon.

The border with Spain is reached at the Rio Guadiana. Facing Spain is **Vila Real de Santo António ❽**, its grid of geometric streets bearing the stamp of the Marquês de Pombal – the man who was responsible for redesigning old Lisbon in the 18th century. Pombal intended this town to be a model administrative, industrial and fishing centre, and he founded the Royal Fisheries Company here, but he lost favour with the court, and his plans never really took off. All the same, fishing remains an important activity.

Just west of Vila Real is the largest touristic development this side of Faro, **Monte Gordo**. The clutch of high-rise buildings over looking a vast flat beach, as yet remains fairly compact.

Moors, mines and marshlands

Further inland along the Guadiana is the architecturally appealing **Castro Marim ❾**. This little town is also one of the oldest and historically most important areas of Algarve. Once a major Phoenician settlement, it also played host to the Greeks and Carthaginians before the Moors and Romans invaded. Portugal's kings later used it as a natural point from which to fight the infidel to the east. The huge castle built by King Afonso III after he dispelled the Moors in 1249 is still standing, overlooking the surrounding valley. In 1319, it was the first headquarters of the Order of Christ. The fort on the hill opposite dates from 1641.

Surrounding the town is the Castro Marim fen or marsh, wetland home of many migratory birds including storks, cranes and flamingos, and a hundred different species of plant life. An area of 2,000 hectares (5,000 acres) is now protected as the **Reserva Natural do Sapal ❿** and information is available at the office inside the castle.

Among the least travelled routes in Algarve is the peaceful road along the Rio Guadiana. It is a soothing meander through golden, furze-covered hills dotted with corks, olive and fig trees. (Road numbers are N122 and 1063 for the riverside drive.) **Alcoutim ⓫** is the northernmost Algarve town, and here it often seems as if time has stood still. Sunning dogs in the only square in town have priority, so you'll have to park around them.

From the promenade that extends along the edge of the Guadiana river you can see the nearby Spanish town of **Sanlucar de Guadiana** reflected in the slow-moving water. Signs to the "castle" are a little misleading, as they lead to an empty shell of walls – but the view from here is worth the short walk.

An inland return route will take you through **Martinlongo ⓬**, where it is possible to make a diversion to the open-air copper mine at Vaqueiros, now transformed into the **Museu Minas Antigas** (open Tues–Sun; entrance charge). Continue through Cachopo to reach Faro.

The village church on the banks of the river in Sanlucar de Guadiana, has interesting bas-relief carving on the baptismal font dating from the 16th century.

BELOW: a new bridge to Spain, near Castro Marim.

Lobster for lunch.

West of Faro

The coastal route out to the west heads towards the main area of tourist development and to some of the most picturesque beaches. First stop outside Faro is at **São Lourenço** 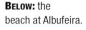 for the small 18th-century church of the same name. Inside it is tiled, from top to bottom, in beautiful blue *azulejo* tiles depicting the life and martyrdom of São Lourenço himself.

All the well-known golf courses, over 17 of them, lie west of Faro, each one an exclusive development with luxury accommodation. Among them are Quinta do Lago, Vale do Lobo and **Vilamoura** ⓮, which has a sixth hole right over the Atlantic. They take up a huge area on the edge of the Ria Formosa reserve, presenting a neat face of colourful flower beds and well-manicured lawns.

Drive on then to the coastal resort town of Albufeira. It is worth a diversion along the way to the small resort-fishing village of **Olhos d'Agua**. The bonus here is that it is too small to attract the large tour operators, otherwise it would be a sell out. Tucked into a small cleft, the fishing village is as picturesque as any in Algarve, with sculptured rock stacks decorating the beach.

Albufeira: holiday heaven

Once a small fishing village favoured by the Romans and Moors, **Albufeira** ⓯ today is a populous and popular tourist spot with an active nightlife, hundreds of bars with a taste for rock music, plenty of restaurants ranging from La Pizza to more typical regional fare, and late-night discos.

The old part of town is still very attractive, as are the rock-protected beaches where the fishermen keep their boats, gaily painted with large eyes (to ward off evil), as well as stars and animals. There is a bustling fish market near the fish-

BELOW: the
beach at Albufeira.

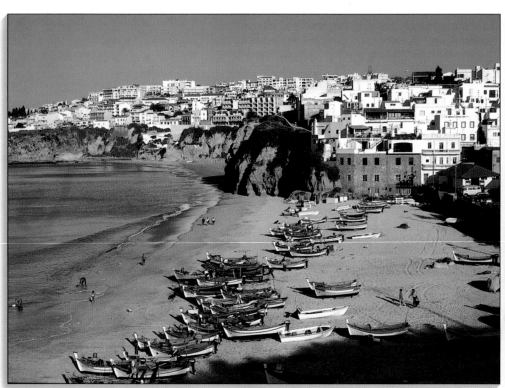

Map
on pages
198–9

ermen's beach and a fruit, meat and vegetable market in the main square. Although development is fairly intense in this region, the coast westward is a delightful symphony of eroded cliffs, stacks, gullies, grottos and arches reaching a crescendo at Lagos. It is still possible to follow your nose and divert off to quiet beaches.

Whichever route you take towards the west, it is likely you will end up in **Alcantarilha** ⑯. It's worth a stop here if only to look in on the parish church, and especially the Capela da Ossos around the corner which is packed with a chilling array of skulls. Head south from here into **Armação de Pêra** ⑰. This drab resort is rescued by an attractive promenade and beach, and it is a good place to eat fish.

All the might and cragginess returns to the coastline and it's a fair descent to reach the beach at **Rocha da Pena**. Sitting on a bluff here between two sandy coves is the simple white church of **Nossa Senhora da Rocha** ⑱ dedicated to the fishermen. Inland from here is **Porches**, famous for its painted pottery.

At the next roundabout on the EN125 is **Lagoa**, where people stop mainly for the lively morning market. This is also where farmers bring their grapes to the central cooperative wine cellar. A left turn at this roundabout leads down to Carvoeiro, a craggy coastline of isolated beaches, like that of Algar Seco. **Praia de Carvoeiro**, which is a lively tourist spot itself, has a pleasant little beach framed by villa-studded cliffs.

Portimão ⑲ (once a Roman harbour, Portus Magnus) lies west of Carvoeiro. An important fishing port, it is also a pleasant shopping town built on the west bank of the Arade estuary. Portimâo is famous for its grilled sardines – have lunch beside the river – and its pastry shops. Facing it is the pretty fishing vil-

Algarve has many spectacular beaches but Praia da Marinha, south of Porches, is one of the most photogenic. For a huge expanse of sand backed by colourful cliffs, try Falésia just west of Quarteira.

BELOW LEFT: a dramatic rock formation at Praia da Rocha
BELOW: flourishing Algarve vegetation.

A street corner in Lagos.

lage of **Ferragudo ⑳**, with its cobbled streets, sidewalk cafés and a good fish market. Close by is ocean-fronted **Praia da Rocha ㉑**, which has a superb, much-photographed beach characterised by strange towering rock formations standing in the blue-green sea. The village itself, however, is a bit of a concrete jungle, although it does have all the facilities a tourist could ask for.

Lagos

Moving west you will come to **Lagos ㉒**, which is believed to have been founded by the Carthaginians, then taken by the Romans in the 5th century BC, when it was called *Lacobriga* (Fortified Lake). The Moors took it over in the 8th century and renamed it *Zawaia* (Lake). The city finally fell to the Portuguese during the reign of Afonso III. In 1434 Gil Eanes left from Lagos and became the first sea captain to round Cape Bojador, off northwest Africa, south of the Canary Islands – then the limit of the known world. Most of Lagos was rebuilt in the 18th century, but some evidence of its darker past still stands in the columns and semicircular arches of Portugal's first slave market in the **Praça da República**. Note, too, the modern monument by João Cutileiro recording King Sebastião's departure to the disastrous battle of Alcácer-Quibir in 1578.

A walk through the city's winding streets will lead you to the **Igreja de Santo António**, on the outside a sober-looking church, but inside an extraordinarily beautiful example of gilded carving. The nave has an impressive painted wooden barrel-vault and baroque paintings on the walls. The **Museu Municipal** has exhibits on archaeology and religious art, and can be entered through the church (open Tues–Sun; closed 12.30–2pm; entrance charge).

Lagos has several pretty coves and beaches, especially **Praia Dona Ana**.

BELOW: the fortifications at Lagos look as though they mean serious business.

Don't miss the rock formations at **Ponta da Piedade** ㉓. From the cliffs you might also hire a boat from a local fisherman to explore the grottoes, with their cathedral-like natural skylights.

Beyond Lagos lie three relatively unspoilt fishing villages, each of a different character and each worth as visit. **Luz** ㉔ is the first of these, and perhaps the most developed, and is followed by **Burgau** and **Salema**. The countryside changes drastically, particularly after Salema, to a rockier and more undulating landscape. The trees look smaller and squatter, permanently bent from the unrelenting wind. Improved roads make driving easier now in this area but the new road actually bypasses the Knights Templar church of **Nossa Senhora de Guadalupe** ㉕, where Henry the Navigator is said to have worshipped. It is easier to spot it when travelling west and visit it on the return.

Map on pages 198–9

Sagres

Sagres ㉖ is a small fishing town, with Baleeira Bay as its port. The attraction to visitors is the fortress at **Ponta de Sagres**, used by Henry the Navigator early in the 15th century. He invited the most renowned cartographers, astronomers and mariners of his day to work here, and thus formed a fund of knowledge unsurpassed at the time, although modern historians believe he did not found a formal School of Navigation. Nothing that Prince Henry built is left so it is hard to be sure. But you can see clues – discovered only in the 20th century – notably a huge, 43-metre (140-ft) compass rose on the stone ground of the fortress. Less pleasing to many is the restoration work which has resulted in old buildings being demolished for the construction of a modern exhibition hall and tourist facilities, and the old fortress walls being painted white. But at least the small white domed church, the **Igreja Santa Maria**, remains unscathed.

It was to Sagres that seafarers returned in 1419 with the news that they had discovered an uninhabited island they called Porto Santo, which was later found to be part of the Madeiran archipelago.

BELOW: Sagres fortress by night.

All that remains now is to continue driving through this windswept terrain passing the small Fortaleza de Beliche, now a small *pousada* and restaurant, to reach **Cabo de São Vicente** ㉗, known to ancient mariners as *O Fim do Mundo*, the End of the World. From within the walls enclosing the lighthouse you can look down upon St Vincent's rocky throne.

Legend has it that in medieval times Christian followers of the martyred St Vincent defied the Moors and buried his body on the cape, with a shrine to honour him. Sacred ravens were said to have maintained vigil over the spot and over the ship that carried the bones of the saint to Lisbon. Here, even on a calm day, waves crash against the cliffs with spray-tossing violence. In spring, the smell of the sea competes with the scent of cistus, the rock-rose bush whose perfumed leaves were once supposedly used by the Egyptians for embalming

The wild west coast

Algarve's Atlantic coast is virtually a continuous sand dune frequently pounded by a restless ocean and almost constantly under surf and spray. Although there are endless beaches, access is usually by a rough track and there are few towns of significance. **Odeceixe**, the most northerly town on this stretch of Algarvian coastline, is a small Moorish-style village that reaches out to long sandy beaches and looming high cliffs. Road improvements are making it easier to reach but few visitors are tempted out just to see it. The most popular west coast circuit starts from Cabo de São Vincente and continues north through the vast, dune-backed Carrapateira to **Aljezur** ❷ – the last town to be taken from the Moors – where there is a castle to visit. Directly west are the **Monte Clérigo** and **Arrifana** beaches. Heading inland from Aljezur towards Monchique leads back into the heart of Algarve.

Mountains and rural villages

Towering above rolling hills, the granite mountains of **Serra de Monchique** attract streams of visitors to enjoy the views from the summit. In spring, Monchique is covered in flowering mimosa, and wild flowers bloom in the valleys between the Fóia and Picota peaks. **Fóia** ❷ is the highest point of Algarve reaching 902 metres (2,950 ft) above sea level. It is easily accessible along a winding road lined with cheerful restaurants selling roast chicken. The summit is heavily forested with aerials and the promised views are revealed only on clear days. Picota is a different challenge and can be reached only on foot.

The town of Monchique is rather disappointing if you merely drive through, but park the car and walk the steep streets to get a better feel for the place. Not to be missed is **Caldas de Monchique** ❸, off to the right heading south, hidden in a deep valley and surrounded by chestnut, cork, pine, orange and eucalyptus trees. The spa has been in use since Roman times and the waters are believed to cure a number of ailments, from convulsions to rheumatism. The springs pour out an estimated 20 million litres (4 million gallons) of water a year.

The eucalyptus trees which now grow in profusion in the Serra de Monchique smell lovely but are unpopular with environmentalists since they are bad for the soil and highly flammable.

BELOW: the Serra de Monchique.

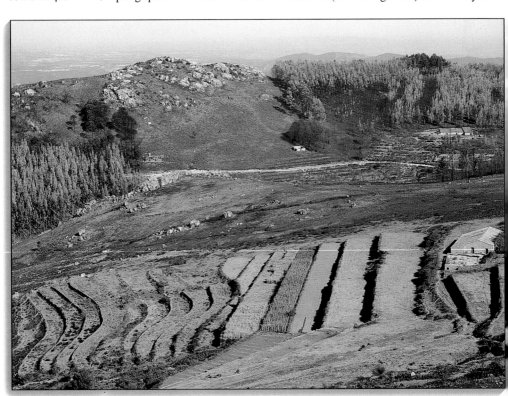

Descending from the heights, but away from the coastal tourist zone, a more rural lifestyle is found in the towns and villages. Here, locals have managed to shrug off the effects of regular visitors and continue their traditional ways. Some of the more interesting places include **Silves** ③, northwest of Albufeira (take the N266 south from Caldas de Monchique then turn left just before Porto de Lagos). Silves was populated as long ago as the 4th century BC; while it was important in Roman times, it reached its greatest splendour under the Moors, who made it capital of Algarve.

In its glory days Silves was the home of some of the greatest Arab poets. They recorded its ruin when the city fell to Portugal's King Sancho I in 1189: "Silves, my Silves, once you were a paradise. But tyrants turned you into the blaze of hell. They were wrong not to fear God's punishment. But Allah leaves no deed unheeded," wrote one. Two years later the Moors occupied Silves again before it was finally reconquered by the Portuguese.

Yemenite Arabs built the walled city, but the castle (atop a Roman citadel, itself built on Neolithic foundations) and the defensive towers were rebuilt in the later Almohad period (12th–13th centuries) and heavily restored in modern times. The Moorish castle and Christian Cathedral dominate the city, the dark-red sandstone contrasting with the soft pinks and faded blues of the older surrounding houses. A sense of history still permeates Silves and the castle – except in June when a beer festival considerably changes the atmosphere.

The Moorish cistern to the north once supplied the city's water, and is architecturally similar to 13th-century cisterns found in Palestine and in Cáceres, Spain. Built by both the Romans and the Moors, the advanced irrigation system transformed Algarve into the garden of Portugal.

Map
on pages
198–9

BELOW:
Silves Cathedral,
rebuilt after the
earthquake of 1755.

Map
on pages
198–9

TIP

Find out the date for
the next Estói market
at the tourist office: it's
the biggest and the
best in Algarve.

RIGHT: testing the
water at Praia
Dona Ana.
BELOW: chickens
for sale at Loulé
market.

The **Sé** (**Cathedral**) is 13th-century Gothic, restored in the 14th century and almost destroyed by the earthquake of 1755. Its apse is decorated with square arches, pyramidal battlements and fanciful gargoyles. The inner chapel of João de Rego dates from the 1400s. Various tombs here are said to be those of crusaders who helped capture Silves from the Moors in 1244. Here, too, for four years lay the remains of João II, who died in nearby Alvor in 1495, aged 40 – from dropsy, according to some doctors, from poisoning according to others.

From Alte to Estói

Northeast of Albufeira (take the E1, the turn right) is **Alte** ㉜, an elegant village lying at the foot of hills and huddled around its parish church. Nossa Senhora da Assunção dates from the 16th century and has magnificent 18th-century tile panels. The tiles in the chapel of Nossa Senhora de Lurdes, among the best in Algarve, are of 16th-century Sevillian origin. Alte is one of the most typical villages of the province with its simple houses, delicate white laced chimneys, and timeless serenity.

A nearby stream has transformed the area into an oasis amid the region's arid landscape. It's a lush garden of oleanders, fig and loquat trees and rose bushes. The blue and white tile panels at Fonte Santa (Holy Fountain) are inscribed with verses by local poet, Cândido Guerreiro. This area is perfect for picnics, or a walk up the Pena hill where you can visit the **Buraco dos Mouros** (Moors' Cave). Further up the mountain is **Rocha dos Soidos**, a cave filled with stalactite and stalagmite formations.

Heading back towards Faro you reach **Loulé** ㉝, a small town whose old quarter – Almedina – is a maze of narrow streets, reminiscent of a North African *casbah*. The interior of the chapel of Nossa Senhora da Conceição (near the tourist office) is tiled with attractive 17th-century *azulejos*, and the Igreja da Misericordia has a fine Manueline doorway. One of Loulé's greatest attractions is the Saturday market, held in the onion-domed market halls, selling food of every kind, from home grown fruit to live chickens.

Take a very slight detour east before you reach Faro and you will come to **Estói** ㉞, a pleasant village with a fine parish church, but best known for its 18th-century **Palácio dos Condes de Carvalhal** (open Tues–Sat; closed 12.30–2pm; entrance charge). With 28 rooms under restoration, some of the palace may not be accessible, but the highly ornamental gardens of this "Queluz of the south", with their statues and rococo fountains, and a splendid tiled staircase, are well worth seeing.

The town has a huge market – more of a country fair, held monthly on Sunday. It is a lively affair where you can buy a horse, sell a few sheep, stock up with fruit and vegetables or just buy sugared cakes to eat as you mingle with the crowds taking in the atmosphere.

Close by is the **Vila Romana de Milreu** ㉟, a Roman site discovered in the late 1800s. There are some lovely mosaics, the remains of thermal baths, and a well-preserved villa dating from the 2nd century. The largest structure, a temple, was consecrated as a Visigothic basilica in the 3rd century. ❑

EVORA AND ALENTEJO

Map on page 216

The Romans left more than a few footprints here, and there are historic towns and castles around almost every corner. Alentejo is one of the country's best-kept secrets

Alentejo, literally "beyond the Tejo" (the River Tagus), has a distinctive character and beauty unlike that of any other Portuguese province. Its vast plains, coloured burnt ochre in summer, are freckled with cork oaks and olive trees which provide the only shade for the small flocks of sheep and herds of black pigs. Nicknamed *terra do pão* (land of bread) because of field upon field of wheat and oats, Alentejo supports acres of grapevines, tomatoes, sunflowers and other plantations.

The largest and flattest of the Portuguese provinces, about the size of Belgium, Alentejo occupies one-third of Portugal's total area yet has only six percent of its population. It stretches from the west coast east to the Spanish border and separates Ribatejo and Beira Baixa in the central regions from Algarve in the south. The open countryside is punctuated by picturesque whitewashed towns and villages, many built on the low hills which dot the horizon.

Alentejo is rich in handicrafts. Rustic pottery with naive, colourful designs can be found everywhere. In addition, certain towns specialise in particular crafts or products: hand-stitched rugs from Arraiolos, loom-woven carpets from Reguengos; cheese from Serpa; tapestries from Portalegre; sugar plums from Elvas. All can be purchased, of course, elsewhere in Alentejo, or in Lisbon or Porto, but for price, selection, freshness and adventure, isn't it more satisfying to go to the source?

Getting familiar

Geographically the province is split into two regions, Upper (*Alto*) and Lower (*Baixo*) Alentejo. Evora is the capital of the former and Beja of the latter. To the east are two low mountain ranges, the Serras of São Mamede and Ossa. Some of the towns in these ranges, particularly Marvão, have breathtaking, even precipitous settings. Portugal's third longest river, the Guadiana, flows through the province and in places provides the border between Portugal and Spain. This is by no means the only waterway. The region is criss-crossed by a network of small rivers and dams.

Roads which connect the towns are excellent. Most of the traffic is local and slow moving. You will need to equip yourself with a reliable road map; signposting is limited, and without a map you could drive miles before discovering you've taken a wrong turn.

The Portuguese in general are not renowned for their tidiness but the Alentejanos are the exception. The towns are litter-free and there is always a *dona de casa* in view whitewashing her already pristine home. Cool and simple is the theme for Alentejo architecture; low, single-storey buildings are painted white to deflect the sun's glare, with a traditional blue or yellow skirting. Large domed chimneys indicate chilly

PRECEDING PAGES: a typically busy scene in Monsaraz' main street. **LEFT:** looking at life. **BELOW:** a local handyman.

Evora and Alentejo

0   20 km

0   20 miles

winters. This practical style is followed from the humblest cottage to the large hacienda-style homes of the wealthy landowners; ornate and impressive architecture is reserved for cathedrals and churches.

Inland, Alentejo's temperature in the summer can reach inferno level: what little wind there is blows hot and dry from the continental land mass – no cooling sea breezes here. Temperatures can drop dramatically in winter, resulting in bitterly cold nights.

Alentejo is steeped in history which goes back to the days of Roman colonisation. Later, it was the seat of the great landed estates (*latifundia*) of the Portuguese nobility and home to former kings. Even as late as 1828, Evora – the capital of the Alto Alentejo – was considered the second major Portuguese city, an honour which was first bestowed on it by King João I (1385–1433).

Estremoz, whose ancient castle has been converted into a comfortable *pousada*, was a nerve centre of medieval Portugal. Vila Viçosa was the seat of the dukes of Bragança, whose royal dynasty began in 1640 with the coronation of João IV and ended in 1910 with the fall of the monarchy.

You'll find evidence of Alentejo's long history all over the region. This ancient pottery is from the town of Mértola.

Politics, pastimes and and popular song

Modern Alentejo is a far cry from the days of aristocratic domination, although farming techniques in the smallholdings have changed little. The greatest change is political: after the restoration of democracy in 1974 Alentejo became the heartland of Portuguese communism. Many of the great estates – so vast that they included villages, schools and even small hospitals – were taken over by the farm workers during the revolution. Some of the landowning families were forcibly ejected, but the majority were absentee landlords anyway, living in

BELOW: walking the sheep.

properties nearer Lisbon or Porto. There is now a new landowning generation with a modern approach to agriculture and skilled at effective farm management.

Farming is the pulse of Alentejo, and the lives of its people revolve around the seasons. Aside from Evora the towns are small and the population is scattered in hamlets linked to farms. Secondary schools are restricted to the larger towns; in the more remote areas the general practice among young people is to leave school early to work in the fields, or head to the cities.

Throughout the year, but particularly at harvest time, you will see the field workers making their way to and from work on foot, by bicycle or crammed into open-topped trucks. Most rural Alentejanos adopt the traditional dress: black wide-brimmed hats for both men and women, black trousers, waistcoats, jackets and white collarless shirts for men, black shawls and thick black skirts for women, or trousers for field work. Neckerchiefs for extra protection against sun and dust are loosely knotted around the men's necks, while women favour head-squares worn under their hats. The faces of the old people are extraordinary – leathery skins baked a deep brown, furrowed like tree bark and coloured like walnuts.

One of the traditional pastimes for the menfolk is a wild boar hunt near the Spanish border. During the season (October–February), you will often see men out with their shotguns, pouches and a gaggle of dogs.

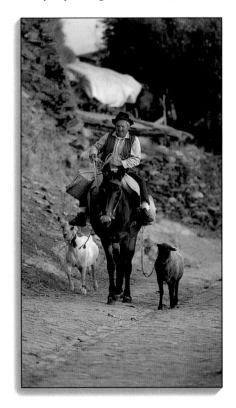

Map on page 216

Singing and dancing are popular across the length and breadth of Portugal, and Alentejo does its share. Here, the folk songs are the domain of the men. The songs are slow, rather melancholic, but of a completely different style from the haunting *fado* which is heard elsewhere. A slow tempo is set by the stamping of the men's feet as they sing in chorus, swaying to the rhythm by the time they reach the end of the song. A performance is well worth listening to; ask at an Alentejo tourist office about where to hear the *ceifeiros*.

Evora is the largest and most important of all Alentejana towns. It is a superb city, full of fascinating sights, all of which are in a good state of preservation. They are likely to remain so as the entire city has been proclaimed a world heritage site by UNESCO, therefore qualifying for financial aid.

It takes about two and a half hours to drive from Lisbon to Evora, and a tour could comfortably be managed as a day trip. But that would not leave time to see the lovely towns and villages along the way. To base yourself in Evora is easy; there are plenty of small guest houses and hotels.

Evora is one of nine sites in Portugal to have been designated a UNESCO World Heritage Site. (See Travel Tips for a complete list).

The route from Lisbon

To reach Evora leave Lisbon via the Ponte 25 de Abril and head down towards the *auto-estrada* for Setúbal, and then turn eastwards on the A6 (IP7) past Montemor-o-Novo for Evora. You will not need a welcome billboard to tell you that you have just reached Alentejo; suddenly the road is broad and less pot-holed, and you will find yourself at the edge of the rolling plains. Look for the jumbles of twigs on top of the high walls and buildings – homes to the storks that flourish in the province. As you drive further inland you will also notice the waning breeze and the increase in temperature.

BELOW: the Temple of Diana, Evora.

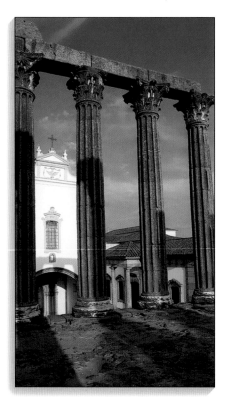

Pegões is the first small Alentejo town on the route. It's a rather dry, dusty and deserted town nowadays, especially as it is by passed by the new highway. A little further along is **Vendas Novas**, also off the new road. Shady, neat and with an air of affluence, it is typical of modest Alentejo towns.

Montemor-o-Novo ❶ can be seen from quite a distant approach, its ruined medieval castle crowning its low *monte* (hill). The castle ramparts are thought to date from Roman times. The town is divided into the upper old town and lower new town. As you might expect the old town is more interesting. It was here that St John of God (São João de Deus) was born in 1495. He was baptised in the ruined parish church, of which only the granite Manueline portal is still intact. In the square outside the church is a statue commemorating the saint, a Franciscan monk of great charity and humility. Although it does not have the population to support them, the town has five churches, three convents and two monasteries.

Evora: Alentejo's city

As you enter **Evora ❷** on the main Lisbon road, there is a small tourist office just before the Roman walls, where you can pick up a street map marked with suggested walks that take in the most important sights. The best place to park is outside the walls and walk to **Praça do Giraldo ❹** at the centre of the city. This

Maps:
Area 216
City 219

large square is arcaded on two sides and has a 16th-century church and fountain at the top. From here you can explore the inner city with ease.

The city's history can be traced back to the earliest civilisations on the Iberian peninsula. Evora derives its name from *Ebora Cerealis*, which dates from the Luso-Celtic colonisation. The Romans later fortified the city, renamed it *Liberalitas Julia*, and elevated it to the status of *municipium,* which gave it the right to mint its own currency. Its prosperity declined under the Visigoths, but was rekindled under Moorish rule (711–1165). Much of the architecture, with arched, twisting alleyways and tiled patios, reflects the Moorish presence. Evora was liberated from the Moors by a Christian knight, Geraldo Sem-Pavor ("the Fearless"), in 1165, in the name of Afonso Henriques I, Portugal's first king.

For the next 400 years Evora enjoyed great importance and wealth. It was the preferred residence of the kings of the Burgundy and Avis dynasties, and the courts attracted famous artists, dramatists, humanists and academics. Great churches, monasteries, houses and convents were also built. The splendour peaked in 1559, when Henrique, the last of the Avis kings (and also Archbishop of Evora), founded a Jesuit university. In 1580, following the annexation of Portugal by Spain, Evora's glory waned. The Castilians paid little attention to it, except as an agricultural and trading centre and even after Portuguese independence was restored in 1640, it did not regain its former brilliance.

Evora: the sights

The oldest sight in Evora is the **Temple of Diana (Templo Romano) B**, off Praça do Giraldo, which dates from the 2nd or 3rd century AD. The temple is presumed to have been built as a place of imperial worship. The Corinthian

There's nothing austere about the pousada *in the old Convento dos Lóios in Evora.*

columns are granite, their bases and capitals hewn from local marble. The façade and mosaic floor have disappeared completely, but the six rear columns and those at either side are still intact. The temple was converted into a fortress during the Middle Ages, then used as a slaughterhouse until 1870, an inelegant role which nevertheless saved the temple from being torn down.

From a good viewpoint in the shady garden just across from the rear of the temple, you can look down over the lower town and across the plains: the tiny village of Evoramonte is just visible to the northeast. To the right of the temple is the **Convento dos Lóios** ● and the adjacent church of **São João Evangelista**. The convent buildings have been converted into an elegant *pousada* but the church is still public. Founded in 1485, its style is Romano-Gothic, although all but the doorway in the façade was remodelled after the 1755 earthquake. The nave has an ornate vaulted ceiling and walls lined with beautiful tiles depicting the life of St Laurence Justinian, dated 1771 and signed by António de Oliveira Bernardes. There are guided tours of the church, cloisters and chapterhouse.

The Cathedral

The nearby **Sé** (**Cathedral**) ● is a rather austere building. Its granite, Romano-Gothic-style façade was built in the 12th century, while its main portal and the two grand conical towers – unusual in that they are asymmetric, with one tower adorned with glittering blue tiles – were added in the 16th century. Before going inside, take a close look at the main entrance, which is decorated with magnificent 14th-century sculptures of the apostles. With three naves stretching for 70 metres (230 ft), the Cathedral has the most capacious interior in Portugal, and the vast broken barrel-vaulted ceiling is quite stunning.

BELOW: 14th-century apostles at the entrance to the Cathedral in Evora.

Once you've seen the cathedral, it is worth paying the nominal sum to see the cloisters, choir stalls and **Museu de Arte Sacra** (open Tues–Sun from 9am, closed 12.30–2pm and public holidays). The latter, in the treasury, contains a beautiful collection of ecclesiastical gold, silver and bejewelled plate, ornaments, chalices and crosses. The Renaissance-style choir stalls, tucked high in the gallery, are fashioned with a delightful series of wooden carvings with motifs both sacred and secular. From the choir stalls you get a good bird's-eye view of the Cathedral. The marble cloisters are 14th-century Gothic, large and imposing, more likely to inspire awe than meditative contemplation.

Next door to the cathedral is the **Museu de Evora ❺** (open Tues pm, Wed–Sun, closed 12.30–2pm; entrance charge), formerly the Bishop's Palace and now home to a fine collection of paintings, both Portuguese Primitives and Flemish. There is also interesting local sculpture and furniture.

More Evora landmarks

At the old **Jesuit University ❻**, some elegant and graceful cloisters are visible. You have to follow a short road down to the east of the city to reach it. The marble of the broad cloisters seems to have aged not at all since the 16th century, and there is still the peaceful atmosphere of the serious academic.

The classroom entrances at the far end of the cloister gallery are decorated with *azulejos* representing each of the subjects taught. If you take a slow walk back up the hill and head for the Igreja São Francisco, you'll pass by another church, the **Misericórdia ❼**, noted for its 18th-century tiled panels and baroque relief work. Behind it is the Casa Soure, a 15th-century Manueline house formerly part of the Palace of the Infante Dom Luís.

Map on page 219

Particularly interesting carvings in the cathedral choir stalls are those of everyday life: wine pressing, wheat threshing, singing and feasting.

BELOW: bones lying in wait in the Capela dos Ossos.

A MOTHER'S CURSE

The church of São Francisco (*see next page*) dating from the late 15th or early 16th centuries, has a remarkable chapel, the *Capela dos Ossos*. This bizarre and macabre room is entirely lined and decorated with the bones of some 5,000 people. It was created in the 16th century by a Franciscan monk. The skulls and bones have not merely been stored here in a random fashion; a lot of creative thought has gone into their placement. At the entrance you will see the inviting inscription: *Nós ossos qui estamos, pelos vossos esperamos* – "We bones lie here waiting for yours."

Hung at the far end of the chapel are the corpses of a man and a small child. These centuries-old bodies are said to be the victims of the curse of a dying wife and mother. Father and son were supposed to have made her life a misery and their ill treatment eventually killed her. On her death bed she cursed them, swearing that their flesh would never fall from their bones. The corpses are far from fleshy, but there is plenty of leathery substance attached to their bones.

Braids of human hair dating from the 19th century are hung at the entrance of the chapel – votive offerings placed there by young brides.

As you walk, take notice of the houses. Nearly all have attractive narrow wrought-iron balconies at the base of tall rectangular windows. An odd tradition in Evora as elsewhere in Portugal, is that visiting dignitaries are welcomed by a display of brightly coloured bedspreads hung from the balconies.

When you reach the Misericórdia church, take a brief detour to **Largo das Porta de Moura **. The gates mark the fortified northern entrance to the city, the limit of construction and safety as it was in medieval times. This picturesque square is dominated by a Renaissance fountain, built in 1556.

Heading west along the Rua Miguel Bombarda, keep an eye out for the church of **Nossa Senhora da Graça** ❶ (Our Lady of Grace), just off the Rua Miguel Bombarda. Built in granite, it is a far cry from the austerity of the cathedral. A later church (16th-century), its influence is strongly Italian Renaissance. Note the four huge figures supporting globes which represent the children of grace.

The most interesting thing about the **Igreja de São Francisco** ❶ is the Capela dos Ossos (*see previous page*), but the chapterhouse that links the chapel to the church is worth seeing, too. It is lined with *azulejos* depicting scenes from the Passion and contains an *altar dos promessas* (altar of promises) on which are laid wax effigies of various parts of the body. Ailing people, or their friends and relatives, go to the altar and pray for a cure. If it is granted, then an effigy of the relevant part is placed in thanks on the altar. The church also has an interesting Manueline porch.

Evora's public gardens – the **Jardim Público** – near the church provide a very pleasant walk; if you're lucky you may catch the band playing on the park's old-fashioned wrought-iron bandstand. The delightful **Palácio de Dom Manuel** ❸ (1495–1521), or what remains of it, stands in the park. It has paired

TIP

If you're visiting Evora during the summer and want to cool off, go to one of the local swimming pools on the edge of town. Although well patronised because they are inexpensive, they are spotlessly clean, with plenty of lawn on which to stretch out and dry off.

BELOW: the view over Evora is impressive.

windows in horseshoe arches, typical of the style which gained its name from Dom Manuel. Exhibitions are held in the long Ladies' Gallery.

If you're not intent on going inside Evora's monuments, a night stroll reveals its exterior architecture admirably. Nearly all the monuments are floodlit until midnight, and the winding narrow streets are very inviting on a balmy evening.

During the last week of June, Evora is filled with visitors who come to enjoy the annual **Feira de São João** (24–30 June). This huge fair fills the grounds opposite the public gardens. There's a local handicraft market, an agricultural hall, a display of local light industry, the general hotchpotch of open-air stalls, as well as folk singing and dancing, and restaurants serving typical cuisine.

Evoramonte and Estremoz

Alentejo has a number of megalithic monuments scattered across its plains, and some of the most important are just outside Evora. (*Turismo* will give you a map.) The best preserved and most significant stone circle, or cromlech, on the Iberian peninsula is 12 km (7 miles) west of the city. Close to the hill of Herdade dos Almendres, the **Cromeleque do Almendres ❸** has 95 standing stones.

Near to the Agricultural Department of the University of Evora in Valverde, just southwest of Evora, is the largest dolmen on the peninsula. The **Zambujeiro Dolmen** stands some 5 metres (17 ft) high with a 3-metre (10-ft) diameter and is dates from about 3000 BC.

On the road from Evora to Estremoz lies **Evoramonte ❹**, a village at the foot of a recently renovated 16th-century castle. It was here that the convention ending Portugal's civil war was signed on 26 May 1834. A plaque commemorating the event is placed over the house where the historic event took place.

Maps:
Area 216
City 219

The ruins of Evora's Palácio de Dom Manuel, built by the creator of the "Manueline" style – of which the palace's arched windows are a fine example.

BELOW: the ancient standing stones at Almendres.

Evoramonte Castle perches high on a hill and offers remarkable views: well worth the detour and the clamber up to the top of the castle which, despite its refurbished appearance and Manueline knots, dates from 1306.

Estremoz: steeped in history

About 22 km (14 miles) northeast lies the lovely town of **Estremoz ❺**. Although much smaller than Evora, it has some fascinating monuments. The old part of town, crowned by a castle now converted into a *pousada*, was founded by King Afonso III in 1258, but is most often associated with King Dinis, whose residence it was in the 14th century. His wife, the saintly Queen Isabel of Aragon, is honoured by a statue in the main square, and a chapel dedicated to her can be seen in one of the castle towers (ask at the *pousada*).

Estremoz is famous for its pottery, which is on sale in shops all over town, and also at the Saturday market in Rossio, the main square of the lower town.

The chapel is at the top of a narrow staircase; small, and highly decorated, it is where she is said to have died. Mind you, some also say that she died in the nearby King's Audience Chamber. The chapel walls are adorned with 18th-century *azulejos* and paintings depicting scenes from the queen's life. Behind the altar is a tiny plain room bearing a smaller altar on which the Estremoz faithful have placed their ex votos, or offerings.

The most impressive part of the castle is the wonderful 13th-century keep which is entered via the *pousada*. To get to the top you need to be fairly fit – or make a slow and steady ascent. The second floor has an octagonal room with tre-foil windows. From the top platform there is a breathtaking view. The red rooftops contrast beautifully with the whitewashed houses and the green plains beyond, much of which are planted with rows of olive trees.

BELOW: the rooftops of Estremoz.

Across the square from the *pousada* is King Dinis's palace. It must have been a beautiful place, but all that remains standing after a gunpowder explosion in the palace arsenal in 1698 is the Gothic colonnade and star-vaulted **Audience Chamber**. It is used nowadays for exhibitions of work by local artists.

Having survived the narrow roads and hairpin bends on the drive up to the castle, the descent seems easy. The upper town is connected to the lower by 14th-century ramparts and fairly modern buildings: the wrought-iron balconies here are decorated with coloured tiles.

If you like Portuguese wines then you may be familiar with the name Borba, where a co-operative produces a good red wine. The ancient village of **Borba** (about 11 km/6 miles from Estremoz), which is said to date back to the Gauls and Celts, does not have much to show except for a splendid fountain, the Fonte das Bicas, built in 1781 from local white marble.

Vila Vicosa: Bragança's base

Down the road from Borba is **Vila Viçosa ❻**, the seat of the dukes of Bragança. It comes as quite a surprise after the Moorish-influenced towns perched on the hilltops. It is cool and shady, its large main square (Praça da República) is filled with orange trees, and elsewhere there are lemon trees and lots of flowers. Viçosa means lush, and its luxuriant boulevards are a pleasure to walk.

A lovely, if rather overgrown, medieval castle overlooks the town square. It is very peaceful there, the only sound being the cooing of the white fan-tail doves which nest in the ramparts. The drawbridge is lowered across the (dry) moat and the first floor has become a modest archaeological museum.

Vila Viçosa is best known for the **Paço Ducal** (the Ducal Palace of the Braganças), a three-storey building with a long façade, which is open to the

Map on page 216

Old-fashioned street light in Estremoz.

BELOW:
a sleepy afternoon in Vila Viçosa.

Alentejo is full of unexpected buildings such as this Moorish inspired oddity in Monsaráz.

public for guided tours. Its furniture, painting and tapestries are very fine, and definitely worth seeing. The palace also contains an excellent collection of 17th- to 19th-century coaches.

The palace overlooks a square in which stands a bronze statue of João IV, the first king of the Bragança dynasty. To the north of the square is a striking gateway, the Manueline **Porta do Nó** (Knot Gate), a stone archway which appears to be roped together, and is part of the 16th-century town walls.

From Elvas to Monsaraz

Heading east for about 28 km (17 miles) along the main road to the Spanish border from Estremoz, you will come to the strongly fortified town of **Elvas 7**. Founded by the Romans, it was long occupied by the Moors and finally liberated from them in 1230 – about 100 years later than Lisbon. The town was of great strategic importance during the wars of independence in the mid-1600s. The fortress of **Santa Luzia**, south of town, was built by a German, Count Lippe, for the purpose of repelling the Spanish. The older castle above the town was originally a Roman fortress, rebuilt by the Moors and enlarged in the 15th century.

If you walk around the ramparts that once encircled the town you cannot fail to be impressed by the effective engineering. The town itself is very attractive, from the triangular "square" of Santa Clara, with its 16th-century marble pillory, to the main Praça da República, with its geometric mosaic paving.

Elvas has a country house-style *pousada,* whose restaurant is particularly popular with Spanish visitors. One of its specialties is a *bacalhau dourado –* slivers of salted cod fried with potatoes, onions, olives and scrambled egg. (If you stay overnight, be sure to ask for a quiet room – the *pousada* is close to the main A6/E90 highway.)

The **Aqueduto da Amoreira 8**, just outside the town, was designed by a great 15th-century architect, Francisco de Arruda. Its 8 km (5 miles) and 843 arches took nearly 200 years to complete. The cost was borne by the people of Elvas under a special tax named the *Real de Agua.*

Handwoven rugs used to be manufactured throughout Alentejo, but nowadays the small town of **Reguengos 9** is the only place where they are still made, in a factory that has been using the same looms for the past 150 years. To reach it, return to Borba then travel south for about 60 km (38 miles). Reguengos is a nucleus of megalithic stones and dolmens, found at several sites near the town.

About 16 km (10 miles) northeast of Reguengos is the delightful walled town of **Monsaraz 10**, so small it can easily be explored on foot – leave your car at the gate. It was originally fortified by the Knights Templar, when the Moors were the enemy. Later, its proximity to the Spanish border combined with its height made it of great strategic importance. Once the threat from Spain had passed, however, Reguengos became gradually more influential and Monsaráz less so, which helped it become the relaxed and peaceful village it is today. Its main street, Rua Direita, is all 16th- and 17th-century architecture, yet the town still maintains a distinctly medieval atmosphere.

Portalegre

The lush countryside which surrounds **Portalegre ⑪** is rather different from that in the low-lying lands. This area is in foothills of the **Serra de São Mamede**, and the cooler and slightly more humid climate makes it much greener. To get there, return to Evora and take the N18/E802 north.

Quite a large town by Alentejo standards, Portalegre is unusual in that it is not built on top of a hill, but on the site of an ancient ruined settlement called Amaya. In the mid-13th century, King Afonso III issued instructions that a new city was to be built. He called it Portus Alacer: Portus for the customs gate which was to process Spanish trade and Alacer (*álacre* means "merry") because of its pleasing setting. King Dinis ensured that the town was fortified in 1290 (although only a few of those ruins can be seen today) and João III gave it the status of a city in 1550.

The lofty 16th-century interior of the **Sé** (**Cathedral**) is late-Renaissance style. The side altars have fine wooden *retábulos* and 16th- and 17th-century paintings in the Italian style. The sacristy contains lovely blue-and-white *azulejo* panels from the 18th century depicting the life of the Virgin Mary and the Flight to Egypt. The cathedral's façade is 18th-century, and is dominated by marble columns, granite pilasters and wrought-iron balconies.

Portalegre's affluence began in the 16th century, when its tapestries were in great demand. Continued prosperity followed in the next century with the establishment of silk mills. You should not miss the opportunity to see the tapestry workshops in the former Jesuit Monastery in Rua Fernandes (guided tours are available). The looms are still worked by hand.

Portalegre was home to one of Portugal's major writers: poet, dramatist and

Map on page 216

BELOW: plenty of time for reflection in Monsaraz.

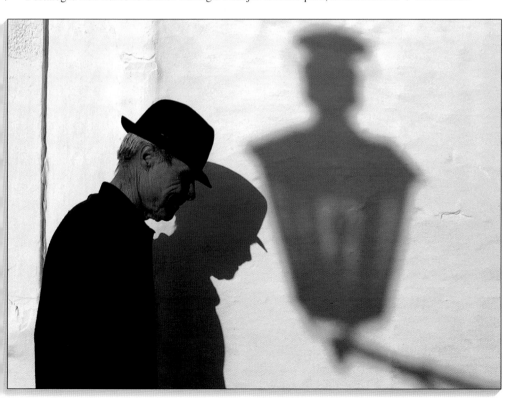

novelist José Régio (1901–69). His house has been opened as a museum. Of particular interest is his collection of regional folk and religious art. Also of note is the 17th-century Yellow Palace, where the 19th-century radical reformer, Mouzinho da Silveira lived. The ornate ironwork is quite remarkable.

Spectacular Marvao

Marvão ⑫ is one of the most spectacular sights of Alentejo. About 25 km (15 miles) north of Portalegre, it is a medieval fortified town perched on one of the São Mamede peaks. Its altitude (862 metres/2,830 ft) affords it an uninterrupted view across the Spanish frontier. The precipitous drop on one side made it inaccessible to invaders and an ideal defensive situation.

At this height the land is barren and craggy. The seemingly impenetrable castle was built in the 13th century from the local grey granite. Clinging to the foot of the castle is the tiny village, a few twisting alleyways flanked by red-roofed whitewashed houses. Close by the church of Espírito Santo, on the street of the same name, is a baroque granite fountain. On the same street is the sober-looking Governor's House, its only decoration two magnificent 17th-century wrought-iron balconies.

On the road to Castelo de Vide are the ruins of the Roman settlement of **Medóbriga**. Many artifacts have been found here, although most of these have been taken to Lisbon.

BELOW: Marvão, bathed in early morning light.

Castelo de Vide: fort and spa

Completing the triangle of noteworthy upper Alentejo towns is **Castelo de Vide** ⑬, a delightful town built in the shadow of an elongated medieval castle

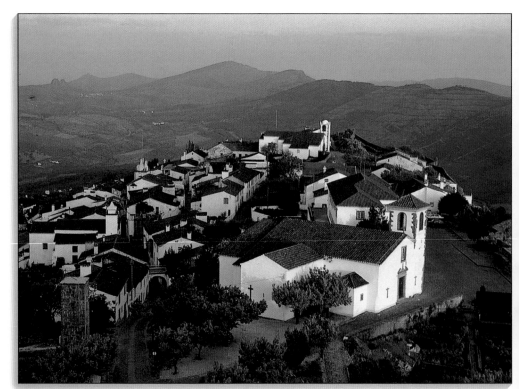

situated on the summit of a foothill on the northern *serra*. The town was originally a Roman settlement. Alongside it ran the major Roman road which traversed the Iberian peninsula. The settlement was sacked by the Vandals at the beginning of the 4th century, occupied by the Moors during their domination of the southern part of the peninsula, and fortified by the Portuguese in 1180.

Castelo de Vide is a spa town. You can drink its curative waters from plastic bottles which are sold in the supermarkets, or sip from one of the numerous fountains located in the town and environs. Perhaps its prettiest outlet is the quadrangled, covered fountain (Fonte da Vila), set in the small square below the Jewish Quarter. The baroque fountain has a pyramid roof supported by six marble columns. The central urn is carved with figures of boys and the water spills from four spouts.

As in nearly all fortified Alentejo towns, Castelo de Vide has two very distinct faces. The first is the older one, situated next to the castle. The most interesting and picturesque is the medieval **Judiaria** (Jewish Quarter). This host of back alleys, cobbled streets and whitewashed houses is splashed with green, as potted plants sprout their tendrils from every available niche, windowsill and step. Notice the doors: this section of Castelo de Vide has the best-preserved stone Gothic doorways in Portugal. It also has the oldest synagogue, dating from the 13th century. The majority of the inhabitants of this neighbourhood appear to be elderly people who sit in the doorways of their homes calmly watching the world go by.

Further down the hill is the newer part of town: essentially 17th- and 18th-century buildings with wider, less steep streets, more space, more order and more elegance. On the main square, **Praça Dom Pedro V**, stands the grandiose

Map on page 216

Carrying greenery in the Jewish Quarter of Castelo de Vide.

BELOW: Igreja Santa Maria, Castelo de Vide.

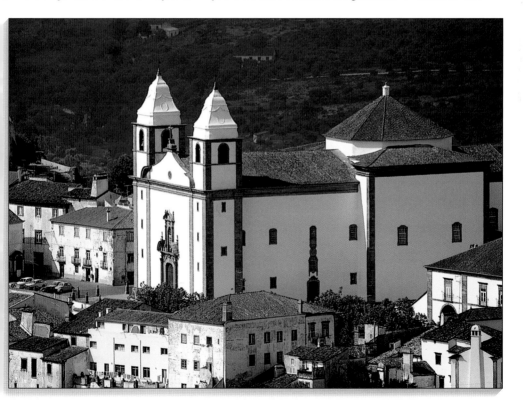

18th-century parish church and the old town hall, **Paços de Concelho**, remarkable for the huge 18th-century wrought-iron gate securing the main entrance.

Near Castelo de Vide you will find still more megalithic stones: these *pedras talhas* seem to be everywhere, standing in fields, in open scrubland or in local villages, inscrutable and ageless.

Flor de Rosa used to be a thriving pottery centre. The trade has dwindled in recent years, but pots are still made in the traditional way.

Portalegre's western neighbours

Nisa is a small, rather rambling town northwest of Castelo de Vide. It has the mandatory medieval castle, walls and an unusual squat, round-towered chapel. Homemade cheese is Nisa's speciality.

Some 24 km (15 miles) south of Nisa on the road back to Estremoz is **Flor da Rosa**, where you may be able to buy local pots. But the most interesting place to see is the Convento de Flor da Rosa, dating from 1356 and founded by the Order of Knights Hospitallers of St John. An eclectic building, with a solid Gothic cloister, it was in use as a monastery until the end of the last century.

Two royal marriages took place in **Crato**, a couple of kilometres down the road. The first was that of Manuel I, who married Leonor of Spain in 1518 (his third marriage); the second was seven years later when King João III married Catarina of Spain. The main square is dominated by a splendid 15th-century stone veranda, the **Varanda do Grão-Prior**, which is all that survives of the former priors' residence.

Some 13 km (8 miles) further south, in countryside filled with olive groves, is **Alter do Chão**, a medieval town that is interesting for its equine traditions. It is from here that the Alter Real horse takes its name. The Alter stud farm (*coudelaria*) was founded in 1748 by José I (as he became two years later). Based on Andalusian stock, the animals thrived until the Napoleonic Wars when the best animals were stolen and the royal stables abolished. Happily, the breed has been revived to a highly respected standard. There are guided tours of the stud farm, which horse lovers will find fascinating.

BELOW: the picturesque Jewish Quarter in Castelo de Vide.

Unspoiled beaches

If you like unspoiled cliffs and beaches, quiet roads and villages, then you will delight in the Alentejo coast, although more and more tourists are discovering it. It borders on the open Atlantic and the ocean is therefore much rougher than on the south coast. But there are plenty of sheltered bays for swimming, although the water is chilly.

Alentejo's coast is not renowned for its nightlife. Bars, discos, and fancy restaurants hardly exist; nor do large hotels, except at Vila Nova de Milfontes. There are campsites, however, and all the villages have at least one *pensão*. You'd better bring along your phrase book. Where tourists are relatively rare, so are natives who speak English.

Most people approach the coast from Lisbon, from where access is easy thanks to the extended motorway network. Heading south, the IP8 branches southwest just before Grândola to **Santiago do Cacém**, crowned by a castle built by the Knights Templar, which gives good views over the town and coast. Any-

one interested in things Roman should consider a trip to nearby **Miróbriga**
(open Tues–Sun; entrance charge). This Iron-Age/Roman site is quite extensive
and has been well excavated. There's also an interesting little Museu Regional
nearby, concentrating mainly on the local cork industry.

Map on page 216

Now it's just a short hop to Alentejo's largest coastal town, **Sines**, which
is famous for being the birthplace of Vasco da Gama in 1460. It's not what you
would call a beauty spot. The old part is still picturesque, but the nearby oil
refinery and power station is hard to ignore.

Leaving Sines in a hurry, you can clear your lungs at the village of **Porto
Covo**. The road which takes you there is tree-lined and virtually traffic-free.
Several tracks lead from the main road down to shingly beaches. Porto Covo is
a tiny village, with cobbled streets swept scrupulously clean. The main square,
grandly named Largo Marquês de Pombal, is very small, bordered by houses and
the tiny parish church. A few small trees and plentiful benches surround the
square. Down by the sea you can find shops, cafés and a restaurant.

Just off the coast of Porto Corvo is the fortified **Ilha do Pessegeiro** (Peach
Tree Island), which in bygone days provided protection from raids by Dutch and
Algerian pirates. Returning to the main road, some 15 km (9 miles) south of
Porto Corvo is the small town of Cercal, beyond which you reach **Vila Nova de
Milfontes**, the busiest of the coast's resorts – and very pleasing it is, too. The
only time it gets really busy is in high summer when many Alentejanos and
Lisboetas come for their annual holiday at the large campsite.

Again, there is little nightlife but there are a few more seafood restaurants and
a range of accommodation that includes the pricy Castle Hotel, converted from
an ivy-clad fortress – drawbridge and all – which overlooks the sea.

BELOW: some
things look better
with age.

Vila Nova de Milfontes is set at the mouth of the Rio Mira, whose estuary provides long golden beaches and a calm sea. Park out at the headland overlooking the ocean, and you can turn back to see the town to your left, the winding river and the hills beyond – all very idyllic. If you are planning a day or two on this coast, then this is the place to stay.

Almograve and Zambujeira do Mar offer more stunning, deserted beaches and some fine clifftop viewpoints across the basalt cliffs to the sea. Of the two very small villages, Almograve is by far the nicer. Between these two beaches is another, Cabo do Girão, but it is naval property and access is prohibited.

Southern Alentejo

You may well choose to start an exploration of the Lower Alentejo from a base in Lisbon, but you can start from here by going inland to the pretty town of **Odemira ㉒**, set on the banks of the Rio Mira, after which it's named. It is full of flowers and trees, so green that you are apt to forget that it is in Alentejo at all. Nearby, **Barragem de Santa Clara ㉓**, a huge dam on the Mira, where water sports are popular.

Ourique ㉔ is an agricultural town north of the dam. In its surrounding fields (Campo do Ourique), fruit, olives and cork trees grow. These fields, however, have seen far more than mere farming in their time. In the nearby hamlet of **Atalaia**, archaeologists have excavated an extraordinary Bronze-Age burial mound. And it was on the site of a battle called Ourique in 1139 (which may or may not have taken place) that a fateful encounter was fought between the Portuguese and the Moors. Afonso Henriques had just become the first king of Portugal, and the victory on this battlefield strengthened his determination to dis-

BELOW: cork trees dot the Alentejo plain.

pel the Moors from all Portuguese soil, and gave a tremendous boost to the flagging morale of his battle-weary forces.

Map
on page
216

Beja: a hot place

The capital of Lower Alentejo, **Beja** ㉕, is the hottest town in Portugal during the height of summer. It is a three-hour drive from Lisbon and an hour or so from Evora, or, if you are following the route from Ourique, it's about 60 km (38 miles) on the E802. A town existed on the present-day site as early as 48 BC, and when Julius Caesar made peace with the Lusitanians the settlement was named after this event, Pax Julia. During the 400-year Moorish occupation the name was adulterated to Baju, then Baja, until it finally became Beja.

It is now a fairly prosperous town, its income derived from olive oil and wheat. A long-time German Air Force base has been turned over to the Portuguese. Beja is not a beautiful town, but it does have some interesting sights.

The 15th-century **Convento da Conceição** is a fine example of the transition between Gothic and Manueline architecture. The baroque chapel is lined with carved, gilded woodwork. The chapterhouse which leads to the cloisters is tiled with superb Hispanic-Arabic *azulejos* dating back to the 1500s. Their quality is rivalled only by those to be found in the Royal Palace at Sintra. The convent also houses the Museu Regional (open Mon–Sat; closed 1–2.30pm; entrance charge).

Storks on a stalk, in Serpa.

The small and modest **Santo Amaro** is the oldest church in Beja. It is thought to date back to the 7th century and is a rare example of Visigothic architecture. The **Misericórdia** church in the Praça da República is also worth a look. Beja's 13th-century castle keep still stands, and its castellated walls run around the town perimeter. The tall keep contains a military museum, and a narrow balcony

BELOW: dressed for the fiesta in Beja.

on each side from which you can enjoy a remarkable view across the plains.

Driving in to **Serpa ㉖** (about 30 km/18 miles east of Beja) is – as with so many small Alentejo towns – like driving into a time warp. The castle and fortified walls were built at the command of King Dinis. A difference here from other 13th-century walls is that these have an aqueduct built into them.

A well-preserved gateway is the **Portas de Beja**, which, along with the rest of the walls, were almost sold by the town council in the latter half of the 19th century. Cooler heads prevailed and the walls were saved, though a great part of them had been destroyed in 1707 when the Duke of Ossuna and his army occupied the town during the War of the Spanish Succession.

José Maria Eça de Queiroz, a diplomat and a graduate of Coimbra University, wrote passionate, biting novels which attacked the upper-class mores of his day.

There are several churches worth seeing (notably the 13th-century Santa Maria), as well as the delightfully cool and elegant palace belonging to the Counts of Ficalho, the **Paço dos Condes de Ficalho**. It was built in the 16th century and has a majestic staircase and lovely tiles. The present Marquise, incidentally, is the granddaughter of José Maria Eça de Queiroz (1845–1900), one of Portugal's great 19th-century novelists.

The Rio Guadiana is considered the most peaceful of Portugal's three big rivers (the others being the Tagus and Douro), but an exception is at **Pulo do Lobo** (Wolf's Leap) between Serpa and Mértola. This is a stretch of high and wild rapids, which can be reached by road and is worth a visit if you're in the area – you'll probably find you are the only tourist there.

Mértola

The ancient fortified town of **Mértola ㉗**, set in the confluence between the Guadiana and the Oeiras rivers, is one of Alentejo's hidden gems. To get here

BELOW: local colour.

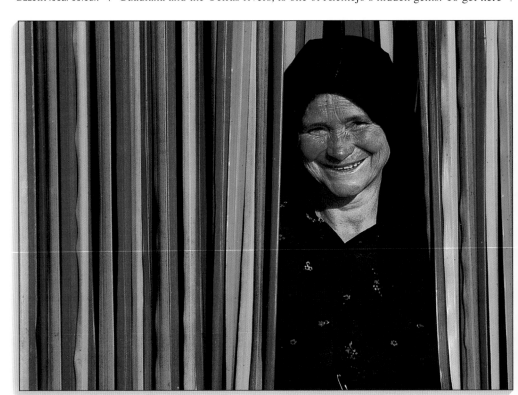

from Serpa you can either take a secondary road to the south, or return to Beja, then take the main road south and turn off to the left. Whichever way you approach, the sight of the town's strongly built walls crowned by a **castelo** (open Tues–Sun; closed 12.30–2pm; entrance charge) is as impressive as it is unexpected. Mértola has a long history reaching back to Roman times. For five centuries under the Romans it was an important port on the then navigable Guadiana for exporting mineral ores from the nearby Minas de São Domingos, near the Spanish border. Its importance continued under the Visigoths and later the Moors. Twice in the 11th and 12th centuries it was capital of a kingdom which included Beja. With the growth of agricultural produce in the region Mértola was active in exporting grain to North Africa. When the river eventually silted up the town slipped quietly into oblivion.

Map on page 216

Alentejo produces some fine wines. Its reds are full-bodied and mature well in the bottle.

Leave plenty of time to explore the astonishing remains of the Roman port, the parish church, the castle and museums, and the **Igreja Matriz**, originally a mosque and one of the few in Portugal to have survived virtually intact. The exhibition of Islamic pottery in the **Núcleo Islâmico** (Museum of Islamic Art) is the finest in Portugal, and the **Núcleo Romano** (Roman Museum), born from a twist of fate, is very sophisticated. The town hall here burned down some years ago, and during the clearing operation the remains of a Roman villa were discovered. After finishing a thorough excavation, the town hall was rebuilt and the Roman villa tuned into an elegant basement museum.

Mértola does not get too many visitors and its excellent museums are somewhat under-staffed. If they are closed, ask at *Turismo*, the tourist office (open Tues–Sun; closed 12.30–2pm). They will usually open on request.

BELOW: Moorish influence in Mértola.

Food and drink

Alentejo's culinary specialities should not be missed. Try *sopa Alentejana* – a filling soup of bread, with lots of coriander (a herb used a great deal in Alentejo cooking), garlic and poached eggs. One of the classic meat dishes is *carne de porco à Alentejana* – chunks of pork seasoned in wine, coriander and onions and served with clams. Two much heavier but delicious stewed dishes are *ensopada de cabrito* – kid boiled with potatoes and bread until the meat is just about falling off the bone, and *favada de caça*, a game stew of hare, rabbit, partridge or pigeon with broad beans. The best Alentejo cheese comes from Serpa. Made from sheep's and goat's milk it has a creamy texture and a strong, slightly piquant flavour. Evora has its own goat cheese which is hard, salty and slightly acid. It is preserved in jars filled with olive oil.

Alentejo is a *região demarcada* – a demarcated wine region. Most towns have their own co-operative winery from which you can buy stocks at rock-bottom prices, and most restaurants have a low-priced co-operative house wine. In Lisbon, Alentejo reds are often drunk with *bacalhau*, instead of the more usual white. To appreciate really good Alentejo wines, try the reds from the Reguengos co-operative or those from Borba (*see page 225*). White wines from the Vidigueira co-operative are far superior to any of the other Alentejo whites. ❏

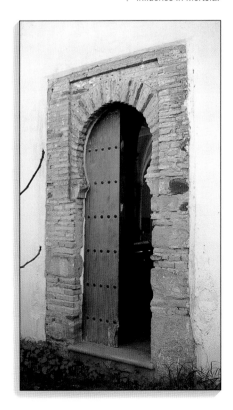

THE FIGHT TO PRESERVE ARTS AND CRAFTS

Local customs form a thread of continuity in rural Portugal, and none are stronger than the craft skills which are found throughout the country

Portugal is a land rich in tradition, and in rural areas the skills and artistry of local craftspeople have been passed from generation to generation. Most skills are specific to one locality: pottery is perhaps the only national craft – although with important variations in design and decoration. Craft work is a significant cottage industry, but there is a danger of skills dying out, especially in regions with few visitors. To prevent this, EU funding has been channelled towards promoting the work of artisans to save skills, create employment, and retain life in dying villages.

There are plenty of craft shops in the large towns, but the real joy is to stop in tiny villages and discover the spinning and weaving co-operatives formed by women, as in Mértola, see bobbin lace work, watch ceramics in the making, buy jute dolls, and marvel at the basket creations made from leaves of the dwarf fan palm.

The products of some regions have gained national importance. Arraiolos in Alentejo has a centuries-old tradition of rug and carpet-making which has grown into a major industry; and the hand-embroidered bedspreads of Castelo Branco, which have been made since the 17th century, are also popular throughout Portugal, and now in demand by tourists.

◁ **MERTOLA BLANKETS**
The women of Mértola specialise in making traditional brown and white blankets and other woollen goods.

◁ **TAPESTRY WORK**
Home-grown flax is often used for tapestry work. The fibre must be soaked, combed, spun and whitened before use.

▽ **MOORISH LAMPS**
Decorative white lamp shades, an Algarvian speciality seen in many homes, retain a marked Moorish influence.

THE GALO DE BARCELOS

There is no escape from the Barcelos rooster. Its fame arises from a legend (as colourful as the little figure itself), which has been embroidered and enlarged with every telling. The central theme relates the story of a murder committed in the northern town of Barcelos many centuries ago. A certain Galician pilgrim came under suspicion as the perpetrator, and no matter how strong his protest, his pleas of innocence fell on deaf ears, and he was sentenced to death.

Before his execution he was granted a last wish: to make a final plea before the judge, who, in the midst of entertaining guests to dinner, agreed to see him. In desperation, the condemned man pointed to the roast fowl on the dinner table and cried "As surely as I stand innocent, so will that cock crow". Miraculously, the rooster obliged. The judge forfeited his dinner, but the pilgrim gained his life.

Ceramic figures of the Barcelos cock are on sale everywhere. The symbol now also adorns everything from T-shirts to tea towels, and finds a place in most visitors' luggage.

△ **A LOAD OF COCKERELS**
A profusion of cockerels can be found in shops and stalls all over Portugal, but nowhere more so than in Barcelos, where the legend originated (*see side panel*).

◁ **LOCAL INDUSTRY**
Estremoz is renowned for its clay pots and figurines. You will find the best displays at the Saturday market in the town square.

△ **VILA REAL POTTERY**
This distinctive black pottery is made by a simple but effective method: covering pots with soil and ashes to exclude oxygen and burning brushwood above them.

▷ **BASKETWARE**
Sweet chestnut, willow, the leaves of the dwarf fan palm and the giant reed are favoured materials in basketware (*matosinhos*).

ESTREMADURA AND RIBATEJO

Although ribboned with silver sand, the coast is not the major attraction in this region. It is inland that you'll find some of the country's finest and best loved monuments

Map on page 242

The region north of Lisbon's environs reaching up towards Coimbra has not managed to establish itself as a tourist destination with a clear brand image in spite of its many attractions. Bordered by an endless ribbon of silver sand, the Costa de Prata – the Silver Coast – seemed a promising promotional aid, except that the coast, Nazaré apart, has only small resorts. Most of the region's attractions, the famous monasteries at Alcobaça, Batalha and Tomar, the religious sanctuary at Fátima and the spectacular deep caves in the limestone *serras* are all inland.

With its points of interest fairly widespread, it is an area tailor-made for touring. Allow around three days to take in most of the major sites and longer if you are intent on savouring everything the region offers. The circular tour described here follows an anti-clockwise route from Lisbon up to Batalha and back.

North from Lisbon

Easily the quickest way to escape Lisbon is to take the A1 and follow it north. The alternative for a slower but more interesting journey is to cross the Rio Tejo on the Ponte Vasco de Gama and take the road on the eastern side of the river.

Santarém ❶ is the central town of Ribatejo. It was named after Santa Iria, a young nun who was accused of being unchaste, and martyred in 653 near Tomar. Her body, thrown into the river, washed ashore here. A riverbank shrine has a statue whose feet act as a sacred gauge to the water level – if they are touched by floods, even Lisbon is in danger.

Among several fine churches, the Romanesque-Gothic church of **São João de Alporão** contains a fine archaeological museum (open Tues–Sun; closed 12.30–2pm; entrance charge), as well as the beautifully carved tomb of Duarte, a son of Pedro I who died in the Battle of Alcácer-Quibir in 1458. It contains just one of Duarte's teeth, the sole relic which was delivered to his wife.

In northeastern Santarém is the church of **Santa Clara** (open Tues–Sun; closed 12.30–2pm), originally part of a 13th-century convent, containing the elaborate tomb of Dona Leonor, daughter of Afonso III. The church of **Nossa Senhora da Graça** (open Tues–Sun; closed 12.30–2pm), a bold Gothic structure with a beautiful nave, holds several tombs, among them that of Pedro Alvares Cabral, discoverer of Brazil. In Alpiarça, across the river, look for the 19th-century architectural gem of the Casa dos Patudos, today a wonderfully eclectic museum.

PRECEDING PAGES: a proud owner. **LEFT:** Obidos. **BELOW:** hard-working donkey.

A diversion to Abrantes is worthwhile, if only to see the nearby Castelo de Almourol, romantically located on an island in the middle of the Tejo. The road on the east of the river offers the most interesting route. **Abrantes ❷** itself is well sited above the Tejo but it has little to offer visitors except perhaps for the castle of **Santa Maria do Castelo**.

Foreign visitors often prefer Portuguese bullfights (touradas) *to those in Spain since Portuguese bullfighters do not kill their bulls – at least not in public.*

Turn back along the north bank just before Tancos and look for the sign to **Castelo de Almourol ❸**. It crowns a rocky island in the river and a ferryman is usually on hand to row visitors across for a small fee. The Romans recognised the importance of the site on this key communication route and built a castle, although there may well have been an earlier settlement. Later, the castle experienced a succession of tenants, the Visigoths, the Moors and finally the Christians. Afonso Henriques entrusted it to the Knights Templar in 1147 for their help in fighting the Moors. The Grand Master Gualdim Pais rebuilt the castle leaving an inscription over the door, and it remained garrisoned for a time. When the Moors were finally expelled from Portugal the strategic importance of the castle declined and it eventually fell into disuse. It takes only a few minutes to wander around the walls of this irregular-shaped fortress (entrance free).

Tomar: the haunt of knights

From the castle it is a fairly short run north to **Tomar ❹**, a delightful town with a host of good points: a setting on the banks of the Rio Nabão; the splendid Convento do Cristo, which is a UNESCO World Heritage Site; and medieval streets paved with stone and fancifully patterned with exuberant flowers. With its pleasing ambience and rich culture, its ancient legends and appealing daily life, Tomar is a town in which to linger and explore for a couple of days.

Estremadura and Ribatejo

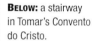

Map on page 242

Tomar was the headquarters of the Knights Templar in Portugal, an order which was formed in 1119, during the crusades. The order spread quickly throughout Europe, gaining extraordinary wealth. It also made powerful enemies, and in the early 1300s, amid accusations of heresy and foul practices, and finally the suppression of the order altogether, the Knights took refuge in Tomar, where Grand Master Gualdim Pais had built a castle back in 1162. They re-emerged in 1320, reincarnated as the Order of Christ, whose proud symbol, the Cross of Christ, became the banner of the Age of Discoveries. In Tomar they left behind the marvellous ruins of the old castle and, within its walls, the still-intact church and cloisters. The castle is set on a hill above the city, a 10-minute walk, and commands a view over the rooftops of the old town.

The monastery and other Tomar sights

The **Convento do Cristo** (open Tues–Sun; closed 12.30–2pm) is a maze of staircases, passages, and nooks and crannies. The seven cloisters (just four are open to the public) have been added at irregular angles and over several centuries, and even the beautiful main entrance is oddly tucked into a corner. The original Templar church is on the right, just inside the entrance . Begun in 1162, the octagonal temple was modelled on Jerusalem's Church of the Holy Sepulchre. Here, the knights would hear services while seated on their horses, and pray for victory in battle.

The chapterhouse and Coro Alto, added much later, provide a sharp contrast to the original temple, as does the adjoining 16th-century cloister with 17th-century tiles. Some of the tombs of the knights are found here. From here there is access to the upper level and then into the other cloisters. From the terrace of the small Claustro de Santa Bárbara, there is a view of the amazing ornate Manueline window, structured around two deep relief carvings of ships' masts and knots, cork, coral, and seaweed. The whole is topped by a shield, crown and cross, symbol of the union of church and king.

From the opposite side of the building there is a view of the surrounding forest and the castle yard where the knights trained their horses and spent their off-duty hours. Also on this side lies an unfinished chapel: bad luck during construction persuaded the superstitious knights to abandon it.

Tomar's **Synagogue** (open Thurs–Tues; closed 12.30–2pm) is in Rua Joaquim Jacinto. Although up to 70 percent of Portuguese people have Jewish ancestry, and Tomar was once the home of a thriving Jewish community, there are very few Jews left. When the King Manuel I married Isabella of Castile in 1497, a condition of the marriage contract was their expulsion. But they were allowed to remain, if they converted, although laws governing fair treatment were not closely monitored. Later, the Inquisition would legitimise brutal discrimination against them. The synagogue/museum is simple and moving, decorated with gifts from all over the world.

The church of **São João Baptista** has a dark wood ceiling and a rather sombre atmosphere. Sixteenth-century wood panel paintings on the walls depict

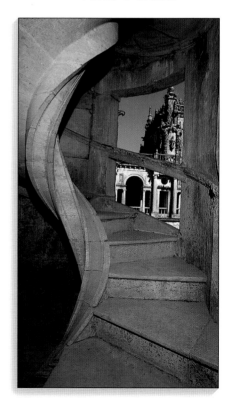

BELOW: a stairway in Tomar's Convento do Cristo.

scenes such as the Last Supper and Salome with the head of John the Baptist. On the left is a delicately carved pulpit.

Standing alone on the edge of town, **Santa Maria dos Olivais** is a simple church dating from the 12th century and containing many Templar tombs. Tourist offices are located on Avenida Dr Cândido Madureira, near the road to the castle, and at 1 Rua Serpa Pinto.

En route from Tomar to Fátima, it is well worth a stop at **Ourém 5**, or more particularly at Ourém Velha the fortified site on top of an easily defended hill. The history of the castle is known only from the time it was recovered from the Moors in 1148 by King Afonso Henriques. Little was attempted in the way of restoration until King Dinis (1279–1325) arrived on the scene. He rebuilt this as he did many other castles in Portugal.

The Lourdes of Portugal

Fátima 6, some 12 km (8 miles) from Ourém, is not a place for non-believers, and there is even a notice to advise you of this. It is a place for pilgrims – of which there are up to 2 million a year. On 13 May 1917, three shepherd children had a vision of the Virgin here. Thereafter, she appeared before the children and, on one occasion, as a shining light to the townspeople who gathered with them on the 13th of the subsequent months (*see page 77*). The two younger children died shortly after the apparitions, but one, Lucia de Jesus Santos, lived well into her eighties in a convent near Coimbra. The processions that now take place each year draw thousands of people from around the world.

A vast white basilica, consecrated in 1953, was built in recognition of the importance of this site to pilgrims, but with little attention to aesthetics. In front

The most important days of pilgrimage to Fátima are 13 May and 13 October, when the roads around are crammed with weary pilgrims travellng to the shrine on foot.

BELOW: Fátima, one of the best-known shrines in the world.

of it is a huge esplanade large enough hold 100,000 worshippers. Inside lie the tombs of the two visionary children who died, Jacinta and Francisco Marto.

Today, Fátima has capitalised on its massive appeal with ubiquitous merchandising of religious souvenirs. Many thousands of pilgrims still walk for days suffering penitential hardship.

Castles and caves

West of Fátima, along scenic well-paved roads, lies the pleasant town of **Porto de Mós** ❼, worth a brief stop even if only to look at the castle, capped with green cones and standing on a hill. The castle has a fairly long pedigree and still contains some original Roman stonework. As with Ourém castle, King Afonso Henriques recovered it from the Moors in 1148. After several restorations, it remained in military use at least until the Battle of Aljubarrota in 1383 when João I is said to have rested his troops here before the fight. Afterwards the king rewarded his captain, Nuno Alvares Pereira, with the gift of this fortress for leading his troops so bravely. It was his grandson, Afonso, a cultured and much travelled man, who endeavoured to convert the castle into a palace and disguise the strong military lines.

As a change from monuments, a diversion into the **Parque Natural das Serras de Aire e Candeeiros** ❽ offers fine limestone scenery and a chance to visit three caves. Take the N243 towards Torres Novas to find Grutas Mira de Aire, Grutas de Santo António and Grutas de Alavdos. The latter two lie on a spur off the main road. All three are open to the public and are different enough to be worth visiting. If only one is possible then perhaps Grutas Mira de Aire might be the best choice, if you can face descending more than 600 steps

BELOW: the great monastery at Batalha.

A characteristically graceful vaulted dome inside the monastery at Batalha.

through well-illuminated caverns with imaginative and descriptive names, to the underground river. At least the return is by elevator.

Batalha: an essential stop

Batalha is one of Portugal's most beautiful monuments, and another UNESCO World Heritage Site. The origins of **Mosteiro de Santa Maria da Vitória**, to use its full name, lie in Portugal's struggle for independence from Castile. One of the decisive battles for independence was fought at Aljubarrota, which was not far from Batalha.

The Castilian king, Juan, who based his claim to the throne on his marriage to a Portuguese princess, invaded Portugal in 1385. The 20-year-old Dom João, Master of the Order of Avis and illegitimate son of Pedro I, promised to raise a monastery to the Virgin Mary if the Portuguese won. With his young general, Nuno Alvares Pereira, João defeated the Castilian, and became João I. The monastery was constructed between 1388 and 1533.

Enter the large front portal. Inside, the arches sweep upward to a sculpture representing the hierarchy in the heavenly court, as it was perceived in the Middle Ages. In the centre is Christ surrounded by the four gospel writers. Though the outside of the monastery is ornate, the interior is endowed with a simple Gothic elegance and dignity. Vaulted ceilings arch above a slender nave which is illuminated through stained-glass windows. To the right is the **Capela do Fundador** (Founder's Chapel), built around 1426 by João I, and here are the tombs of João and his English queen, Philippa, effigies eloquently holding hands. Tombs of their children, including that of Prince Henry the Navigator, are set into the walls under regal arches. The room is topped by a dome supported by star-shaped ribbing.

BELOW: exquisite carving at Batalha.

On the other side of the building you may enter the **Claustro Real** (Royal Cloister). Arches filled with Manueline ornamentation surround a pretty courtyard and are patterned with intricate designs. The chapterhouse is the first room off the cloister. It has an unusual and beautiful ceiling, with no support other than the walls. The impression is of precarious balance. The window is filled with a stained-glass Christ on the Cross, remarkably rich in colour. This chamber holds the tombs of two unknown soldiers, whose remains were returned to Portugal from France and Africa after World War I. The sculpture of "Christ of the Trenches" was given by the French government. An armed guard of honour seems out of place in this peaceful setting.

To reach the **Capelas Imperfeitas** (Unfinished Chapels), go outside the monastery. This octagonal structure is attached to the outside wall and its abrupt rooflessness is a shock. Ordered by King Duarte I to house the tombs of himself and his family, the chapel was begun in the 1430s but construction was never finished. No one is quite certain why. The shell contains simple chapels in each of seven walls. The chapel opposite the door holds the tomb of the king and Leonor, his wife. The eighth wall is a massive door of limestone, with endless layers of beautifully detailed ornamentation in carved Manueline style.

Alcobaça

Twelve km (8 miles) south of Batalha is the town of **Alcobaça** , named after two rivers, the Alcoa and the Baça. At its heart is the magnificent **Cistercian Abbey** (open daily from 9am), yet another UNESCO World Heritage Site. The first king of Portugal, Afonso Henriques, founded it to commemorate the capture of Santarém from the Moors. He laid the foundation stone himself in 1148.

The Cistercian monks were energetically productive. Numbering, it is said 999 ("one less than a thousand"), they diligently tilled the land around the abbey, planting vegetables and fruit. In Sebastião I's reign, the exceedingly wealthy and powerful Santa Maria Abbey, as it is also known, was declared by the Pope the seat of the entire Cistercian order. The monks here were particularly known for their lively spirits and lavish hospitality. They ran a school, perhaps the first public school in Portugal, and a sanctuary and hospice as well. In 1810, however, the abbey was sacked by French troops. In the Liberal Revolution of 1834, when all religious orders were expelled from Portugal, the abbey was again pillaged.

The long baroque façade, added in the 18th century, has twin towers in the centre, below which are a Gothic doorway and rose window, surviving from the original façade. Directly inside the serene and austere church, the largest in Portugal, three tall aisles and plain walls emphasise the clean lines. In the transepts are the two well-known and richly carved tombs of Pedro I and Inês de Castro (*see page 30*). Off the south transept are several other royal tombs, including those of Afonso II and Afonso III, and a sadly mutilated 17th-century terracotta of the Death of St Bernard. To the east of the ambulatory there are two fine Manueline doorways that were designed by João de Castilho.

Map on page 242

There is little else to see in the village of Batalha other than the monastery. The shopping mall next to the monument has tourist-oriented "handicraft" shops and a tourist office.

LEFT: Alcobaça's Cistercian abbey from without… **BELOW:** …and from within.

An entrance in the north wall of the church leads to the 14th-century **Claustro de Silencio** (Cloister of Silence). Several rooms branch off the cloister, including the chapterhouse and a dormitory. There is a kitchen, with an enormous central chimney and a remarkable basin through which a rivulet runs: it supposedly provided the monks with a constant supply of fresh fish. Next door is the refectory, with steps built into one wall leading to a pulpit. At left of the entrance is the **Sala dos Reis**, with statues, probably carved by monks themselves, of many of the kings of Portugal. The panel in the same room, which tells the history of Alcobaça Abbey, is a rare example of a manuscript *azulejo* panel.

Alcobaça today is the centre of a porcelain and pottery industry. There are many shops around the central square, and some factories welcome visitors.

Mending nets, a task that doesn't change.

The Silver Coast

From Alcobaça, it is a relatively short drive out to the coast to reach **Nazaré** ⓫, a fishing port which nestles along a sweeping mile-long bay. In summer, thousands of holidaymakers pack the beach in rows of peaked, brightly-striped canvas tents that create a rather romantic atmosphere of a Moorish battle camp.

The abundance of tourists vitiates some of Nazaré's charm, but it also assures that all the visitor's desires will be catered to. Pleasant seafood restaurants and small hotels line the sandy bay; esplanade cafés, bars and souvenir shops abound. But the life of the hardy fishermen goes on.

Because they had no natural harbour, the fishermen used to launch their boats from the beach. They managed this by pushing their craft down log rollers into the sea then clambering aboard and rowing furiously till they overrode the incoming breakers. When they arrived home again, the boats were winched

BELOW:
looking down on a
boatyard at Nazaré.

ashore by oxen and later by tractors. The building of a modern anchorage to the south of the beach has relieved the Nazaré fishermen of this arduous task.

The Nazaré fisherfolk's traditional dress is today seen more in souvenir shops than on the street. Some women still wear coloured petticoats under a wide black skirt and cover their heads with a black scarf; the men still favour woollen shirts in traditional plaids, but few wear the distinctive black stocking bonnets.

Nazaré, named after a statue of the Virgin that a 4th-century monk brought to the town from Nazareth, lives literally on two levels. In the lower part of town, small, white-walled fishermen's cottages line the narrow alleyways. High above on the cliff that towers 109 metres (360 ft) above the old town is the quarter known as **Sítio**. Reached by a funicular that climbs the tallest cliffside in Portugal, Sítio is dominated by a large square, and on its edge a tiny chapel, built to commemorate a miracle in 1182 when the Virgin saved the local lord by stopping his horse plunging off the cliff as he pursued a deer.

The 17th-century **Nossa Senhora da Nazaré** on the other side of the square is the focus of the annual religious festivities during the second week of September that include processions and bullfights in the Sítio bullring. The steep, narrow pathway and steps from the lighthouse west of the church afford stirring views of Atlantic breakers.

Calm waters and a walled town

The road south out of Nazaré leads first past the new fishing harbour and then down the coast to **São Martinho do Porto ⓬**. Here a huge encircling sand bank creates virtually a lagoon, although there is a small opening to the sea. These calm shallow waters are readily warmed by the sun, but on the downside,

Map on page 242

BELOW: the Romeria of Nossa Senhora da Nazaré.

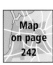

Map on page 242

Between Obidos and Peniche some delightful coastal scenery and excellent restaurants make it worth taking a short detour to Baleal. For golfers, the Praia d'el Rei course offers a splendid challenge.

RIGHT:
Nazaré fishing fleet at dawn.
BELOW:
a gilded statue in Obidos church.

with only a limited exchange of water, the risk of pollution in the bay is much higher. Moving south again, the road sweeps grandly by the university town of **Caldas de Rainha** (Queen's Spa) and on to Obidos.

A picture-postcard view of town walls crowned by a castle announces **Obidos ⓭**. The old walled town, its streets tumbling with bougainvilleae, presents a well-groomed appearance to the steady influx of day trippers. At least the town retains some authenticity, as there has been no new building, and only existing structures within the walls are used as tea houses, residences and gift shops. Everything in the narrow jumbled streets is painted white, with blue or yellow trimmings and some colourful window boxes.

The town has a long history: it was occupied by the Moors before falling into Christian hands. The indefatigable castle-builder King Dinis tidied it up and restored the **castelo** early in the 14th century. Damaged in the great earthquake of 1755, the castle was subsequently restored and today is used as a *pousada*. It is the place where everyone wants to stay, and gets booked up well in advance. Apart from wandering around unprotected town walls and enjoying the ambience of the town, there is little to see in the way of monuments. The 17th-century **Igreja de Santa Maria** dominating the market square attracts the most attention, chiefly for the religious paintings by Josefa de Obidos (1634–84).

Back to the coast

Like many of Portugal's coastal towns, **Peniche ⓮** has no natural harbour, only a bay sheltered by the rocky promontory of **Cabo Carvoeiro**, the second most westerly point in Europe. A sea wall has been built to protect the bay. Peniche is an uncompromising town of around 18,000 people. Here, the spare white houses cling to the slopes for shelter from the sweeping northwesterly winds. Too stark and exposed for tourism to have taken hold, the town typifies life in Portuguese fishing communities.

The **Fortaleza** physically dominates the town. The veteran leader of Portugal's Communist Party, Alvaro Cunhal, escaped from this notorious prison in 1960 by climbing down the cliffs to a waiting boat that reportedly took him to a Soviet-bloc submarine. Today, the building serves as a local museum.

You can get a sense of the Atlantic swell that is the fisherman's constant companion by taking the ferry from Peniche to **Ilha Berlenga ⓯**, 7 km (4 miles) offshore. The ferry takes an hour and runs from June to September. Once out of the shelter of the peninsula, the powerful current rocks the boat with unexpected force, but it's well worth the slight discomfort. A 17th-century fortress, now converted to an inn, the lighthouse and a few fishermen's cottages are the only buildings. The entire island has been designated a national bird sanctuary, and seagulls and eider are everywhere. Officials patrol the makeshift paths to ensure that visitors don't disturb the birds. The greatest excitement lies in taking a trip around the reefs, caves and smaller islands, past a breathtaking sea tunnel called the **Furado Grande**.

The return to Lisbon is best made via the new highway from Obidos, entering Lisbon via the A8. ❑

COIMBRA

Coimbra grows old but never grows up. University freshers arrive each year to revitalise traditions and pour their souls into fado. *For visitors it's a great mix of history and youthful exuberance*

Maps:
Area 266
City 256

Perched on a hill overlooking the Rio Mondego, **Coimbra ❶** is surrounded by breathtakingly beautiful countryside. The city itself is a mixture of ancient and new, rural and urban. The tourist office in the centre of the lower town in Largo de Portagem will provide you with a good map of the city.

The university is the most stalwart guardian of Coimbra's colourful past. Students clad in black capes, the traditional academic dress, resemble oversized bats as they flit around town. The hems of the capes are often ripped, a declaration – at times – of romantic conquest. But these capes have only recently come back into style, since for a time they were associated with Salazar's New State, and therefore not worn in the years after the 1974 revolution.

In May each year, the university celebrates the *Queima das Fitas*, the "burning of the ribbons", when graduating students burn the ribbons they have been wearing, the colour of which signify their faculty – yellow for medicine, and so on. The celebrations last a week, and their grand finale is a long drunken parade.

Another Coimbra tradition is *fado*, a more serious cousin of the Lisbon variety. The sombre Coimbra *fado* theoretically requires you to clear your throat in approval after a rendition, and not applaud. It is performed only by men, often cloak-wrapped graduates of the university.

The country's third-largest city, Coimbra lies at the centre of an agricultural region and has a large market. The students are not the only ones in black: it is the traditional dress of many of the rural women who come to town as well. Coimbra also has a considerable manufacturing industry.

Roman roots

Coimbra traces its roots to the Roman municipality of *Aeminium*. It gained in importance because the city of Conímbriga, a few miles south, proved vulnerable to invasion. Convulsions in the empire and various invasions brought an end to Roman rule in the city. The Moors took over in 711, ushering in 300 years of Islamic rule, with a few interruptions. One such occurred in 878 when Afonso III of Asturias and León captured the city. But Coimbra was not permanently retaken by Christian forces until 1064. It then became a base for the reconquest of other parts of Portugal, and it was at this time that the city was walled. From 1139 to 1385 Coimbra was the capital of Portugal.

The 12th century was an age of considerable progress for Coimbra – including the construction, which began in 1131, of the city's most important monastery, Santa Cruz, still standing today. The city was a lively commercial centre and included both Jewish and Moorish quarters. Division was not only by religion, but by class as well. Nobles and clergy lived inside the

PRECEDING PAGES: playing cards is a serious business. **LEFT:** a university student. **BELOW:** a fraction of Coimbra's library.

Decorative doorway in Coimbra.

walls, while merchants and craft workers lived outside in what is today known as the Baixa, the "lower area".

The university was founded in 1290 – not in Coimbra, but in Lisbon. In 1308 it moved to Coimbra, only to return to Lisbon in 1377. These shifts were the result of continual political conflict between the monarchy and the academic hierarchy. It was not until 1537 that the university settled permanently in Coimbra. A few years late, it moved to its present site at the top of the hill.

Most areas of interest are easily reached on foot – that is, if you're willing to do some uphill walking. There is an extensive bus system, although the bus maps are difficult to read. Don't try to drive within the city. The old city and the university crown Coimbra's central hill, and the Baixa, which is the main shopping district, lies at the foot of the hill along the Rio Mondego. Santa Clara lies across the river, while the tourist office, *Turismo*, is handily located at the northern end of the bridge.

The old city

Once enclosed within walls, the old city is a tangle of narrow streets and alleys, lined by ancient buildings and filled with squares and patios – and cars. The university buildings are a compelling mix of styles, from the odd baroque **Torre**, a clocktower known to the students as *a cabra* (the goat), to bleakly Salazarist faculty blocks. The passage of centuries is evident. The modern centre of the university is the statue of King Dinis, its founder, on the site of an earlier castle in **Praça Dinis A**. Nearby are the buildings that house the Faculties of Science and Technology, Medicine and Letters and the New Library.

Of more historical interest than these stolidly functional buildings is the Pátio

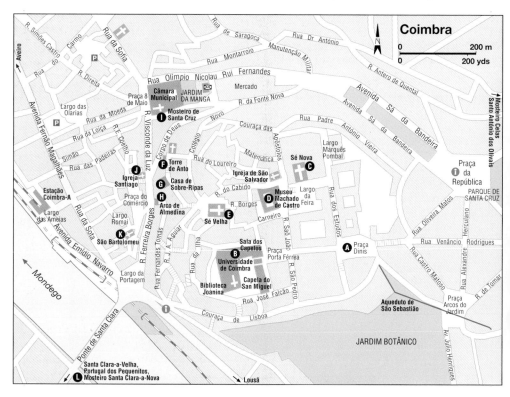

das Escolas (Patio of the Schools), within the **Universidade Velha** , the Old University. To enter the patio, pass through the 17th-century Porta Férrea, a large portal decorated in the Mannerist style, to a large, dusty courtyard, which is used for parking. Here are some of the oldest and stateliest buildings of the university. The figure of João III, who installed the university in Coimbra, still reigns from the centre of the patio. Behind him, there is a magnificent view of the river.

The building in the farthest corner from the Porta Férrea is the **Biblioteca Joanina**, among the world's most resplendent baroque libraries. To enter, ring and wait for the caretaker to open the door (closed for lunch, noon–2pm). The three sumptuous 18th-century rooms were built during the reign of João V, whose portrait hangs at the far end. Bookcases, decorated in gilded wood and oriental motifs, reach gracefully to an upper galleried level; even the ladders are intricately decorated. Note the frescoes on the ceilings. More than 30,000 books fill the cases and are still consulted by scholars.

Next door is the **Capela do San Miguel** (St Michael's Chapel), which was begun in 1517, and remodelled in both the 17th and 18th centuries. The chapel is notable for its carpet-style tiles, the painted ceilings, the altar, and the baroque organ. Beside the chapel is a museum of sacred art.

The arcaded building to the right of the Porta Férrea on the Via Latuna houses the **Sala dos Capelos**, where degrees are conferred and academic ceremonies take place. Portraits of the kings of Portugal hang from its walls. Other rooms which you may enter are the Rectory and, right by the bell tower, the Private Exam Room.

A short walk down from the university grounds takes you to the **Sé Nova** (**New Cathedral**) , whose sand-coloured façade presides over a rather uninteresting square. Built for the Jesuits in 1554, it became a cathedral in 1772.

Coimbra's greatest contribution to traditional folk music is the soulful and expressive fado. *This style of singing is an instinctive expression which springs from the soul in the form of a lament about love or life.*

BELOW: the Old University is a dominant feature in Coimbra.

Inside, the altar and much else is of lavish gilded wood. Many of the paintings around the altar are copies of Italian masters.

The **Museu Machado de Castro** (open Tues–Sun; closed 1–2.30pm; entrance charge) is housed in the old episcopal palace and the neighbouring 12th-century church of São João de Almedina. Constructed over the city's Roman forum and *cryptoporticus* (underground galleries), the palace was the residence of Coimbra's early bishops. The museum is named after Portugal's greatest sculptor Joaquim Machado de Castro (1732–1822), who was born in Coimbra. It holds an excellent collection, both extensive and varied, of medieval sculpture, as well as later work. Unfortunately, much of it is unlabelled. Nevertheless, the museum is well worth a visit: there are also Roman artifacts on display, a large collection of Portuguese paintings from the 15th century onwards, gold work, ceramics, tapestries, furniture, and two coaches. From the courtyard there is also a grand view of the Romanesque Old Cathedral and the roofs of the old city.

The Old Cathedral

The **Sé Velha** (**Old Cathedral**) ❸, renovated in the 20 century, was built between 1162 and 1184. It served as cathedral until 1772, when the episcopal See was moved to the Sé Nova. The fortress-like exterior is relieved by an arched door with an arched window directly above. The intricate Gothic altar within is of gilded wood, created by two Flemish masters in the 15th and 16th centuries. Sancho I was crowned king here in 1185, and João I in 1385. There are several tombs in the cathedral, including those of the 13th-century Bishop Dom Egas Fa'es (to the left of the altar) and Dona Vetaça, a Byzantine princess who was a governess in the Coimbra court in the 14th century. The cloister is early Gothic and its construction began in 1218.

BELOW: the Old Cathedral of Coimbra, built in the 12th century.

Work on the **Colégio de Santo Agostinho**, on Rua Colégio Novo, was started in 1593. The ecclesiastical scholars and monks who first occupied it would probably be astonished by its present-day purpose, for this pleasant building, lined with pretty *azulejos*, is now home to the university's Psychology Department.

Nearby, on Rua Sobre-Ripas (confusingly, also called Sub-Ripas), the medieval **Torre de Anto** ❺ (Anthony's Tower) was once part of the 12th-century walls of the city. Much later it was the home of poet António Nobre (1867–1900) during his undergraduate days. Today, it displays and sells traditional crafts from the Coimbra area, sponsored by the city council.

The **Casa de Sobre-Ripas** ❻, on the same street, is an aristocratic 16th-century mansion. Note the archetypal Manueline door and window, but don't bother knocking: it is the Faculty of Archaeology, and not open to the public. Here, according to tradition, Maria Teles was murdered by her husband João (eldest son of the tragic Inês de Castro) who had been convinced by the jealous Queen Leonor Teles that his wife – the queen's sister – was unfaithful to him.

Arco de Almedina ❼, an entrance to the old city just off Rua Ferreira Borges (the main downtown street) was also part of the Coimbra walls.

Baixa Coimbra

The Baixa is the busy shopping district. Rua Ferreira Borges, with many fashionable shops, is the principal street. Although this district lay outside the walls of the old city, it dates back to nearly the same time. The **Mosteiro de Santa Cruz ❶** in Praça 8 de Maio (a continuation of Rua Ferreira Borges) was founded in 1131 by Portugal's first king, Afonso Henriques. The façade and portal, now sparkling after a major face lift, date from the 16th century, when the monastery church was restored. Inside, although the church is small, it is light and spacious. Eighteenth-century *azulejos* adorn either wall: the right side depicts the life of Saint Augustine; on the left, scenes relate to the Holy Cross.

Another striking work by a major 16th-century artist is the exquisite pulpit on the left-hand wall, by sculptor Nicolau Chanterène. The **sacristy** (open daily 10am, closed 12.30–2pm; entrance charge) contains several paintings including *The Pentecost* by the notable 16th-century painter Grão Vasco, a silverwork collection, and some vestments. You can see the tombs of the first two kings of Portugal, Afonso Henriques and Sancho I, who are ensconced in regal monuments. The chapterhouse and the lovely Cloister of Silence may also be visited.

Behind the church of Santa Cruz lies the **Jardim da Manga** (Garden of the Sleeve), so named because Dom João III reputedly drew this oddity of a garden on his sleeve – although the design has also been attributed to João de Ruão, a French sculptor working in Portugal in the 16th-century. Curiously modernistic, this monumental garden was completed in 1535, and intended as a representation of the fountain of life.

If you wander down the Rua da Sofia, which turns off 16th-century Praça 8 de Maio, you may be struck by the fact that it is extraordinarily wide for a street

Map on page 256

BELOW: Coimbra students take part in the annual ritual of "the burning of the ribbons".

Map on page 256

The Jardim Botânico, created in 1772 for the study of natural history, contains some 1,200 species of plants, many rare and exotic. It is open daily.

BELOW: a statue in Santa Clara-a-Nova.
RIGHT: part of the Jardim Botânico.

of that period. It was the original base for several colleges of the university before they were moved to new homes.

Praça do Comércio, off Rua Ferreira Borges, is an oddly-shaped square lined with 17th- and 18th-century buildings. At the north end stands the sturdy **Igreja Santiago ❶**, a church dating from the end of the 12th century. The capitals are decorated with animal and bird motifs. At the square's south end is the **Igreja de São Bartolomeu ❶**, built in the 18th century.

Santa Clara

The Santa Clara section of town lies across the river. **Mosteiro Santa Clara-a-Nova ❶** (New Santa Clara Monastery) is worth a visit if only for the view of Coimbra. Inside, in a wildly baroque setting, is the tomb of the Holy Queen Isabel, who was canonised in 1625 and became the city's patron saint. Closer to the river, too close for its own comfort in fact, is **Santa Clara-a-Velha**, the old Santa Clara Monastery. This 12th-century edifice is simpler and lovelier than its replacement, for which it was abandoned in 1677. Waterlogged for centuries, its value has now been realised and money found for its restoration.

Quinta das Lágrimas, where Inês de Castro is believed to have been murdered (*see page 30*), lies not far from Santa Clara-a-Velha. The family home has been restored into a tasteful small hotel and the grounds contain the **Fonte das Lágrimas**, the spring which is said to have risen on the spot where the luckless Inês met her violent end.

Nearby, **Portugal dos Pequenitos** is an outdoor museum displaying small-scale reproductions of traditional Portuguese houses and famous monuments, popular with children and with those who like miniatures. To the east of the city, the Mosteiro Celas is notable for its cloister, and the pretty church of Santo António dos Olivais was once an old Franciscan convent.

Shops, parks and canoes

If you are interested in traditional ceramics and handicrafts, the place to go is the **Torre de Anto**, in the old city. For a different shopping experience, visit the covered market on **Rua Olimpio Nicolau**, not far from Baixa, which is open every morning but is best on Saturday. The market vendors hawk fish, bread, fruit, vegetables, flowers and live chickens and rabbits. You'll get an authentic taste of Coimbra life here.

Coimbra's numerous parks are agreeable resting places. The **Jardim Botânico** (Botanical Garden), on Alameda Dr Júlio Henriques, next to the 16th-century Aqueduto de São Sebastião, is a lovely garden, which was originally laid out in the 18th century. Unfortunately, not all of its grounds are open to the public, but there's much to see.

Other parks are Santa Cruz, off the Praça da República, and Choupal, west of the city – a larger park which is good for walks and bike rides. The tiny Penedo da Saudade has a nice view.

If you want some physical exercise, and a complete change from historical monuments, you could rent a canoe from the municipal boat club near the Ponte Santa Clara, on the far side of the river. ❑

SIDE TRIPS FROM COIMBRA

*Within easy reach of Coimbra you will find gleaming
lagoons, colourful fishing villages, exotic forests, and the
most extensive Roman ruins in the country*

Map
on page
266

Coimbra **❶** might be the main focus of interest in this vicinity, but there are
plenty of opportunities for short excursions to other places of interest.
The countryside towards the coast is especially bucolic and an old rural
way of life can still be seen. The coast also has plenty of interest, especially
Aveiro with its canals and lagoons. Castles and palaces feature too, not to
mention Roman ruins.

Conímbriga: the Romans were here

Portugal's largest excavated Roman ruins are at **Conímbriga ❷**, 15 km (9 miles)
south of Coimbra, near the town of Condeixa; the drive is easy, and there is also
a bus service. The site (open daily from 10am, closed 1–2pm; entrance charge)
is complemented by one of the country's finest museums (closed Mon).

Only a few hundred metres of the estimated 13-hectare (32-acre) site have
been excavated. A glance out on to the hot, dusty field that is still off-limits to
tourists reveals signs of further ruins, and, happily, the beginnings of more
excavation. Archaeologists believe remains may be found as far away as the
main highway and even under the homes of people in the nearby village of
Condeixa-a-Velha.

Conímbriga was probably settled as early as the
Iron Age (800–500 BC), and it was not until the latter
part of the 2nd century BC that the Romans arrived.
Conímbriga profited from its location by the Roman
road between Olisipo (Lisbon) and Bracara Augusta
(now Braga). Some time around AD 70, the Roman
Empire designated Conímbriga a *municipium*.

Conímbriga's prosperity was not to last. Crises in
the empire and Barbarian incursions into Iberia
prompted the construction of the defensive wall which
is still prominent today. To take advantage of the natural defensive position of the area, the inhabited area
of Conímbriga had to be reduced. Despite the new
wall, in 464 the Suevi successfully attacked the city.
Conímbriga continued to be inhabited, but it lost its
status as an important centre to its neighbour, the more
easily defensible *Aeminium* (Coimbra).

As you enter the site, you are walking down the
road that gave Conímbriga its original importance:
the highway from *Olisipo* to *Bracara Augusta*. In
front of you is an enormous wall. Passing through the
main entrance and continuing along the path to the
right, you'll come to the arch of the aqueduct (rebuilt),
parts of the aqueduct itself, and the remains of several
buildings which may have been small shops.

The building known as Cantaber's House stretches
to the south (on the left if you have your back to the
entrance). The house is full of ornamental pools, but

PRECEDING PAGES:
Mira beach, where
little changes.
LEFT: the remains
of Conímbriga.
BELOW: a Roman
mosaic, Conímbriga.

perhaps the most interesting part are the baths, which lie at the extreme south end. They are easily recognisable by their hexagonal and round shapes, and by the piped heating system (that great Roman innovation), which is visible through the stone grid covering the floors. Around the other side of the wall you can see more baths: public ones. For Romans, bathing was an important daily ritual, and the bathroom was also a place to discuss politics. Beyond the baths is an area of marvellously-patterned mosaics. The colours were once much brighter than the pleasing pastels to which they have mellowed today.

The museum is small but carefully designed. A long case displays ceramics, jewellery, and artifacts relating to weaving, agriculture, lighting, writing, hygiene and so on. There are also statues and a model of the forum and temple.

After taking a bath, the Romans would cover themselves with olive oil and then scrape their skins clean with a curved blade.

Serra do Buçaco

Northeast of Coimbra lies the **Serra do Buçaco** ❸ (Buçaco Forest), a darkly haunting area which for centuries has been protected, enabling 700 varieties of

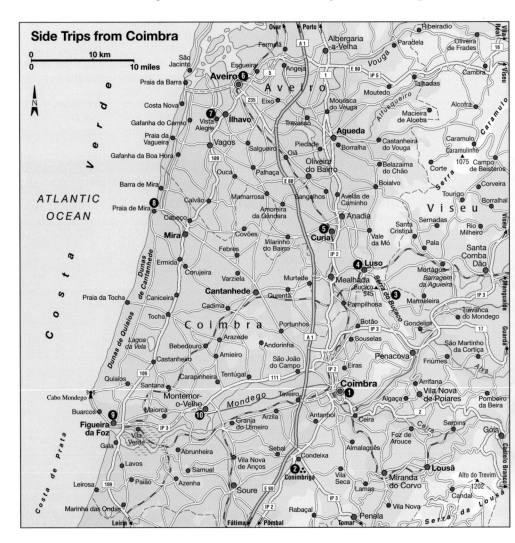

Side Trips from Coimbra

native and exotic trees to flourish. Benedictine monks established a hermitage here in the 6th century. The Carmelites, who built a monastery in 1628, began cultivation of the forest, planting species brought back from the Portuguese voyages, including Himalayan pines, monkey-puzzles, Japanese camphor trees, huge Lebanese cedars, and ginkgoes. In 1643 the Pope threatened to excommunicate anyone harming the trees.

Map on page 266

A royal hunting lodge was built in neo-Manueline style at the end of the 19th century next to what remained of the convent. The Italian architect, Luigi Manini, somehow managed to inject his own interpretation of Romantic Revivalism into the construction and the intended modest hunting lodge turned into a sumptuous palace. After the fall of the monarchy in 1910, it became the spectacular and luxurious **Hotel Palace Buçaco** (where you may still, at a price, lodge in the suite of the last king, Manuel II.) A small church, the cloister, and several monks' cells remain from the monastery. In one of these cells the Duke of Wellington spent the night before the Battle of Buçaco on 27 September 1810. His victory in this battle was the first serious setback suffered by Napoleon's army, as the French attempted for the third time to conquer Portugal. The victory is still celebrated annually on the anniversary, with a re-enactment of the battle, in full period costume. A military museum is among a host of sights.

Flowers seem to drip from every wall in Buçaco.

A wine of incredibly good quality is produced on the estate and is available in the restaurant. If you are keen to try it, book yourself in for lunch at the hotel and enjoy a real treat.

Downhill from Buçaco is the village of **Luso ❹**, renowned as a spa for the water which flows freely from fountains and is available bottled throughout

BELOW: the sumptuous Hotel Palace Buçaco.

Portugal. A common sight here is locals overburdened with an assortment of plastic water bottles jostling to fill them at Fonte São João (St John's Fountain).

Taking the N1 north towards Aveiro leads through the heart of the Barraida wine country. A slight diversion into **Curia** ❺ allows the opportunity of picking up a special map of the region from *Turismo*. Armed with the map you can find your way to one of the three wineries, Caves Borlido, Caves Aliança and Caves Império, which offer free wine tasting without prior appointment.

Visitors will find it hard to forget that Luso is a spa town.

To the coast and Aveiro

Aveiro ❻ has been described as "the Venice of Portugal", but in truth it is nothing like the Italian city. The comparison stems from the canals that traverse the city and the boats that ply them. The canal system is modest, however: there is only one main canal, with two smaller ones along the edges of town. But they are linked with the Ria, the lagoon that extends 47 km (29 miles) just inland of the Atlantic Ocean and is fringed by dunes and long sandy beaches. Known to the Romans as Talabriga, Aveiro once lay directly on the ocean. However, over the centuries a strip of sediment has built up, creating the Ria but blocking ships and trade.

The lagoon plays a significant part in Aveiro's economic importance as an expanding port for fishing fleets and industrial cargoes. Other important local industries include wood, cork, and ceramics from nearby Vista Alegre. Next to the canals are large saltpans, another local resource. Particularly conspicuous are the brightly painted *moliceiros*, the boats with large graceful prows that were once widely used to gather *moliço* (seaweed) for fertiliser (*see page 86*), and which can still occasionally be spotted today.

BELOW: a graceful bridge over the canal in Aveiro.

Map on page 266

Aveiro was a small settlement during the Middle Ages. It was designated a town in the 1200s, and in 1418 was encircled by fortified walls, at the suggestion of Infante Prince Pedro after whom the city park is named. Shortly after this, Aveiro was granted the concession of a town fair, and the March Fair still goes on to this day.

The 16th century was a time of growth and expansion for the town. With dredged access to the sea and to the interior, Aveiro became a trade centre from which products of the entire Beira region were exported. In 1575, a violent storm shifted the sandbanks in the lagoon, blocking the canal from the sea. The inevitable decline in Aveiro's importance encouraged emigration, which caused a dramatic decrease in population (to about one-third). In 1808, another storm reopened the sea passage, but it was not until the last half of the 19th century that Aveiro's fortunes picked up.

In 1472, Joana, daughter of King Afonso V, entered the Convento de Jesus of Aveiro, against her father's will. Several miracles have been attributed to the princess, who is now known as Santa Joana Princesa.

Exploring Aveiro

Aveiro makes a good base for a trip on the Ria or to nearby beaches, but there are things worth seeing in the city as well. Aveiro is divided into two parts by the principal canal. The southern part is where the aristocracy once lived; the northern half is the old fishermen's section.

The southern half centres around the **Praça da República**. In the simple square, the nicest building is the solid and rather prim town hall. On the east side of the square, the 16th- and 17th-century **Misericórdia** church has a lovely Renaissance portal and 19th-century tiles on its façade. In a square further south the 17th-century **Carmelite Convent** once housed the barefoot Carmelite order. Note the paintings on the ceiling which depict the life of Saint Teresa.

BELOW: Aveiro's waterfront.

Aveiro's **Museu Regional** (open Tues–Sun; closed 12.30–2pm; entrance charge) is housed in the 15th-century **Convento de Jesus**. Although the labelling of exhibits in the museum is poor, guides will take you through and can answer questions. The convent church is a riot of gilded wood. Arching over the choir are lovely hand-painted ceilings, and off the choir is a chapel with beautiful tiles. Just outside is the tomb of Santa Joana Princesa, a 15th-century miracle-working nun; it is done in intricately carved coloured marble with statues supporting and crowning it. The tomb took 12 years to construct.

The **São Domingos Cathedral** is near the museum. Its baroque façade has twisted columns and sculpted figures of Faith, Hope and Charity. Inside, an enormous skylight over the altar lends the church an airiness that many baroque churches lack. The huge blue altar rises strikingly in the all-white interior. The tomb of Catarina de Atalide is here, a woman honoured, under the name Natércia, by the poet Luis Camões in his sonnets. The church was founded in 1423 and remodelled during the 16th and 17th centuries.

Several blocks away is the refreshing **Parque Dom Infante Pedro**, in the grounds of the old Franciscan Monastery. Colourful flowers, lush trees, fountains, and a small lake where you can rent paddle boats make this a nice spot for a break.

Map on page 266

TIP

The tourist office runs a boat tour to the Ria area daily between 15 June and 15 September. Trips last from 10am to 5pm.

RIGHT: a day's sardine catch.
BELOW: collecting weed in the Ria.

The old quarter

North of the canal lies the fishermen's section, where narrow houses support façades that sometimes rise beyond roof levels. The arches and curves on the tops of these false fronts are reminiscent of the fishing boats and their curved prows. The fish market, where the catch is sold each morning, is in this area. There is also the bright white, oddly shaped chapel of **São Gonçalinho** and the church of **São Gonçalo**. Inside this 17th- and 18th-century building gleam a gilt altar and newly placed tiles.

The beautiful Ria is a prime reason for coming to Aveiro. You can tour its length by boat, car or bus, although boat is by far the most rewarding. The lagoon and its subsidiary canals extend as far south as Mira and as far north as Ovar. There is a fair range of hotels in the area and many camp sites. You will see traditional colourful *moliceiros,* shorelines dotted with saltpans, forests and villages, glorious sea birds plummeting into the water, and the sandbar which blocks the city's access to the sea. A new road bridge takes you over the mouth of the estuary to **Costa Nova** where there are brightly coloured traditional houses and excellent fish restaurants. Whether you boat or drive, you will see why this region also bears the name of **Rota da Luz**, the Route of Light.

Castles and candy stripes

From Aveiro a good road leads south to Figueira da Foz and back to Coimbra along the riverside. Things to grab your attention along the way include a famous pottery factory, candy-striped houses and a castle. Fairly soon after leaving Aveiro, divert right to **Vista Alegre ❼** for its porcelain factory. Famous throughout Portugal, it started production in 1842 and is still run by the same family. There is a shop and small museum (open Tues–Fri; closed 12.30–2pm).

Mira lies close to the road a little further south. Keep going through the town and head for **Praia de Mira ❽** on the coast. This is the most southerly point of the lagoon and canal system which surrounds Aveiro. Candy-striped beach huts add a jaunty air to the resort but the main attraction is the inland lagoon where there is safe boating and where picnickers enjoy shade from the surrounding pine trees.

Although industrialised around the mouth of the Mondego, **Figueira da Foz ❾** has become an important holiday resort favoured by both Portuguese and Spanish visitors. To find the attractions, turn a blind eye to the high rise blocks and look at the broad expanse of beach and the gaily coloured beach huts, again in delightful candy stripes.

There is a fast road along the north side of the river to **Montemor-o-Velho ❿** dominated by a castle on a prominent mound. Like many in Portugal, it was held by the Moors before being taken by the Christians in the 11th century. Within the walls are some well-manicured gardens, the ruins of a 16th-century Manueline palace and the restored **Igreja de Santa Maria da Alcáçova** which was built around the time the castle was restored. To enjoy a rural atmosphere on the return to Coimbra, take the road from here along the south side of the river. ❑

PORTO

Maps
on page
276

*Once a river community, Porto is now a great commercial city,
but life still centres on and around the Rio Douro. The north bank
offers culture, and the south port wine*

Porto ❶ is the commercial centre of northern Portugal and the hub of the
lucrative port wine trade. Like Lisbon, Porto is clustered on hills overlooking a river, but unlike Lisbon, with its pastel walls and soft light,
Porto is a northern European city with granite church towers, stolid dark buildings, narrow streets and hidden baroque treasures. There is keen rivalry between
the two cities. Lisbon's hosting of Expo '98 and the resulting investment in
infrastructure was keenly felt. This has been compensated for by Porto's nom-
ination as European Cultural Capital in 2001.

Posed majestically on the rocky cliffs overlooking the Rio Douro, Porto is
linked by four bridges to Vila Nova de Gaia, an industrial area where most of
the wine lodges are located. These days large ships often dock at the seaport of
Leixões because of frequent silting of the Douro estuary, but coal barges, fishing trawlers and other small vessels still sail up the river. The climate in town
is temperate and the Portuenses, as the inhabitants are called, are traditionally
industrious. The population of Greater Porto is about one million.

In Roman times, the twin cities at the mouth of the Douro were known as
Portus on the right bank and Cale on the left. During the Moorish occupation,
the entire region between the Minho and Douro rivers was called Portucale.
When Afonso Henriques founded the new kingdom
in 1143, he took the name of his home province and
called it Portucalia.

Porto prospered from the seafaring exploits of the
golden epoch of discoveries. Its shipyards, adapting
Douro river *caravelas*, produced caravels that sailed
around the world. Prince Henry, who initiated and
inspired exploration, was born here.

The wine trade

England's close connections to the city (known in English as Oporto) developed with the wine trade. According to some, it was in fact the English who invented
port. It is said that in 1678 two sons of a rich English
merchant stayed for a while in a monastery on the
Upper Douro. They discovered that by adding a little
brandy to the sweet wine of the Douro it was suffi-
ciently fortified to withstand temperature changes and
long sea voyages. When the brothers returned to England, they reportedly took back large quantities of this
fortified wine, which came to be known as port.

Inevitably, there are different versions of this story:
in the 17th and 18th centuries, the wines of the Upper
Douro were robust table reds. Then, in 1820, a "climatic accident" occurred, with very warm weather
producing unusually sweet grapes, and a wine appreciated by the British. In the following years, amid
much controversy, the wine companies added

PRECEDING PAGES:
Cais da Ribeira
houses in Porto.
LEFT: life on the
banks of the Douro.
BELOW: a cooper
making port barrels.

Flower sellers add colour to the streets of Porto.

aguardente, or brandy, to stop the fermentation and fix the sugar content. This was the beginning of the sweet fortified nectar as it is known today.

In any event, the Methuen Treaty of 1703 opened English markets to Portuguese wines, and the British shippers of Porto became increasingly rich and powerful. In 1727 they established a Shippers' Association, which regulated the trade and controlled prices paid to Portuguese growers. To combat the English monopoly, the Marquês de Pombal founded the Alto Douro Wine Company in 1757, which provided a measure of Portuguese control.

In her delightful book, *They Went to Portugal,* Rose Macaulay describes whimsically how British port wine shippers virtually "captured and occupied" the city. She notes that the "Oporto families, some of them established in Oporto or Viana do Castelo since the 17th century, have the air of owning the city, so Britannically, so unconsciously arrogantly". The British presence can still be felt, although it is no longer overbearing.

Portugal's liberal revolution began with a revolt in Porto in 1820, and it was here, too, that the forces of King Miguel's brother and antagonist, Dom Pedro, landed in 1832, although it was to be another two years before the absolutist king went into exile.

Today, Porto is an energetic and lively commercial city with an individual taste in food and drink. Regional specialities include roast pork, fresh salmon, lamprey, trout and tripe (Portuenses are sometimes referred to as *tripeiros*). Generally, it is a sober city. Apart from dining out, there's not much nightlife. You may hear *fado* at some restaurants such as Mal Cozinhado or Taverna de São Jorge. The younger set frequents discos around Ribeira or in suburbs such as Foz do Douro.

The old city

The heart of the city is the **Praça da Liberdade** Ⓐ, with an equestrian statue of Pedro IV in the centre. On the north side of the square is the broad Avenida dos Aliados, with bright flower-beds and mosaic walks, leading up hill to the **Câmara Municipal** Ⓑ (Town Hall). Here stands the modern statue of Almeida Garrett (1799–1854), liberal poet and novelist, and native son of Porto.

To the southeast of Praça da Liberdade lies the Praça da Almeida Garrett, where the railway station, the **Estação São Bento** Ⓒ, has a fine entrance hall, decorated with traditional *azulejos* depicting historical scenes. From here you can catch a train for a journey along the Rio Douro to Pocinho.

Heading south, you arrive at the **Sé (Cathedral)** Ⓓ, dating from the 12th century and with its square towers and small domes (open Mon–Sat; closed 12.30–2pm). It was here that King João I wed the English Philippa of Lancaster in 1387, the year after the Treaty of Windsor was signed with England. The Gothic cloister is decorated with fine tiles. Nearby, on Pena Ventosa, the site of an ancient citadel, stands the impressive 18th-century **Palácio do Bispo** Ⓔ, the Bishop's Palace. Just beyond, is the **Casa Museu de Guerra Junqueiro** Ⓕ (open Tues–Sat, Sun pm; closed noon–2pm; entrance charge), in the house of the highly-regarded poet of that name, who died in 1923. His memorabilia and furnishings are on display, and the house itself is lovely.

Across the avenue stands the 15th-century church of **Igreja Santa Clara** Ⓖ, next to one of the best preserved sections of the old city wall. Santa Clara has been rebuilt several times but is noted for its splendid gilded wood choir stalls and altars. Sacheverell Sitwell wrote: "After it, every other building in Porto, even São Francisco, is drab and dull".

Map on page 276

BELOW: the Douro snakes through the city.

*The well-known
Sandeman silhouette
is hard to avoid in
Porto .*

BELOW: celebrating
the Dia de São João
on 24 June.

To the west, the **Igreja São Lourenço ❽**, better known as Igreja dos Grilos (after the crickets that lodge there), was built in 1570 and is one of the earliest examples of Portuguese baroque.

The western side

At the end of Rua Infante Dom Henrique stands the bastion of English life, the **Feitoria Inglesa (Factory House) ❶**. Here, the old British port wine shippers do their business, play billiards or cards, read English newspapers and enjoy English cuisine, as they have for the past 200 years. Outsiders must obtain special authorisation from the British Port Wine Shippers' Association to visit.

Around the corner, on Rua da Alfândega, stands the much restored **Casa do Infante ❶**, where Prince Henry the Navigator was born in 1394. For a time it served as the customs house; it is now a museum (open weekdays 9am, closed 12–2pm; entrance charge).

Going by the Praça do Infante Dom Henrique, you reach the **Igreja São Francisco ❻**, founded by King Sancho II in 1233 and rebuilt in the 14th century (open Mon–Sat). The interior glitters in baroque splendour with gilded columns, arches and statues. On the site of a convent, which burnt down in 1832, is the **Palácio de Bolsa ❶** or Stock Exchange, noted for its opulent neo-Moorish reception hall (open daily). Up the hill is the **Instituto do Vinho do Porto (Port Wine Institute) ❿**, a government agency established in 1932 to control the quality of port. The Institute closely regulates virtually every aspect of port production.

Following the Rua Belmonte past old homes with balconies and tiled walls, you arrive at the church of **São João Novo ❿**, built in 1592. Across the way

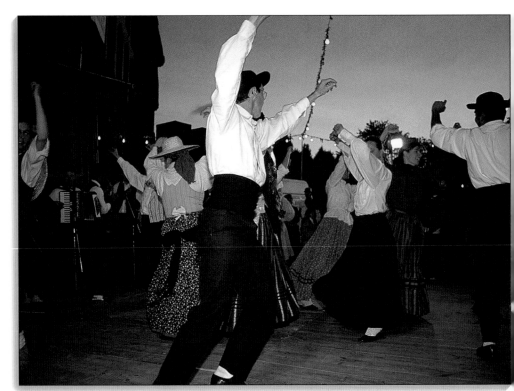

stands the 18th-century **Palácio de São João Novo O**, a whitewashed and granite building that houses the Museu de Etnografia e História (tel: 200-2010 for opening hours when current renovation is completed). The collection includes archaeological finds, wine presses and wine boats, fishing equipment, ceramics, costumes, jewellery and folk art, as well as a pharmacy.

The road leads to the singular 18th-century **Torre dos Clérigos P** (open daily), the tallest granite tower in Portugal. This was designed, along with its church, by Nicolau Nasoni, who was also architect of the fine baroque Solar de Mateus near Vila Real. Unless you really have no head for heights it's worth climbing the 225 or so steps for the view over the city. Just north of the tower lies the main **university** building, a handsome granite structure built in 1807 as the Polytechnical Academy.

East of São Bento railway station, lies the busy **Praça da Batalha Q**, with a statue of Pedro V in the middle, and the imposing 18th-century church of São Idelfonso with a façade of bright blue-and-white tiles. The main shopping street is **Rua Santa Catarina**, where bargains may be found in a variety of goods, from shoes to pottery. Rua das Flores has the best gold and silver shops.

Cais da Ribeira

Returning to the river, you might spend some time strolling along the river bank or riding on the *eléctrico*, the tram which runs from Boavista out to Castelo do Queijo on the coast and back, past the restored Alfandega (Customs House) to the **Cais da Ribeira R**, the liveliest part of the city. Many small shops and restaurants are built right into what remains of the old city wall. The area has recently been declared a UNESCO World Heritage Site.

Map on page 276

BELOW: *azulejos* adorn a church wall in Porto.

Map on page 276

On the Dia de São João (24 June), the most popular festivities take place near the Ponte Dom Luís I. People sing and dance around bonfires, drink vinho *and feast on roast kid and grilled sardines.*

RIGHT: beneath the Torre dos Clérigos
BELOW: catching up on the news, Rua de Santa Catarina.

The splendid steel arch farther up-river is a railway bridge, **Ponte de Dona Maria Pia**, built in 1876 to a plan by Alexandre Gustave Eiffel and only recently put out of use by the new São João Bridge. In the centre of Oporto is the handsome **Ponte Dom Luís I ⑤**, built in 1886, which provides splendid views. This two-storey iron bridge carries two road tracks and leads directly to Vila Nova de Gaia (see below),

Outside the old town

On the western side of the city, in the old royal Palácio dos Carrancas is the **Museu Nacional Soares dos Reis ⑦** named after a 19th-century sculptor (open Tues 1pm, Wed–Sun; closed 12.30–1.30pm; entrance charge). It has a fine collection of archaeological artifacts, religious art, regional costumes, ceramics and contemporary paintings, as well as sculpture. Paintings by Grão Vasco are on display, among them pictures of St Catherine and St Lucy.

On the western side of the Jardim do Palácio de Cristal is the **Solar do Vinho do Porto ⓤ** (entered from Rua Entre Quintas), where you can taste a wide variety of port wines (open Mon–Fri 10am–11.30pm, Sat 11am–10.30 pm; closed holidays). It is located in the old wine cellar and stable of the Quinta da Macieirinha, which is where the former King Charles Albert died in 1849, after abdicating the throne of Sardinia. Now an intriguing **Museu Romântico** (open Tues–Sat; entrance charge), the mansion is set in a rose garden and contains most of its original furnishings.

To the northwest, in Boavista, is the art deco **Casa de Serralves** (open Tues–Fri pm, Sat, Sun from 10am; entrance charge), set in an attactive 18-hectare (44-acre) estate. The mansion holds exhibitions of modern art, but is likely to be outshone soon by the new **Museu de Arte Contemporânea** in the grounds nearby, also run by the Fundaçao de Serralves. As well as a large exhibition space, the building comprises an auditorium, a restaurant and a library.

South of the river

Vila Nova de Gaia, across the Ponte Dom Luís I, is an industrial zone with ceramic, glass, soap and other factories. But above all, Gaia is the true seat of the port wine industry, where most warehouses or lodges are to be found. There are about 60 port wine lodges: many of them welcome visitors to tour the installations and taste their wines. The Sandeman, Ferreira and Ramos Pinto companies employ full-time guides.

In spring, the new wine is brought down from the Upper Douro by truck, less picturesque but far more practical than the *barcos rabelos*, the flat-bottomed sailing boats that were once used. In the Gaia lodges, the wine is left to mature in 530-litre (140-gallon) oak casks, or pipes. Here the blending takes place, with wines from different vineyards and years blended to produce a distinctive aroma, taste and colour before the wine is bottled and again left to mature.

Like museum pieces, a few *barcos rabelos* are kept docked at Gaia near the Dom Luís I Bridge. Once a year, during the Dia de São João on 24 June, the boats participate in a colourful regatta. ❏

THE DOURO VALLEY

Renowned worldwide for the wine it produces, the Douro valley is graced by its centuries-old vineyards growing on steeply terraced hillsides

Map on pages 286–7

The romantic history of port wine has endowed the Douro region with unrivalled respect. Douro means "of gold" and the river, on certain glowing days, does resemble a twisting golden chain as it winds through the narrow valley between the steep hills and terraced vineyards. The countryside is exceptionally beautiful, particularly in spring and autumn, and is enhanced by the neat rows of vines which grace the hillsides.

Although the Douro stretches from Spain to the Atlantic at Porto, only the inland part of the valley, the Alto Douro, is recognised for growing the grapes used for port wine. The demarcated region starts some 100 km (60 miles) upstream from Porto at Barqueiros, just before Régua and follows the river all the way to Spain. Some of the tributaries of the Douro, the Corgo, Torto, Pinhão and Tua, are included in the area. It was Portugal's authoritarian Marquês de Pombal who staked out the Douro in 1756, making it the first officially designated wine-producing region in the world. Subsequent legislation designated the Upper Douro as the port wine region.

Characteristically, the schistose soils are stony and impoverished and the climate extreme. Summers are very hot and dry, and made hotter by the direct rays of the sun reflected on the crystalline rock, winters are cold and wet. The large lumps of surface schist act as storage heaters, absorbing the sun's heat in the day and releasing it throughout the night. The slopes nearest to the river grow the finest grapes and this land is highly prized.

PRECEDING PAGES: the sleepy Rio Tâmega. **LEFT:** port wine lodges on the banks of the Douro. **BELOW:** Amarante's historic bridge.

Choosing a base

Pinhão is regarded as the centre of the wine industry, and this is where all the famous names have their farms. It is a handy place to stay although it is hardly bristling with hotels. Taylors have restored and extended a *quinta* on the banks of the Douro and in 1998 it opened as the Vintage House Hotel, providing quality accommodation. The area does have a number of restored houses and farms which are part of the Manor House system (*see page 129*), some of them in very fine locations.

Casa de Casal de Loivos, above Pinhão, has a fine overview of the Douro or, if you prefer to bury yourself in the country, Casa da Lavada, a restored 14th-century fortified manor house provides modern comforts. It is high in the mountains of the Serra do Marão in a village where visitors are still a curiosity. Traditional hotels are found in the surrounding towns of Amarante, Vila Real or Lamego. Régua (*see page 288*) is well located but unattractive as a base.

If your intention is to go on brief excursions into the area, then **Porto ❶** is well geared with organised trips. Coach trips are well advertised but it is easy enough to catch a train from São Bento station on the Douro line. The end of the line is Pocinho, not too far from the Spanish border. There are branch lines to Amarante, Vila Real and Mirandela. The river is now navigable for much of its length and boat trips up the river are a regular feature and a pleasant way to see the countryside. One option is to boat as far as Pinhão and return by train.

Out from Porto

Balconies overhang the Rio Tâmega in Amarante.

There is little to detain the motorist between Porto and Amarante so the fast A4 is the best way to travel. It speeds an otherwise very slow journey through *vinho verde* growing countryside. The main area for *vinho verde* lies to the north in Costa Verde and Minho.

Amarante ❷ on the banks of the Rio Tâmega, is delightful, at least in the old part of town. Geese paddle contentedly amongst punts and trailing willow trees on the river while afternoon tea-takers look on from overhanging wooden balconies. Dominant in the town is the three-arched **Ponte de São Gonçalo** built in 1790. It became a battle ground in the Peninsular War in 1809 when General Silveira, supported by Beresford's troops, successfully fought off the French. The bridge leads to the **Convento de São Gonçalo**, named after the local patron saint, protector of marriages.

Amarante's association with fertility rites reaches back into the mists of time and some claim the town's name is derived from *amar*, meaning "to love". These ancient beliefs have empowered São Gonçalo, beatified in 1561, to assist believers in everything pertaining to love and marriage. He is honoured every June by a festival, a particularly raucous occasion with the local men out in the streets offering distinctly phallic cakes to any women prepared to accept them.

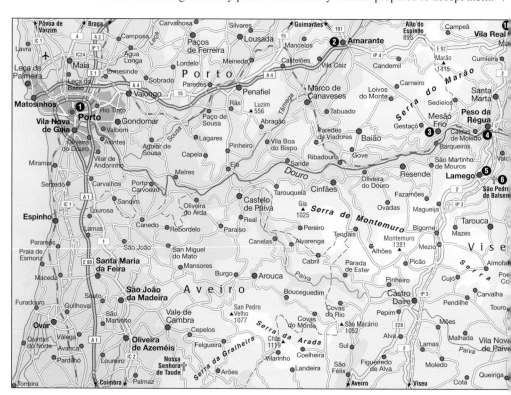

The convent, however, is much more sombre. It was begun in 1540 but not completed until 1620. Inside is the tomb of São Gonçalo, who died about 1260, and some lush gilded carved woodwork. Anyone aspiring to love and marriage need only touch the effigy of the saint to be blessed within the year. Sadly, the limestone effigy is now quite worn in places.

Map below

Above the rear cloister is the **Museu Municipal Amadeo de Souza-Cardosa** (open Tues–Sun; closed noon–2pm; entrance charge), which has some interesting modern Portuguese paintings – Souza-Cardosa was a Cubist artist who came from Amarante.

Nearby is the **Quinta da Aveleda**, seat of one of Portugal's main wine empires and a leading exporter of *vinho verde*. The *quinta* is included on some wine-tasting tours. Individual visitors are welcome but advised to make prior arrangements at the company's office in Porto. A tour of the 200-hectare (500-acre) Aveleda estate includes a visit to the family chapel, which was built in 1671. The luxuriant gardens contain a ruined window said to be from the palace of Prince Henry the Navigator in Porto. You can also observe contemporary *vinho verde* production: mile upon mile of grapes; climbing poles, trellises and crosses; and mechanical crushers, modern concrete storage vats and mechanised bottling and labelling. At the wine lodge you can taste different types of *vinho verde* and buy a bottle or a case from the old distillery, now converted to a store.

Port wine country

Beyond Amarante the road turns abruptly south to twist and climb through the Serra do Marão. *Vinho verde* vines climb the trees here and huge granite tors stand in the summit region. Beyond is a descent to the small village of **Mesão**

Ready to pour.

Frio and a sweeping view of the Upper Douro winding peacefully through the gorges of the port wine country. The road follows the river's north bank, passing through the small spa town of **Caldas de Moledo** before reaching **Régua** ❹ (its full name is Peso da Régua), a busy river port and the headquarters of the **Casa do Douro**, an organisation which has a great deal of power in the regulation of port wine production. In this area lie some of the oldest British and Portuguese estates. Here the road crosses the Douro and runs along the southern bank.

South of the river

Before following along the south bank towards Pinhão, there is a worthwhile diversion to **Lamego** ❺, which is a city of historical importance. Although the Lusitanians had finally been subjugated by the Romans (*circa* 200 BC), the tribespeople of this area arose in revolt, refusing to pay the heavy taxation. In retaliation, the Romans burned the town to the ground. But it was an important defensive location, so Emperor Trajan ordered it rebuilt.

By the 4th century AD, the town had turned to Christianity, and was granted the status *civitas*, the Roman equivalent of a city franchise. Then came the invasions of the Suevi and Visigoths – and then the Moors. Finally, in the same sweep that won him Viseu, Fernando of León and Castile took the city, aided by the legendary El Cid. Fernando allowed the Muslim *wali* to continue to govern Lamego, as long as he converted and paid tribute to the king.

Perhaps the city's most significant moment in Portugal's history was in 1143, when the *cortes* met for the very first time. At this meeting, the nobles declared Afonso Henriques to be Afonso I, first king of Portugal.

BELOW: pilgrims' stairway at the Nossa Senhora dos Remédios church in Lamego.
BELOW RIGHT: fountain at the same church.

Lamego's 12th-century castle, on one of the city's two hills, preserves a fine 13th-century keep, with windows that were added later, and a very old and unusual vaulted cistern, possibly Moorish, with monograms of master masons.

Atop Lamego's other hill is its most visually striking building, the pilgrimage church of **Nossa Senhora dos Remédios** crowning a vast stairway reminiscent of Braga's Bom Jesus. The first chapel of the sanctuary was founded by the Bishop of Lamego in 1361, and dedicated to St Stephen. In 1564, it was pulled down, and a new one built. From that time, there has been a steady stream of the faithful seeking cures. The first week in September is the time of the major pilgrimage, and there's a very jolly accompanying festival which seems to have little to do with healing or piety. The present sanctuary was started in 1750, and was consecrated 11 years later – but the magnificent baroque-style staircase leading up to it, begun in the 19th century, was completed only in the 1960s. Fountains, statues and pavilions decorate each level of the 600 or so steps.

The **Sé** (**Cathedral**), a Gothic structure, was built by Afonso Henriques in 1129. Only the Romanesque tower is left from the original building. The city museum, housed in the 18th-century Bishop's Palace, has a collection which includes 16th-century Flemish tapestries and works by Grão Vasco.

Just outside Lamego (start on the Tarouca road) in the valley of the Rio Balsemão, is the tiny **São Pedro de Balsemão ❻**, a Visigothic church believed to be the oldest in Portugal and second oldest in Europe.

Following the south bank of the Douro towards Pinhão is a rewarding drive as you can enjoy the flowing lines of vineyards patterning the hillsides and broken only by signs displaying such well-known names as Sandeman, Barros and Quinta Dona Matilde.

Map on pages 286–7

TIP

The best time to visit the Douro Valley is during the *vindima*, in late September and early October, when the grapes are being collected.

BELOW: ageing the wine at the Sandeman *quinta*.

Backbreaking work in the vineyards.

BELOW: a port wine *quinta* in an idyllic spot on the Douro river.

Pinhão ❼, on the north side of the river, seems an unlikely town to lie at the heart of the port wine region. There is little to visit but it is worth a stop at the railway station to see the *azulejo* panels depicting scenes of the Rio Douro.

A scenic circular tour

A tasty sampler of typical Douro scenery and traditional villages can be enjoyed on a short circular tour from Pinhão, taking around half a day. It starts on the south side of the river, along the road climbing the hillside to **São João da Pasqueira ❽**. This village has some fine 18th-century houses mixed with surprisingly modern property. Follow left turns signposted Barragem de Valeira to drive through dilapidated, overgrown vineyards ravaged by the Phylloxera scourge many years ago and never replanted. Watch out on the descent towards the *barragem* for the pointed hill, **São Salvador do Mundo ❾**, littered with churches and chapels.

The **Barragem de Valeira ❿** is where Baron Forrester, the 19th-century English pioneer, lost his life in 1862: in those days the river here tumbled over dangerous rapids. Born in Hull in 1809, Joseph James Forrester came out to Portugal as a young man to work for his uncle in Porto. He was fascinated by the wine industry and spent many years boating up and down the river making a detailed map. His widely acclaimed work won him his title in 1855, the first foreigner ever to earn such an honour.

It was the river that eventually claimed his life at the age of 51. He was out boating with Antónia Adelaide Ferreira and others when they ran into trouble at the rapids known as Cachão de Valeira. The boat capsized and Baron Forrester drowned, dragged down, it is said, by the weight of his money belt. Antónia

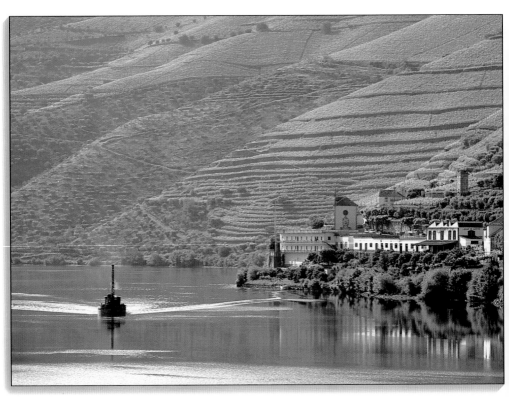

Adelaide Ferreira survived, helped by the buoyancy of her crinoline dress.

Cross the *barragem* to regain the north shore and zigzag up the hillside towards Linhares. Vineyards make the patterns and create the scenery for much of the way towards Tua and Alijó. **Alijó ⓫** is one of the bigger towns in the area and is the location of a *pousada* named after Baron Forrester. The route back heads through Favaios to Pinhão.

Map on pages 286–7

Rock art

Winding eastwards from Pinhão through **São João da Pasqueira** and along the hill contours, past quaint churches and villages, you will come to Vila Nova de Foz Côa and the valley of the Rio Côa. Work in the 1990s to build a dam in this remote region uncovered a remarkable collection of rock paintings. In 1996 the Portuguese government declared the Côa Valley protected as the **Parque Arqueológico do Vale Côa ⓬** (open daily; closed 12.30–2pm; visits must be reserved, tel: 079-765258). In 1998, the park was declared a UNESCO World Heritage Site.

At present, only three rock art sites, at Penascosa, Ribeira de Piscos and Canada do Inferno can be visited, not by individuals, but on a guided tour. Tours to Canada do Inferno start from the Park Office in Vila Nova de Foz Côa; tours to Ribeira de Piscos start from the Visitor Centre at **Muxagata ⓭**, while tours to Penascosa leave from the Visitor Centre in **Castelo Melhor ⓮**.

North to Vila Real

Going from Pinhão to the north leads to **Sabrosa ⓯**, the birthplace of Fernão de Magalhães, better known as Ferdinand Magellan, the man who led the first

BELOW: even the tiles depict the vineyards.

ESTAÇÃO VITI-VINÍCOLA
DO DOURO RIO TORTO

Map
on pages
286–7

circumnavigation of the world between 1519 and 1522, under the Spanish flag. Just before Constantim, look out on the right for a diversion to the sanctuary of **Panóias** ⓰. All there is to see is a field with a series of enormous carved stones, believed to have been used as altars for human sacrifice. Inscriptions in Latin invoke the ancient god Serapis, known to both Greek and Egyptian mythology.

Beyond Constantim but before Vila Real is the village of **Mateus** ⓱, with its celebrated palace and gardens. It was built by Nicolau Nasoni in 1739–43 for António José Botelho Mourão. Today, an illustration of the palace graces the distinctive label of the less-than-distinctive rosé wine from this area. The exquisite building with its striking baroque façade, double stairway, and huge coat of arms is open for visits, and frequently hosts musical events.

Vila Real

An ancient settlement in the Terra de Panóias, **Vila Real** ⓲ was founded and renamed by Dom Dinis, the sixth king of Portugal, in 1289. Its name, literally "royal town", is appropriate, as Vila Real once had more noble families than any city other than the capital. Ignoring the modern city, and walking through ancient streets, you will see many residences marked, often above the main entrance, with the original owners' coats-of-arms. As likely as not, descendants of the same family will still be still living there. The 19th-century writer Camilo Castelo Branco lived in Vila Real, and wrote many of his most enduring works using the town as a backdrop.

"In what century are we on this mountain?" asks one of his characters.

"In what century?" comes the reply. "Why, it is the same 18th century here as it is in Lisbon."

"Oh!" says the first. "I thought time here had stopped in the 12th century."

FOLLOWING PAGES:
bringing home the
vegetables.
RIGHT: setting off
for the local fair.
BELOW: strange
things happen in
the countryside.

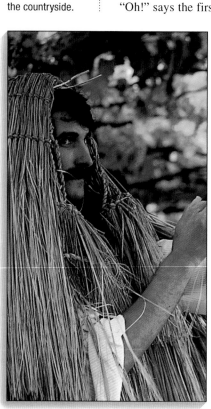

Vila Real became a city proper only in 1925, but the importance of the region dates from 1768, when the vineyards were first developed commercially: the area has good red and white wines, but it is the rosé that is best known – especially Mateus, which is exported to more than 150 countries. Now a lively bustling industrial centre, Vila Real is one of the largest towns in the region.

The **Sé** (**Cathedral**) was originally the church of a Dominican convent. Although much of the present building dates from the 14th century, Romanesque columns still remain from an earlier structure.

Vila Real's oldest church is the ancient **Capela de São Nicolau**, on a promontory of high land behind the municipal hall, overlooking the valley of the Rio Corgo. Another church of note is **São Pedro**, whose baroque touches were completed by Nicolau Nasoni (1691–1773), the Tuscan-born architect who designed the manor house in Mateus.

Among fine houses dating from the 15th to 18th centuries is the **Casa de Diogo Cão**, an Italian Renaissance-style building that was the birthplace of Cão, the navigator who discovered the mouth of the River Congo in 1482.

As far aslocal crafts are concerned, the Vila Real region is particularly noted for the black pottery of Bisalhães and the woollen goods of Caldas do Alvão and Marão. ❏

PORT WINE - TREASURE FROM STONY SOIL

The story of port wine is one of triumph over adversity. From bare, inhospitable terrain came a wine that some prize above all others

Upstream from Porto lies the Cinderella of harsh regions, which, at the pop of a wine cork, was transformed into a beautiful princess.

Dry and stony, with barely a covering of dusty soil, and with excessively high summer temperatures combined with months of drought, the Upper Douro seems an unlikely area to enjoy a fairy-tale transformation into a global producer of a unique wine – port.

The source of encouragement that provided the life force for this industry's growth was the high-quality wine already being produced by the locals. Exploiting the region to produce wine in commercial quantities was beset by huge problems, but it seemed that every disadvantage, every deterrent, contributed to its success. The soil, or rather the lack of it, was just one. Vines planted into the schist (rock) sent their roots searching deep down through the cracks and crevices to find water. The vast root system which developed allowed the plants to survive burning summers without irrigation, so yielding grapes high in sugar.

The Rio Douro, steep banked and virtually unnavigable, was another apparent drawback which proved essential to the region's success, for without it there would have been no means of exporting the wine. Grapes harvested at the steep higher levels were transported to the split-level factories below, and the resulting wine was then lowered to the river for transportation on the distinctive flat-bottomed *barcos rabelos*.

△ **MATURING PROCESS**
The length of time port spends in wood is one factor which determines its variety. Vintage port does most of its ageing in glass.

▽ **BARCOS RABELOS**
The flat-bottomed *rabelos*, designed to suit the shallow waters of the Douro, carried the port barrels down-river. Accidents were common.

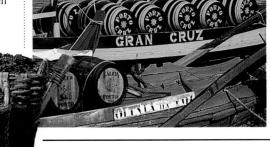

▷ **INFINITE VARIETY**
More than 80 varieties of grape have been used in port wine but modern plantings are limited to about six varieties.

◁ GRAPE PICKING
Teams of women spread along the rows and sweep systematically across the vineyard, leaving men to carry away the baskets.

△ TREADING GRAPES
Once all grape juice for port wine was extracted by the old treading process, but nowadays most of this work is done mechanically.

△ VINTAGE PORT
Vintage port on display at Sandeman's Wine Lodge in Vila Nova de Gaia, where most of the prestigious lodges are now found.

◁ QUINTA DO CRASTO
The close-packed vineyards create geometric green patterns on the hillsides transforming the dusty landscapes of this region.

BRINGING IN THE HARVEST

The Upper Douro is a pleasure to visit at any point during the summer, but harvest time is the most rewarding. The harvest (*vindima*) usually starts towards the end of September – the exact date being dictated by the conditions of any particular year – and by this time temperatures have cooled to a pleasant heat.

In spite of recent mechanisation, grape picking is still largely done by hand. Extended families of itinerant workers from surrounding villages often return year after year to the same farms to bring in the harvest. Traditionally, men and women adopt different roles in the field, but they all come together at meal times. Lunch is almost party time: the estate owners provide a fulsome meal and the pickers relax and enjoy it.

When the mood is right, and with a contented team of workers, the sound of singing can be heard emanating from the vine terraces. It is a time of great celebration, of relief that the crop has survived the vagaries of the weather and of thanksgiving for a harvest, even in years when it is not at its most bountiful.

COSTA VERDE AND THE MINHO

Map on page 300

Verdant and lush, this is a land of vineyards, tranquil riverside towns, busy markets, and Europe's last great wilderness, the Peneda-Gerês National Park

The Minho region north of Porto is often described as Costa Verde, or the Green Coast, a reference to the vineyards and lush green of its well-watered landscape. In reality it is a much bigger area than just the coast. It extends northwards to the Rio Minho, the boundary with Spain, eastwards to include the Parque Nacional da Peneda-Gerês and south to encompass Braga and Guimarães. It is a region of great natural beauty, especially the verdant Lima Valley and the wild and mountainous Peneda-Gerês, where farming techniques and lifestyles pass from generation to generation without perceptible change.

Grapes are grown everywhere. They hang from trees, pergolas and porches, and climb along slopes and terraces. They grow in poor rocky soil where little else flourishes. To get the most out of the land, the Minhotos train their vines to grow upwards, on trees, houses and hedges, leaving ground space for cabbages, onions and potatoes. This free-wheeling system has made it difficult to modernise grape production, but in recent years the larger farms have begun to use a system of wire-supporting crosses which are called *cruzetas*.

LEFT:
the unusual grain
stores of Soajo.
BELOW:
Vila do Conde.

The *vindima,* or grape harvest, is still done by hand and is a wonderful sight to behold. Harvesting takes place in September and October and lasts until early November. It is often a hazardous task, requiring towering 30-rung ladders to get at the elusive treetop grapes, though most vines now are trained at lower levels. In the hilly country, men still carry huge baskets of grapes weighing as much as 50 kg (110 lb) on their backs. On some back roads, squeaky oxcarts transport the grapes to winepresses. In these modern times, however, the fruit is generally transported in trucks.

While harvest is a festive occasion, it is no longer quite the unbridled merry-making of yore. In the old days, workers used to perform a kind of bacchanal dance, their arms linked, stamping on the grapes with their bare feet. It was said that this was the only way to crush the fruit without smashing the pips and spoiling the flavour of the wine. This was often accompanied by music and clapping, glasses of spirits and a good deal of sweat. Nowadays, mechanical extractors often remove the pips and presses are generally used to crush the grapes, although treading still takes place in some vineyards.

North from Porto

A good way to visit the Minho is to drive up the coast from Porto and return by an inland route. The Atlantic beaches are generally broad with fine sand, but the sea is cold and rough. A fishing town and resort, **Vila**

do Conde ❶ is the site of the vast Convento de Santa Clara, which was founded in 1318, the 16th-century parish church of São João Baptista and a lovely 17th-century fortress. Travellers are welcome to watch how fishing boats are made and to visit the lace-making school. Nearby, **Póvoa de Varzim ❷** is another popular fishing port-resort, with an 18th-century fort and a parish church. There's also a casino and a modern luxury hotel, the Vermar, with heated pools and tennis courts. Further north, **Ofir ❸** is a delightful seaside resort amid pine forests. Just across the Rio Cávado lies the town of **Esposende ❹** with the remains of an 18th-century fortress. There are many new, often garishly-painted houses in towns and villages along the way which have very often been built by emigrants returned from France, Germany and elsewhere.

A lively fishing and ship-building port, **Viana do Castelo ❺** was called Diana by the Romans. This was the centre of Portugal's wine trade until the port declined in the 18th century and Porto became pre-eminent. There is a good deal to see in Viana, starting with the 18th-century Palácio dos Távoras, now the

Costa Verde and the Minho

main tourist office. In the central Praça da República there's a beautiful 16th-century fountain and the remarkable Misericórdia hospital, with its three-tiered façade supported by caryatids. Nearby stands the handsome 15th-century parish church with a Gothic portal and Romanesque towers. The town is dominated by **Monte Santa Luzia ❻**, with a large and inappropriate modern basilica. To the west of the town, the baroque Nossa Senhora da Agonia church is the site of a popular pilgrimage each August. Dancers, musicians, and other celebrants, wearing vivid embroidered traditional costumes, come from all over the Minho to take part in the three-day *festa*, which is among Portugal's most spectacular.

Along the Rio Minho

Continuing north, the road leads to **Caminha ❼** on the banks of the Rio Minho, an attractive town with echoes of its past as a busy trading port. The church, dating from the 15th century, has a beautiful carved-wood ceiling. There are several lovely 15th- and 16th-century buildings near the main square.

At the estuary of the Minho, the road turns inland and follows the water, which forms the border with Spain. **Valença do Minho ❽** is a bustling border town with shops and markets. Spaniards come here regularly to purchase items that include table linen and crystal chandeliers. The Portuguese, on the other hand, cross the border to Tui or Vigo to buy canned goods such as asparagus and artichokes, and ready-made clothing. The old town of Valença is still fairly intact with cobbled streets and stone houses with iron balconies, surrounded by 17th-century granite ramparts. Outside them, near the station, is a railway museum. The ancient convent, with a splendid view of the Minho and of Spain, is now a *pousada*.

Grapes grow everywhere, even on telegraph wires.

BELOW: Valença do Minho's cheerful town square.

From **Monção ❾**, a fortified town known for its spring water and classy *vinho verde*, there is a difficult choice to make. Either you take the road south through the heart of the Minho or continue along the riverside and cross over the mountains of Serra da Peneda and sense the isolation. Either way the routes meet at Ponte da Barca.

The mountain route

Follow the river as far as **Melgaço ❿**, another fortified town, and turn inland for **Castro Laboreiro ⓫**, an ancient settlement with an 11th-century castle, but more famous for a large breed of dog which was originally introduced to protect the villagers from marauding wolves. Take the road to **Senhora da Peneda ⓬** to find an amazing "Bom Jesus" style church seemingly in the middle of nowhere. A long flight of steps ascending to the church is adorned with 14 chapels, each containing a tableau depicting a major event in the story of Christ.

Dramatic mountain scenery opens up as you pass through a number of villages, including Rouças and Adrão, to meet the road outside the village of **Soajo ⓭**, where there is a colourful market on the first Sunday of the month. Of particular interest are the communal *espigueiros*, granite -built grain stores built on mushroom-shaped legs, grouped around a threshing floor. Note that the roads are of poor quality.

The road onward leads to **Lindoso** (from *lindo* meaning beautiful) and a finely situated border castle keeping watch for invaders from Spain. Below the castle ramparts lies another cluster of *espigueiros*. Return from Lindoso on the road to Ponte da Barca.

You'll see lush countryside, crisscrossed by rivers with medieval stone bridges; simple white churches with elaborate granite doorways and windows; and, of course, unending vineyards. Due to the high population density, the land has been divided and sub-divided for generations, so the average property is just an acre or two.

Feeding the hens.

The road passes **Arcos de Valdevez** ⓯, a charming hillside town built on the banks of the Rio Vez, with a magnificent view of the valley. Just to the south, **Ponte da Barca** ⓰, on the south bank of the Rio Lima, has a lovely 15th-century parish church and an old town square, but the principal attraction is the fine arched bridge, built in 1543 and often restored. This is a possible starting point for a tour of the nearby **Peneda-Gerês National Park** (*see below*).

The Lima Valley and the south

Here you might turn westward, along the beautiful valley of the Lima river, which the Romans believed to be the *Lethe*, the mythical River of Forgetfulness. The area has numerous great estates or *solares,* which stand as a tangible reminder of the glories of the old empire. Some are now guesthouses, and arrangements to visit or stay in these manors should be made beforehand, if possible (*see page 128*).

BELOW: waterfall in Peneda-Gerês.

Ponte de Lima ⓱ is one of the loveliest towns in Portugal, mainly because of its location on the south bank of the Lima; its market, held every other

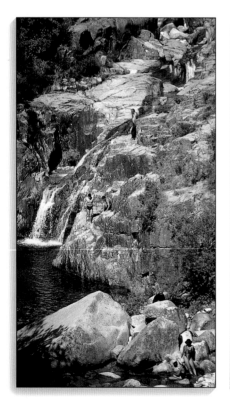

A TOUR OF THE PARQUE NACIONAL DA PENEDA-GERÊS

With the relaxing of border controls it is easy to make a round trip by car, taking in some of the most spectacular scenery on both sides of the frontier with Spain. From Ponte da Barca take the road east towards Lindoso, past the new hydro scheme to the border at Madaleina. Cross over – there are no formalities – and continue alongside the reservoir until you come to a right turn signposted Lobios and Portela do Homen. Take this turn and you eventually cross back into Portugal.

On the Portuguese side you have a choice: continue straight down the "main" road to the old spa town of Caldas do Gerês then towards Braga, or, shortly after crossing back into Portugal, take the right turn down a dirt track which follows the Vilarinho reservoir to Campo do Gerês (a metalled road again). Campo do Gerês has an excellent visitor centre portraying traditional life in Vilarinho das Furnas, the village submerged by the reservoir. Then drive towards Covide, passing a well-stocked craft shop, then west to Vila Verde. Of the two options, the latter is the more interesting. Note that roads can get very busy at weekends in summer and at peak times the park authority may impose traffic restrictions.

Monday, is a splendidly colourful "tent city" on the riverbank. The town faces a magnificent Roman bridge with low arches, and remains of the old city wall still stand. A 15th-century palace with crenellated façade is now the town hall. Across the river, the 15th-century **Convento de Santo António** has beautiful woodwork, including two baroque shrines.

Continuing towards Viana do Castelo, you pass more manor houses, such as the Solar de Cortegaça, with its great 15th-century stone tower. This is a working manor, with wine cellars, flour mill and stable. Guests are welcome to take part in the farm life.

Barcelos: cock and bull

Heading south from Ponte de Lima, you reach the charming market town of **Barcelos ⑱**, on the north bank of the Rio Cávado. Barcelos has 15th-century fortifications, a 13th-century church and a 16th-century palace, but more than that, it has one of the best craft markets in the country. Every Thursday, traders and artisans display their folk art and other goods in the centre of town.

It was here that the late Rosa Ramalho, the most famous folk art sculptress in Portugal, created her world of fanciful ceramic animals and people – a style that has been continued by her grand-daughter. There is a crafts exhibition and shop in the medieval keep next to the tourist office in the **Largo da Porta Nova**. It displays copperware, hand-made rugs, wooden toys, bright cotton tableware, and, of course, the *galo de Barcelos* – the ubiquitous Barcelos cockerel. A monument, the so-called Senhor do Galo cross, is the most apt reminder of the extraordinary legend that lies behind the rooster's elevation to Portugal's unofficial national emblem (*see page 237*).

Map on page 300

There's no escaping the Barcelos cockerel.

BELOW: lovely Ponte de Lima.

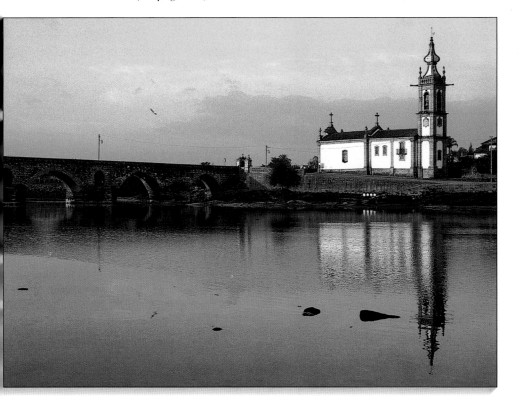

Guimarães: birthplace of a nation

A busy manufacturing town noted mainly for textiles, shoes and cutlery, **Guimarães** still possesses many reminders of its past glory as birthplace of the Portuguese nation. Around the year 1128, an 18-year-old boy named Afonso Henriques proclaimed independence for the region of Portucale from the kingdom of León and Castile. In the field of São Mamede, near Guimarães, the young Afonso Henriques defeated his mother's army, which was battling on behalf of Alfonso VII, king of León and Castile.

Guimarães' Festival of Saint Walter, the Festas Gualterianas, dates from the middle of the 15th century. This three-day celebration, on the first weekend in August, includes a torchlight procession, a fair with traditional dances, and a medieval parade.

Guimarães has long been the centre of the Portuguese linen industry. It still produces high quality, coarse linen from home-grown flax naturally bleached by the sun. The region is also known for its hand embroider, though unfortunately machines are gradually taking over.

A good place to begin a tour is at the 10th-century **Castelo** (open Tues–Sun; closed 12.30–2pm; entrance charge), on the northern side of town. It is believed that Afonso Henriques was born here in 1110, the son of Henri of Burgundy, Count of Portucale, and his wife Teresa. The castle is a large mass of walls and towers on a rocky hill with a magnificent view of the mountains. The dungeon and fortifications were restored many times. Early in the 19th century, the castle was used as a debtors' prison; it was restored again in 1940. At the entrance stands the small Romanesque chapel of **São Miguel do Castelo** with the original font where Afonso Henriques was baptised in 1111.

BELOW: the cross of the Senhor do Galo, Barcelos.

Heading into town, you pass the 15th-century Gothic **Paço dos Duques**, the palace of the Dukes of Bragança, now occasionally used as an official residence by the President of the Republic. This massive granite construction consists of four buildings around a courtyard and has been completely restored. Outside is a fine statue of Afonso Henriques by Soares dos Reis. Visitors may also view the splendid chestnut ceiling of the Banquet Hall, the Persian carpets, French tapestries, ancient portraits and documents.

The Rua de Santa Maria, with its cobblestones and 14th- and 15th-century houses with wrought-iron balconies leads to the centre of town. On the left lies the **Convento de Santa Clara**, built in the 1600s and now used as the Town Hall.

The church of **Nossa Senhora de Oliveira**, dating from the 10th century, was rebuilt by Count Henri in the 12th century and has undergone several restorations. Still visible are the 16th-century watchtower and 14th-century western portal and window. The church takes its name from a 7th-century legend of an old Visigoth warrior named Wamba who was tilling his field nearby when a delegation came to tell him he had been elected king. Refusing the office he drove his staff into the ground, declaring that not until it bore leaves would he become king. It turned into an olive tree and the church was later built on the spot.

Adjacent to the church of Oliveira, the convent has been converted into the **Museu de Alberto Sampaio** (open Tues–Sun; closed 12.30–2pm; entrance charge), displaying the church's rich treasury of 12th-century silver chalices and Gothic and Renaissance silver crucifixes as well as 15th- and 16th-century statues, paintings and ceramics.

The busiest square in Guimarães is the Largo do Toural. Just beyond, the **Igreja São Domingos** was built in the 14th century and still has the original transept, rose window and lovely Gothic cloister. The latter houses the Museu Martins Sarmento (open Tues–Sun; closed noon–2pm; entrance charge), with objects from Briteiros (*see below*) and other *citânias* (ancient Iberian fortified villages) of northern Portugal, as well as Roman inscriptions, ceramics and coins.

Continuing along the broad garden called the Alameda da Resistência ao Fascismo, you reach the **Igreja São Francisco**, founded in the 13th century. There is little left of the original Gothic structure, but the sacristy has an impressive 17th-century gilt woodwork and ceiling.

High on the outskirts of the city stands **Santa Marinha da Costa**, founded as a monastery in the 12th century and rebuilt in the 18th century. The church functions regularly and may be visited. The cells of the monastery, which were badly damaged by fire in 1951, have recently been restored and turned into a luxury *pousada*. Visible in the cloisters are a 10th-century Mozarabic arch and vestiges of a 7th-century Visigothic structure. The veranda is decorated with magnificent 18th-century tile scenes and a fountain.

Citânia de Briteiros

After the Briteiros exhibit at the Martins Sarmento museum, you could visit the original site, 11 km (7 miles) north of Guimarães. At first, the **Citânia de Briteiros** ⑳ appears to be nothing more than piles of stones on a hillside, but it is in fact one of Portugal's most important archaeological sites. Here are the remains of a prehistoric fortified village said to have been inhabited by Celts. It was discovered in 1874 by archaeologist Francisco Martins Sarmento.

Map on page 300

A knight rides into battle.

BELOW: the Pousada de Santa Marinha da Costa in Guimarães.

*Splendid wooden
doorway of Braga
Cathedral.*

Near the summit, two round houses have been reconstructed. Also visible are the remains of defensive walls, ancient flagstones and the foundation walls of over 150 houses. The houses were circular with stone benches running around the walls. A large rock in the centre supported a pole which would have held up a thatched roof. Several of the houses are larger, with two or more rectangular rooms, presumably the homes of prominent members of society. The town evidently had an efficient water system: spring water flowed downhill through gutters carved in the paving stones to a cistern and a public fountain.

Braga

Some people still refer to **Braga** ㉑, somewhat wistfully, as "the Portuguese Rome". In Roman times, as Bracara Augusta, it was the centre of communications in north Lusitania. In the 6th century two synods were held here. Under Moorish occupation, Braga was sacked and the cathedral badly damaged. But in the 11th century, the city was largely restored to its former eminence by Bishop Dom Pedro and Archbishop São Geraldo. The Archbishop claimed authority over all the churches of the Iberian peninsula, and his successors retained the title of Primate of the Spains for six centuries.

Like a Renaissance prince, one of his successors, Archbishop Dom Diogo de Sousa, encouraged the construction of many handsome Italian-style churches, fountains and palaces in the 16th century. Zealous prelates restored many of these works in the subsequent two centuries, but often with unfortunate results. Braga lost its title as ecclesiastical capital in 1716, when the Patriarchate went to Lisbon. But it is still an important religious centre, and the site of Portugal's most elaborate Holy Week procession.

BELOW: the
grand stairway
of Bom Jesus.

A visit to Braga usually begins at the **Sé**, the cathedral built in the 11th century on the site of an earlier structure destroyed by the Moors. Of the original Romanesque building there remains only the southern portal and the sculpted cornice of the transept. Although it has been greatly modified by various restorations, the cathedral is still imposing. The interior contains some fine tombs, including those of the founders, Count Henri and his wife Teresa, a fine granite sculpture of the Virgin, an 18th-century choir loft and organ case, and richly decorated chapels and cloister. The cathedral treasury is now the **Museu d'Arte Sacra** (Museum of Sacred Art; open daily, closed 12.30–2pm; entrance charge), with a fine collection of 15th-century vestments and silver chalices and crucifixes dating from the 10th and 12th centuries.

Nearby, with plain west walls set off by an 18th-century fountain, is the **Palácio de Arzobispo** (Archbishop's Palace), built in the 14th century. It, too, has been reconstructed several times. The palace now houses the Public Library, with city archives dating back to the 9th century, 300,000 volumes and 10,000 manuscripts. On the western side of Praça Agrolongo stands one of Braga's Rome-inspired churches, **Nossa Senhora do Pópulo**, built in the 17th century and remodelled at the end of the 18th. It is decorated with *azulejos* depicting scenes from the life of St Augustine.

The **Casa dos Biscainhos**, across the way, is a 17th-century mansion with lovely garden and fountains. It is now a museum, and the collection includes 18th-century tiles, ceramics, jewellery and furniture. Part of the museum has been set aside for artifacts from recent excavations on the site of a protected zone established in 1977, after some damage from modern construction. The University of Minho is directing the excavations, which have uncovered Roman baths, a sanctuary called Fonte do Idolo and the remains of a house called Domus de Santiago.

On the northern side of the city, the church of **São João de Souto** was completely rebuilt in the late 18th century. But here is the superb **Capela do Conceição**, built in 1525, with crenellated walls, lovely windows and splendid statues of St Anthony and St Paul.

Bom Jesus

There are many other churches and chapels of interest in the religious centre, but the best known is **Bom Jesus ㉒**, which is conspicuously set on the wooded Monte Espinho, about 5 km (3 miles) outside the city. This popular pilgrimage centre is remarkable, not so much for the building but for its grandiose stairway and the view from its terrace of the Rio Cávado valley and the mountains in the distance. The double flight of stairs is flanked by chapels, fountains and often startlingly bizarre figures at each level, representing the Stations of the Cross.

If you don't wish to climb the steps, there's a funicular, and a winding road to the top. There, among oak trees, eucalyptus, camelias and mimosa, stands the 15th-century church, rebuilt in the 18th century. In its **Capela dos Milagres** (Chapel of Miracles) are votive offerings and pictures left by past pilgrims. Several hotels, souvenir shops and restaurants are also located in the vicinity of the sanctuary. ❑

Map on page 300

BELOW: the Café Brasileira in Braga.

TRAS-OS-MONTES

Isolated by distance and mountains, Trás-os-Montes has developed an individuality which distinguishes it from the rest of Portugal

Map on page 312

To most Portugues, the remote northeastern province of Trás-os-Montes ("behind the mountains") could be on the other side of the moon. Most Lisboetas are inclined to look at it as from a vast distance – albeit with fierce affection. The word *"trás"* – "back" or "behind" – fits the region like a glove. Before Portugal joined the EU, this region was backward in almost every aspect: cut off from the rest of the country by mountains, poor road and rail systems, and grinding poverty which has driven the workforce of almost every village to migrate to urban areas, or emigrate to the more advanced economies of northern Europe, or overseas. Now, improved roads, better communications and farming subsidies have led to rapid improvements in living standards, although pockets of poverty still exist.

Regional differences

There has been higher emigration from the north of Portugal than from the south, and one of the principal reasons is the division of land. The south is an area of *latifúndios* – large landholdings – while the north has *minifúndios* – smallholdings. A farmer's land in the north is often insufficient to provide him and his family with a living. The northern people are conservative, and resist such cooperative farming as operates in the southern province of Alentejo. Another reason for *minifúndios* is the terrain – high mountains and steep-sided valleys make it difficult to organise large-scale farming.

A more subtle factor affecting Portugal's conservative north is the Church. While all Portugal is Roman Catholic, the sheer remoteness of the northeast corner has meant that national government has little impact, while tradition and religion predominate. This has affected education, particularly; until recently, often the only educated man in a village was the priest, whose wisdom and opinion would be sought on every matter ranging from the spiritual to crop harvesting.

Geographically, Trás-os-Montes covers the extreme northeast corner of the country, from Bragança in the north to the Rio Douro in the south and, as far as this chapter is concerned, west to Chaves and Montelegre. Climatically, the region is different, too. Cut off from the influence of the Atlantic, it is hotter and drier in summer and colder in winter, especially in the norteastern region which is known as the *Terra Fria*, the cold lands. In contrast, the southern part is called, *Terra Quente*, the warm lands. Vines on a commercial scale are not viable in the *Terra Fria* so their place is taken by grain crops, which changes the landscape appreciably. It remains one of the most interesting areas of the country, for its towns, its countryside and its historical connections.

LEFT: *al fresco* spinning in Barroso.
BELOW: proud of his wooden-wheeled cart.

Who will buy?

Entering the region

You can enter the region, which includes the Alto Douro from a number of directions. Northern border crossings from Spain are at Vila Verde da Raia, on the road leading south to Chaves (this is a historical invasion route – employed by the armies of Napoleon in the early 1800s); at Portelo, in the Parque Natural de Montesinho; from the east at Quintanilha, east of Bragança; and at Miranda do Douro and Bemposta, where the Douro forms the frontier. From inside Portugal, the main routes into the region are from Porto or Lamego via Vila Real; or from Guarda via either Torre de Moncorvo or Freixo de Espada à Cinta.

This itinerary enters the region at Vila Real and follows a meandering route to absorb the sights and atmosphere of the area without ignoring the major points of interest.

Serra de Alvão

Two scenic routes lead north out of Vila Real, one on each side of the high Serra da Padrela – to Chaves in the north, and Bragança in the northeast. But the adventurous traveller may strike northwest into the rugged Serra de Alvão, and be treated to one of the most lavish vistas the country has to offer. The road leads through a small natural park and across the Rio Olo to **Mondim de Basto ❶** on the banks of the Rio Tâmega. There it forms the border between Trás-os-Montes and the Minho.

Granite gives way to slate – many of the houses are roofed by it – and in the high passes you can hear the rushing of mountain waters, the tinkle of goat bells, or the calling of a herder to his dogs. In the winter there is snow here, but at other times of the year you are likely to encounter a profusion of wild flowers and pine forests. Pine resin, which is used in the manufacture of paints and turpentine, is a major product of this area.

A side trip of some 12 km (8 miles) from Mondim de Basto will take you to **Atei ❷**, a delightful little village containing numerous archaeological remnants of Roman occupation. From here a curious subterranean passage of either Roman or Arab construction leads down to Furaco on the banks of the Tâmega.

Leaving Mondim de Basto, the road winds northwards to **Cabeceiras de Basto**, which is actually in the Minho province, at the head of a small "peninsula" that juts up into Trás-os-Montes. Stop at the imposing baroque **Mosteiro Refójos** before heading into the high Serra de Cabreira and back into Trás-os-Montes at Póvoa.

Barroso district

You soon join the main Braga–Chaves road that runs beside **Barragem do Alto Rabagão ❸**, a gigantic expanse of lake formed behind a dam, but here again another side trip could take you north – to Montalegre, the towering Serra do Larouco, and the primitive villages of the Barroso district.

As the largest town in the area, **Montalegre ❹** might be considered the capital of Barroso. Given a charter in 1273 by King Afonso III, and restored and expanded in turn by King Dinis and King Manuel I, Montalegre (*monte* meaning hill, *alegre* meaning happy or cheerful) is thought to have enjoyed its status from a much earlier time, for the pillory in the centre of town carries the coat-of-arms of King Sancho I, who reigned from 1185 to 1211.

The hill on which the town stands commands a view over an extensive area, so it's hardly surprising that this has been a military centre for dozens of centuries. Montalegre is rich in archaeological finds. Ancient Lusitanians, the Romans, Suevi and Visigoths were all here.

BELOW: storks' nest near Bragança.

A magnificent four-towered castle stands at Montalegre, much used during the many wars that Portugal fought against Spain. North of the region rises the **Serra do Larouco**, the second highest range of mountains in the country (after the Serra da Estrela), with a number of passes leading into Spanish Galicia.

The district of Barroso stretches from the foothills of the Serra do Larouco southeast towards the city of Chaves. There is no absolute boundary, but it would include such villages as Meixido, Padornelos and Tourém, to name a few. If you can shut out the "emigrant architecture" – uncontrolled modern housing that is built with money saved by the Portuguese who work abroad – you will find in these settlements a sense of history utterly remote in time.

The ancient houses are built of enormous granite or slate blocks. Doors, windows and balconies are of weathered antique wood. Until recently, many houses were thatched. Once common, dirt streets are rapidly becoming paved, and electricity has only recently been installed. Almost every church is Romanesque, with the typical façade rising to a twin-columned peak to house the church bell.

For centuries the people of Barroso lived out their lives cut off from the outside world. They developed

Map on page 312

their own customs, songs, festivals and habits. In many corners of the world under similar circumstances, local people may treat outsiders with suspicion or alarm. This is certainly not the case in Barroso. It is hard to imagine a more warm-hearted, hospitable people, willing to share the peculiarities of their daily lives with those who come to visit them.

Communal bulls

One of the region's most colourful festivals is the annual **Chega dos Toiros**, an inter-village competition which means "The Arrival of the Bulls". Each village takes enormous pride in its own bull, a communally-owned animal bred especially for the purpose of covering the various cows owned by the individual farmers. This bull, by both tradition and breeding, is the biggest and fiercest animal imaginable, intended as much to gain the honours at the annual competition as it is for stock purposes.

Held in June, July and August, the Chega is essentially a bullfight, where the bull of one village is pitted against another in a fierce battle. Each animal is decorated and fêted by his villagers, and paraded to the accompaniment of noisy bands and crowds. The fight itself is in deadly earnest, with the champions of each bull goading their animal into combat. The fight continues until one animal is injured, or turns and runs. The victor is led away by his villagers with much celebration.

At the end of the season there will be a regional champion, and this is the lucky animal who'll be put out to pasture with the region's cows. He is a source of great pride to the residents of the village from which he comes, even if he doesn't know what all the fuss is about. He's just doing what comes naturally.

BELOW: an example of Barroso's archaic building methods.

Wine of the dead

Boticas ❺ is the place to drink *vinhos mortos*, "wine of the dead". In order to protect their wine stocks from the French during the Peninsular War in the early 1800s, the villagers buried it in the ground. When it was later retrieved, the wine was found to be much improved. The practice is still followed, with good results. For another regional drink, divert a short way west to the spa village of **Carvalhelhos ❻**. The spring water here is particularly sweet and is sold all over the country. Most refreshing is *com gas*, the sparkling version.

Map on page 312

Chaves

Chaves ❼, just a few kilometres down the road from Barroso, seems a world away. An ancient city, the fortified Lusitanian village of the present site was captured by the Romans in the year AD 78. The Emperor Flavius founded the city of *Aqua Flaviae* there, inaugurating the still popular hot springs and baths. Chaves is now a bustling town with a population of about 15,000. An agricultural and textile centre, it is famous for its *presunto*, smoked ham; you could taste it, with a glass of wine, at Faustino's which claims to be the largest taverna, or *tasca,* in Portugal.

Situated on the Rio Tâmega, Chaves commands a strategic position in a wide valley that extends from the Spanish frontier into the heart of Trás-os-Montes. Just about every invader who set his heart on Portugal, or chunks of it, routed his armies through this channel. Thus, at one time or another, Chaves has hosted Celts, Lusitanians, Romans, Vandals, Suevi, Moors, Spanish and French.

Here the Romans built one of the largest of their bridges in the Iberian peninsula. Completed in AD 104, it has 20 arches, is 140 metres (150 yards) in

Dom Afonso, standing proud in the centre of Chaves.

BELOW: a novelty store in Chaves.

length, and is still very much in daily use. In the middle of the bridge are two inscribed Roman milestones.

Chaves means "keys" in Portuguese, but this is probably not what the name is derived from. The ancient *Aqua Flaviae* was much later shortened to *Flavias*, and local mispronunciation eventually produced the current name.

Sights include the parish church, originally rebuilt in the 16th century; and the former Bragança ducal palace, now the Museu Regional, in the **Praça de Camões**. Prior to the formation of Portugal, the fortified city was a part of the original County of Portucale. Various of Portugal's early kings added significantly to its castle, one of the most important in the land. A second castle, in its day also an integral part of the defences of this strategic valley, still stands at **Monforte ⑧**, about 12 km (8 miles) northeast.

East from Chaves

Heading eastwards towards Bragança you will pass the old town of **Vinhais ⑨**. Its castle is barely more than a ruin, though there was a significant population here. The town is set high in the Serra de Montesinho, on the south flank of the **Parque Natural de Montesinho ⑩**, a wildly rugged park, the habitat of wolves, boars and foxes. The area survives on agriculture, particularly vines, woodwork, weaving and basket-making.To explore the region, first stop at the tourist office in Bragança and ask for a book about the park, which contains a detailed map of the area. Not all of the roads are paved. Whichever direction you take, you will have a journey through spectacular country.

A mountain, **Cidadela**, rises behind Vinhais. Over it passed the Roman road that led from Braga to Astorga; today this ancient route is rich in archaeologi-

BELOW: the Corgo railway runs from Chaves to Régua.

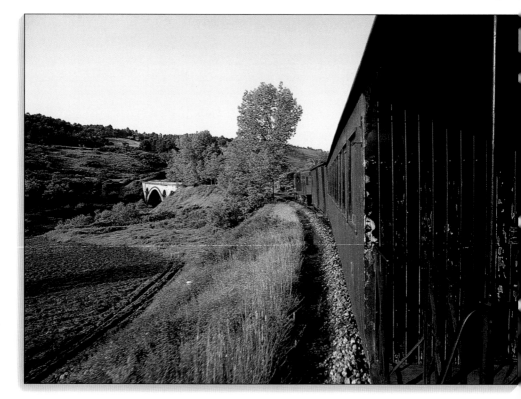

cal discoveries. In the 11th and 12th centuries there was a general movement by the population of this area towards the more fertile farm lands of the south. To prevent this, various monasteries were founded and encouraged by the early rulers of the region to develop their own agriculture and cottage industries.

One of the most important of these was the **Mosteiro de Castro de Avelãs ⓫**, a few miles west of Bragança. Parts of the church of the Benedictine abbey have been incorporated into the present-day parish church.

Bragança: a fascinating city

With a population of some 30,000, **Bragança ⓬** is the administrative capital, a university town, and also an agricultural trade centre (livestock, vineyards, olive oil, grains). It has a thriving textile industry, and has been famous for its ceramics since prehistoric times (in a nearby cave at Dine, archaeologists have found pottery dating from the Paleolithic period).

Known as *Brigantine* to the Celts and *Juliobriga* to the Romans, Bragança received its first *foral* (royal charter) from King Sancho I in 1187 – when the family from which the dukes of Bragança are descended started building their feudal castle there. The Braganças – still pretenders to the throne of Portugal – provided the land's kings and queens consistently from 1640 until the formation of the Republic in 1910, and the emperors of Brazil from 1822 to 1889. In 1662, Catherine of Bragança, daughter of the first Bragança king João IV, became Queen to Charles II of England, thus renewing the long alliance between the two nations. Since the fall of the monarchy, a foundation, the Fundação da Casa de Bragança, has managed all royal properties including the family's 16th-century ducal palace in Vila Viçosa.

Map on page 312

BELOW: Bragança's medieval skyline.

Bragança's ancient castle still stands – with a Princess's Tower full of tragic ghosts. The keep of the castle houses a military museum. You can also see an unusual medieval *pelourinho* (or pillory), its shaft piercing a granite boar. Nearby, still within the castle walls, you will find the 12th-century five-sided **Domus Municipalis**, the oldest municipal hall in the land. The town walls with their 18 watchtowers are still largely intact, and the city has a fine cathedral and fascinating museum, the **Museu do Abada de Baçal** (open Tues–Sun; closed 12.30–2pm; entrance charge) in what used to be the Bishop's Palace.

You will see people in the fields working with traditional agricultural tools, beasts of burden and wooden-wheeled carts – things that are rarely seen in the rest of Europe.

Excursions north

Basing yourself in this historic city, it is relatively easy to make short day trips out into the surrounding region.

First, to the north, in the farthest corner of Portugal, there is **Rio de Onor ⓭**, a tiny village that straddles the border with Spain. Only recently, after a rare presidential visit, did the village acquire its first bus service. The people of Rio de Onor developed their own dialect and intricate communal social system. In their music and folk dances a common instrument is the *gaiteiro* – a bagpipe, with Celtic associations similar to those of Scotland and Ireland.

A good time to visit the villages that extend in an arc from Vinhais, across Bragança, and down as far as Miranda do Douro and Freixo de Espada-à-Cinta, is between Christmas Day and Epiphany (6 January), when the local population celebrates a number of feasts connected with the Christian calendar – but incorporating ferocious masks and unearthly costumes. These celebrations date back to the dawn of time, when the agrarian people of these pastoral regions practised fertility rites and paid more than passing attention to magic. Carnival, in

BELOW: a woman carries a traditional farm implement.

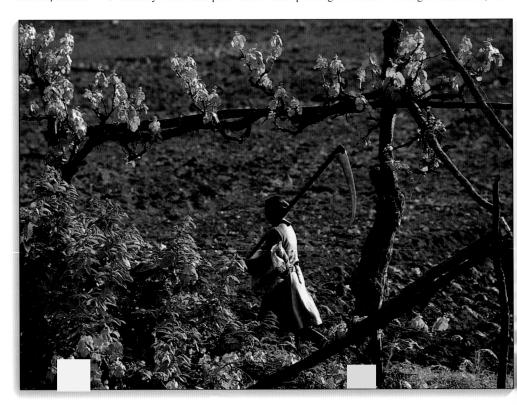

February, is another good time to visit. Forty days before Easter the masks come out again, and you cannot be sure if it is the Christian spirit or the bogey-man that dominates the season. As in so many places, the Catholic Church incorporated pagan elements in order to appease the local people, and the rites became entangled.

Map on page 312

Excursions south

South of Bragança you may head towards the Spanish frontier at **Miranda do Douro** ⓮. This fortified town sits above a craggy gorge overlooking the Douro. Like many of the country's border towns, it has suffered a turbulent history in its attempts to keep out the Spanish. These days invaders from across the river are welcomed with open arms – provided they bring a supply of pesetas.

Fifteenth-century houses with granite doorways, a 16th-century cathedral with a sequence of gilded wood altarpieces, an excellent folk museum, the **Museu da Torre de Miranda** (open Tues–Sun; closed noon–2pm; entrance charge), and the medieval street called the Rua da Costanilha make it a worth-while stop.

It is possible to make a circular tour by following the road on to sleepy **Mogadouro** ⓯, which slumbers in the shadow of a 12th-century castle built by King Dinis on earlier Roman foundations.

If you like castles, you will not want to miss the impressive ruins at **Algoso** ⓰, on the way back to **Vimioso** ⓱. Since the 12th century, this fortress has guarded the area surrounding its lofty perch – a hill called Cabeça da Penenciada – while 500 metres (1,650 ft) below, the Rio Angueira flows west-wards until it joins the Rio Maçãs. ❏

FOLLOWING PAGES: the hill village of Monsanto in Beira Baixa. **BELOW:** the church at Miranda do Douro.

BEIRA ALTA AND BEIRA BAIXA

Map on page 324

This is region of extreme contrasts, incorporating the Serra da Estrela (the highest mountain range in Portugal), an area of cattle-raising plains, and a line of defensive castles

The provinces of Beira Alta and Beira Baixa, the Upper and Lower Beiras, constitute a large rural section of eastern Portugal – a modest and hardy geographical region in a country that is among the poorest in Western Europe. But it is rich historically, marked over centuries by the invasion routes of both the Spanish and Moors, in defensive castles and remnants of fortresses. The area has its natural attractions as well: the dramatic mountains of the Serra da Estrela and the stark plains and plateaux of the Baixa are some of the most beautiful natural landmarks in Portugal. The region is bounded by the Spanish frontier to the east, the Rio Douro to the north, and the Tagus to the south. The western boundary is a ragged line 60 km (38 miles) east of Oporto.

Beira Alta

Guarda ❶ is the principal city and administrative capital of the Beira Alta's eastern district. The charter of Guarda was granted by Sancho I, Portugal's second king, in 1199, although the city had been established by 80 BC, when it had a role in the attempted secession from Rome. There are still traces of Roman occupation: ruins of the period can be found just outside town, near the Romanesque chapel of Póvoa de Mileu, notable itself for a small rose window and nicely carved capitals. Three town gates from the 12th- and 13th-century castle and town walls still stand: the Torre de Ferreiros (Blacksmiths' Tower), the Porta da Estrela (Star Gate), and the Porta do Rei (King's Gate), along with the castle keep. From the top there is a magnificent view of the mountains, and the broad plains to the north.

The **Sé** (**Cathedral**) was built of granite cut from the surrounding area. An earlier cathedral, close to the city's original walls, was destroyed before this one was begun, because it was believed to be in an unsafe position. Work on this "new" edifice started in 1390 and was not completed until 1540, so that there were many Renaissance and baroque elements added to the original Gothic architecture. The renowned builder Diogo Boytac (1494–1520) worked on the cathedral, which bears some resemblance to Batalha. The exterior has flying buttresses and fanciful gargoyles. Inside, the 16th-century stone *retábulo*, later highlighted with gilt, represents scenes in the life of Christ; the stone carving is the work of João de Ruão, also known as Jean de Rouen (1530–70). A beautiful Renaissance doorway, off the north aisle, leads to the Capela dos Pinas, which contains the late Gothic tomb of a bishop.

LEFT: in the Serra da Estrela.
BELOW: a local sanctuary.

Guarda has been dubbed the city of four Fs – *fria, farta, forte e feia*, which means: cold, plentiful, strong and ugly. The predominance of heavy grey granite may be ugly to some, but the old parts of the city are pleasant. Strong alludes to Guarda's history as a defence point against the Moors and Castile. Plentiful refers, no doubt, to the rich land surrounding the town, noted particularly for its sheep farming. Cold it certainly is, in winter: situated some 1,066 metres (3,500 ft) above sea level, Guarda is Portugal's highest city – high enough for frost and snow during winter months.

Around Guarda

South of Guarda lie two handsome castle-towns: on the main road to Castelo Branco is **Belmonte ❷**, birthplace of Alvares Cabral, who discovered Brazil, and on the narrower N233 is **Sabugal**. About half-way between the two is the oddly enchanting **Sortelha ❸**, a tiny village with a castle surrounded by rocky crags, within a "magic ring" of stone. Ancient civilisations may have shaped

Beira Alta and Beira Baixa

Map on page 324

some of the rocks, and they certainly mined in the area – there are entrances to mines that have been closed for centuries.

Stretching southwest is the **Serra da Estrela**, the highest mountains in the country and the source of Portugal's most highly-rated cheese. The highest point is the over-commercialised **Torre ❹**, at nearly 2,000 metres (6,500 ft). Nearby is a pilgrimage site, a statue of the Virgin carved into the rock, to which the faithful journey on the second Sunday of August.

The Serra offers skiing in winter and pleasant walking (or driving) with grand views in all directions. The prime winter resort is **Covilhã ❺**, southeast of Torre. It is too low to receive much snow itself, but it is a short drive to the ski area at **Penhas da Saúde ❻**.

Viseu: hub of Beira Alta

The western district of Beira Alta is governed by the city of **Viseu ❼**, about halfway between Guarda and Aveiro. In the 2nd century BC the Romans built a fortified settlement here, and some of their road system can still be seen, along with a number of Latin-inscribed stones.

A thorn in the side of the colonisers was a rebel Lusitanian named Viriathus, who harassed Roman legions until he was finally betrayed and killed. A monument to him lies at the edge of a park – the Cova do Viriato – on the site of a Lusitanian and Roman military encampment. Here, you can still see the old earthworks once used by the Romans. Viseu was made a bishopric during the 6th century AD, the time of the Suevian-Visigothic kingdom, and a record still exists: a signature of the Bishop of Viseu, dated AD 569.

The city suffered alternating invasions of Moors and Christians from the 8th to the 11th century. Fernando the Great of Castile and León captured it for the Christians in 1057. Teresa, mother of the first king of Portugal, granted the city its first charter in 1123. From the 14th to the 16th century, building in Viseu seems to have been concentrated in the upper part of town. About this time an active Jewish colony evolved here. In 1411 the Infante Dom Henrique (Prince Henry the Navigator) became Duke of Viseu, and towards the end of that century the town walls were completed. But the surrounding area was becoming a centre of vigorous agricultural activity, and by the 16th century the walled area was becoming depleted.

Perhaps this was fortunate, because over the next two centuries much of this space was filled with a lavish assortment of baroque churches, chapels, mansions and fountains. Today the architectural richness lends a dignified air to the enclosed city.

Pure baroque

You should not miss the 13th-century **Sé** (**Cathedral**). The ribbed vaulting is beautifully carved to look like knotted cables, and the ceiling of the sacristy is extravagantly painted with animals and plants. The twin-towered **Igreja da Misericórdia** across the square is whitewashed granite and pure baroque. You should also save some time for the **Museu Grão Vasco** (open Tues–Sun; entrance charge), in the old

BELOW:
a woman with
her faithful friend.

Bishop's Palace in the same square. Many of the works represent the fine school of Portuguese Primitive painting that flourished here in the 16th century, and of which Grão Vasco Fernandes (*see page 125*) was the acknowledged master.

The **Feira de São Mateus**, the fair held annually in August and September, is a major event in Viseu, and St John the Baptist is celebrated on 24 June. A Tuesday market is held all year round, with plenty of fresh produce, cloth, pots and pans, and crafts. Viseu is well-known for its lace, carpets, and black pottery.

Around Viseu

Successive members of Portugal's royal family used to visit the spa at São Pedro do Sul, but whether it cured what ailed them is not known.

Northwest of Viseu is the small town of São Pedro do Sul and, some 4 km (2½ miles) southwest, the **Termas de São Pedro do Sul** ❽ – possibly the oldest, the best known and most frequented hot springs in the country. Sinus problems, rheumatism, hangovers or a foul temper – the springs are said to cure all ailments. There are other delightful villages in the area, too. Just south of São Pedro do Sul is **Vouzela** ❾, with a lovely 13th-century church, and close by is the village of **Cambra**, clustered around the remnants of its castle.

South of Viseu, just off the secondary road to Nelas, **Santar** ❿ is a little gem of a place, once known as "the Court of the Beiras". Due south you'll find **Oliveira do Hospital** ⓫, a small town which once belonged to the Hospitallers. As a mark of this, tombs of the Ferreiros in the parish church (the Igreja Matriz) are crowned by a carving of an equestrian knight on the wall above.

To the southwest (continue down the main road in the direction of Coimbra), in the village of **Lourosa** ⓬, is the ancient church of São Pedro. King Ordoño II ordered its construction in 911; it has a central nave, horseshoe arches, Moorish windows, and Visigothic decoration.

BELOW: a wall of *azulejos* in Viseu.

Beira Baixa

Travelling south now toward the Beira Baixa, you come to the Rio Zêzere, which roughly divides Beira Alta from Beira Baixa.The river flows most swiftly from early April to late June. A good place for water sports is the **Barragem de Castelo do Bode**, a long, many-armed lake that runs south into the province of Ribatejo. (The most direct route is to take the IC3/N110, then turn left about 8 km/5 miles south of Tomar.) Both the river and the lake have fine fishing, with canoeing in places.

The Rio Tejo (Tagus) marks the southern limit of Beira Baixa. Upstream the Tejo crosses into Spain. On both sides of the border, is desolate scrub country. The gorge formed by the river is steep-sided and virtually inaccessible for vehicles other than four-wheel-drives. Along much of the Portuguese side of the river runs an ancient Roman road. Originally it was the route from Vila Velha de Rodão to the Spanish town of Santiago de Alcántara. Water now conceals large chunks of the work, but where the road rises above the surface, you will see that instead of building the road with flat stones, the entire way is paved with local slate stood on edge, its upper surfaces rutted by centuries of cart traffic.

Castelo Branco: ancient capital

The capital of Beira Baixa is **Castelo Branco** ⑬ (25,000 inhabitants), which stands at the junction of the IP2/E802 and the N112. It is an ancient city whose origins, like those of so many communities in Portugal, are lost in time. Its "modern" history dates back to 1182, when it and the surrounding area were given as a gift to the Knights Templar by Dom Fernão Sanches. It received a charter in 1213, and became a city in 1771, in the reign of José I.

The battlements of the old Templar castle – the "white castle" which gave the city its name – provide a fine view, though the castle itself is not noteworthy. The old town is delightful, with narrow winding streets. Points of interest include two churches, São Miguel, and Misericórdia Velha, the latter a 16th-century structure with a notable doorway; and the **Praça Velha**, also known as the Praça de Camões – a fine medieval square off which you can find the ancient municipal library.

The most important thing to see in Castelo Branco is the splendid **Palácio Episcopal**, built on the orders of the Bishop of Guarda, in 1596. It served as the winter residence of the bishops of the diocese. It now houses the **Museu de Francisco Tavares Proença Júnior** (open Tues–Sun; closed noon–2pm; entrance charge), which displays archaeological and regional items, but is most interesting for its large collection of *colchas*, the beautiful hand-embroidered bedspreads for which the town is famous.

In 1725, Bishop João de Mendonça commissioned a garden to be laid out at the side of the palace. Athough it is not very large – you can walk around it in a matter of minutes – it is considered one of Portugal's finest formal gardens, and it is an extraordinary sight, with a multitude of statues, fountains and pools.

These statues are all named, and have been placed in homage to just about everybody and everything the

BELOW: there are numerous pretty villages in the region, including Monsanto.

Map on page 324

bishops thought important: the kings of Portugal, of course (the two hated Spanish rulers of Portugal, Felipe I and II, are represented, but by smaller figures); the saints, apostles and evangelists, along with the virtues; and the seasons of the year, the signs of the zodiac and the elements of the firmament. There once were even more statues, but the invading French armies of 1807 carted off the best. The plinths have been left standing in their places, in many cases with the name of the missing item clearly engraved.

If you have been impressed by the bedspreads you saw in the museum, you might be inspired to buy a modern version to take home with you. Since the 17th century it has been the custom for brides-to-be to hand-embroider their wedding bedspreads. From this practice and skill, a cottage industry was born. Traditionally the spreads were white, but in recent years, they have become available in interwoven colours. Earlier patterns were geometric, echoing Persian carpets, but other decorative themes have become popular as well.

Monsanto: the typical village

From Castelo Branco it is easy to get to **Idanha-a-Velha** ⑭, northeast of the city. This was an Episcopal See until 1199, when the See was moved to Guarda. There remains a strange, ancient basilica with dozens of Roman inscriptions inside. It is said that Wamba, the legendary king of the Visigoths, was born here. A Roman bridge in the village is still in use, and various coins, pottery and bones have been found.

BELOW: the garden of Castelo Branco's Palácio Episcopal.

Nearby is the granite village of **Monsanto** ⑮, once declared "the most typical Portuguese village", with many of its houses tucked between giant boulders. Built around and atop a steep rocky mass in a broad valley some 50 km (30

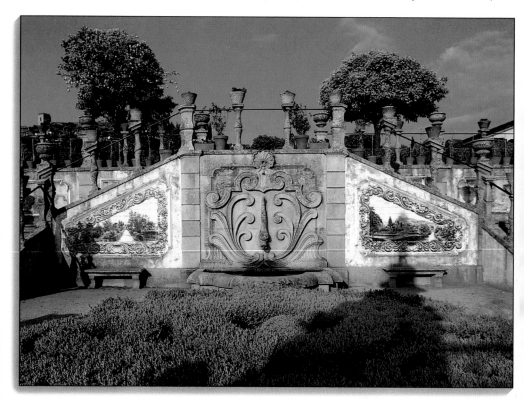

miles) northeast of Castelo Branco, Monsanto is located in the middle of a major invasion route. Its intriguing castle commands a superlative view in every direction. It is thought that this *monte* has been fortified since neolithic times, and the castle is so well integrated into the natural rock it looks as if it grew here.

Map on page 324

Some say it was during the Roman invasion in the 2nd century BC, others claim it was some 1400 years later during a Moorish invasion, that the people of Monsanto, under a long siege and nearly out of food, fooled their attackers by killing a calf, filling its belly with rice, and hurling it off the ramparts to the soldiers below. The attackers were so impressed with the evidence of ample supplies that they packed up and left. Today one of the biggest feast days is the 3rd May, when young villagers toss down pitchers filled with flowers from the battlements, symbolically re-enacting the event.

Much of the castle was destroyed at the beginning of the 19th century. One Christmas Eve there was a tremendous thunderstorm, and a bolt of lightning hit the gunpowder magazine. The gunpowder exploded, and the irons flew from the hearth and struck dead the governor, and unpopular figure who that year had forbidden the traditional burning of a tree trunk in front of the parish church. Divine retribution, the people of the village believed.

The folk music of the Monsanto area is charming if strange. Half chanted, half sung, there is nothing quite like it elsewhere in the country. Its rhythm is beaten out with the assistance of a square tambourine known as an *adufe*.

The great Idanha plain stretches south from here, beyond Castelo Branco, where there are large areas of pine and eucalyptus. It's a vast area of cattle-raising country: bitterly cold in winter, scorching hot in the summer months, it is not a region that is much visited by tourists.   ❑

BELOW: ruins of the fortifications at Monsanto.

MADEIRA

Map on page 334

The archipelago has an individuality that marks it off from the rest of Portugal. Its beauty is varied, from the flowery elegance of Funchal to the remote inland craters

The discovery of the Madeiran archipelago, 608 km (380 miles) west of Morocco, was an early triumph for the ambitious seafaring inspired by Prince Henry the Navigator. In 1418, while sailing south to explore the West African coast, the caravels of João Gonçalves Zarco and Tristão Vaz Teixeira were blown west by storms – eventually finding shelter on a low-lying, uninhabited island they gratefully called Porto Santo (Holy Port). Two years later the navigators returned, to discover a large mountainous island 37 km (23 miles) to the southwest which they named Ilha da Madeira – the Island of Wood.

Modern explorers, now arriving by jet and cruise ship, will find Madeira is still a wild and idyllic place to visit. Its great forests may have gone – burnt down by the first settlers with fires that got out of control and are said to have raged for years – but man has contributed his own wonders to an Atlantic island whose natural splendour has earned it such titles such as "God's Botanical Gardens" and "The Floating Flower-pot".

The city of Funchal

A statue of Zarco now stands as a central landmark in **Funchal ❶**, the capital of Madeira and home to a third of the 280,000 islanders. The city squats in the centre of a wide bay on the sunnier south side of the island, its name inspired by the wild fennel (*funcho*) that the discoverers found growing on the surrounding plain. Behind it rises an amphitheatre of terraced hills and mountains that provides shelter from the north-easterly winds that frequently blow over the island – rain, storms and consolatory rainbows are the price you pay for Madeira's splendid verdancy.

New Year's Eve is the best time to appreciate Funchal's panoramic setting, and the climax in a busy calendar of island festivities. On that night the bay is crowded with brightly-illuminated cruise liners and pleasure boats, and the city is adorned with Christmas decorations and a haze of 300,000 coloured lights. At midnight Funchal erupts – as if sending some hedonistic signal to outer space – in a cacophony of fog-horns, sirens, fireworks and flashing lights. Up on hotel rooftops sunseeking Finns embrace overwintering English aristocrats, while in the streets below families celebrate the annual return of the emigrants from Venezuela or South Africa with dancing, wine and specially-made editions of the islanders' rich molasses-based cake, *bolo de mel*.

If you can't get to this party, there are plenty of other memorable ways to appreciate the island capital. Cruise ship passengers and tourists with limited time usually settle for the two essential Madeiran experiences, the Monte toboggan ride and tea at Reid's

PRECEDING PAGES: fertile islands in the Atlantic.
LEFT: seafront at Funchal, with Reid's Hotel at the far end.
BELOW: face beaten by the Atlantic sun.

Madeira

0   10 km

0   10 miles

N

Ilha do Porto Santo **14**
Serra de Dentro
Camacha
Campo de Cima
15 Vila Baleira
Ponta
Ilhéu de Baixo ou da Cal

Arquipélago da Madeira

A T L A N T I C   O C E A N

Deserta Grande **16**
Ilhas Desertas
Bugio **17**

Ponta de São Lourenço

Ilha da Madeira

Ponta de São Jorge
São Jorge
Santana
Faial
Arco de São Jorge
9
Ponta Delgada
Seixal
7
São Vicente
Ribeira da Janela
Porto Moniz
Ponta do Tristão
Achadas da Cruz
Ponta do Pargo
8
Ponta do Pargo
Fajã a Ovelha
Paúl do Mar
Jardim do Mar
Calheta
Magdalena do Mar
Arco da Calheta
Canhas
Estreito da Calheta
Prazeres
Ramal
Ruivo do Paúl 1640
Parque Natural da Madeira
Ruivo 1320
Serra da Água
Paúl da Serra
Boca de Encumeada 1007
12 Curral das Freiras
6 Ribeira Brava
Campanário
Cabo Girão
Câmara de Lobos **3**
Ponta da Cruz
Ponta do Garajau
CPico Ruivo 1862
4 Pico do Areeiro 1818
5
10 Santo António da Serra
Ribeiro Frio
São Roque
Porto da Cruz
Cancal
Machico **13**
Água de Pena
Santa Cruz
Gaula
Caniço
Monte **2**
Camacha **11**
1 Funchal

Madeira

Lisboa

A T L A N T I C   O C E A N

Madeira

Hotel. The first of these involves driving up to **Monte ❷**, a cool and leafy hill-top resort with *quintas*, sanatoriums and chapels once frequented by the ailing rich, titled exiles and upper-class travellers in need of a brief period of respite. From here you can descend to Funchal by *carro de cesto*, a kind of wicker sofa attached to wooden runners that is guided down the steep lanes by a pair of drivers wearing boaters and white flannels. This unique form of transport was invented by an English resident looking for a speedy way to get down to his office from his *quinta* (don't ask if he had been at the Madeira when he had the idea) and is similar to the tobòggan runs once used around the island to slide farm produce grown on the terraces to the harbours below.

Tea at **Reid's Hotel** is far less strenuous, and simply involves climbing into a wicker armchair, ordering a pot of Earl Grey tea and some crustless cucumber sandwiches, then falling asleep with a copy of yesterday's *Times* over your face. A world-famous five-star hotel with a prestigious site overlooking Funchal harbour, Reid's was opened in 1891 to cater for the growing number of well-to-do visitors to the island – particularly the British who liked to stop over en route to and from their colonies.

Their presence on the island has proved influential in many ways – besides endorsing Madeira's reputation as a refined holiday destination acclaimed for its civility and hospitality, the English taste for cane furniture, acquired in the Orient, stimulated the islands' wicker industry. Centred on the eastern town of Camacha (*see page 339*), this now employs some 2,000 islanders. Another important cottage industry, the production of an intricate and understandably expensive kind of embroidery (*bordados*), is also indebted to an Englishwoman, Elizabeth Phelps, who introduced it to supplement local incomes after disease devastated the island's vines, with disastrous effects on the islanders' living standards, in the 1850s.

Lomquats and scabbard fish

Funchal's true pleasures, however, are not its nostalgic tourist attractions, which can get crowded and histrionic, but the more modest sights woven into the everyday life of the city. A visit to its cornucopious **Mercado dos Lavradores** (Workers' Market) costs nothing – unless, of course, you are tempted to buy some lomquats, tomarillos, pittangas or any of the many other exotic fruits and vegetables now grown on or imported to the island.

Venture into the Mercado's inner halls and you can gaze in safety upon the gloriously ugly *espada* (scabbard fish) that frequently features on Madeiran menus (not to be confused with the equally common traditional dish called *espetada* – beef cooked on a skewer over a wood fire scented with laurel twigs). Despite its vicious teeth and eel-like appearance, *espada* tastes good and is something of a rarity as it is only caught here and off the coast of Japan. The most important catch in the archipelago, the fish lives at a depth of up to 760 metres (2,500 ft) and is hunted year-round by fishermen from **Câmara de Lobos ❸**, just west of Funchal. They use lines with baited hooks and flies spaced at regular intervals that can be over 1.6 km (1 mile) in length.

Map on page 334

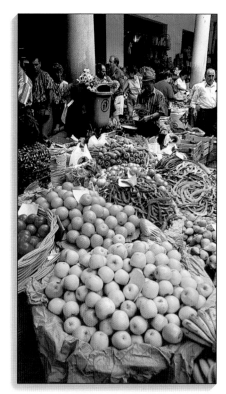

BELOW: Funchal's Mercado dos Lavradores.

You'll find flowers for sale in many corners of Funchal.

For a rewarding insight into Madeira's past, there are two places which are worth a visit: one is the **Museu de Fotografia Vicentes** in Rua da Carreira (open Tues–Sun; closed noon–2pm; entrance charge), which houses a collection of old photographs of life on the island as recorded since 1865 by the Vicente family. The second is the **Quinta das Cruzes** (Calada do Pico 1), a stately home once owned by a wine-shipping family and now packed with art treasures. The *quinta's* attractive gardens stay open throughout the lunch break, and are one of several exotic oases around the city, the largest being the **Jardim Botânico** (Botanical Gardens), which you will find on Caminho do Meio.

Most of Madeira's hotels are located in a zone on the west side of the capital – only a short bus or taxi ride away from Funchal's main square, **Praça do Município**. Decorously paved with black and white stones, this is bordered by imposing buildings with whitewashed façades and dark basalt outlines that remind visitors how church and state have lorded it over this Portuguese outpost. A Jesuit church and college, founded in 1569, fills its north side, while the 18th-century **Câmara Municipal** (Town Hall) to the east was once the palace of the Conde de Carvalhal. The Count's country residence was at **Quinta do Palheiro Ferreiro**, 8 km (5 miles) east of Funchal, which is now a 320-hectare (800-acre) estate owned by the Blandy family, with magnificent gardens open to the public.

On the south side of Praça do Município, the former Bishop's Palace houses Madeira's principal art museum, the **Museu de Arte Sacra** (Museum of Sacred Art). Amongst its exhibits is a fine collection of 15th- and 16th-century Flemish paintings acquired during the island's profitable trade in sugar with Flanders. "White gold" was the spur that provoked Madeira's rapid colonisation – by the 1450s merchants from Lisbon had established lucrative plantations on the island, worked by slaves brought over from Africa and the nearby Canary Islands, 416 km (260 miles) to the south. By the 17th century, most of Madeira's terraces had been given over to producing its eponymous fortified wine, originally derived from Cretan vines introduced to the island by Henry the Navigator. Amongst these was the sweet *malvoisie* grape, which gave rise to the malvasia or malmsey wines that so besotted Europe in the 16th century. In Shakespeare's *Henry IV*, Falstaff is accused of selling his soul for "a cup of Madeira and a cold capon's leg".

Map on page 334

Wine routes

Madeira's fortunes have long been entwined with those of its famous sherrylike drink, and the names of English, Scottish and Irish immigrant families like Leacock, Cossart, Gordon and Blandy have become synonymous with its history. In the 18th century it was discovered that long sea voyages through the heat of the tropics, far from spoiling the wine, improved its quality. This lengthy process of maturation that has now been replaced by the *estufagem* system, where the young wine is stored in hot-houses (*estufas*) for several months. Four main types of Madeira are produced today: a dry *Sercial* and medium-dry *Verdelho*, both ideal as aperitifs, and the richer *Bual* and dark, sweet *Malmsey*, both often served with desserts.

Madeira wine travels well and keeps well, and few visitors leave for home without a bottle or two. Funchal has many invitingly fusty wine lodges and tasting bars where you can indulge in some serious research. **D'Oliveiras** and **Henriques & Henriques**, both in Rua dos Ferreiros, are two worth seeking

BELOW: into the mountains.

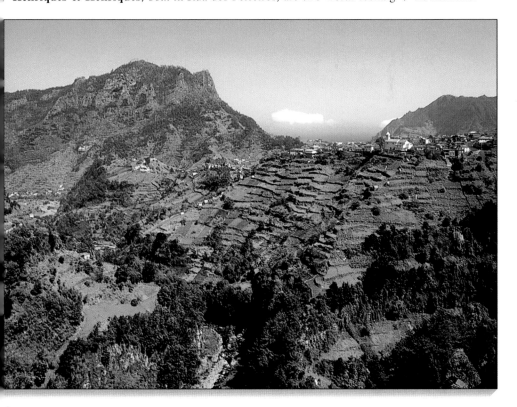

out, though the best initiation into the history and production of Madeira wine is provided by the **Adegas de São Francisco** (Avenida Arriaga 28).

Take any road out of Funchal, and the arduous work required to produce the island's wines, fruit and other crops soon becomes apparent. The true heroes of Madeiran history are its farm labourers and their enslaved predecessors, who over the centuries have toiled to win cultivable land from the island's steep and irregular terrain. Unaided by beasts of burden, who cannot keep a steady foothold on the sheer cliffs and valley walls, workers have resolutely sculpted the island with staircases of tiny stone-walled fields – sometimes built by suspending men on ropes from above, with baskets of soil carried up from the river beds far below. These *poios*, or terraces, are fed by a phenomenal network of irrigation channels, known as *levadas*, that today run for over 2,000 km (1,240 miles), including 40 km (25 miles) through tunnels.

The maintenance paths running alongside the irrigation channels or levadas *that water the terraces provide long, level walks into the silent heart of Madeira, with the stream of water serving as a faithful companion.*

Peaks, cliffs and villages

Even without the terracing that has transformed the island's landscape into a precipitous work of art, Madeira would be staggeringly attractive. A range of volcanic mountains runs east–west across the island, rising to a central conference of peaks of which the highest is **Pico Ruivo ❹** at 1,800 metres (6,000 ft). The nearby summit of **Pico do Arieiro ❺**, which can be comfortably reached by car, provides a physical and spiritual high point. From here, providing you have prayed away the clouds, you can follow an exhilarating on-top-of-the-world path across the peaks to **Achada do Teixeira**.

From all sides of these central mountains, deep ravines run seawards to boulder-strewn beaches where small villages have grown up – most spectacu-

BELOW:
traditional lifestyles
prevail in Santana.

larly at **Ribeira Brava ❻** and **São Vicente ❼**, directly opposite each other on the south and north coasts respectively. The ridges above them invariably culminate in sheer cliffs that are among the highest in the world. If you have the head for it, a viewing platform at **Cabo Girão** enables visitors to contemplate a vertical drop of 580 metres (1,900 ft).

Along Madeira's wild north coast, narrow roads have been stitched into the cliffsides, threading through tunnels, round hairpin bends and under waterfalls that provide a free and unexpected car wash. **Porto Moniz ❽**, a remote and weatherbeaten town on the island's northwestern tip with a couple of small hotels, fish restaurants and volcanic rock sea pools, provides a welcome goal for adventurous motorists searching for the raw side of Madeira.

For all this natural drama, Madeira is a fundamentally benign and relaxing island. Blessed with fertile soil, abundant water and an equable subtropical climate, the countryside is graced with a profusion of native plants and flowers that have been supplemented by exotic imports. The island is a heaven for walkers and the botanically-inclined, with the mountain pass at **Boca da Encumeada** and the **Parque das Queimadas** popular starting points for hikers.

Getting around the island used to be hard work, but with the advent of new roads (including a motorway), purpose-built viewpoints and a plethora of old footpaths, Madeira's appeal is widening. Driving along some of the older intestinal roads can still be tiring and time-consuming, but it is possible to stay overnight at one of several mountain *pousadas* and there is now a good small hotel in virtually every village on the island.

Among the most popular points of call are the village of **Santana ❾**, on the northern coast, where the islanders' traditional A-shaped thatched cottages have been colourfully restored; the forest resort of **Ribeiro Frio ❿** on a winding road which traverses the island between Funchal and Santana; and, closer to the capital, the wicker-making centre of **Camacha ⓫** towards the east of the island.

Off the beaten track

Like all good islands, Madeira has plenty of secrets. An easy and worthwhile trip from Funchal is up to **Curral das Freiras ⓬** (Corral of the Nuns), a secluded crater-like valley that until the late 1950s could only be reached by the narrow mountain paths that still snake down its sides. It gets its name from the nuns of Funchal's Santa Clara convent, who fled here in 1566 when French pirates sacked the capital. Another pleasant surprise lies to the west of Ribeira Brava – a plateau of austere and often misty moorland known as the **Paúl da Serra**, where a tiny white statue, Nossa Senhora da Serra, supervises the grazing sheep and cows.

The east side of Madeira is less mountainous and is consequently the most developed part of the island. Here you can find the airport, two golf courses, stretches of intensive farmland and **Machico ⓭**, which can claim to be Madeira's second city even though it only has 13,000 inhabitants, one high-rise hotel and a seafront commandeered by a sandy football pitch.

Map on page 334

Basket-making is a traditional industry on Madeira.

BELOW: a classic A-shaped cottage in Santana.

Map
on page
334

*São Lourenco
fortress in Funchal.*

RIGHT: a willow-
worker in Curral
das Freiras.
BELOW: splashes of
vivid bougainvillea.

In the northeastern corner of the island the mood changes again as the land narrows to a low-lying, sandy peninsula called **Ponta de São Lourenço**, reached through a tunnel to the north of Machico. Here Caniçal was, until 1981, the island's principal whaling station.

Continue to the end of the headland, which offers good views and blustery walks, and you will often meet old men selling souvenirs carved from redundant stocks of whalebone.

Porto Santo and other islands

The arid landscape of Ponta de São Lourenço provides a foretaste of that found on Madeira's neighbouring island, **Porto Santo ⑭**. The sleepy world of Porto Santo is a relatively accessible one, connected daily by ferry and aeroplane. The island is a complete contrast to Madeira: while the former has a surplus of mountains, water and vegetation but no beaches to speak of, Porto Santo has just a few parched volcanic hills and a south coast that is one long, 7-km (4½-mile) stretch of unspoilt sand. It is as if God was planning to add beaches to Madeira but, like a builder who leaves a pile of sand outside your front door then disappears, He somehow forgot.

This divine oversight is a blessing both for beach-lovers and for connoisseurs of small-island life. Plagued by rabbits and erosion, and vulnerable to attack by pirates, Porto Santo has always been ignored in favour of its lush and fertile neighbour, but it is nevertheles well worth a visit. The capital, **Vila Baleira ⑮**, makes a virtue out of such inertia, and has only recently made efforts to cash in on its most famous resident, Christopher Columbus. The explorer was amongst the many sugar buyers who came to the islands in the 1470s, and later married the daughter of Porto Santo's first governor, Bartolomeu Perestrello.

During the summer, holidaymakers from Funchal and mainland Portugal flock to Porto Santo, giving it the semblance of a seaside resort. But even at the height of the season there is space enough to wander along its magnificent beach – following in the footsteps of Columbus.

Porto Santo is linked underwater to another separate group of islands, the barren **Ilhas Desertas**. Only 16 km (10 miles) southeast of Madeira, they rise as high as 480 metres (1,570 ft) and can easily be seen from the main island's southern shores. Despite repeated attempts over the centuries, settlement of the two islands – **Deserta Grande ⑯** and **Bugio ⑰** – has proved impossible.They are now a nature reserve where seabirds, wild goats, poisonous black spiders and a colony of monk seals live in curious harmony. The Ilhas Desertas can sometimes be visited by boat trips from Funchal, and if you are interested in wildlife and wilderness regions it is worth enquiring at the tourist office.

Another set of islands also belong to the Madeiran archipelago and are even more inhospitable than the Ilhas Desertas. Known as the **Ilhas Selvagens**, these lie 215 km (135 miles) to the south of Madeira. Despite being closer to the Spanish Canaries, they remain under Portuguese jurisdiction. ❏

THE AZORES

Time seems to have stood still in the beautiful Azores islands. Way out in the Atlantic Ocean, they have a character of their own, yet are redolent of Portugal's maritime history

Map
on page
346

T he nine islands of the Azores floating in the Atlantic ocean are gratifyingly rich in romantic history, cryptic legend and stunning natural beauty. You cannot ignore their volcanic origins – deep craters or *caldeiras* are their most outstanding feature. But greenery and trim, patchwork fields impose order and a surprising gentleness. With their tall cliffs and farm-quilted countryside, their tiny homesteads sprinkling the lush landscape, the islands are a magical presence in a volatile ocean.

To Portuguese explorers, who first mapped them in the 15th century, the Azores (Açores in Portuguese) became vital stepping stones in an expanding empire. Christopher Columbus, returning from his momentous 1492 voyage to the New World, took on water at the eastern island of Santa Maria. For centuries the Azores have offered a safe haven and restful stopover to other mariners. This remote island group has an extra dimension if you share the view that the 650-km (400-mile) long archipelago's two tiny, westernmost islands, Flores and Corvo, more than a third of the way across the Atlantic, mark the true outermost limit of Europe. The Azores' capital, Ponta Delgada, is on São Miguel, the largest island in the group. The islands are meteorologically important to weather forecasters – an Azores High (high-pressure area) extending to the east means fine weather for western Europe.

PRECEDING PAGES: fishing boats and houses on São Miguel, the largest island. **LEFT:** patchwork fields on the coast. **BELOW:** a windmill on Faial.

Origins

The name Açores, was bestowed on the archipelago by Gonçalo Velho Cabral who, with Diogo de Silves, landed at Santa Maria in 1427. These daring seafarers mistook the many buzzards there for hawks, which are called *açores* in Portuguese. But from myth, fable and fanciful charts, another legend persists. Here, some believe, is the lost Atlantis, from Plato's account of a sunken empire lying beyond the Pillars of Hercules. Yet chroniclers wrote that all the islands were uninhabited when the Portuguese arrived.

In 1439, settlement officially began on the seven then-known islands (Flores and Corvo were not discovered until 1452) through the efforts of Prince Henry the Navigator. His colonisation policy was so zealous that he offered land to Flemish farmers (the connection was through his sister, Isabel, who was married to the Duke of Burgundy and ruler of Flanders). Prince Henry not only foresaw the role of the islands in his larger purpose of African discovery but, in his businesslike way, realised they could be productive and profitable, and organised the planting of wheat and sugar cane.

Throughout Portuguese history, the islanders have held themselves apart from Lisbon, and have often chosen an opposing path. In the 19th-century War of the Two Brothers – the Miguelist Wars – between two sons of King João VI, islanders supported the liberal Dom Pedro IV against his absolutist brother, Dom Miguel, who had the support of most of Portugal.

Hardy islanders today still live by farming and fishing. There's a significant dairy industry. You'll see cows milked on steep hillsides, their milk occasionally still carried in churns by farmers on horseback. But there are more cerebral pursuits, too, and from the Azores have emerged many of the finest poets, novelists and philosophers in Portuguese culture. One of several daily newspapers, *O Açoriano* is the third oldest in Europe. The islands' identity was established long ago; autonomous government came in 1976, two years after the coup which toppled the dictatorship.

Island attractions

In recent years, the Azores have become a modestly expanding tourist destination. Great for walking holidays, they are full of pleasant surprises, and invite the visitor to explore. In other words, a dream world for anyone seeking unspoilt nature, tranquillity and the chance to "get back to basics". What they are not, though, are bland resorts for sophisticates or sun-worshippers. There are relatively few sandy beaches, and these are mostly volcanic black – which some find oppressive. The weather is mild (the winter averages 14°C/57°F, summer 23°C/74°F) but except for June to September, it is often wet and windy.

Island pleasures are unpretentious and relaxed. You will discover awe-inspiring scenery of stunning beauty, a luxurious vegetation with exotic plants (50 of 850 species are endemic), enchanting lakes amidst extinct craters, tranquil hill country with rolling fields and lush meadows, magnificent coasts lined by

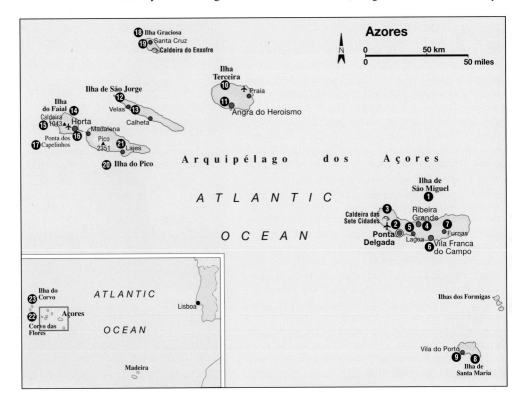

picturesque villages and historical towns, and spectacular hydrangea hedges criss-crossing the landscape. There is also much to see in the daily working life, which has still a rather traditional aspect. Entertainment is generally limited to discos and bars. Custom and religion are served by frequent *festas*, and the striking baroque churches carved from basalt.

On the island of Terceira, gaudy chapels (*impérios*) reflect the islanders' ardour for the Espírito Santo cult, which originated in medieval Germany and was promulgated in Portugal through the teachings of the 17th-century Jesuit priest, António Vieira. On Whit Sunday, the day of the Holy Spirit, there are processions in towns and villages throughout the island, and many villages have regular Sunday celebrations. Local people believe that worship of the Holy Spirit – whose insignia, a crown, sceptre and a white dove are kept in the *impérios* – will protect their communities from volcanic eruptions, earthquakes, and damage from storms.

You can see the relics of a long tradition of whaling, and will encounter the sons and grandsons of whaling men – and, in summer, numerous emigrant families on annual trips home. The Azores are worth a visit even if you only have time to see São Miguel. The Government Tourist Office (*Turismo*) is very friendly and helpful, and the Portuguese Tourist Board in London will provide plenty of information, including a free guide book and a list of accommodation.

The islands are ideal for walking. The more ambitious can climb Pico (Peak) on Pico island: at over 2,300 metres (7,550 ft), this is Portugal's highest mountain, but there are numerous less demanding hikes. Additionally, an expanding number of sports facilities range from deep-sea fishing, whale-watching and diving to golf and tennis.

The islands divide naturally into three groups: São Miguel and Santa Maria in the east; Terceira, São Jorge, Graciosa, Faial and Pico in the centre; and Flores and Corvo to the west.

São Miguel

São Miguel ❶ is perhaps the most varied of the islands. It is also the largest, measuring 65 km by 16 km (40 miles by 10 miles), and the most populated, with nearly half the archipelago's population of 250,000.

On the south coast, the capital of **Ponta Delgada ❷** sprawls behind the waterfront – the Avenida Infante Dom Henrique – with its arcades and 18th-century city gates. The town is dramatically set off against numerous small volcanic cones rising on the distant hills. City sights include several fine baroque churches, among them the 16th-century parish church, Igreja Matriz de São Sebastião. Also of architectural interest are the Palácio da Conceição which nowadays houses the government; and the curious baroque Casa de Carlos Bicudo with its mermaid façade.

For a view that overlooks the city, head for the **Reduto da Mãe de Deus**, where in 1944 an ill-informed anti-aircraft battery shot at an aircraft carrying General Eisenhower on his way home. There's a good museum, the **Museu Carlos Machado** (open Tue–Fri; closed 12.30–2pm; entrance charge), in Rua João Moreira, west of the redoubt.

Map on page 346

TIP

The main tourist office in the Azores is on Avenida Inf. Dom Henrique, in Ponta Delgada, São Miguel island, tel: 096-25152.

BELOW: a market vendor in Ponta Delgada.

In the west of the island are the enchanting twin lakes within the **Caldeira das Sete Cidades ❸**. This "Cauldron of the Seven Cities" is best viewed from Vista do Rei (The King's View), but you will be able to spot only one sleepy village in the crater. In sunlight, one lake is blue, the other green – stemming, legend has it, from the tears of a princess forced to part from her shepherd lover. A half-day circuit of the island might take you past pineapple plantations (visitors welcome) just north of the capital, on to Sete Cidades and the promontory of **Ponta dos Mosteiros**, eastwards to Capelas and its tobacco fields, and finally to the historical town of **Ribeira Grande ❹**. Further east are the Caldeiras da Ribeira Grande, a small spa in picturesque surroundings, and the tea plantations of Gorreana (open to the public).

Eastwards from Ponta Delgada, past sandy beaches, are the potteries of **Lagoa ❺** and the underwater diving centre at Caloura, and, beyond, the attractive town of **Vila Franca do Campo ❻** with three ornate baroque churches. The municipal museum has a good collections of musical instruments and pottery. Above Vila Franca, the pilgrimage chapel of **Senhora da Paz** affords a splendid view over the south coast. Just offshore, accessible from the pretty harbour, is the tiny crater island of **Ilheu**, with a natural seawater swimming pool.

Northeast and inland, past the crater lake of Lagoa das Furnas, is the village of **Furnas ❼**, with its hot springs and boiling mud cauldrons that give off the rich stink of sulphur. But here too is a famous botanical park, a volcanically heated lake you can swim in, and a pleasant hotel and restaurant, the **Terra Nostra**. The dish of the house is *cozido à Furnas* – meats and vegetables steamed in underground ovens. For a picnic, you can boil your own eggs in the hot springs beside the crater lake.

BELOW: Ponta Delgada's city gates.

Santa Maria and Terceira

The island of **Santa Maria ❽**, only 17 by 9 km (10 by 5 miles), has peaceful fields and red-roofed whitewashed houses in a southern Portuguese style (initially settlers came from the Algarve and Alentejo). Apart from the underlying volcanic massif, there is also sedimentary rock, and the beaches therefore are a shining gold, in bright contrast to the more usual volcanic black. Santa Maria is the driest, sunniest island, often called the "Algarve of the Azores". Just north of the airport in Anjos is the reconstructed church, where Christopher Columbus once knelt in prayer. The main town is **Vila do Porto ❾**.

In the central group, **Terceira ❿** (29 by 17 km/18 by 10 miles) derives its name from the fact that it was the third island in the archipelago to be discovered. All the settlements stretch along the coastline, while the unpopulated interior of the island – a wild and rugged landscape partly covered with native brushwood of tree heather, juniper and mosses – is often enveloped in clouds. Terceira is distinguished by its capital **Angra do Heroismo ⓫**, which is, deservedly, on UNESCO's World Heritage list as it is undoubtedly the most beautiful town in the archipelago.

Once the capital of the Azores, it was granted its heroic title by Queen Maria II, the daughter of Dom Pedro IV, whose regency the island stoutly supported. Severely damaged by an earthquake in 1980, Angra is gradually recovering. Its cathedral, several churches, castles and palaces are of considerable interest. A circuit of the island encompasses stunning views of green patchwork fields subdivided by stone walls. Terceira's most boisterous *festas* are around 24 June, the day of São João (St John the Baptist), and include *touradas à corda,* the running of rope-restrained bulls.

Map on page 346

At Ponta do Raminho on Terceira Island there is an old whalers' lookout post.

BELOW: Furnas, where the ground is hot enough to cook a meal.

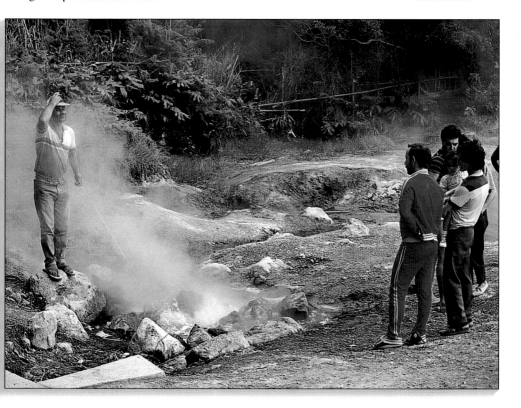

From São Jorge to Corvo

Beautiful **São Jorge** ⓲, 56 km (35 miles) long by only 8 km (5 miles) wide, rises abruptly from the sea and culminates in a mountain ridge that is often shrouded in mist. Besides its glorious natural setting, São Jorge affords magnificent views of all the central islands. Almost all the villages are set on small coastal plains (*fajãs*) at the foot of tall cliffs; some hamlets can only be reached via narrow footpaths. **Velas** ⓳, with stunning views across to Pico, is the main town and a good base to explore the island.

Faial ⓴ rises almost symmetrically on all sides to the central **Caldeira** ⓯, an eerie crater with a depth of some 300 metres (1,000 ft). Faial's epithet, "Blue Island", was inspired by its hydrangea hedgerows running like blue ribbons over the countryside – a stunning sight for people used to seeing these bushes only in neat parks and gardens.

The lively capital of **Horta** ⓰ is extremely pleasant, with some interesting museums and churches. Its harbour is a port of call for transatlantic sailors, with each crew commemorating their journey by painting a picture on the *mole* (breakwater). **Ponta dos Capelinhos** ⓱ is a dramatic contrast to the lively town and flowery countryside: here, in 1957–58, an undersea volcanic eruption rumbled and grumbled and left vast, grim dunes of dark cinder.

Graciosa ⓲ is as gracious as its name suggests, with soft sloping hills and peaceful villages scattered over the island. Yet it also has a volcanic heritage: in Caldeira do Enxofre you may descend 182 stone steps to a huge cavern (*furna*) with a sulphurous subterranean lake. In the small, tidy capital of **Santa Cruz** ⓳ it becames obvious why Graciosa was known as the "White Island": all its houses are traditionally white-washed.

BELOW:
typical white-
washed houses
on Santa Maria.

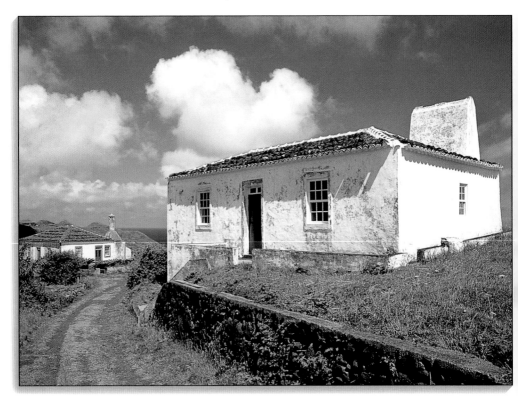

The towering peak which gives the island its name is the main reason to visit **Ilha do Pico** ⑳, but a look round the island reveals fertile countryside in the east and bizarre rocky regions (called *mistérios*) in the west which have been flooded by lava comparatively recently. In the sheltered enclosures between dry-stone walls, grapevines are grown to produce the local wines.

In **Lajes** ㉑, a small whaling museum, the **Museu dos Baleeiros** (open Tue–Fri; closed 12.30–2pm; entrance charge) recalls the all-too-recent past, when men went out hunting the giant creatures: Herman Melville's *Moby Dick* is set in these waters. Rising to over 2,350 metres (7,700 ft), majestic Pico is the highest mountain not only in the Azores but in the whole of Portugal. To climb the main peak (this is best done in summer), you will need proper gear and a reliable route-finder.

Ilha das Flores ㉒ (17 by 12 km/10 by 7 miles) does not abound in flowers, as its names suggests. But it is the most humid island of the Azores, its wet climate accounting for the lush evergreen vegetation. Flores offers some wild landscapes which are quite different from those of the other islands: basalt predominates, in the form of high-lying, boggy plateaux where waterfalls plummet down over steep rock faces.

From Flores, a boat runs daily, weather permitting, to **Ilha do Corvo** ㉓ (*corvo* is "cormorant" in Portuguese), which measures only 6 by 3 km (4 by 2 miles). It is the smallest and quietest island in the archipelago, with its 300 inhabitants all living in **Vila Nova**, which is the only village. Corvo's prime sight is a tranquil lake embedded in an isolated crater, whose swampy islets reputedly resemble a map of the Azores. The voracious birds after which the island was named can still be seen around the shores. ❑

Map on page 346

TIP

Between May and September, daily whale-watching trips are organised by the Museu dos Baleeiros in Lajes on Ilha do Pico. The departure time is normally 10am daily, but call ahead to check: (092) 672617.

BELOW: island delivery service.

INSIGHT GUIDES
Travel Tips

Insight Guides portray destinations in depth, providing the complete picture and the top photography

Insight Pocket Guides focus on the best choices for places to see and things to do and include large fold-out maps

Insight Compact Guides' portability makes them the perfect books to carry with you for on-the-spot reference

Three types of guide for all types of travel

INSIGHT GUIDES Different people need different kinds of information. Some want *background information* to help them prepare for the trip. Others seek *personal recommendations* from someone who knows the destination well. And others look for *compactly presented data* for on-the-spot reference. With three carefully designed series, Insight Guides offer readers the perfect choice. Insight Guides will turn your visit into an experience.

The world's largest collection of visual travel guides

CONTENTS

Getting Acquainted

The Place 354
Climate 354
Geography 354
Government 354
Public Holidays 355
Etiquette 355

Planning the Trip

Visas & Passports 355
Money Matters......................355
What to Bring........................356
Health & Insurance...............356
Tourist Offices Abroad 356
Getting There 356

Practical Tips

Business Hours 358
Media 358
Postal Services 358
Telephone 358
Local Tourist Offices..............359
Embassies & Consulates.......359
Security & Crime...................359
Medical Matters 360
Weights and Measures..........360

Getting Around

By Air....................................361
By Train.................................361
By Bus 361
Driving 361
Transport in Lisbon 362
Taxis 362

Where to Stay

Choosing a Hotel...................362
Hotels Listings 363
Manor Houses.......................367
Pousadas 368

Where to Eat

What to Eat 370
Restaurant Listings 370
Drinking Notes 373

Nightlife

After Dark 373
Music.....................................373
Discos and Clubs 374
Cinema 375

Great Outdoors

National Parks.......................375

Sport

Participant Sports..................376
Spectator Sports 376

Shopping

What to Buy 377
Where to Shop 377

Language

Getting By 378
Basic Communication 378
Eating and Drinking...............378
Sightseeing............................379
Shopping 380
Travelling 380
Health 380
Numbers................................380

Further Reading

Portuguese Works 381
Books about Portugal 381
Other Insight Guides..............381

Getting Acquainted

The Place

Area: 92,072 sq. km. (33,549 sq. miles) including Madeira and the Azores.
Capital: Lisbon
Principal rivers: Douro, Guadiana, Lima, Minho, Mondego and Tejo (Tagus).
Population: 10.5 million
Language: Portuguese
Religion: Roman Catholic (97 percent)
Time Zone: GMT (summer time March–October GMT + 1); the Azores are 1 hour behind continental Portugal.
Currency: escudo/euro
Weights and measures: metric
Electricity: 220 volts AC, continental-style round plugs.
International dialling code: outgoing 00; incoming 351

Climate

Spring and summer are definitely the best times of year to visit Portugal. Winter brings a distinct north–south divide in the weather. Southernmost Algarve enjoys mild winters with many fine sunny days. Sheltered, south-facing beaches provide ideal sun traps which allow sun-bathing throughout the year. Evenings might have a chill in the air but the weather is kind enough to attract a significant number of tourists, and Algarve is especially popular for long-stay holidays.

Around Lisbon, winters are mild with an unpredictable mixture of sunny and showery days. The weather is just about good enough on balance to attract some tourism along the Estoril coast.

In the northern and central regions winters are rainy, and while not freezing, are surprisingly chilly. Spells of fine, clear weather between rainy periods provide excellent walking conditions but there is no reliability. In the mountains it's even colder, and variable snow falls on the Serra da Estrela and mountains to the north and east between November and February (sometimes enough for ski enthusiasts, although conditions are far from ideal). Winters are short, beginning in November or December and ending in February or March, averaging 12°C/53°F.

Generally, the weather starts getting warm in May and June throughout the country, and usually stays warm to very hot until September. Weather patterns are changeable and difficult to predict from year to year: winters can be considerably shorter or longer; the rainy season heavy or light.

Apart from in the Algarve, nights can be cool even in summer, especially along the Cascais/Estoril coast of Lisbon. Along the western coast, the Atlantic tends to be cool (22°C/72°F) until July. It warms up earlier along the southern coast.

Summers are generally hot throughout the country with endless days of sunshine. The north enjoys the same high temperatures as the rest of the country, although there is always the risk of more rainy days. Some inland areas experience extremely high temperatures – Alentejo in the south and the Upper Douro in the north often top 40°C/104°F for long periods. Algarve is moderately hot in summer (31°C/88°F) enjoying the benefit of cooling westerlies.

Geography

Continental Portugal is roughly rectangular in shape, bordered on the east and north by Spain and the west and south by the Atlantic. It measures about 560 km (360 miles) north–south and 220 km (130 miles) east–west. A 840-km (522-mile) coastline borders the country.

The mountainous northern half of the country is more populated. The intense greens of the northern valleys, with their winding riverbeds and mountain peaks (the highest of which is the Serra da Estrela, at 2,000 metres/6,500 ft), make central and northern Portugal extraordinarily beautiful. But it's a matter of taste: there are those who prefer the great open spaces of the south.

Portugal is divided into eight principal regions: in the north and northwest are the rich wine lands of the Minho and the Douro valley; in the northeast the distant Trás-os-Montes, ("Behind the Mountains"). The Beiras – the litoral, Alta and Baixa ("upper" and "lower") – reach across north-central Portugal. In the middle, Estremadura and the Ribatejo encompass the areas just above Lisbon. In the southern part of the country the dry, flat and under-populated Alentejo (administratively divided into Alto and Baixo) occupies a third of Portugal. The far south, Algarve, is hilly, and has long stretches of beautiful beaches, most of which have been discovered by visitors.

UNESCO Heritage Sites

- Angra do Heroismo (Azores)
- Belém tower and Jerónimos monastery (Lisbon)
- Batalha Monastery
- Convento do Cristo (Tomar)
- Evora – historic centre
- Alcobaça Monastery
- Sintra
- Porto – historic centre
- Vila Nova de Foz Coa

The Government

Portugal is a democratic republic, with an executive president elected for a five-year term. The 230-member assembly is directly elected for four years. Appointed by the president, the prime minister commands a majority in the assembly. A council of ministers (cabinet) is responsible to the assembly. Portugal has 18 districts and two autonomous regions.

Public Holidays

1 January New Year's Day
25 April Anniversary of the
Revolution (1974)
mid-to late February Carnival
(preceding Lent)
1 May Labour Day
10 June Portugal and Camões
Day
early June Corpus Christi
15 August Day of the
Assumption
5 October Republic Day
1 November All Saints' Day
1 December Restoration of
Independence
8 December Day of the
Immaculate Conception
25 December Christmas Day

Local municipal holidays are as
follows:
Aveiro – 12 May
Beja – 8 May
Braga – 24 June
Bragança – 22 August
Castelo Branco – 1 April
Coimbra – 4 July
Evora – 29 June
Faro – 7 September
Guarda – 26 November
Leiria – 22 May
Lisbon – 18 June
Porto – 24 June
Porto Alegre – 23 May
Santarém – 19 March
Setúbal – 15 September
Viana do Castelo – 20 August
Vila Real – 13 June
Viseu – 21 September

The Economy

About 15 percent of the labour
force works in agriculture, but there
is little real investment in farming.
Major crops are wheat and maize,
along with tomatoes, potatoes, cork
and forestry products. Grapes are
cultivated for wines – table wine as
well as port and Madeira.

Away from the land, the main
exports are textiles and clothing.
Other products include footwear,
processed food and, increasingly,
electrical appliances and petro-
chemicals.

Tourism and foreign exchange,
primarily from Portuguese working
abroad, are major foreign-currency
earners. Portugal remains among
Western Europe's poorer countries,
despite economic development
begun after the revolution in 1974
and significant advances since
joining the European Union in 1986.

Etiquette

The Portuguese are usually
courteous and hospitable. Taking a
short while to learn the language
basics, and liberal use of these
thereafter, will serve you well. (*Turn
to the Language section on page
378 for some useful words and
phrases.*)

Here are a few helpful hints:
• If you are invited to someone's
house, it is polite to bring flowers
for the hostess or a small toy or
sweets if there are young children.
• There are always orderly queues
at bus stops. Be certain to respect
them.
• For some reason, stretching in
public (on the street or at the table)
is considered rude. Otherwise, use
common sense and a smile and you
shouldn't go far wrong.

Planning
the Trip

Visas & Passports

European Union nationals may
enter Portugal with a national
identity card. Citizens of Great
Britain and Australia need nothing
more than a valid passport for a
three-month stay. The same applies
to Americans and Canadians
staying for 60 days or less.

All other non-EU visitors must
show a valid passport to enter
Portugal. On arrival, your passport
will be stamped with a 60-day
tourist visa. No one with a tourist
visa is permitted to work.

Bureaucracy is a serious
problem, so you should apply for an
extension at least one week before
your time runs out.

Visas or extended stay visas can
be obtained at any Portuguese
consulate abroad, or contact the
Serviço de Estrangeiros (Foreigners'
Service) at Rua Conselheiro José
Silvestre, 22, Lisbon, tel: (01)
7141027.

The British office which deals
with extensions to visas is at 62
Brompton Road, London SW3 1BY,
tel: (0171) 581 8722 (prefix 171
with 00 44 if calling from Portugal).

Money Matters

Currency
The escudo, which divides into 100
centavos, is the basic unit of
currency. The coin with the smallest
denomination is the 1 escudo
piece, which is of little value; the
largest is the 200 escudos coin
(but this could change); 1,000
escudos is usually called a *conto*.
Notes are as follows: 500$00;
1000$00; 2000$00; 5000$00;
10,000$00.

If this looks confusing, it is because the symbol for the escudo is the same as the dollar sign. But note that it is written after the number of escudos (and before the number of centavos). Thus, 75$00 means 75 escudos; and 75$50 means 75 escudos and 50 centavos. Centavos have long since disappeared as a unit of currency but they still appear in shop prices.

Exchange

While you may want to buy a small amount of escudos before you leave home, you'll get a better exchange rate if you wait until you are in Portugal. Once you have bought escudos, however, it may be costly to re-exchange them for foreign currency. The best policy is to change money as you require it.

Money is best changed at banks, rather than at hotels or travel agencies. Outside normal banking hours, ATMs (Automatic Teller Machines), usually called *Multibanco*, are widely available and there are currency exchanges at Lisbon's Santa Apolónia railway station as well as at the airports. Visa, American Express, MasterCard, and Eurocheque are acceptable. ATMs taking all the major cards, including Cirrus, are widespread throughout the country.

Exchanging money at a bank or cashpoint – some banks have even installed – automatic exchange machines for various currencies – works out far cheaper than paying the higher rate of commission on travellers' cheques.

Travellers' Cheques and Credit Cards

Travellers' cheques are accepted in all banks, although, as already mentioned, the commission charge is higher than for changing cash. It is best not to use them in stores, where, if they are accepted at all, you can be certain you are being charged at a disadvantageous rate. Major credit cards can be used in the more expensive hotels, restaurants and shops, but check in advance to avoid embarrassment.

Convenience Cards

If you are driving through Portugal, remember that you can use Visa cards (and sometimes charge cards) to buy fuel, at least in the major petrol stations. A 100$00 tax is added to card purchases but it can be far more convenient than using cash then having to stop to exchange more.

What to Bring

You should bring your own film and photographic equipment, which will almost certainly be cheaper outside Portugal.

Toiletries and personal effects are all available locally, and are often much cheaper than in other countries. Most common methods of contraception are available, but some might be difficult to obtain in remote areas.

Health & Insurance

Portugal enjoys a healthy climate and no vaccinations or other special health precautions are necessary. Bring enough prescription medication to last through your stay, if only to avoid confusion with brand names and/or language. Although the Portuguese health service has reciprocal emergency treatment arrangements with other EU countries (take your E111 form with you) it is advisable to have additional health insurance in case of serious problems, as well as insurance against loss, theft, etc.

All narcotics and illegal drugs are banned. Be warned: customs keep a close watch.

Portugese Tourist Offices Abroad

CANADA

(Montreal)
Délégation Commerciale et du Tourisme du Portugal,
2075 University, Suite 1206
Montreal, Quebec H3A 2L1
Tel: +1-514-282 12 64
Fax: +1-514-499 14 50

(Toronto)
Portuguese Trade and Tourism Commission, 60 Bloor Street West Suite 1005, Toronto, Ontario M4W 3B8
Tel: +1-416-921 73 76
Fax: +1-416-921 13 53

IRELAND

Portuguese Trade & Tourism Board, 54, Dawson Street, Dublin 2
Tel: +353-1-670 91 33/34
Fax: +353-1-670 91 41

SPAIN

(Barcelona)
Oficina de Comercio y Turismo de Portugal, Calle Bruc, 50, 4ª,3ª, 08010 Barcelona
Tel: +34-3-301 44 16/301 45 62
Fax: +34-3-318 50 68

(Madrid)
Oficina de Turismo de Portugal, Gran Via, 27, 1ª, 28013 Madrid
Tel: +34-1-522 93 54/522 44 08
Fax: +34-1-522 23 82

UNITED KINGDOM

Portuguese Trade & Tourism Office, 22–25A Sackville Street, London, W1X 1DE
Tel: 0171-494 1441
Fax: 0171-494 1868

UNITED STATES

(New York)
Portuguese National Tourist Office, 590 Fifth Avenue, 4th Floor, New York, NY 10036 - 4704
Tel: +1-212-354 44 03/44 04
Fax: + 1-212-764 61 37

(Washington)
Portuguese Trade & Tourism Office, 1900 L Street NW, Suite 310, Washington DC 20036
Tel: +1-202-331 82 22
Fax: +1-202-331 82 36

Getting There

BY AIR

Scheduled Flights

TAP Air Portugal is Portugal's national airline and it has wide international links. Generally speaking, the service is good with a modern fleet of aircraft. But be aware that TAP flights, particularly from Paris, can get very heavily booked by returning immigrants in the summer (July/August) and around Christmas and Easter.

Many major airlines make non-stop direct flights to Lisbon from capital cities in Europe and other continents. There are several flights a week from New York, and from Boston.

You may also, from some countries, fly directly to Porto in the north and Faro in the south. Links with London are particularly good, and the privately owned Portugália Airlines offers flights from Manchester to Porto and Lisbon with onward flights to Faro. Portugália also has a growing network of routes to regional airports in Spain, France and Germany; their service is of a consistently high standard. British Airways subsidiary GO operates between London Stansted and Lisbon.

Between regular airlines and charter companies the choice is considerable – and ticket prices vary a great deal.

Charter flights

Because Portugal is a popular tourist destination, charter flights from Britain and continental Europe to Lisbon and Faro are very frequent in summer, less so in winter. There are similar flights from the United States. Although primarily intended for holidaymakers buying a complete package, including accommodation, spare capacity is sold off as seat only, and often at a discounted rate.

Airports

In Lisbon and Porto the international airports are on the outskirts of the city. Taxis will take you to the city centre. All have meters and lists of charges for out-of-town journeys. In Lisbon, taxi drivers are entitled to charge an excess for luggage over 30 kg (66 lb). All three airports also have bus services to their city centres and good air links with each other. The main airports are:

Aeroporto de Lisboa,
Tel: (01) 8485974/8494323

Aeroporto Dr Francisco Sá Carneiro (Porto)
Tel: (02) 9412534/9482141
Aeroporto de Faro
Tel: (089) 818582

If you are visiting the islands you may also fly to the Aeroporto de Santa Maria in the Azores or the Aeroporto des Horta in Madeira.

BY RAIL

An extensive rail network covers the country and most trains have first- and second-class carriages. Restaurant cars are provided on long-distance services and mini-bars can be found on most of the other trains. Seats must be reserved in advance on international and express trains. Children under 4 travel free, 4- to 12-years-olds, half the adult fare.

Nowhere in Portugal is yet linked to the superfast TGV system, which so far only reaches Irun on the Spanish-French border, but there's a busy international (and national) train service. A daily train makes the Paris–Lisbon run (around 24 hours; about 2 hours less if you take the TGV to Irun); and the Paris–Porto route (from Paris to the Spanish border it's the same journey as above). The Madrid to Lisbon/Porto service (usually twice a day) is a sleeper and takes around 10 hours.

There are also routes from northern Spain (Galicia) or southern Spain (Seville) into Portugal. These last services tend to be slow and time-consuming. Once in Portugal, you have a good, fast north–south route (Porto–Lisbon–Faro) as well as slow, scenic rides, if you care for them, especially in the north. You'll find that on some routes trains have been replaced by bus services.

Special Tickets

A variety of tickets and discount cards are available, including group tickets, Senior Citizens' cards, Inter-rail cards, Rail-Europe Senior tickets, and International Youth tickets. There are also Tourist tickets for periods of 7, 14 and 21 days and a Family card which allows

a minimum of three people to travel and is valid for single journeys over 150 km (95 miles).

The main categories of train in Portugal are:
Regional – slow
Inter-regional – fast
Inter-cidades – very fast
Rápidos (ALFA) – express

For more information on train services, call: (01) 8884025.

BY ROAD

By Car

Good roads link Portugal with its Spanish neighbour at numerous border points. Main east–west routes to Lisbon are from Seville via Beja; from Badajoz via Elvas; from Salamanca via Viseu (via the notoriously dangerous IP5 motorway).

If driving from England, using the channel ferries, or the *Shuttle* through the Channel Tunnel, allow three days; or, via Plymouth–Santander or Portsmouth–Bilbao, two. There are drivers who boast of doing the journey faster, but don't try it. Road accident figures are appallingly high.

By Bus

There are regular bus/coach services between principal cities, linking with Madrid and Paris. These get very congested in summer months as immigrants return home for holidays, and they can be hard work, but they are cheap. For information phone (01) 354 54 39 (*also see page 361*).

Practical Tips

Business Hours

Most stores open for business Monday–Friday 9am–1pm, and from about 3–7pm. Stores are open on Saturday from 9am–1pm, and are closed Sunday and holidays (hypermarkets remain open all day Saturday and half-day Sunday and holidays). Major banks are open Monday–Friday 8.30am–3pm and are closed Saturday, Sunday and holidays.

Media

NEWSPAPERS & MAGAZINES

Portugal has many daily newspapers, two of which are dedicated solely to football!

The principal general newspapers are now published in both Lisbon and Porto and tend to have a regional bias, as indicated: *Diário de Notícias* (Lisbon), *Jornal de Notícias* (Porto), *Público* (Lisbon and Porto), and *Diário Económico* (Lisbon and Porto).

Weeklies include the *Expresso* and the *Independente* (both up to Sunday Times/Observer standard. There is a weekly English language newspaper – the *Anglo-Portuguese News*.

TELEVISION

RTP, the state-owned corporation, operates two national television channels (RTP 1 and RTP 2), two regional stations and one international (RTP Madeira, RTP Azores, RTP International). There are also two other commercial stations (**Sic** and **TVI**).

Films are transmitted in the language of origin, with sub-titles, as are many serials and document-aries. There tends to be a high content of Brazilian soap operas and quiz shows, which are not known for their quality.

News bulletins are broadcast at 8pm (RTP1/SIC); 9pm (TV1) and at 10pm (RTP2). Most hotels have satellite/cable TV, which will include Sky News, Eurosport, CNN and CNBC.

RADIO

There are four national and five regional **RDP** (state-owned) radio stations as well as more than 300 local radio stations. Among them are Antenna I, which broadcasts popular music and news, and Antenna 2, which is a classical music station. There are also commercial radio stations, **TSF** and **RR**, which offer a similar mix of news and popular music.

Tipping

A tip of 10 percent is sufficient in restaurants and for taxi drivers. Barbers and hairdressers expect to receive the same, or a little less.

Postal Services

Postal services, both international and domestic, are generally reliable and efficient. Allow five days for delivery within Europe. For next day delivery within Portugal, use Correio Azul, an internal express service.

Post Offices

These open Monday–Friday 9am–6pm; smaller branches close for lunch from 12.30–2.30pm. In district capitals , the main branch is usually open on Saturday morning. Mail is delivered Monday to Friday.

To buy stamps, stand in any queue marked *Selos* (Stamps). To mail or receive packages, you need to go to the queue marked *Encomendas*.

Be certain to write Via Aérea on all airmail items. To send large parcels home, if speed is not important,

consider the less expensive alternative of surface mail.

The Post Office also provides services such as express mail (*Expresso* and *Correio Azul* – see above), postal money orders (*vales*), general delivery (*poste restante*), registered mail (*registos*), insurance on packages (*seguro*), and telegraph, telephone and fax services.

Telephone

Phones equipped for international calls are located in all areas and accept coins, Telecom cards or credit cards, although the older phones taking coins are fast disappearing.

A Telecom phone card can be bought at kiosks and many shops. Instructions for using the phone are written in English and other major languages. You can also make calls (international and local) from post offices. Go to the window for a cabin assignment and pay when the call is finished. In Lisbon there is also a phone office in the Rossio railway station, open daily from 9am–11pm; in Porto, there is one in Praça da Liberdade (same hours).

Many village stores and bars in Portugal have metered telephones. Phone first, pay later, but be prepared to pay more than the rate for call box or post office calls. As elsewhere, calls made from hotels are higher still.

For US phone credit card holders, the major access numbers are:
• **AT&T**: tel: 05017–1288.
• **MCI**: tel: 05017–1234.
• **Sprint**: tel: 05017–1877.

Mobile Phones

Mobile phones with reciprocal GSM network arrangements will function throughout most of the country. Alternatively, the three national cellular networks (Telecel, TSM and Optimus) have short-term rental facilities at the main airports.

Telegrams

You may place telegrams by phone (tel: **10**) or from a post office, but the rates are high.

Another way to make fast contact outside Portugal is to use the fax/telecopy machines which operate in all major post offices (**Corfac**) and most hotels. Your message will be charged per page. If you make an arrangement with a private firm the cost is usually a great deal less.

Useful Numbers

To reach an English-speaking international operator, dial **098** (intercontinental service) or **099** (European service). To call direct to the US or Canada, dial **097–1**, plus the area code and phone number. For the UK, dial **00 44** plus the full phone number (minus the first zero of the code). Dial slowly or it won't connect.

Note: telephone numbers in Portugal change with infuriating frequency. To obtain a current number, dial **118**. But be warned: that could change, too.

Tourist Offices

The main tourist offices are known as **Regiao de Turismo** (Regional Tourist Office). They can be found in the main towns and will provide information about the whole region.

Aveiro
Rua João Mendonça, 8
Tel: (034) 23680
Fax: (034) 28326
Azores
Casa do Relfices, Colónia Alemã,
9900 Horta, Faial
Tel: (092) 23801
Fax: (092) 22004, or
Avenida Infante Dom Henrique,
9500 Ponta Delgada, São Miguel
Tel: (092) 25743
Fax: (092) 22211
Beja
Rua Capitão João Francisco
Sousa, 25
Tel: (084) 23693
Fax: (084) 22300
Braga
Avenida da Liberdade, 1
Tel: (053) 22550
Fax: (053) 613660

Bragança
Edifício do Principal, Largo do Principal
Tel: (073) 331078
Fax: (073) 331913
Estoril
Arcadas do Parque
Tel: (01) 4680113
Fax: (01) 4672280
Castelo Branco
Alameda da Liberdade
Tel: (072) 21002
Fax: (072) 23073
Coimbra
Largo da Portagem
Tel: (039) 33028
Fax: (039) 25576
Elvas
Praça da República
Tel: (068) 622236
Fax: (068) 629060
Evora
Rua 24 de Julho-1-1oD
Tel: (066) 742535
Fax: (066) 742534
Faro
Avenida 5 de Outubro
Tel: (089) 800400
Fax: (089) 800489
Guimarães
Al. Resistência Fascismo, 83
Tel: (053) 515123
Fax: (053) 515134
Lagos
Praça Marquês de Pombal
Tel: (082) 763031
Leiria
Jardim Luís de Camões
Tel: (044) 823773
Fax: (044) 33533
Lisbon
Praça dos Restauradores
Tel: (01) 3463643
Fax: (01) 3425231
Madeira
Avenida Arriagas, 18
Tel: (091) 229057 or 225658
Fax: (091) 232151
Porto
Rua Clube Senianos, 25
Tel: (02) 323303
Fax: (02) 2084548
Setúbal
Travessa Frei Gaspar, 10
Tel: (065) 524284
Fax: (065) 36745
Tavira
Casa Municipal, Praça da República
Tel: (081) 22511

Tomar
Rua Serpa Pinto, 1
Tel: (049) 32311
Fax: (049) 314677
Viana do Castelo
Rua do Hospital Velho
Tel: (051) 82787
Viseu
Avenida Gulbenkian
Tel: (032) 422014
Fax: (032) 421864

Embassies/Consulates

Australia
Avenida da Liberdade 244, 4º,
Lisbon
Tel: (01) 523350

Canada
Edifício MCB, Avenida da
Liberdade 144–156, 4º, Lisbon
Tel: (01) 3474892

Great Britain
Lisbon: Rua São Domingos
à Lápa 37
Tel: (01) 3961191
Porto: Avenida da Boavista
3072, 4100
Tel: (02) 6184789

Ireland
Rua da Imprensá Estrela 1, 3º,
Lisbon
Tel: (01) 3961569

United States
Lisbon: Avenida Forças Armadas
Tel: (01) 7266600
Porto: Rua Júlio Dinis 826, 3º,
4000
Tel: (02) 6063094

Security and Crime

Portugal has a well deserved reputation for non-violence. It remains one of the few developed countries where you can both feel and be safe when walking almost anywhere at any time of day or night. This is changing in one or two of the larger cities, though, and petty theft is becoming a problem in some of the more run-down areas of Lisbon and Porto, and close to some of the larger shopping centres. Foreign registered cars or cars obviously rented may be targets for thieves if left unattended in out of the way locations.

However, with common sense and the usual degree of attention you should normally be able to take a fairly relaxed attitude towards security.

Help!

Police, fire and ambulance
Tel: 112 (toll free)
Credit card theft/SOS:
Tel: (01) 44 44 50.

Stolen property

In the event of theft you must report it to the police within 24 hours in order to reclaim on insurance. The Lisbon police station most used to dealing with foreigners' problems is in the Rua Capelo (tel: 3466141) in the Bairro Alto, beside the São Carlos opera house.

Lost property

To claim lost property, go to Anjos police station in Lisbon, Rua dos Anjos, 56A (Anjos Metro). For property left on buses, go to the Carris office at the top of the Santa Justa lift, between 3–7pm.

Medical Matters

As mentioned before, there are no special health precautions necessary for visitors to Portugal. Beware of sunburn, especially on misty days when the combination of a cool breeze and filtered sunshine can cause serious burning. Take sunscreen with you, or buy it when you get there, and wear a hat if the sun is fierce.

Tap water is generally potable but often not very palatable, so it is best to use bottled water (*água mineral*).

Insect bites (usually by mosquitos) can be a problem in the summer so bring repellents. Out in the countryside, snakes are not uncommon but they are rarely a problem: apart from one species of

viper in the north, the other venomous snakes have fangs at the back of their mouths, so even if you encounter one, and even if it were to strike, it is unlikely to poison you. There is no rabies in Portugal.

Useful Numbers

Ambulance (Portuguese Red Cross)
Tel: (01) 3017777
Poisons unit
Tel: (01) 7950143
Linha Vida (for information on drug use and abuse)
Tel: (01) 7267766
Linha Sida (AIDS help line)
Tel: (01) 7599943

CHEMISTS

When closed, all chemists (*Farmácias*) have a list on their doors highlighting the nearest one that is open. Newspapers also publish a list of chemists open late each day.

HOSPITALS

Lisbon

There are half a dozen large hospitals in Lisbon. The following have accident and emergency departments:
Hospital Cruz Vermelha, Rua Duarte Galvão 54 (situated behind the zoo), tel: (01) 783003 or 7786141
Hospital de Santa Maria, Avenida Prof Egas Moniz (in the Cidade Universitária area not far from Sete Rios), tel: (01) 775171 or 775191
Hospital São Jose, tel: (01) 8860131.
The British Hospital, Rua Saraiva de Carvalho 49 (overlooking the British cemetery near the Jardim de Estrela), tel: (01) 3955067, has no casualty department, but takes outpatients and may be able to help since all staff speak English. This hospital also operates a clinic at Cascais, tel: (01) 4836343.

Porto

Hospital Santo António, Rua José de Carvalito, tel: (02) 2007354.

PRIVATE CLINICS

Lisbon

Clinica de Santo António, Avenida Hospitais Civis Lisboa 8, Reboleira, 2720 Amadora, tel: (01) 4952541.

Porto

Hospital da Ordem Trindade, rua Trindade, tel: (02) 2003378.

Weights and Measures

Portugal uses the metric system of weights and measures. Listed below is a conversion table which may be useful.

Temperatures

To convert Celsius temperatures to Fahrenheit, multiply the Celsius temperature by 1.8 and add 32. Thus, 20C x 1.8 + 32 = 68F. If this sounds too complicated, don't worry about it. After all, you're on holiday, and you'll know whether it's hot or cold.

Conversions

1 metre	=	1.09 yards
1 yard	=	0.92 metres
1 km	=	about 5/8 mile
1 mile	=	1.6 km
1 kilo	=	2.2 pounds
1 pound	=	about 0.46 kilo
1 litre	=	1.76 pints
1 pint	=	about 0.57 litre
1 cm	=	about 0.3 inch
1 inch	=	2.56 cm

Getting Around

By Air

TAP Air Portugal is the national airline. There is daily service between Lisbon, Porto and Faro.

Aerocondor flies several times weekly between Lisbon and Bragança. The airline **Portugália** also operates a growing domestic and international service, and has a good reputation. The offices are located at Avenida Almirante Gajo Coutinho 88-1700 Lisbon, tel: (01) 8486693.

By Train

Trains in Portugal range from the comfortable and speedy *rápidos* to the painfully slow *regionais*. Generally, the most efficient routes are the Lisbon–Coimbra–Porto and the Lisbon–Algarve lines. There will be a direct link from Lisbon to the Algarve from April 1999; prior to this Algarve trains depart from the south side of the Tejo, (*see below*).

Rápidos (ALFA), which run only on the two routes mentioned above, are fast and punctual and cost more. Some *rápidos* have first-class carriages only; others have a very comfortable second-class as well. Next in line are the *directos intercidades*, which make more stops and travel more slowly. These have both first- and second-class compartments; second-class here is likely to be less comfortable than in the *rápidos*.

Finally, the *semi-directos* and especially the *regionais*, seem to stop every few metres and take longer than you could have believed possible. On *directos*, *semi-directos* and *regionais*, second-class seats are not assigned, and the train

company, **Caminhos de Ferro Portugueses (CP)**, has no qualms about issuing more tickets than seats if the need arises. If you want to be certain of a seat, board early. On rural routes, trains are almost always regional.

Furthermore, to reach more remote – or even not-so-remote – destinations, it may be necessary to change trains, and schedules are seldom coordinated. Unless you are catching *rápidos* (and *intercidades*), which are punctual, leave yourself plenty of time between transfers.

See also Getting There By Rail page 357.

Stations in Lisbon

There are four railway stations in Lisbon. Cais do Sodré and Rossio are commuter stations. International and long-distance trains to the north and east leave from Santa Apolónia, just to the east of Praça do Comercio. For trains to Alentejo and Algarve, take a ferry boat at the Terreiro do Paço station (the popular name of the Praça do Comércio). The price of the boat is included in the train ticket, which you can buy at the boat station. Just be certain to buy the right one; there are two boat stations next to each other. For the train link-up, use the eastern station, i.e. the one to the left as you face the river.

Stations in Porto and Coimbra

Porto and Coimbra each have two railway stations. Porto's São Bento and Coimbra A are located in the respective town centres. Most long-distance trains, however, arrive and leave from Porto's Campanhã station and Coimbra B station, outside the cities, and there are shuttle services between the central and outlying stations.

By Bus

Bus networks are privately-run but many systems have adapted their name from the former Rodoviária Nacional so that, for example, the main bus company in the far north is now **Rodoviária Entre Douro e**

Minho. Only the Algarve bus company dropped the word Rodoviária, calling itself **Eva Transportes**. Except for routes between major cities, the bus is often faster than the train, and the system is certainly more extensive. This is particularly true in the north and between the smaller towns in Algarve and Alentejo.

There are quite a few private bus lines which specialise in particular areas of the country. Often they have more direct routes to smaller towns. Many travel agencies can book tickets on a private line, or may even run their own.

Driving

Portugal is a trying place for drivers. In the cities, traffic is heavy, road construction hinders movement, parking is close to impossible, and cars and pedestrians regularly ignore the rules of the road.

Outside cities, conditions vary enormously – from good, broad north–south and east–west highways (a network of new toll roads numbered Al to A8) to smaller roads which are often in poor condition. Many minor roads are narrow, making it difficult to pass slow-moving rural trucks and tractors. On mountain roads, driving takes skill and concentration. Portugal's accident rate is high: drivers too often pass at the last minute on two-lane highways.

Car Hire

If you're determined to drive, the Yellow Pages are full of car rental firms. The big three – Hertz, Avis, and Europcar – have offices in Portugal, along with many other smaller (and often cheaper) companies. You can book a car before leaving home, which is often much less expensive. Transhire in London, tel: 0171-978 1922, is one of the most competitive.

It's advisable to shop around, as costs vary and many agencies offer special packages from time to time. There are various options to choose from, including having a driver. For

Petrol in Portugal is cheap by European standards, but is still expensive by American ones.

more information look up car rentals in the local Yellow Pages under *Automóveis Aluguer com e sem Condutor* (which means cars to rent, with or without driver).

To rent a car in Portugal, most agencies require you to be at least 21 years old and to have had a valid drivers' licence for a minimum of one year. An international licence is not necessary.

Transport in Lisbon

Trains
Commuter trains to Cascais (stopping in Carcavelos, Estoril and other towns along the western coast) depart from Cais do Sodré station, west of the Praça do Comércio. Trains depart roughly every 15 to 20 minutes; the journey to Cascais (the end of the line) takes 35–40 minutes.

Trains to the northwestern suburbs, including Sintra, leave from the Rossio station at 15-minute intervals. The trip to Sintra takes about 45 minutes. This station houses an information centre for national services.

Buses and Trams
The city bus company, **CARRIS**, runs an extensive system of buses, trams (*eléctricos*) and funiculars. Bus stops are clearly marked by signposts or shelters. All stops display a diagrammatical map of the bus route; many have a map of the entire city system.

Pre-World War I trams ply the smaller, steeper streets where buses are unable to navigate. Some of them are quite beautiful, inside and out; they are slower and cheaper than the buses and are a good way to see the city. The tram is also supplemented with some larger, more modern vehicles operating along the riverside.

CARRIS also runs two funiculars

and an elevator. The Santa Justa Elevador, near the Rossio, leads to the Bairro Alto. One funicular climbs the steep Calçada da Glória from Praça dos Restauradores, the other is in São Bento. You pay after you've boarded.

Tickets and Passes
It is worth considering buying a 3-day or 7-day tourist pass, which gives unlimited access. If you have no pass, you pay a flat rate when you board, which works out more expensive. Less expensive are the pre-paid *modulos* that you can buy in packs of 20 from the kiosks. Don't board the bus without paying, as ticket inspectors appear from time to time and the fine is steep.

The CARRIS information kiosks scattered all over the city provide information and sell tickets and passes. If you're lucky, they may even have bus maps in stock. Two of the most convenient kiosks are in Praça da Figueira, near the Rossio, and near Eduardo VII Park.

Metro
Extended for Expo '98, the metro is principally useful for travel in the central zone of the city. The system is easy to use and very cheap.

A tourist pass valid for 4 or 7 days can be used on the Metro and buses. Metro passes valid for periods of 1, 7 and 30 days are also available. You can also buy singles or books of 10 tickets, and validate your ticket at the machines next to the ticket booths.

Taxis

In all Portugal's cities, taxis are plentiful and cheap. The great majority of them are cream, while older ones are black with cream roofs. In the city, they charge a standard meter fare, with no additions for extra passengers. (They carry up to four people.) Outside city limits, the driver may use the meter or charge a flat rate per kilometre, and is entitled to charge for the return fare (even if you don't take it). You should tip taxi drivers about 10 percent.

Where to Stay

Choosing a Hotel

Accommodation ranges from luxury hotels to basic private rooms. The middle range of reasonably priced accommodation has been considerably expanded thanks to an increase in the number of both Portuguese- and foreign-owned hotels. The French Ibis chain, for example, has opened hotels in several popular locations.

Pousadas and Manor Houses
Pousadas are state-run inns, which provide stylish and comfortable accommodation. They are to be found in most parts of the country, some in historic castles, and the majority serve excellent regional food (see Pousadas and Manor Houses, *page 128–9*). For reservations, contact the *pousadas* directly, or book through a travel agent or the central agent: **ENATUR**, Rua Santa Joana Princesa 10A, 1700 Lisboa, tel: (01) 848 9078, fax: (01) 848 4349.

Manor houses offer a pleasant rural alternative to hotels, pensions or *pousadas*. They are private properties which have been adapted, or totally converted, for use by guests. Government supervised, the network comes under an inclusive heading of *Turismo de Habitação*, or *Turismo no Espaço Rural* ("Tourism in the Country"). The range includes centuries-old manor houses – variously described as *paços* (palaces), *quintas* (estates), *solares* (manor houses) in the north, *montes* (in Alentejo), or simply *casas* (house), which can be modern lodgings, farmhouses, and even mills. All have bathrooms and a few are still owner-occupied.

You can book directly or through owner associations, which will give more details and prices. These are:
• **Solares de Portugal Turihab** (Assoc. de Turismo de Habitação), Praça da República, 4990 Ponte de Lima.
Tel: (058) 942 729 or 741 672
Fax: (058) 741 444. Strong on northern Casas Antigas, Quintas and Casas Rústicas.
• **Promoções e Ideas Turísticas** (PIT), Rua Frederico Arouca, Alto da Pampiliteira, Torred 2oA, 2750 Cascais.
Tel: (01) 483 7958. Country-wide representation.
• **PRIVETUR** (Assoc. Portuguesa de Turismo de Habitação), The Manor Houses of Portugal Promotion Company, Apartado 596, 4900 Viana do Castelo.
Tel: (0351) 588 35065.
Fax: (058) 741 493 (internet site: manorhouses.com for property details and reservations).
• **ANTAR** (Assoc. Nacional de Turismo no Espaço Rural), Rua 24 de Julho No. 1, 7000 Evora.
Tel: (066) 744555.

Hotels

Hotels in Portugal come in several guises:
• **Hotels** offer amenities such as restaurants and room service. All rooms have bathrooms. They are rated from 1–5-stars:
5-stars: a luxury hotel.
4-stars: not luxury but close.
3-stars: good value but sometimes slightly run-down.
1- and 2-stars: basic and often depressing places to stay.
• **Albergarias** are essentially hotels offering 4-star comfort and meals.
• **Estalagems** are very similar but may be 4- or 5-star.
• **Residencials** have star gradings and are like small hotels but generally do bed and breakfast only. They usually have an "R" on a sign outside.
• **Pensions** are more basic, and again do bed and breakfast only. You can find 4-star *pensions*, but the majority are less comfortable than that.

Hotel Listings

The list below includes a small sample of the wide variety of hotels in Portugal. Remember that you will probably have difficulty finding a decent room in July and August if you haven't made an advance reservation.

The following hotels are listed by area, beginning with Lisbon and the immediate area, and then running from north to south. In each place, they are listed in order of comfort, beginning with the most luxurious.

Note that *pousadas* and manor houses are listed separately.

Price Categories

Price categories are based on the cost of a double room for one night in high season.
**$$$$** = above 22.000$
**$$$** = 15.000$–22.000$
**$$** = 10.000$–15.000$
**$** = up to 10.000$

LISBON

5-star

Alfa Lisboa Hotel
Avenida Columbano Bordalo Pinheiro
Tel: (01) 726 2121
Fax: (01) 726 73031
Very modern but rather out of the way. **$$$$**

Hotel Altis
Rua Castilho, 11
Tel: (01) 314 2496
Fax: (01) 354 8696
Amenities include indoor pool and sauna. **$$$$**

Hotel Avenida Palace
Rua 1º de Dezembro
Tel: (01) 3460151
Fax: (01) 3422884
A grand 19th-century building, smack in the old town centre, between the Rossio and Praça dos Restauradores. **$$$$**

Hotel da Lapa
Rua do Pau de Bandeira, 4
Tel: (01) 3950005
Fax: (01) 3950665
Glamorously restored 19th-century mansion in the best residential quarter. **$$$$**

Hotel Sheraton Lisboa
Rua Latino Coelho, 1
Tel: (01) 3575757
Fax: (01) 3547164
Good for short stays and business trips, but there are several better hotels for the price. **$$$$**

Meridien Park Atlantic Hotel
Rua Castilho, 149, Lisbon
Tel: (01) 3830900
Fax: (01) 3833231
Elegant. Overlooking the park. **$$$$**

Hotel Ritz Intercontinental
Rua Rodrigo Fonseca, 88
Tel: (01) 3850939
Fax: (01) 3831783
High-quality rooms and service. Overlooking Eduardo VII Park. The top of the luxury range. **$$$$**

Hotel Tivoli Lisboa
Avenida da Liberdade, 185
Tel: (01)3530181
Fax: (01) 3579461
Big, handsome and handy for all parts of town. Friendly. **$$$$**

4-star

Albergaria Senhora do Monte
Calçada do Monte, 39
Tel: (01) 8866002
Fax: (01) 8877783
Beautiful views overlooking São Jorge castle, Alfama and down to and across the Tejo River. **$$$**

Hotel Diplomático
Rua Castilho, 74
Tel: (01) 3862041,
Fax: (01) 3862155.
Centrally located. **$$$**

Hotel Lisboa Plaza
Travessa do Salitre, 7
Tel: (01) 3463922
Fax: (01) 3471630
Just off Avenida da Liberdade. Attractively decorated interior. **$$$$**

Hotel Príncipe Real
Rua da Alegria, 53
Tel: (01) 3460116
Fax: (01) 3422104
Small and quiet; a few blocks from Avenida da Liberdade in an interesting area below the Bairro Alto. **$$$**

Hotel Tivoli Jardim
Rua Julio C. Machado, 9
Tel: (01) 3539971
Fax: (01) 3556566
Run by the same company as the 5-star Tivoli. **$$$**

Pensão York House,
Rua Janelas Verdes, 32
Tel: (01) 3962544/3968143
Fax: (01) 3972793
In a class by itself: comfort and
charm combined. The great
favourite of, among others, Graham
Greene. In an interesting
neighbourhood, about 15 minutes
by bus from the Rossio. Reserve
well in advance. The annex is down
the street at number 47. **$$$$**

3-star
Hotel Botânico
Rue da Mãe d'Agua, 16–20
Tel: (01) 3420392
Fax: (01) 3420125
Between the Bairro Alto and the
Avenida da Liberdade; pleasant and
comfortable. **$$$**
Hotel Britânia
Rua Rodrigues Sampaio, 17
Tel: (01) 3155016
Fax: (01) 3155021
Clean, if slightly shabby, and on a
nice quiet street near Avenida da
Liberdade. **$$$**
Hotel Dom Carlos
Avenida Duque de Loulé, 121
Tel: (01) 3539071
Fax: (01) 3520728
On a busy, centrally located street.
$$$
Hotel Eduardo VII
Avenida Fontes Pereira de Melo, 5
Tel: (01) 3530141
Fax: (01) 3533879
Next to the park of the same name.
A good view from the restaurant
and the front rooms. Slightly dark,
but clean. **$$$**
Hotel Flamingo
Rua Castilho, 151
Tel: (01) 3862191
Fax: (01) 3861216
Near the Marquês de Pombal, but
on a quieter street. **$$$**
Hotel Miraparque
Avenida Sidque, 13862191
Tel: (01) 3524286
Fax: (01) 3578920
Decent rooms; a good location on a
quiet street overlooking the park.
$$$
Hotel Rex
Rua Castilho, 169
Tel: (01) 3882161
Fax: (01) 3887581

For those who can't afford the Ritz
or the Meridian, the Rex is a nice
hotel next door. **$$$**
Residencial Dom João
Rua José Estêvão, 43
Tel: (01) 3144171
Fax: (01) 3524569
In a quiet residential neighbour-
hood, slightly off the beaten track,
but only a 15-minute walk to the
Praça Marquês de Pombal. **$$$**

2-star
Pensão Fluorescente
Rua das Portas de Santo Antão, 99
Tel: (01) 3426609
Fax: (01) 3427733
Tiled hallways and bright, clean
rooms, some with full baths. Very
centrally located, near Praça dos
Restauradores. **$**
Pensão Roma
Travessa da Glória 22-A
Tel/fax: (01) 3524569.
Has many of the amenities of a
hotel, including private bath and TV
in every room. Don't let the rather
shabby exterior put you off; the
inside is well kept and clean. **$**

AROUND LISBON
Sintra
Estalagem de Colares
Estrada Nacional, 247, Colares
Tel: (01) 9282942
Fax: (01) 9282983
Modern hotel on the main road.

MINHO
Arcos de Valdevez
Pensão Costa do Vez
EN 101 Silvares
Tel: (058) 51 11 90
Fax: (058) 52 28 51
Comfortable *residencial* situated
half a kilometre out of town towards
Monção. **$**

Braga
Hotel Elevador
Bom Jesus do Monte
Tel: (053) 60 34 00
Fax: (053) 67 66 79.
Just 4 km (2 miles) from Braga;
recently renovated. **$$$**
Hotel Tourismo de Braga
Praceta João XXI

Tel: (053) 61 22 00
Fax: (053) 61 22 11.
Near the centre; modern and
comfortable. **$$$**
Albergaria da Sé
Rua Gonçalo Pereira, 39-51
Tel: (053) 21 45 02
Fax: (053) 21 45 01.
Central, modern; near Cathedral. **$$**
Albergaria Senhora Branca
Largo Senhora a Branca, 58
Tel: (053) 26 99 38
Fax: (053) 26 99 37
Comfortable modern hotel in the
centre of town. **$$**

Guimarães
Hotel de Guimarães
Rua Eduardo de Almeida Guimarães
Tel: (053) 51 58 88
Fax: (053) 51 62 34
Modern; 10 minutes' walk from the
city centre. **$$$**
**Hotel Fundador D. Pedro
(Residencial)**
Av. D. Afonso Henriques, 740
Tel: (053) 51 37 81
Fax: (053) 51 37 86
Next door to the Hotel de
Guimarães; rather run-down. **$$**

Viana do Castelo
Estalagem Caso Melo Alvim
Av. Conde Carreira, 28
Tel: (058) 810 82 00
Fax: (058) 810 82 20
Very comfortable *estalagem*
installed in a restored period house
near the railway station. **$$$$**
Viana Sol Hotel
Largo Vasco da Gama
Tel: (058) 82 89 95
Fax: (058) 82 34 01
Near the old docks, 10 minutes'
walk from town centre. **$$**
Jardim (Residencial)
Largo 5 de Outubro, 68
Tel: (058) 82 89 15
Fax: (058) 82 89 17
By the river-front gardens, near the
centre of town. **$**

TRAS-OS-MONTES
Bragança
Pensão Classis (Residencial)
Avenida João da Cruz, 102
Tel: (073) 33 16 31
Fax: (073) 2 34 58. **$$**

Pensão Bragança
Av. Sá Carneiro
Tel: (073) 33 15 78
Fax: (073) 33 12 42. **$$**

DOURO
Pinhão
Vintage House Hotel
Tel: (054) 73 02 30
Recently opened, beautifully
situated in the heart of port wine
region. **$$$**

BEIRA LITORAL
Aveiro
Hotel Afonso V
Rua Dr. Manuel das Neves, 65
Tel: (034) 2 51 91
Fax: (034) 38 11 11
Near the city centre. **$$**
Hotel Imperial
Rua Dr Nascimento Leitão
Tel: (034) 2 21 4 1
Fax: (034) 2 41 48
Very modern and central. **$$**
Hotel Pomba Branca
Rua Luís Gomes de Carvalho, 23
Tel: (034) 38 19 92
Fax: (034) 38 18 44
Charming converted villa near town
centre. **$$**
Pensão Estrela (Residencial)
Rua José Estevão, 4
Tel: (034) 2 38 18. **$**

Buçaco
Palace Hotel
Tel: (031) 93 01 01
Fax: (031) 93 16 09
Luxury hotel in an old hunting lodge
set in a forest. Nearby is the
military museum featuring exhibits
from the Peninsular War. **$$$$**

Coimbra
Hotel Tivoli Coimbra
Rua João Machado
Tel: (039) 2 69 34
Fax: (039) 2 68 27
On the western outskirts, new and
very comfortable. **$$$**
Hotel Astória
Av. Emídio Navarro, 21
Tel: (039) 2 20 55
Fax: (039) 2 20 57
Belle Epoque, river front, across
from the tourist offfice. **$$**

Price Categories

Price categories are based on
the cost of a double room for one
night in high season.
**$$$$** = above 22.000$
**$$$** = 15.000$–22.000$
**$$** = 10.000$–15.000$
**$** = up to 10.000$

Hotel D. Luís
Santa Clara Coimbra
Tel: (039) 44 25 10
Fax: (039) 44 91 56
Tall, modern, on southern bank of
the Rio Mondego with grand view of
Coimbra. **$$**
Pensão Rivoli
Praça do Comércio, 27
Tel: (039) 2 55 50
Central. A beautiful courtyard,
friendly management: slightly run-
down. **$**

Leiria
Hotel Eurosol
Rua Dom José Alves Correia da
Silva Leiria
Tel: (044) 81 22 01
Fax: (044) 81 12 05
Modern, with views over the old
town and castle. **$$$**

ESTREMADURA
Obidos
Albergaria Josefa d'Obidos
Rua Dom João d'Ornelas
Tel: (062) 95 92 28
Fax: (062) 95 95 33
Near the old town, very
comfortable. **$$$**
Mansão da Torre
Tel: (062) 95 92 47
Fax: (062) 95 90 51
Modern hotel, 2 km (1 mile) out of
town on the road towards Caldas da
Rainha. **$$**

Tomar
Hotel dos Templários
Largo Cândido dos Reis, 1
Tel: (049) 32 17 30
Fax: (049) 32 21 91. **$$$**
Estalagem de Santa Iria
Parque de Mouchão
Tel: (049) 31 33 26
Fax: (049) 32 10 82. **$$**

UPPER ALENTEJO
Evora
Albergaria Vitória
Rua Diana de Lis, 5
Tel: (066) 2 71 74
Fax: (066) 2 09 74
Modern, on outskirts of town. **$$**
Hotel D. Fernando
Av. Dr Barahona, 2
Tel: (066) 74 17 17
Fax: (066) 74 17 16
Well appointed modern hotel. **$$**
Hotel Évorahotel
Quinta do Cruzeiro, EN 114
Tel: (066) 73 48 00
Fax: (066) 73 48 06
Modern and comfortable. **$$**
Pensão Riveira
Rua 5 de Outubro, 47–49
Tel: (066) 2 33 04
Fax: (066) 2 04 67
Small, slightly old-fashioned; near
the centre. **$$**
Solar de Monfalim
Largo da Misericordia
Tel: (066) 75 00 00
Fax: (066) 74 23 67
In a converted mansion. **$$**
Hotel Sta Clara
Travessa da Milheira, 19
Tel: (066) 2 41 41
Fax: (066) 2 65 44
Good value, very central. **$**
Pensão Diana
Rua Diogo Cão,2
Tel: (066) 2 20 08
Fax: (066) 2 04 67. **$**
Pensão Monte das Flores
Monte das Flores
Tel: (066) 74 96 80
Fax: (066 74 96 80. **$**

Redondo
Hotel Convento de São Paulo
Serra de Ossa, Aldeia da Serra
Tel: (066) 99 91 00
Fax: (066) 99 91 04
Gorgeous furnishings and beautiful
gardens set in a national forest.
$$$$

ALGARVE
Albufeira
Hotel Rocamar
Largo Jacinto D'Ayet, 7
Tel: (089) 58 69 90
Fax: (089) 58 69 98
Perched on cliff top; fine views. **$$$**

Hotel Apart. Brisa Sol
Cerro da Algoa
Tel: (089) 58 94 18
Fax: (089) 58 82 54
Re-opening in the year 2000. **$$$**

Faro
Hotel Eva
Avenida da République, 1
Tel: (089) 80 33 54
Fax: (089) 80 23 04
Make sure your room overlooks the harbour, not the noisy street. **$$$**
Hotel Faro
Praça Dr Francisco Gomes, 2
Tel: (089) 80 32 76
Fax: (089) 80 35 46 **$$$**
Estalagem Aeromar
Av. Nascente, 1, Praia de Faro
Tel: (089) 81 75 42
Fax: (089) 81 75 12
Not in Faro itself but nearer the airport, on the beach. **$$**
Pensão Samé
Rua do Bocage, 66
Tel: (089) 82 43 75
Fax: (089) 80 41 66
In the centre of town. **$$**

Lagos
Hotel Belavista da Luz
Praia da Luz
Tel: (082) 78 86 55
Fax: (082) 78 86 56
Fine modern hotel with good sports and entertainment facilities. **$$$**
Hotel de Lagos
Rua Nova da Aldeia, 83
Tel: (082) 76 99 67
Fax: (082) 76 99 20
Short walk from town centre; pool, beach club and tennis courts. **$$$**
Hotel Golfinho
Praia Dona Ana
Tel: (082) 76 99 00
Fax: (082) 76 99 99
Somewhat dated, but well set among coves and beaches. **$$$**
Hotel de Meia Praia
Meia Praia
Tel: (082) 76 20 01
Fax: (082) 76 20 08
Overlooking Meia Praia beach near Lagos. **$$$**

Loulé
Hotel Loulé Jardim
Praça Manuel Arriaga
Tel: (089) 41 30 95

Fax: (089) 46 31 77
In an old building near the centre; no restaurant. **$$**

Portimão
Hotel Delfim
Praia dos Três Irmãos
Tel: (082) 45 89 01
Fax: (082) 45 89 70
Set high above the sea; modern, with good sports facilities. **$$$**
Hotel D. João II
Torralta
Portimão
Tel: (082) 45 91 35
Fax: (082) 45 93 63
Modern; good sports and recreational facilities. **$$$**
Pensão Alcaide
Praia do Vau, Portimão
Tel: (082) 40 14 62
Fax: (082) 40 16 95. **$$**

Praia da Rocha
Hotel Algarve
Avenida Tomás Cabreira
Praia da Rocha
Tel: (082) 41 50 01
Fax: (082) 41 59 99
Grand hotel on gorgeous beach. **$$$$**
Hotel Bela Vista
Avenida Tomás Cabreira
Tel: (082) 45 04 80
Fax: (082) 41 53 69
Small and comfortable; no restaurant. **$$$**

Sagres
Hotel de Baleeira
Baleeira, Sagres
Vila do Bispo
Tel: (082) 62 42 12
Fax: (082) 62 44 25
Ocean views, a seawater swimming pool, and tennis court. **$$**

Tavira
Convento de Santo Antonio
Atalaia, 56
Tel: (081) 32 56 32
Fax: (081) 32 56 32
An old Franciscan convent virtually in the centre of the village. **$$$**

Vale de Lobo
Hotel Dona Filipa
Tel: (089) 39 41 41
Fax: (089) 39 42 88. **$$$$**

Vilamoura
Hotel Atlantis Vilamoura
Tel: (089) 38 99 77
Fax: (089) 38 99 62
Very comfortable; comprehensive sports facilities. **$$$$**
Hotel Dom Pedro Marina
Rua Tivoli
Tel: (089) 38 98 02
Fax: (089) 31 32 70
Modern; near the waterfront and marina. **$$$$**

PORTO
Hotel Infante de Sagres
Praça D. Filipa de Lencastre, 62
Tel: (02) 200 81 01
Fax: (02) 205 49 37.
Splendid old hotel right in the centre; full of character. **$$$$**
Hotel Le Meridien Park Atlantic
Av. Da Boavista, 1466
Tel: (02) 600 19 13
Fax: (02) 600 20 31
A little farther out of town than the above. **$$$$**
Hotel Ipanema Park
Rua de Serralves, 124
Tel: (02) 610 41 74
Fax: (02) 610 28 09
Excellent service and beautiful views over the River Douro. **$$$$**
Hotel Porto Palácio
Av. Da Boavista, 1269
Tel: (02) 608 66 00
Fax: (02) 609 14 67. **$$$$**
Hotel Apart. Tuela Torre
Rua Gonçalo Sampaio, 282
Tel: (02) 607 18 00
Fax: (02) 607 18 10
Modern; conveniently situated near Boavista. **$$$**
Hotel Mercure da Batalha
Praça da Batalha, 116
Tel: (02) 200 05 71
Fax: (02) 200 24 68
Near the centre. **$$$**
Hotel Castor
Rua das Doze Casas, 17
Tel: (02) 57 00 14
Fax: (02) 56 60 76
A little way from the centre. **$$**
Hotel Dom Henrique
Rua Guedes de Azevedo, 179
Tel: (02) 200 57 55
Fax: (02) 201 94 51. **$$$**
Hotel Inca
Praça Coronel Pacheco, 52

Tel: (02) 208 41 51
Fax: (02) 205 47 56
Central; well-placed for shops. **$$$**
Hotel Ipanema
Rua do Campo Alegre, 156/174
Tel: (02) 606 80 61
Fax: (02) 606 33 39
Comfortable; slightly gloomy but
conveniently placed for buses to
centre. **$$$**
Hotel Beta Porto
Rua do Ameal, 607
Tel: (02) 82 50 45
Fax: (02) 82 52 20. **$$$**
Hotel Boa Vista
Esplanada do Castelo, 58, Foz do
Douro
Tel: (02) 618 31 75
Fax: (02) 617 38 18
Well located near mouth of the Rio
Douro. **$$**
Grande Hotel do Porto
Rua Santa Catarina, 197
Tel: (02) 200 81 76
Fax: (02) 205 10 61
Close to the main square. **$$**
Holiday Inn – Garden Court
Praça da Batalha, 127
Tel: (02) 339 23 00
Fax: (02) 200 60 09
In the centre of town. **$$**
Hotel Tuela
Rua do Arquit. Marques da Silva,
200
Tel: (02) 600 47 47
Fax: (02) 600 37 09
Near Boavista; next door to the
Tuela Torre. **$$**
Pensão Pão de Açucar
Rua do Almada, 262
Tel: (02) 200 24 25
Fax: (02) 205 02 39. **$**
**Residencial Castelo Santa
Catarina**
Rua Santa Catarina, 1347
Tel: (02) 509 77 81. **$**
Residencial Rex
Praça da República, 117
Tel: (02) 200 45 48
Fax: (02) 208 38 82. **$**

South of Porto
Hotel Ibis Porto
Lugar de Chãs, Afurada
Vila Nova de Gaia
Tel: (02) 772 07 72
Fax: (02) 772 07 88
Easy access from motorway. **$$**

Price Categories

Price categories are based on
the cost of a double room for one
night in high season.
**$$$$** = above 22.000$
**$$$** = 15.000$–22.000$
**$$** = 10.000$–15.000$
**$** = up to 10.000$

Manor Houses

AROUND LISBON
Sintra
Pátio do Saloio
Rua Padre Amaro Teixeira Azevedo,
14, Várzea, 2710
Tel: (01) 9241520
Fax: (01) 9241512. **$$$**
Quinta da Capela
Estrada de Monserrate, 2710
Tel: (01) 9290170
Sixteenth-century house with a
chapel and superb views. **$$$**
Quinta de São Tiago
Estrada de Monserrate, 2710
Tel/Fax: (01) 9232923
Comfortable and quiet. **$$$**

MINHO
Arcos de Valdevez
Casa do Adro
Lugar de Eiró Soajo
Tel/Fax: (058) 57 63 27
Fine old granite house in the centre
of this mountain village, 15 km
(9 miles) from Arcos. **$$**

Guimarães
Casa de Sezim
Rua de Sezim
Santo Amaro
Tel: (053) 52 30 00
Fax: (053) 52 31 96
Splendid 18th-century façade. Well
known for the high quality of its
white wine. **$$$**

Ponte de Lima
Paço de Calheiros
Calheiros
Tel: (058) 94 71 64
Fax: (058) 94 72 94
Located 7 km (4 miles) outside
Ponte de Lima, this is a splendid
country manor house full of
character. **$$$**

Casa do Antepaço
Lugar de Antepaço, Arcolezo
Tel: (058) 94 17 02
Fine old Minho-style house
overlooking the Rio Lima, on a
farming estate. **$$**
Casa de Castro
Lugar do Castro, Ribeira
Tel: (058) 94 11 56
Fine granite kitchen and tower in a
17th-century house near Ponte de
Lima. **$$**
Casa do Outeiro
Lugar do Outeiro
Tel: (058) 94 12 06
Sixteenth-century country house,
2km (1 mile) from town. **$$**
Casa das Torres
Lugar de Arribão Facha
Tel: (058) 94 13 69
Eighteenth-century house with fine
views and impressive gateway. **$$**
Império do Minho
Av. Dos Plátanos
Tel: (058) 74 15 10
Fax: (058) 94 25 67
Very comfortable and near the town
centre, but in a quiet position
overlooking the river. **$$**

Viana do Castelo
Quinta do Paço d'Anha
Lugar dos Penedos, Vila Nova de
Anha
Tel: (058) 32 24 59
Fax: (058) 323 39 04
Farming estate which produces its
own *vinho verde*. Apartments in
converted farm buildings. **$$$**
Casa Barros
Rua de S. Pedro, 28
Tel: (058) 82 37 05
Fax: (058) 82 81 37
An old town house right in the
historic centre. **$$**

DOURO
Amarante
Casa da Lavada
Travança do Monte Amarante
Tel: (055) 43 38 33
Fax: (02) 618 15 16
There are superb rural views from
this 16th-century house. **$$**

Lamego
Vila Hostilina
Tel: (054) 6 23 94

Fax: (054) 65 51 94
Samll *quinta* on Lamego-Porto road.
Pool, and health facilities. **$$**
Quinta de Vista Alegre
Tel: (054) 65 61 71
Fax: (054) 65 61 80
Has good views – as its name
suggests. **$$**

BEIRA LITORAL
Coimbra
Hotel Quinta das Lágrimas
Quinta das Lágrimas
Tel: (039) 44 16 15
Fax: (039) 44 16 95
Eighteenth-century palace
converted to a small, tasteful hotel,
set in the park where Inêz de
Castro is said to have met her
violent end. **$$$$**

ESTREMADURA
Porto de Mós
Quinta do Rio Alcaide
Tel: (044) 40 21 24
A small group of houses set within
an active *quinta* in the Parque
Natural das Serras de Aire e
Candeeiros. **$$**

Santarém
Casa de Pedra
Rua das Pedras Negras, 16
Tel: (043) 76 97 54
Fax: (01) 495 30 03
Quinta da Sobreira
Vale de Figueira
Tel: (043) 42 02 21
Fax: (1) 342 47 33
Thirteen km (8 miles) from
Santarém. An old house with
swimming pool and gardens. **$$$**

UPPER ALENTEJO
Alendroal
Casa de Terena
Rua Direita, 45
Tel: (068) 4 51 32
Fax: (068) 4 51 55
Restored 200-year-old house in
centre of Terena, 10 km (6 miles)
from Alendroal. **$$**
Herdade Dom Pedro
Tel: (068) 4 591 37
Old house, peaceful country
location. **$$**

Price Categories
Price categories are based on
the cost of a double room for one
night in high season.
**$$$$** = above 22.000$
**$$$** = 15.000$–22.000$
**$$** = 10.000$–15.000$
**$** = up to 10.000$

ALGARVE
Faro
Quinta de Benatrite
Santa Bárbara da Nexe
Tel/Fax: (089) 9 04 50

Pousadas
AROUND LISBON
Setúbal
Pousada de Palmela
2950 Palmela
Tel: (01) 2351226
Fax: (01) 2330440
Near Setúbal. Spectacularly set,
inside castle walls. **$$$$**
Pousada São Filipe
2900 Setúbal
Tel: (065) 523844
Fax: (065) 532538
In an old fortress, with lovely views
overlooking the harbour. **$$$$**
Pousada Vale do Gaio
Barragem Tito Morais, 7595 Torrão
Tel: (065) 669610
Southeast of Setúbal. Small
pousada beside a lake. **$$$**

MINHO
Amares
**Amares Pousada de Santa Maria
do Bouro**
Tel: (053) 37 19 70
Fax: (053) 37 19 76
Splendidly converted 12th-century
monastery. Conveniently
situated for exploring the Peneda-
Gerês National Park. **$$$$**

Caniçada
Pousada de São Bento
Estrada N.304
4850 Vieira do Minho
Tel: (053) 64 71 90
Fax: (053) 64 78 67
A restored hunting lodge on the

edge of (and with fine views of)
Peneda-Gerês National Park. **$$$$**

Guimarães
Pousada de Nossa Sra De Oliveira
Rua de Santa Maria Guimarães
Tel: (053) 51 41 57
Fax: (053) 51 42 04
A manor house in the centre of the
city in the old district. **$$$**
Pousada de Santa Marinha
Penha
Tel: (053) 51 44 53
Fax: (053) 51 44 59
Just outside Guimarães in an ex-
quisitely renovated convent. **$$$$**

Valença do Minho
Pousada de São Teotónio
Tel: (051) 82 42 42
Fax: (051) 82 43 97
Modern *pousada* situated within the
walls of the old fortress town on the
border with Galicia. **$$$**

Viana do Castelo
Pousada do Monte Santa Luzia
Monte de Santa Luzia
Viana do Castelo
Tel: (058) 82 88 89
Fax: (058) 82 88 92
Elegant 19th-century refurbished
pousada with magnificent views of
the coast and inland along the Rio
Lima towards the mountains. **$$$**

Vila Nova de Cerveira
Pousada de D. Dinis
Praça da Liberdade
Tel: (051) 79 56 01
Fax: (051) 79 56 04
Situated inside the wall of the
town's old castle with fine views
over the Rio Minho. **$$$**

TRAS-OS-MONTES
Alijó
Pousada de Barão de Forrester
Rua José Rufino
Tel: (059) 95 92 15
Fax: (059) 95 93 04
Famous town house, a *pousada*
since 1983. Near Vila Real. **$$$**

Bragança
Pousada de São Bartolomeu
Estrada de Turismo
Tel: (073) 33 14 93

Fax: (073) 2 34 53
Constructed in the late 1950s,
recently refurbished. Overlooking
the old walled town and castle. **$$$**

Miranda do Douro
Pousada de Santa Catarina
Estrada da Barragem
Tel: (073) 43 12 05
Fax: (073) 43 10 65
High above the Rio Douro with
views across to Spain. **$$**

DOURO
Amarante
Pousada de São Gonçalo
Curva do Lancete Asiães
Tel: (055) 46 11 23
Fax: (055) 46 13 53
In the Marão mountains, between
Amarante (24 km/15 miles) and
Vila Real (20km/12 miles). **$$$$**

BEIRA LITORAL
Agueda
Pousada de Santo António
Mourisca do Vouga Serém
Tel: (034) 52 32 30
Fax: (034) 52 31 92
Very comfortable *pousada* 10 km
(6 miles) north of Agueda. **$$$**

Murtosa
Pousada da Ria
Estrada Nacional 327, Torreira
Tel: (034) 83 83 32
Fax: (034) 83 83 33
Situated on an isthmus between
the ocean and the lagoon. Peaceful
setting overlooking the estuary. **$$$**

Oliveira do Hospital
Pousada de Santa Bárbara
Pousada de Santa Bárba Oliveira do
Hospital
Tel: (038) 5 95 51
Fax: (038) 5 96 45
Between Coimbra and the Serra da
Estrela. **$$$**

BEIRA ALTA
Almeida
Pousada da Senhora das Neves
Tel: (071) 57 42 83
Fax: (071) 57 43 20
East of the Serra da Estrela,

northwest of Guarda, within small
fortress town. **$$$**

Caramulo
Pousada de São Jerónimo
Tel: (032) 86 12 91
Fax: (032) 86 16 40
A small *pousada* between Aveiro
and Viseu. Swimming pool. **$$**

BEIRA BAIXA
Manteigas
Pousada de São Lourenço
Tel: (075) 98 24 50
Fax: (075) 98 24 53
High in the Serra da Estrela. **$$$**

ESTREMADURA
Batalha
Pousada do Mestre Afonso
Domingues
Tel: (044) 76 52 60
Fax: (044) 76 52 47
Right next to the abbey. **$$$**

Obidos
Pousada do Castelo
Paço Rea
Tel: (062) 95 91 05
Fax: (062) 95 91 48
In the castle, within the walled
town. **$$$$**

UPPER ALENTEJO
Elvas
Pousada de Santa Luzia
Avenida de Badajoz
Tel: (068) 62 21 94
Fax: (068) 62 21 27
Close to main road; good food. **$$$**

Estremoz
Pousada da Rainha Santa Isabel
Largo Dom Dinis
Tel: (068) 33 20 75
Fax: (068) 33 20 79
Very dramatic setting, in a former
castle. **$$$$**

Evora
Pousada dos Lóios
Largo dos Condes de Vila Flor
Tel: (066) 2 40 51
Fax: (066) 2 72 48
Former monastery. Very popular, so
book early. **$$$$**

Marvão
Pousada de Santa Maria
Rua 24 de Janeiro, 7
Tel: (045) 9 32 01
Fax: (045) 9 34 40
Near Portalegre, within walled town
with border fortress. **$$$**

Sousel
Pousada de São Miguel
Tel: (068) 55 11 60
Fax: (068) 55 11 55
Small country house style with
facilities for hunting parties. **$$$**

LOWER ALENTEJO
Santa Clara-a-Velha
Pousada de Santa Clara
Tel: (083) 88 22 50
Fax: (083) 88 24 02
On the Algarve–Alentejo border,
overlooking a reservoir. **$$$**

Santiago do Cacém
Pousada de São Tiago
Tel: (069) 2 24 59
Fax: (069) 2 24 59
A few miles east of Sines. **$$**

Serpa
Pousada de São Gens
Tel: (084) 5 37 24
Fax: (084) 5 33 37
East of Beja. **$$$**

Vila Viçosa
Pousada de Dom João IV
Tel: (068) 9 87 42
Fax: (068) 9 87 47
Located in a 15th-century convent
in the historical area of the town.
$$$$

ALGARVE
Sagres
Pousada do Infante
Tel: (082) 62 42 22
Fax: (082) 62 42 25
Near Cape St Vincent in the village
of Sagres, with sea views. **$$$**

São Brás de Alportel
Pousada de São Brás
Tel: (089) 84 23 04
Fax: (089) 84 17 26
Twenty minutes from Faro airport;
comfortable, with good views. **$$$**

Where to Eat

What to Eat

Portuguese food is simple and fresh, abundant and filling, with few complicated sauces, but strong flavours and lots of garlic, olive oil and herbs. Canned and frozen foods are scorned. Portions are more than filling, and you'll often have to work hard to clean your plate. Shellfish is popular and is usually served by the gram: about 300 grams is enough for one.

Meal times are relaxed: lunch is between 1 and 3pm; dinner usually between 8 and 9.30pm.

REGIONAL SPECIALITIES

All regions in Portugal are known for particular culinary specialities. Some of the best known of these include:

Coimbra & Aveiro
Chanfana (kid stew); *leitão* (roast suckling pig); *pastéis de Santa Clara* (pastries).
Douro & Minho
Port and *vinho verde*; *tripas á moda do Porto* (tripe with butter beans).
Serra da Estrela
Queijo da serra (cheese); roast kid.
Trás-os-Montes
Chouriços de sangue (blood sausage); *feijoada* (bean stew); goat; rabbit; trout; lamprey.
Alentejo
Açorda de alhos (bread soaked in broth heavily spiced with garlic); *carne de porco á Alentejana* (clams and pork with coriander).
Algarve
Ameijoas na cataplana (clams with ham and sausage, spiced with parsley and pepper); fried sardines; snails; seafood in general.

Favourite Foods

- *Caldo verde*, a cabbage and potato soup with *chouriço* (sausage)
- *Bacalhau* (salt-cod) is a national obsession. There are, supposedly, 365 ways to prepare it,
- *Carne de porco á Alentejana* (clams and pork with coriander) is a favourite meat dish.
- Sardines: fat, fresh and ubiquitous near the coast.
- *Doces de ovos*, or egg sweets, made with egg yolk, sugar and cinnamon and served at the end of a meal.

Restaurant listings

Restaurants in Portugal are rated on a scale of one to four stars, depending on expense, decor and service. The quality of food does not necessarily relate to the rating: there are plenty of 1- and 2-star neighbourhood places that serve great food.

Below are a few recommended restaurants, but there are, of course, many more. Some recommended restaurants are attached to hotels. *Pousada* dining rooms are of consistently high quality (and are also usually expensive).

LISBON

It is wise to reserve a table at the more expensive restaurants.

Expensive ($$$)
Avis
Rua Serpa Pinto, 12b
Tel: (01) 3428391
Chic atmosphere, international menu.
Casa da Comida
Travessa das Amoreiras, I
Tel: (01) 3885376
Casa do Leão
(in St Jorge castle)
Tel: (01) 8875962
Portuguese cuisine at its best. A grand view.
Conventual
Praça das Flores, 45
Tel: (01) 609196
Pleasant decor, good food with interesting sweets.
Escorial
Rua das Portas de Santo Antão, 47
Tel: (01) 3464429
Shellfish specialities.
Gambrinus
Rua das Portas de Santo Antão, 23
Tel: (01) 3421466
Famous for its seafood.
Tágide
Largo Academia das Belas Artes
Tel: (01) 3420720
Blue-and-white tiled setting, and a view. Food is both international and Portuguese.
Tavares Rico
Rua da Misericelas Artes
Tel: (01) 3420720
Lisbon's oldest and most sumptuous restaurant.

Moderate ($$)
Adega do Tia Matilde
Rua do Beneficência, 77
Tel: (01) 7972172
Friendly atmosphere.
Casa Transmontana
Calçada do Duque, 39
Tel: (01) 3420300
Regional dishes from the north.
Pap' Açorda
Rua da Atalaia, 57 (in the Bairro Alto)
Tel: (01) 3464811
Modern, with an excellent reputation.
Antonio
Rua Barroca, 17 (in the Bairro Alto)
Tel: (01) 3422345
Smart, soothing; international food.
Porto de Abrigo
Rua Tomás Ribeiro-63
Tel: (01) 3538780
Not far from Marquês de Pombal, this place enjoys a very good reputation and it's been open since the 1970s. Pleasant atmosphere and wonderful cuisine.
Xele Bananas
Praça das Flores, 29
Tel: (01) 3952515

Inexpensive ($)
Bota Alta
Travessa da Queimada
Tel: (01) 3427959
Popular restaurant in Bairro Alto.

Bomjardin
Travessa de Santo Antão 12
Tel: (01) 3427424
Some say it's the best roast
chicken in town.
Casa do Alentejo
Rua das Portas de Santo Antão, 58
Tel: (01) 3428011
Huge Alentejo meals in lavishly tiled
dining rooms.
Cervejaria da Trindade
Rua Nova da Trindade, 20c
Tel: (01) 3423506
Classical wall-to-wall tiles – a large
and very popular restaurant. Go
early at weekends.
Malmequer Bemmequer
Largo de São Miguel 25
Tel: (01) 8876535
In the heart of the Alfama.
O Bichano
Rua Atalaia, 78.
Tiny place in the Bairro Alto
Solar dos Presuntos
Portas de Santo Antão, I50
Tel: (01) 3424253
Hearty Minho food in the street-of-
many-restaurants.
Sol Dourado
Rua Jardim do Regador, 19–25 (off
Restauradores)
Tel: (01) 3472570
Cheerful setting, tasty food.
Tasca do Manel
Rua da Barroca, 24.
Another Bairro Alto favourite.

SINTRA
Hotel Palácio de Seteais
Avenida Barbosa du Bocage, 8
Tel: (01) 9233200
Marvellous style, frescoed walls, a
good meal. **$$–$$$**
Solar de São Pedro
Praça Dom Fernando II, 12 (in the
village of São Pedro)
Tel: (01) 9231860
Very popular regional food. Packed
during fairs. **$$–$$$**

COSTA VERDE AND THE MINHO
Braga
Hotel Elevador
Bom Jesus do Monte
Tel: (053) 676548
Fax: (053) 676679

Excellent regional cuisine in a hotel
at the sanctuary (*see Where to
Stay*). **$$–$$$**
Inácio
Praca Conde S. Joaquim, 4
Tel: (053) 613235
Regional food, very pleasant. **$$**

Viana do Castelo
Estalagem da Boega
Quinta do Outeiral, Gondarém, near
Vila Nova da Cerveira
Tel: (051) 795231
Distinguished Minho cuisine. Best
to book. **$$$**
Pousada de Monte Santa Luzia
Monte de Santa Luzia
Viana do Castelo
Tel: (058) 82 88 89
Fax: (058) 82 88 92
This hilltop hotel with a grand view
serves international food. **$$–$$$**
Os Três Potes
Beco dos Fornos, 9
Tel: (058) 829928
Traditional setting; regional food. **$$**

Price Categories

The restuarants are divided into
the following price categories
based on a meal for two:
$$$ (Expensive) above 10.000$
$$ (Moderate) 5–10.000$
$ (Inexpensive) below 5.000$

TRAS-OS-MONTES
Bragança
Hotel Bragança
Avenida Sá Carneiro
Tel: (073) 331578
Classy and varied. **$$$**
Lá em Casa
Rua Marquês de Pombal, 7
Tel: (073) 22111
Regional cooking. **$$**
Solar Bragançano
Praça da Sé, 34
Tel: (073) 23875
A cosy place, rustic decor, popular
among the locals. **$$**

Chaves
Hotel Aquae Flavia
Praça do Brasil, 5400
Tel: (076) 332911
Fax: (076) 26497

Modern, good views overlooking the
riverfront. **$$–$$$**

Macedo de Cavaleiras
Estalagem do Caçador
Largo Manuel Pinto de Azevedo
Tel: (078) 421356
Fax: (078) 421381
Good food in a delightful inn. **$$**

Mogadouro
A Lareira
Av. Nossa Senhora do Caminho
Tel: (079) 32363
A large restaurant in a small town,
owned by a French-trained chef.
Excellent value. **$$$**

Porto
Portucale
Rua da Alegria, 598
Tel: (02) 570717
Fine restaurant with a view. **$$$**
Aleixo
Rua da Estacão
Tel: (02) 570462
A very popular place, family-run. The
locals consider it one of the best in
the city. **$$**
Gambamar
Rua do Campo Alegre, 110
Tel: (02) 6092396
Informal, very pleasant, excellent
seafood. Open late. **$$**
Mercearia
Cais da Ribeira
Tel: (02) 2004389
One of the best typical Portuguese
places in Porto. **$$**
Tripeiro
Rua dom Passos Manuel, 195
Tel: (02) 2005886
Good food and huge portions. **$$**

BEIRA LITORAL
Aveiro
A Cozinha do Rei
Hotel Afonso V, Rua Dr Manuel das
Neves, 66
Tel: (034) 26802
The freshest of fish and eels from
the lagoon. **$$$**
Imperial
Rua Dr Nascimento Leitão 9 (in
hotel of the same name)
Tel: (034) 22141
Very good. **$$$**

Centenário
Praça do Mercado 10
Tel: (034) 22798
Good Portuguese cooking. **$$**

Coimbra
Marquês de Marialva
Cantanhede (about 2l km/12 miles northwest of Coimbra)
Tel: (039) 420010
Varied cuisine. **$$$**
O Alfredo
Avenida João das Regras (south of the river)
Tel: (039) 441522
Seafood, regional cooking. **$$**
Real das Canas
Vila Mendes, 7 Santa Clara
Tel: (039) 814877
South of the river, good food and lovely view; very popular. **$$**

BEIRA ALTA

Covilhã
Solneve
Residencial Solneve, Rua Visconde de Coriscada, 126
Tel:/Fax: (075) 323001
Large and cheerful. **$**

Guarda
Hotel de Turismo
Tel: (071) 223366
Fax: (071) 223399
Well-maintained old hotel with good cooking and service. **$$**

Seia
Camelo
Avenida 1 de Maio
Tel: (038) 25555
On the main street. Large, with a pleasant atmosphere and good food. **$$**
O Júlio
Travessa do Loureiro, 1
Tel: (038) 42142
Cosy family-run place. Excellent food and friendly service. **$$**

Viseu
Trave Negra
Rua dos Loureiros 40
Tel: (032) 26138
Roast kid and codfish on a regional menu. **$$**

Price Categories

The restuarants are divided into the following price categories based on a meal for two:
$$$ (Expensive) above 10.000$
$$ (Moderate) 5–10.000$
$ (Inexpensive) below 5.000$

ALENTEJO

Évora
Fialho's
Travessa das Mascarenhas, l4
Tel: 066-23079
The Portuguese favourite for classical regional food. **$$$**
Típico Guião
Rua da República, 81
Tel: 066-23071.
Very good value. Tour groups eat here, but in a separate room. **$$**

ALGARVE

Almost the entire coast caters to holiday-makers, so there are numerous restaurants. The following is just a small selection:

Albufeira
Castel do Bispo
Estrado do Ourada
Tel: (89) 586754
Perched on a cliff; good Italian food. **$$$**
Fernando's Hideaway
Tel: (082) 541618
On the road from Albufeira to Montechoro towards Ferreiras. Family-run, serving excellent traditional Portuguese food. **$$**
Os Arcos
Rua Alves Correia
Tel: (089) 513460
Roof terrace and traditional Portuguese cooking. **$**

Almancil
Duas Sentinelas
Cascalheira, near Quatro Estradas
Tel: (089) 389522
A popular Portuguese restaurant near the big Vale do Lobo and Quinta do Lago resorts. **$$**
Les Lauriers
Just off the by- pass in Almancil
Tel: (089) 397575
Good French food. **$$**

Faro
Hotel and Restaurant La Réserve
Santa Bárbara de Nexe
Tel: (089) 90234
The best in the region, a few minutes' drive inland from Faro. It's the only *Relais & Chateaux* establishment in Portugal. No credit cards. **$$$**
Cidade Velha
Behind the Cathedral
Tel: (089) 27145
Small, stylish and intimate; in the old town. **$$–$$$**
Dois Irmãos
Tel: (089) 823337
The oldest restaurant in Faro, in the large and cheerful town centre. Good rustic cooking. **$$**

Lagos
Alpendre
Rua António Barbosa Viana, 17
Tel: (082) 762705.
Pleasing, dark-beamed place. High-quality food. **$$**
O Galeão
Rua da Laranjeira, l
Tel: (082) 763909.
Pleasant place to eat. **$$**
O Lamberto
Rua 25 de bril 21
Tel: (082) 763746
Family-run restaurant; good food, mostly fish. **$$**
Quatro Aguas
Tel: (081) 325329
Fish and seafood and a terrace with a view over the lagoon. **$$**
O Alcatraz
Santa Luzia-Tavira
Tel: (081) 381092
Great fish and seafood. Closed Monday. **$**

Loulé
Aux Beaux Enfants
Rua Engenheiro Duarte Pacheco (near the post office)
Tel: (089) 62096
Small restaurant. Good French cooking. **$$**

Olhão
O Escondidinho
Rua José Leonardo
Tel: (089) 702674
In the delightful town centre. **$$**

Portimão

A Lanterna
East of the old bridge
Tel: (082) 414429
The nicest place to dine (no lunch).
The duck is home-grown, the
seafood excellent. **$$**

O Bicho
Largo Gil Eanes 12
Tel: (082) 22977
Mostly fish; good *bacalhau*. **$$**

Sagres

A Tasca
Tel: (082) 64177
A large and popular restaurant
above the fishermen's bay: its
shellfish is good and still sold at
reasonable prices. **$$**

O Telheiro
Praia da Mareta
Tel: (082) 64179
Right beside the lovely beach. Good
value. Shellfish a speciality. **$$**

Tavira

Avenida
Rua da Liberdade
Tel: (081) 81113
Good regional cooking. **$$**

Patio
Rua António Cabreira
Tel: (081) 23008
On the east side of the old bridge.
Portuguese and French food. Old
house with roof terrace. **$$**

Drinking Notes

Portuguese wine, at its best, is
superb, and even cheaply-priced
wines can be delicious. (You will
find restaurants' house wines
perfectly acceptable.)

There are basically three types of
table wine: red (often described as
maduro – mature), white, and *vinho
verde* – light and slightly sparkling
(it's usually white; the red is much
rougher).

Port comes in a complexity of
varieties and colours: white is a
good apéritif, dark red aged ports a
grand *digestif,* tawny a pleasure at
any time. Local brandies are widely
available. Wine is drunk at lunch as
well as with dinner.

Beer (*cerveja*) is very popular
and there are several good

Coffee Choices

Coffee connoisseurs have a wide
variety to choose from:
● **bica**: a small cup of strong
coffee.
● **galão**: the same amount in a
large glass filled with milk; you
can have *galão escuro* or *galão
claro*, strong or weaker coffee.
● **meia de leite**: a regular cup of
coffee with milk.
● **garoto**: served in a smaller
cup.
● **Italiana**: an espresso.

varieties. You can order it by the
bottle (*garrafa*), or the glass
(*imperial*) or even a mug (*caneca*).

Nightlife

After Dark

Nightlife in Portugal means
different things to different people.
For some, it's a jug of wine and a
night of *fado* (*see next column*). For
others, it's a flashy disco, or a night
at the neighbourhood café.

Portugal's nightlife is liveliest
in Lisbon, and Lisbon's nightlife –
from *fado* to great bars and discos –
throbs in the Bairro Alto, an odd mix
of the historical and the trendy; and
in a small, smart area behind the
Avenida 24 de Julho.

Towns and smaller cities – anywhere smaller than Porto – tend to
go to sleep soon after 10pm, and
you'll find very little to do apart
from a long, slow dinner or a disco.
There are two exceptions: the tourist towns and resorts in Algarve,
where summer visitors like to stay
up late; and any town or village on
the night of a festival. In particular
Guimarães, Braga, Evora and
Caldas da Rainha are full of fun in
the evenings.

For a list of what's going on
where, look for *Agenda de Lisboa*, a
free monthly magazine which is
available at the airport and tourist
centres. Even if you can't read
Portuguese, the listings are com-
prehensible.

Music

Music, in *fado* houses, concert
halls and nightclubs alike, tends to
start fairly late, around 10pm.

The Portuguese musical tradition
is much broader than simply *fado*.
Folk music, very different from
fado, is surprisingly vibrant in
Portugal, too. Rock music, born
after the Revolution, ranges from
the mediocre to the superb.

Lisbon Musicians

A few musicians you should try to hear while you're in town:

Fado

• **Amália Rodrigues** Her two-volume *Greatest Hits,* released back in 1986, covers a wide range of her work.

Other well-known *fadistas* include Carlos do Carmo, João Braga, Manuel de Almeida and António Pinto Basto.

Folk/Popular

• **Carlos Paredes** Traditional Portuguese guitar. Beautiful instrumentals.
• **Vitorino** Folksy, traditional ballads, many from Alentejo. Janita Salomé. Vitorino's brother sings folk music with an Arabic influence.
• **Júlio Pereira** Portugal's best player of the *cavaquinho,* which looks like a baby guitar and is the ancestor of the ukelele. Popular balladeers include Fausto and Paulo de Carvalho.

Rock

• **Rui Veloso** The "father" of Portuguese rock music, influenced by soul and blues. His first album, from 1980, is Ar de Rock and he has cut many since, all of them good to excellent.
• **GNR** An energetic band whose name, by no coincidence, is the initials of the National Republican Guard.

Other bands include Pontapés, Xutos, Rádio Macau and Trovante.

FADO HOUSES

Fado is a nostalgic – though not necessarily woeful – music, a popular art with a long and mysterious history. Once associated with working-class neighbourhoods, it is now of mixed appeal, and tourists are often a primary commercial target.

The *fadista,* a powerfully voiced singer, is usually backed by *guitarras* – the twelve-stringed Portuguese version, and *violas* –

what we would call a guitar. Sometimes more charming, if less skillful, is *fado vadio,* or spontaneous amateur singing.

Fado is a performance, not a sing-song, and you are expected to be quiet and listen. The *fado* of Coimbra is usually taken far more seriously than that of Lisbon The Portuguese say it takes more than a good voice to become a *fadista* – it takes soul as well.

Lisbon

Many of Lisbon's *fado* houses are located in the Bairro Alto. There are others in the older neighbourhoods – the Alfama, Alcântara and Lapa. They usually serve dinner (optional) and often charge a fairly steep entrance or minimum consumption charge. Singing starts around 10pm. It's best to book in advance.
Adega Machado
Rua do Norte, 91
Tel: 3428713
A Mascote de Atalaia
Rua da Atalaia.
Traditional *fado,* for the neighbourhood, not the tourists. No food, no fancy decor – only wine and *fado.*
Arcadas do Faia
Rua da Barroza 54–56
Tel: 3421923
A Severa
Rua das Gáveas, 51–61
Tel: 3421204
Lisboa Ë Noite
Rua das Gáveas, 69
Tel: 3468557
Senhor Vinho
Rua do Meio, 18 (in Lapa)
Tel: 3972681

Coimbra

This is a university city, full of young people, so there is lots in the way of nightlife. But best of all is the enthusiasm for their own brand of *fado.* Among the best places are:
Boémia Bar
Rua do Cabido, 6
Diligência
Rua do Sofia
Trovador
Largo da Sé Velha

The Teatro Gil Vicente usually has a bright weekly programme of concerts and other events.

Discos and Clubs

Bars with live music – and often dancing – are called *boîtes. Discotecas,* or discos, occasionally have live music as well. "In" places can be "out" very quickly, as fashions change. Try to check what is still open and still popular when you visit.

Lisbon

Most are in or near the Bairro Alto, Rato and São Bento – areas west and up from the Avenida da Liberdade – or in a cluster off the Avenida de 24 de Julho.
Ad-Lib
Rua Barata Salgueira, 28
Tel: (01) 3561717
Sleek, chic and pricey.
Alcântara-Mar
Rua da Cozinha Econtel
Tel: (01) 3561717
Lisbon's largest disco, space for 2,000, and often bursting.
Bairro Alto
Travessa dos Inglesinhos, 48–50
Tel: (01) 3420238
Large, cheerful, tasteful Lisbon decor: a disco plus.
Frágil
Rua da Atalaia, 128
Tel: (01) 369528
Among the trendiest discos in town. Right in the Bairro Alto. Good music.
Jamaica
Rua Nova do Carvalho, 6 (near Cais do Sodré railway station)
Tel: (01) 3421859
American music and dancing with DJs. In the city's red-light district.
Kremlin
Rua das Escadinhas da Praia, 5
Also in the Alcântara area; lively.
Longas Noites
Largo do Conde Baráo, 50 (in the Casa Pia Athletic Club)
Tel: (01) 3964331
The name means "long nights", and if you're here, you've probably had one (it stays open until 4am on Friday. Unpretentious; lots of room, lots of people.
The Plateau
Rua das Escadinhas da Praia, 3
Tel: (01) 3965116
A neighbour to the Longas Noites, costly and exclusive.

Primorosa de Alvalade
Avenida dos Estados, Unidos da
America, 128–D
Tel: (01) 7971913
Disco, which is frequented mainly
by teenagers.

Porto
Postigo do Carvão
Rua Fonte Taurina, 26–34
A restaurant and piano bar.
Aniki-Bobo
Rua Fonte Taurina (next door to the
Postigo do Carvão)
No food but good music.
Rua dos Mercadores, I32
Live music.
Splash/Flying Dutchman
Centro Comercial Dallas (Boavista)
Two lively *boîtes*.
Griffon's
Centro Comercial Brasília, Rua Júlio
Dinis
A disco on one level and quieter bar
on another.
Swing
Praceta Engenheiro Amaro da Costa
Another two-level disco/pub, where
the smart set hangs out.
Twins
Rua do Passeio Alegre, 1000
(at Foz do Douro, to the west)
One of the trendiest places in town.

Cinema

Lisbon is a great place for movies.
There are dozens of cinemas – 10
in the Amoreiras Shopping Complex
alone, at the last count. And all
films in Portugal are sub-titled, not
dubbed, so they're accessible to
non-Portuguese speakers. In towns
elsewhere in Portugal there are
also plenty of cinemas. Seats are
assigned, and the usher should be
tipped 5 or 10 escudos.
  In Lisbon there are several
quaint old cinemas. The oldest is
the Animatógrafo do Rossio, a
beautiful building which opened as
a cinema in 1907, and is one of the
oldest still-operating cinemas in
Europe. It's worth a visit for the
architecture alone.

The Great Outdoors

National Parks

Parque Nacional Peneda-Gerês
The Peneda-Gerês park extends
over some 70,000 hectares (270
sq. miles) and is located in the far
north of the country. The highest
peak in the Peneda-Gerês is 1,544
metres (5,095 ft), with a view of the
Minho, Trás-os-Montes, and across
the border into Galicia.
  The lush plant life is fed by heavy
rainfall. The park is home to 17
species of plants which are found
nowhere else, as well as extensive
forests of oak and pine. Wild
ponies, deer, wolf, golden eagles,
wild boars and badgers, as well as
many other animals, live within the
boundaries.
  You may fish, ride horseback,
hike and mountain climb amid the
breathtaking scenery in the park.
You can also visit picturesque
ancient villages. There are dolmens,
perhaps 5,000 years old, and
milestones that once marked the
old Roman road to Braga.
  Entrance to the Peneda half of
the park – the northern section – is
from Melgaço, at the Galician
border, and Ponte da Barca. The
entrance to Gerês is off the
Braga–Chaves road (take the turn
off to Caniçada). There is a
pousada at the edge of the park, in
Caniçada.
  Tourist offices in the Minho,
especially in Braga, can provide
information about the park.

Parque Natural Montesinho
In the far northeastern corner of
Portugal, Montesinho lies between
Bragança, Vinhais, and the Spanish
border. As in Peneda-Gerês, many
varieties of flora and fauna abound.

There is not only wild, heath-like
scenery but also ancient villages
preserving their age-old customs.
Access is from Bragança or Vinhais.

Parque Natural Serra da Estrela
Granite peaks, glacial valleys and
streams, lakes and boulders lie
within the natural park of the Serra
da Estrela. The highest peaks in
Portugal are also quite accessible
by car (though in winter roads may
briefly be blocked). The prettiest
season, with wild flowers
everywhere, is spring.
  There are places to stay in the
larger towns in or near the Serra,
which include Gouveia, Seia,
Covilhã and Guarda. There is a
pousada in Manteigas. The Serra is
about two hours by car from
Coimbra.

Serra da Arrábida
Just south of Lisbon, the Serra da
Arrábida's natural beauty is
accessible to anyone with a car.
The steep hills, with a wide variety
of flowers and trees, and the blue
ocean for contrast, are beautiful.
The Serra da Arrábida provides
wonderful views all along the
highway 379–1, west from Setúbal.
  A good map will show you
Portugal's several other protected
areas. These include Algarve's
southwestern coast, and a coastal
wetland, the Parque Natural da Ria
Formosa, important to migrating
birds. Rural areas outside parks are
also astonishingly beautiful and rich
in birdlife.

Sport

GOLF

The standard of golf courses in Portugal is very high. Those in the Estoril/Sintra area and in Algarve are particularly popular.

Lisbon

Sil Golf
Quinta da Aroeira, Monte de Caparica (south of the Rio Tagus)
Tel: (01) 2971244
Estoril Golf Club
Avenida da República, Estoril
Tel: (01) 4680176
Estoril-Sol Golf Club
Estrada da Lagoa Azul, 3, Linho,
near Sintra
Tel: (01) 9232461
Lisbon Sports Club
Casal da Carregueira, Belas, near Queluz
Tel: (01) 4310077/4321474
Penha Longa Club
Near Sintra
Tel: (01) 9249011
Praia D'el Rei,
Between Óbidos and Peniche, easily accessible via the A8 motorway
Tel: (062) 905010

Setúbal

Tróia Golf club
Torralta, Tróia
Tel: (065) 44151/44236

Costa de Prata

Vimeiro Golf Club
Praia do Porto Novo, Vimeiro, about 65 km (40 miles) north of Lisbon
Tel: (061) 98157

Porto

Miramar Golf Club
Praia de Miramar, Avenida Sacudura Cabral, Valadares, near Porto
Tel: (02) 7622067

Vidago Golf Club
Vidago, about 2 hours from Porto
Tel: (076) 97106

Algarve

This is a selection from a large number of excellent courses:
Palmares Golf Club
Meia Praia, near Lagos
Tel: (082) 762961 or 762953
Fax: (082) 762534
Penina Golf Club
Penina, near Portimao
Tel: (082) 415415/415500
Fax: (082) 415000
Quinta do Lago Golf Club
Almancil, near Loulé and Faro
Tel: (089) 396002
Fax: (089) 394683
Vale do Lobo Golf Club
Vale da Lobo, near Loulé
Tel: (089) 394145 or 393939
Vilamoura-1 and Vilamoura-2 Golf Clubs
Vilamoura, near Loulé
Tel: (089) 302977 or 302978

TENNIS

In Lisbon, the **Marinha Golf Club** and **Lisbon Sports Club** (*listed above, under Golf*) have tennis courts. Try also:
Club Internacional de Ténis
Compolide Tel: (01) 3882084
Club de Ténis de Monsaonto
Tel: (01) 3648741
Club de Ténis do Estoril
Tel: (01) 4662770
  In Porto, the **Miramar Golf Club** has facilities for tennis.
  In Algarve, there are courts at the **Quinta do Lago**, **Vale do Lobo**, and **Vilamoura-1 Golf Clubs**, and at many hotels. Several towns have their own municipal courts.

WATERSPORTS

There are few facilities for renting equipment outside Algarve. In the Lisbon area you'll find surfboards and other equipment for hire at the beaches. For sailing, there's the **Cascais Naval Club**. Windsurfers head for the long beaches and wild waves at Guincho, further out. For deep-sea fishing, check with the local tourist office.

In Porto, the **Porto Golf Club** (*see above*) has skin-diving facilities. You can also try the Leça da Palmeira Beach (to the north) for sailing.
In Algarve, all the larger tourist beaches and towns have some facilities. Near Lagos, there are windsurfing and waterskiing facilities at Luz, São Roque (Meia Praia) and Alvor beaches; the latter two also have sailing facilities. Praia da Rocha has sailing, windsurfing and waterskiing facilities; sailing and windsurfing are practised at Armação de Pera, near Albufeira. Vilamoura has extensive watersports facilities, as does Vale de Lobo.

The Serra da Estrela is the place for the little that Portugal has to offer in the way of winter sports. Visitors ski here, despite poor facilities, but mostly they *scu* – a combination of the words ski and *cu*, which means rear end in Portuguese. To *scu*, you grab a plastic bag, sit on it, and slide downhill.

FOOTBALL

Football dominates Portuguese sports life. From the 10-year-olds playing in the street to the hundreds of professional, semi-pro and amateur teams, to the massive coverage the sport is given on TV and in the papers, football in Portugal is inescapable.
  The three most important teams in the country are FC Porto, from Porto (the 1987 European champions), Benfica, and Sporting, the latter two from Lisbon. Every Portuguese, no matter where they are from, are loyal fans of one of the three.
  The football season stretches from September or October to July. Tickets for the big three teams are difficult to get, as there are many season-ticket holders. In Lisbon, try the ticket kiosk located in Praça

dos Restauradores; elsewhere, try the stadia themselves. Games are usually held on Sunday afternoons.

BULLFIGHTING

Portuguese bullfighting is different from the Spanish variety. It is considered less violent because the bull is not killed in the ring (although, naturally, it is killed later, out of public view). Nonetheless, it is bloody enough to upset the sensibilities of many people. The star Portuguese bullfighters are on horseback, the horses beautifully bedecked and highly trained. A striking aspect of the Portugese *corrida* is the team of *forcados* – eight unpaid local heroes, colourfully dressed in short coats, tight pants, waistband and stockings – who face the bull bare-handed in an exhibition of pure *machismo*.

Bullfighting is popular primarily in Ribatejo (just outside Lisbon) and in Lisbon itself. The season runs from spring to autumn. In Lisbon, *corridas* are held in the Campo Pequeño bullring. There is also a ring in Cascais. The most famous bullfights, however, are held in Santarém and Vila Franca da Xira, northeast of Lisbon. (Take the train from Santa Apolónia.)

Ribatejo festivals, which are frequent in the summer, almost always feature bullfighting and the freeing of bulls in the streets.

Shopping

What to Buy

Portuguese handicrafts range from hand-carved toothpicks to wicker furniture to blankets and rugs. The most famous items are ceramic tiles (*azulejos*) and pottery, Arraiolos rugs, embroidery and lace (*see pages 236–7*). The beautiful Vista Alegre porcelain and Atlantis crystal bear comparison with the best in the world.

Pottery Different varieties of ceramic work are produced all over the country; in Alentejo, for example, you'll find examples of *barro* pottery, a simple brown clay, sometimes decorated, sometimes glazed. Decorations on ceramics tend to be paintings of fruit or flowers, or sometimes scenes of rural life. Fine pottery from around Coimbra often carries animal motifs, and looks quite intricate in comparison with the simple Alentejano decorations. Farther north, blue-and-white glazed pottery appears.

Rugs Arraiolos rugs, by contrast, come from only one place: Arraiolos, in Alentejo. (They are, however, sold in other parts of the country, especially Lisbon.) The art of designing and stitching these rugs probably goes back to the Middle Ages.

Where to Shop

Lisbon
Lisbon, as befits the capital, has several good shopping areas – in central Baixa, around Rua Garrett and in Avenida da Roma. Two large shopping malls are Amoreiras (uphill from the Praça Marquês de Pombal) and Cascais, off the new expressway near Cascais. A huge

new shopping complex, called Colombo, has also recently opened just opposite the Benfica football stadium.

But while many regional crafts are sold in Lisbon, there is usually a much wider and more authentic selection in the provinces. The following is a list of the traditional crafts produced in particular areas:

Alentejo
Cane and wicker work, cork products (baskets, coasters, sculpture), wool blankets, Arraiolos rugs, ceramics (*barro*), traditional hand-painted furniture, copper goods and lace.

Algarve
Palm and wicker work, copper and brass articles, candles, earthenware pottery.

Coimbra and the Beiras
Ceramics (colourful animal motifs from near Coimbra; elegant Vista Alegre porcelain from the Aveiro region; black clay pottery from the Viseu region); woven rag quilts (from the Serra da Estrela); as well as lace and embroidery.

Douro and Minho
Ceramics, wickerwork, straw baskets and hats; embroidery, crochet, and regional costumes (especially from the Viana do Castelo area), religious art (from Braga). The Thursday market in Barcelos, north of Porto, has lots of handicrafts for sale.

Trás-os-Montes
Blankets; weaving and tapestries; crocheted bedspreads; black pottery from Bisalhóes (near Vila Real).

Language

Getting By

If you speak Spanish you will be able to read Portuguese and understand some, but certainly not all, the spoken language. There are also slight similarities with written, but little with spoken, French. For most English speakers, however, Portuguese, which has many nasal sounds, is not easy to follow.

Many Portuguese speak a second language, and most have the tolerance and courtesy to help resolve problem or queries. At the tourist offices and in virtually all hotels and many restaurants you'll find the major European languages are spoken. Yet learning just a few simple words and phrases in Portuguese will certainly enhance your visit.

Basic Communication

yes *sim*
no *não*
thank you *obrigado/a*
many thanks *muito obrigado*
all right/okay *de acordo/está bem*
please *faz favor, por favor*
excuse me *faz favor*
(to get attention)
excuse me *com licença*
(to get through a crowd)
excuse me *desculpe*
(sorry)
wait a minute *espere um momento*
can you help me? *pode ajudar-me?*
certainly *com certeza*
can I help you? *posso ajudálo/a?*
can you show me? *pode mostrar me?*
I need... *preciso...*
I'm lost *estou perdido/a*
I'm sorry *desculpe-me*

I don't know *não sei*
I don't understand *não comprendo*
do you speak... *fala...*
English *Inglês*
French *Francês*
German *Alemão*
please speak slowly *faz favor de falar devagar*
please say that again *diga outra vez, se faz favor*
slowly *devagar*
here/there *aqui/ali*
what? *o quê?*
when/why *quando/porquê/onde?*
where is the toilet? *onde é a casa de banho?*

Greetings

hello (good morning) *bom dia*
good afternoon/evening *boa tarde*
good night *boa noite*
see you tomorrow *até amanha*
see you later *até logo*
see you soon *até já*
goodbye *adeus*
Mr/Mrs/young lady/girl *senhor/senhora/menina*
pleased to meet you *muito prazer em conhecê-lo/lá*
I am English/American *sou Inglês/Americano (a)*
I'm here on holiday *estou aqui de férias*
how are you? *como está?*
fine, thanks *bem, obrigado*

Questions

Where is...? *onde é...?*
When...? *quando...?*
How much...? *quanto custa?*
Is there...? *há...?*
Do you have...? *tem...?*
At what time...? *a que horas...?*
What time is it? *que horas são?*
Do you have a...? *tem um...?*

Telephone calls

I want to make a telephone call *quero fazer uma chamada*
the area code *o indicativo*
the number *o número*
can you get this number for me? *podia fazer-me uma chamada para este número?*
the line is engaged *está ocupada*
no one replies *ninguém atende*
the operator *a telefonista*

hello? *está lá?*
may I speak to... *posso falar com...*
hold the line please *não desligue, faz favor*
who is that? *uem/onde fala?*
may I leave a message? *posso deixar um recado?*
I will phone later *ligarei mais tarde*

At the hotel

do you have a room available? *há algum quarto disponível?*
I have a reservation *tenho uma reserva*
single/double room *um quarto individual/duplo*
twin/double bed *camas individuais/cama casal*
with bathroom *com casa de banho*
for one night *para uma noite*
two nights *para duas noites*
how much is it per night? *qual é o preço por noite?*
with breakfast? *com pequeno almoço incluindo?*
does it have air conditioning? *o quarto tem ar condicionado?*
it's expensive *é caro*
can I see the room? *posso ver o quarto?*
what time does the hotel close? *a que horas fecha o hotel?*
dining room *sala de jantar*
what time is breakfast? *a que horas será o pequeno almoço?*
please call me at... *acorde-me às...*
the bill please *a conta por favor*
can you call a taxi please? *chame um táxi por favor?*
key *a chave*
lift *elevador*
towel *toalha*
toilet paper *papel higiénico*
pull/push *puxe/empurre*

Eating and Drinking

IN A RESTAURANT

can we have lunch/dinner here? *podemos almoçar/jantar aqui?*
we only want a light meals? *podemos almoçar/jantar aqu*
a table for two/three... *uma mesa para dois/três...*
may we have the menu? *a ementa se faz favor*
we should like... *queríamos...*
what do you recommend? *que recomenda?*

what is this? *o que é isto?*
do you know what this is in English? *sabe o que é isto em Inglês?*
what wine do you recommend? *qual é o vinho que recomenda?*
not too expensive *não muito caro*
I'll have that *quero aquilo*
Is it good? *É bom?*
well cooked/rare *bem passado/ mal passado*
grilled *grelhado*
fried *frito*
boiled *cozido*
vegetables *legumes*
spoon/fork/knife *colher/garfo/faca*
would you like some more? *deseja mais?*
no thank you – no more *obrigado – não desejo mais*
yes please *sim – mais faz favor*
I enjoyed that *gostei muito*
we have finished *acabámos*
the bill please *a conta se faz favor*
toilets (ladies/gents, men/women) *serviços (senhoras/senhores, homens/mulheres)*

Menu Decoder

Entradas (Starters)
amêijoas ao natural clams with butter and parsley
camarão prawn
gambás langoustines
pasteis de bacalhau dried cod fishcakes
presunto smoked ham
rissois de camarão shrimp pies
santola recheada dressed crab

Sopas (Soups)

caldo verde finely chopped cabbage and potato soup
canja chicken broth
creme de marisco seafood soup
sopa de coentros coriander, bread, and a poached egg

Peixe (Fish)
arroz de polvo octopus with rice
atum grelhado grilled tuna fish
bacalhau á Brás fried dried codfish with fried potatoes and scrambled eggs (there is an almost endless variety of dishes with dried codfish)

caldeirada de peixe fish stew
ensopado de enguias eels with fried bread
lagosta lobster
linguado sole
lampreia lamprey
lulas recheadas stuffed squid
robalo sea bass
rodovalho halibut
salmão salmon
salmonete red mullet
salmonetes á moda de Setubal grilled red mullet
sardinhas grelhadas com pimentos grilled sardines and peppers
savel shad
truta trout

Carne (Meat)
arroz à moda de Valência kind of paella
arroz de pato duck with rice
cabrito assado roast kid
carne assada roast beef
churrasco pork cooked on a spit
coelho à caçadora rabbit stew
cozido à portuguesa variety of boiled meats and vegetables
feijoada dried beans with rice and various smoked meats
frango de carril roast chicken with a hot sauce
frango na pucara chicken casserole
leitão assado roast sucking pig
peru turkey
porco pork
tripas à moda do Porto tripe with dried beans
vitela veal

Salada (Salad)
alface lettuce
cebola onion
cenoura carrot
pepino cucumber
tomate tomato

Doces (Desserts)
arroz doce sweet rice
fruta fruit
gelado ice cream
laranja orange
leite creme type of custard
maça apple
marmelada quince marmalade
papos de anjo small butter cakes with syrup
pasteis cakes

Drinks

coffee (black and strong) um café
coffee with milk *um café com leite*
large, weak coffee with milk *um meio de leite/galão*
tea (lemon) *um chá (de limão)*
orange juice (bottled) *sumo de laranja*
orange juice (fresh) *sumo de laranja natural*
mineral water (still) *agua sem gás;* (fizzy) *agua com gás*
chilled/room temperature *fresca/natural*
red/white wine (mature/ "green") *vinho tinto/branco (maduro/verde)*
bottle/half bottle *garrafa/meia garrafa*
beer *cerveja*
milk *leite*
cheers! *saúde!*

pera pear
pudim flan cream caramel
queijo cheese
uvas grapes

Basic Commodities
açucar sugar
alho garlic
azeite olive oil
azeitona olive
manteiga butter
pão bread
pão integral wholemeal bread
pimenta pepper
sal salt
vinagre vinegar
sandwich (ham/cheese/mixed) *sande (fiambre/queijo/misto)*

Sightseeing

what should we see here? *o que podemos ver aqui?*
what is this building? *que edifício é este?*
where is the old part of the city/town? *onde é a zona antiga da cidade/vila?*
when was it built? *quando foi construída?*
what time is there a mass? *a que horas há missa na igreja?*

when is the museum open? *a que horas está aberto o museu?*
is it open on Sunday? *está aberto no domingo?*
how much is it to go in? *quanto custa a entrada?*
admission free *entrada gratuita*
can I take pictures? *posso tirar fotografias?*
photographs are prohibited *é proibido tirar fotografias*
follow the guide *siga o guia*
we don't need a guide *não precisamos de guia*
where can I get a plan of the city? *onde posso obter um plano da cidade?*
how do I get to...? *como se vai para...?*
can we walk there? *podemos ir a pé?*

Shopping

what time do you open/close? *a que hora abre/fecha?*
can I help you? *posso ajudar?*
I'm looking for... *procuro...*
we are just having a look around *queremos ver o que há*
how much does it cost? *quanto custa?*
do you take credit cards? *aceitam cartões de credito?*
have you got...? *tem...?*
can I try it on? *posso experimentá-lo?*
this is not my size *não é a minha medida*
too small/big *é muito pequeno/muito grande*
its expensive *é caro*
I like it/don't like it *gosto/não gosto*
I'll take this *levo isto*

Shops
bakery *padaria*
barber *barbearia*
bookshop *livraria*
butcher *talho*
chemist *farmácia*
department store *armazém*
dry cleaner *lavandaria a seco*
fishmonger *peixaria*
grocer *mercearia*
hardware store *drogaria*
optician *oculista*
post office *correios*

shoe shop *sapataria*
shopping centre *centro comercial*
stationer *papelaria*
tobacconist *tabacaria*

Travelling

airport *aeroporto*
arrivals/departure *schegadas/partidas*
boat *barco*
bus *autocarro*
bus station *centro camionagem*
bus stop *paragem*
car/hire *carautom camionagem rtidasonde*
customs *alfândega*
driving licence *carta de condução*
flight *voo*
motorway *auto-estrada*
railway station *estação de comboio*
return ticket *bilhete de ida e volta*
single ticket *bilhete de ida*
smokers/non-smokers *fumadores/não fumadores*
taxi *taxi*
ticket office *bilheteria*
toll *portagem*
train *comboio*

Health

is there a chemist's nearby? *há uma farmácia aqui perto?*
where is the hospital? *onde é o hospital?*
I feel ill *não me sinto bem*
it hurts here *tenho uma dor aqui*
I have a headache *tenho dor de cabeça*
I have a sore throat *doe-me a garganta*
I have a stomach ache *tenho dores de estômago*
I have a fever (temperature) *tenho febre*
call a doctor *chame um médico*
take this presription to the chemist *leve este receita para a farmácia*
take this note to the hospital *leve esta carta para o hospital*
danger! *perigo!*
look out! *cuidado!*
help! *socorro!*
fire! *fogo!*

Days of the Week

Sunday	domingo
Monday	segunda-feira
Tuesday	terça-feira
Wednesday	quarta-feira
Thursday	quinta-feira
Friday	sexta-feira
Saturday	sábado

Numbers

1	*um/uma*
2	*dois/duas*
3	*três*
4	*quatro*
5	*cinco*
6	*seis*
7	*sete*
8	*oito*
9	*nove*
10	*dez*
11	*onze*
12	*doze*
13	*treze*
14	*catorze*
15	*quinze*
16	*dezasseis*
17	*dezassete*
18	*dezoito*
19	*dezanove*
20	*vinte*
30	*trinta*
40	*quarenta*
50	*cinquenta*
60	*sessenta*
70	*setenta*
80	*oitenta*
90	*noventa*
100	*cem*
200	*duzentos*
1000	*mil*

Further Reading

Portuguese Works

Although the Portuguese have a long and rich literary tradition, few books have been translated into English; even fewer are still in print. The following is a partial list of works available in English.

Baltasar and Blimunda, by José Saramago is a masterly novel by Portugal's leading (and often controversial) writer.

Brother Luis de Sousa, by Almeida Garrett, an important 19th-century poet and playwright.

Fernando Pessoa. This early 20th-century poet is second only to Camões in the long list of illustrious Portuguese poets. Many of his poems have been translated into English; others were originally written in English. Pessoa wrote under other names including Alberto Caeiro, Ricardo Reis and Álvaro de Campos; not simply changing from pseudonym to pseudonym, but transforming his style with each persona as well.

Mountain Doctor, by Fernando Namora. One of the Portuguese "neo-realists" who tried to capture the ordinary texture of life. (Another good neo-realist is Mário Braga, who wrote short stories.)

South of Nowhere (*Os Cús de Judas*), by António Lobo Antunes, an author who writes psychological novels of great intensity.

The Emigrants and The Mission, by Ferreira de Castro. Another modern Portuguese author of interest.

The Lusiads, by Luís de Camões. An epic poem, written in 1572, celebrating the Portuguese Era of Discoveries. Written by Portugal's premier poet and national hero.

The Maias, **The Illustrious House of Ramires**, **The Mandarin and Other Stories**, **The Relic**, and **The Sin of Father Amaro**, by Eça de Queiroz. One of Portugal's best-known and most enjoyable authors. Eça was writing books during the latter half of the 19th century.

Books about Portugal

Again, the selection in English is not wide, and sometimes hard to find. The following is a short compilation of historical, anthropological, and sociological books about Portugal, listed in rough chronological order according to the time periods they cover.

A Portuguese Rural Society, by José Cutileiro. Clarendon Press, 1971. A study of Portuguese village life.

Contemporary Portugal, by Richard Robinson. Allen and Unwin, 1979.

History of Portugal, Vol. I, From Lusitania to Empire, and Vol. II, From Empire to Corporate State, by A.H. Oliveira Marques. Columbia University Press, 1976. The best general history of Portugal.

In Search of Modern Portugal, the Revolution and its Consequences, by Lawrence S. Graham, and Douglas L. Wheeler (eds). University of Wisconsin Press, 1983.

Portugal's Struggle for Liberty, by Mário Soares. Allen and Unwin, 1975. By Portugal's most eminent political figure – a long-serving president and a key personality in post-Revolution events.

Portugal, by Charles E. Nowell. Prentice-Hall, 1973.

Portugal, by H.V. Livermore. A New History of Portugal. Cambridge University Press, 1976.

Portugal: 50 Years Of Dictatorship, by António de Figueiredo. Penguin, 1975. A general survey by a former political exile.

Portugal and Its Empire: The Truth, also by António de Figueiredo. Gollancz, 1961.

The Portuguese Seaborne Empire 1415–1825, by C.R. Boxer. Hutchinson, 1977.

The Portuguese: The Land and Its People, by Marion Kaplan. Penguin, 1992. The first book in years to take a close look at the country, its history, and modern life. Revealing, readable and entertaining.

Other Insight Guides

The award-winning 190-title Insight Guide series covers destinations on every continent. **Insight Guide: Lisbon** provides a real insight on the delights and historic sights of this city.

Insight Pocket Guides

There are also over 100 Insight Pocket Guides, designed specifically for travellers on short visits. The carefully timed itineraries, compiled by local writers, help to make the visit memorable. The books also contain an easy-to-use full-size pull-out map. **Insight Pocket Guide: Algarve** brings to life this beautiful and fascinating area of the country, with its whitewashed churches and peaceful fishing villages. The pull-out map and timed itineraries help to make the most of a short stay.

Insight Compact Guides

More than 70 Compact Guides offer visitors a highly portable guide packed with detailed and cross-referenced text, photographs and useful maps. **Insight Compact Guides: Lisbon** and **Algarve** highlight the best places to go and what to do when you get there.

ART & PHOTO CREDITS

All photography by Tona Arruzza except for:

B & E Anderson 14, 33, 34, 92L, 92R, 134, 136L, 153, 157L, 178, 183, 205R, 217T, 235, 240, 246, 264, 298, 327
Biblioteca Nacional, Lisbon 43, 44, 52
Calouste Gulbenkian Foundation 126
J D Dallet 6/7, 62/63, 130/131, 138/139, 272/273, 279
Empresa Pública dos Jornais Notícias e Capital 54, 56, 58, 59
Gil Galvin/APA 91, 96, 116R, 135, 192R, 197, 198T, 199, 201, 202, 203, 204T, 205L, 206T, 208, 210, 340
J L González Grande/Naturpress 136R
Michael Jenner 231
Martti Kainulainen/Rex Features 60
Marion Kaplan 121, 342/343, 344, 345, 348, 349, 351
J Lightfoot/Robert Harding Picture Library 19
C Lopesino & J Hidalgo/Naturpress 151, 169, 233, 249, 257, 259, 267
Museu da Cidade, Lisbon 22, 25, 48, 49, 50, 127
Museu de Évora, Évora 125L
Museu da Marinha, Belém 38, 55
Museu Militar, Lisbon 4BL, 16/17, 24, 45, 46, 47
Museu Nacional de Arte Antiga, Lisbon 28, 29, 36, 41, 122, 123, 125R
Gunter Oberzill 330/331
Mark Read/APA 2B, 21, 99, 108, 114, 116L, 118R, 175, 182T, 184T, 215, 220T, 224T, 225T,

226T, 229T, 230, 233T, 235T, 241, 242T, 246T, 250, 256T, 258, 260, 261, 265, 267T, 268T, 276T, 278, 278T, 280, 281, 285, 286T, 288L, 288T, 301, 301T, 302, 303T, 302T, 304, 305, 305T, 306T, 307, 312T, 315T, 319, 325
Mick Rock/Cephas 104, 105, 106, 284
Neil Setchfield 150
A Stieglitz 347, 350
Martin Symington 85
Tim Thompson 148/149, 248
Topham Picturepoint 81
Courtesy of the Trustees of the V&A/Paul Rubins 51
Xosé Varela/Naturpress 71, 107
Bill Wassman 2/3, 35, 66, 70, 84, 140/141, 144, 206, 224, 234, 247L, 270, 292, 296/297, 332, 336, 337, 338
Phil Wood/APA 4BR, 5B, 23, 39, 61, 80, 90, 98, 112/113, 117, 119, 120, 155, 155T, 157R, 157T, 158T, 160, 161T, 162, 168T, 169T, 179, 179T, 181, 192L, 223T, 248T, 333, 335, 336T, 339, 339T, 340T, 341

Cartographic Editor **Zoë Goodwin**
Production **Stuart A Everitt**
Design Consultants **Carlotta Junger, Graham Mitchener**
Picture Research **Hilary Genin, Monica Allende**

Picture Spreads

Pages 110/111
Top Row, left to right: Xosé Varela/Naturpress, C Lopesino & J Hidalgo/Naturpress, C Lopesino & J Hidalgo/Naturpress, Mark Read/APA. *Centre Row, left to right:* both Xosé Varela/Naturpress. *Bottom Row, left to right:* B & E Anderson, B & E Anderson, Xosé Varela/Naturpress
Pages 170/171
Top Row, left to right: C Lopesino & J Hidalgo/Naturpress, Tony Arruzza, Phil Wood/APA, Michael Jenner *Centre Row:* Neil Setchfield *Bottom Row, left to right*: Gil Galvin/APA, Phil Wood/APA, Phil Wood/APA
Pages 236/237
Top Row, left to right: Mark Read/APA, B & E Anderson, Mark Read/APA, Phil Wood/APA. *Centre Row, top and bottom:* Cephas, Mark Read/APA. *Bottom Row, left to right:* B & E Anderson, Mark Read/APA, Phil Wood/APA
Pages 294/295
Top Row, left to right: Mark Read/APA, B & E Anderson, Mick Rock/Cephas, Mark Read/APA *Centre Row, left to right*: C Lopesino & J Hidalgo/Naturpress, Mick Rock/Cephas, Mark Read/APA *Bottom Row, left to right*: Mick Rock/Cephas, Neil Setchfield, Mark Read/APA

Map Production Colourmap Scanning Ltd

© 1999 Apa Publications GmbH & Co. Verlag KG (Singapore branch)

Index

Numbers in italics refer to photographs

Abrantes 242
Santa Maria do Castelo 242
accommodation 362–9
booking agencies 129, 363
campsites 230, 231, 270
Casa de Casal de Loivos (Pinhão)
285
Casa da Lavada (Serra do
Marão) 285
Castle Hotel (Vila Nova de
Milfontes) 231
Estalagem dos Cavaleiros (Sintra
Vila) 182
Estremoz castle 217, 224
hotels 362, 363
listings 363–7
manor houses 129, 285, 362–3
listings 367–8
Palace Hotel do Buçaco 107–8,
267
Palácio de Seteais (Sintra) 184
Palmela Castle 128–9, 189
pousadas 128–9, 362–3
listings 368–9
pousada do Castelo (Obidos)
128, *129*, 250
pousada dos Lóios (Evora) *129*
Pousada de São Bento 128
Pousada de São Teotónio
(Valença do Minho) 128, 301
Quinta da Capela (Sintra) 184
Quinta de São Tiago (Sintra) 184
Quinta das Torres (Vila Fresca de
Azeitão) 193
Reid's Hotel (Funchal (Madeira))
333, 335
São Filipe Castle (Setúbal)
189–90
Santa Marinha da Costa
monastery *pousada*
(Guimarães) *305*
Solar de Cortegaça (Lima Valley)
303
Terra Nostra hotel (Furnas
(Azores)) 348
Vintage House Hotel (Pinhão)
285
Afonso II 30
burial place (Alcobaça) 247
Afonso III 29, 203
burial place (Alcobaça) 247
Afonso IV 30, 31

Afonso V 37
Afonso VI 48
Afonso, Duke of Bragança 37
Afonso Henriques *24*, *25*, 24–6,
33, 34, 197, 288, 304
birthplace (Guimarães) 304
agriculture 69, 134, 198
pineapple plantation visits
(Azores) 348
tea plantation visits (Azores) 348
airlines 356
airports 357
Albuquerque, Afonso de 40, *41*
Albufeira 204
beaches *204*
nightlife 204
Alcantarilha 205
Capela da Ossos 205
Alcobaça 247–8
Cistercian Abbey 26, 30, *116*,
247, 247–8
porcelain and pottery factory
tours 248
Alcoutim 203
Alentejo 215–235
see also individual place names
accommodation 365, 368, 369
agriculture 215
beaches 230–2
crafts 215
food and drink 235
geography 215
getting there 218, 230
history 217
music 218
people 217–8
politics 217
Pulo do Lobo (Wolf's Leap) rapids
234
roads 215
Alfonso VI 24
Algarve 197–210
see also individual place names
beaches 199, 204–8
crafts 199
golf 204
history 197–8
Praia de Carvoeiro 205
Praia da Rocha *204*, 206
tourism 199–200
Algés 175
Algoso 319
Alijó 291
Aljezur 208
Almada 189
Cristo Rei monument *189*
Almada, Antão de *47*
Almoçageme 111
Almograve 232

Almourol *33*, 242
castle *33*
Alte 110, 210
Alter do Chão 230
Alter stud farm 230
Alter Real horse *see* **Alter do Chão**
Alvares Cabral, Pedro 40
Amarante *285*, 286–7
São Gonçalo festival 286
wine tasting 287
ancient sites
Atalaia Bronze-Age site (Ourique)
232
Cetóbriga Roman remains
(Setúbal) 191
Citânia de Briteiros prehistoric
site (Guimarães) *21*, 305–6
Conímbriga Roman site *264*,
265–6
Cromeleque de Almendres
(Evora) 223
Medóbriga Roman ruins 228
Miróbriga Iron-Age/Roman site
(Santiago do Cacém) 230–1
Panóias prehistoric site 292
Parque Arqueológico do Vale Côa
291
prehistoric remains (Sortelha)
324
prehistoric stones (Castelo de
Vide) 230
prehistoric stones (Reguengos)
226
Roman bridge (Chaves) 315–6
Roman ruins (Guarda) 323
Sortelha mines 324
Temple of Diana (Evora) *23*, *218*,
219–20
Vila Romana de Milreu (Roman
site) (Estói) 210
Zambujeiro Dolmen (Evora)
223
Angra do Heroismo (Azores) 349
Annunciação, Tomás da 126
architecture 115–20, 215, 217
azulejos see individual entry
baroque 119
Gothic 115–6
Mannerism 118
modern 120
Moorish 219
neoclassicism 120
Manueline 116–7, 190
Renaissance 118
rococo 119–10
Romanesque 115
Romanticism 120
Arcos de Valdevez 302
Armação de Pêra 205

Arraiolos rugs 236, 377
Arrábida Peninula 189, 191–3
see also individual place names
art 123–7
  Flemish influence 124–5
  Humorists 127
  Mannerism 125–6
  Modernism 127
  Naturalism 127
  neoclassicism 126
  Portuguese Primitive 325–6
  Portuguese School 123, 163
  religious art 123–4
  Renaissance 125–6
  rock paintings 291
  Romanticism 126–7
  School of Mafra 185
arts, the 53
  theatre (Lisbon) 156, 162, 168
Atei 313
  Roman remains 313
Aveiro 268–70, *269*
  boat trips 270
  Carmelite Convent 269
  Convento de Jesus 269
  March Fair 269
  Misericórdia church 269
  Museu Regional 269
  Old quarter 270
  Parque Dom Infante Pedro 269
  Praça da República 269
  Ria lagoon 268, *270*
  São Domingos cathedral 269
Azeitão *see* **Vila Nogueira de Azeitão**
Azenhas do Mar 185
Azores 39, 345–51
  see also individual place names
  Angra do Heroismo 349
  agriculture 346
  beaches 346
  Caldeira das Sete Cidades 348
  climate 346
  discovery 345
  history 346
  Ponta dos Mosteiros 348
  tourism 346
  Vista do Rei (King's View) 348
azulejos 18, 161, 170–1 *279, 326*

b

Baleal 250
  Praia d'el Rei golf course 250
Barcelos 97, 303
  Barcelos cockerel 237, 303
  Festas das Cruces 111
barcos rabelos see **boats**
Barragem de Valeira 290

Barril 202
basketware 236, 237
Batalha 32, *80, 114*, 116, *245, 246*
Battle of Alcácer-Quibir 44
Battle of Aljubarrota 32, 245
Battle of Buçaco 267
Battle of Ourique 25
beaches 136, 175, 185, 204
  see also individual place names
  Costa da Caparica 189
  Portinho da Arrábida 191
Beckford, William 80
  Sketches of Spain and Portugal 80
Beiras, Alta and Baixa 67, 323–9
  see also individual place names
  Barragem de Castelo do Bode lake 327
  geography 323
  history 323
Beira Litoral province 86
  see also individual place names
  Ria de Aveiro lagoon 86
Beja 233
Belmonte 324
Beresford, William Carr 51
Bernardes, António de Oliveira and Policarpo 171
birds *see* **wildlife**
Black Death 31, 153
boats 85–7
  barcos rabelos 35, 85–6, *101*, 103–4, 280, 294
  caravel 39, 85
  caravelas 39, 275
  moliceiros 85, 86–7, 268, *270*
  traineiras 87
Bocage, Manuel Barbosa du 190
Borba 225
Borrow, George 81
Boticas 315
  vinhos mortos (wine of the dead) 315
Boytac, Diogo 190
Braga 77, 306–7
  Bom Jesus church 77, 119, *306*, 307
  Café Brasileira *307*
  Capela do Conceição 307
  Capela dos Milagres (Chapel of Miracles) 307
  Casa dos Biscainhos museum 307
  Holy Week procession *75*, 306
  Palacio de Arcebispo (Archbishop's Palace) 307
  Museu d'Arte Sacra (Museum of Sacred Art) 307

Nossa Senhora do Pópulo church 307
  São João de Souto church 307
  Sameiro shrine 77
  Sé (Cathedral) 307
Bragança 316, *317*, 3178
  castle 318
  cathedral 318
  ceramics 317
  Domus Municipalis 18
  military museum 318
  Museu do Abada de Baçal 318
Bragança dynasty 48–53, 55, 217, 225–6, 317
  Catherine of Bragança 35, 48, 317
  Fundação da Casa de Bragança 317
bullfights 377
  Barroso district 314
  Cascais 179
  Lisbon 169
  Nazaré 249
Burgau 207
Byron 80, *81*, 181, 182
  Childe Harold 80, 81, 181

c

Cabeceiras de Basto 313
  Mosteiro Refójos 313
Cabo Espichel 192, *193*
  fishermen's festival 192
  lighthouse *188*
  Nossa Senhora do Cabo church 192
Cabo da Roca 185
Cabo de São Vicente 207
Cabral, Pedro Alvares *38*, 241
  birthplace (Belmonte) 324
  burial place (Santarém) 241
Cacela Velha 203
Cacilhas 189
Caetano, Marcelo 58–9
Caldas das Gêres 302
Caldas de Moledo 288
Caldas de Rainha (Queen's Spa) 250
Caloura (Azores) 348
  diving centre 348
Camacha (Madeira) 339
  wicker-making 339
Cambra 326
Caminha 301
Camões, Luís de 34, 44, *45*, 68, 166, 185
  Os Lusíadas 45, 68, 185
Campo do Gerês 302
Caniçal (Madeira) 340

Cão, Diogo 292
Capela de São Lourenço 171
car hire 361
Carlos I 55, 155
Carmona, Oscar 56
Carrapateira 208
Carvalho e Melo, Sebastião José de see **Pombal, Marquês de**
Carvalhelhos 315
  spring water 315
Cascais 175, 178–9
  beaches 179
  Boca do Inferno (Mouth of Hell) *179*
  bullring 179
  craft market 179
  Museu Castro Guimarães 179
  Nossa Senhora da Assunção 179
  Praia do Guincho *174*, 179
  Praia de Santa Marta 179
Castelo Branco 327–8
  colchas (embroidered bedspreads) 327, 328
  Misericórdia Velha church 327
  Palácio Episcopal and garden 327, *328*
  Praça Velha 327
  São Miguel church 327–8
Castelo Melhor 291
  Parque Arqueológico do Vale Côa 291
Castelo de Vide 228–30
  castle 228
  Fonte da Vila 229
  Igreja Santa Maria *229*
  Judiaria (Jewish Quarter) 229, *230*
  Praça Dom Pedro V 229
  prehistoric stones 230
  spa waters 229
castles 33
  Algoso 319
  Aljezur 208
  Almourol *33*, 242
  Beja 233
  Bragança 318
  Castelo Branco 327
  Castelo dos Mouros (Sintra) 184
  Castelo de São Jorge (Lisbon) 151, 157, *159*, 159–60
  Castelo de Vide 228
  Castro Laboreiro 301
  Castro Marim 203
  Chaves 316
  Elvas 226
  Esposende 300
  Estremoz 224–5
  Evoramonte 224

Guarda 323
Guimarães 33, 305–6
Lamego 33, 289
Mértola 235
Mogadouro 319
Monforte 316
Monsanto *329*
Montalegre 313
Montemor-o-Novo 218
Montemor-o-Velho 270
Nisa 230
Palmela 189
Porto de Mós 245
São Filipe 189–90
São Julião da Barra (Oeiras) 175
Santiago do Cacém 230
Serpa 234
Sesimbra 192
Silves 209
Sortelha 324
Vila do Conde 300
Vila Viçosa 225
Vinhais 316
Castro, Ferreira de 182
Castro, Joaquim Machado de 185, 258
Castro Laboreiro 301
Castro Marim 203
  castle 203
  Reserva Natural do Sapal 203
cathedrals see **churches and cathedrals**
Catherine of Bragança 35, 48
caves
  Buraco dos Mouros (Moors' Cave) (Alte) 210
  Caldeira do Enxofre (Graciosa island, Azores) 350
  Gruta da Santa Margarida 191
  Grutas Mira de Aire 245–6
  Grutas de Santo António 245
  Grutas de Alavdos 245
  Rocha dos Soidos (Alte) 210
Caxias 175
Cercal 231
Chaves 315–6
  castle 316
  Museu Regional 316
  Praça de Camões 316
  presunto (smoked ham) 315
  Roman bridge 315–6
chemists 360
churches and cathedrals
  see also **Monasteries and Convents**
  Basílica da Estréla (Lisbon) *163*
  Bom Jesus (Braga) 77, 119, *306*, 307

Capela do Conceição (Braga) 307
Capela dos Milagres (Chapel of Miracles) (Braga) 307
Capela dos Ossos (Chapel of Bones)
  (Alcantarilha) 205
  (Evora) *221*, 222
Capela dos Ossos (Chapel of Bones) (Faro) 201
Capela do San Miguel (St Michael's Chapel) (Coimbra) 257
Capela de São Nicolau (Vila Real) 292
Espírito Santo (Marvão) 228
Fátima 77, *244*, 244–5
Igreja do Carmo (Faro) *201*
Igreja dos Grilos (Porto) see Igreja de São Lourenço (Porto)
Igreja de Jesus (Setúbal) 190
Igreja de Madalena (Lisbon) 157
Igreja Matriz (Mértola) 235
Igreja Matriz (Oliveira do Hospital) 326
Igreja Matriz de São Sebastião (Ponta Delgada, Azores) 347
Igreja da Misericórdia
  (Aveiro) 269
  (Beja) 233
  (Evora) 221
  (Loulé) 210
  (Tavira) 202
  (Viseu) 325
Igreja de Nossa Senhora da Graça (Lisbon) 160
Igreja de Nossa Senhora do Monte
  (Funchal) *333*
  (Lisbon) 160
Igreja de Santo António (Lagos) 206
Igreja de São Bertolomeu (Coimbra) 260
Igreja Santa Clara (Porto) 277
Igreja São Domingos (Guimarães) 305
Igreja de Santa Engrácia (Lisbon) 119, 160
Igreja São Francisco
  (Evora) 222
  (Guimarães) 305
  (Porto) 278
Igreja São Lourenço
  (Porto) 278
  (Vila Nogueira de Azeitão) 193
Igreja Santa Maria (Castelo de Vide) *229*
Igreja de Santa Maria (Obidos) 250

churches and cathedrals cont'd
Igreja Santa Maria (Sagres) 207
Igreja de Santa Maria da
  Alcáçova (Montemor-o-Velho)
  270
Igreja de São Roque (St Rock)
  (Lisbon) 119, 162
Igreja de São Vicente de Fora
  (Lisbon) 160
Igreja Santiago (Coimbra) 260
Misericórdia Velha (Castelo
  Branco) 327
Nossa Senhora da Agonia (Viana
  do Castelo) 301
Nossa Senhora da Assunção
  (Alte) 210
Nossa Senhora do Cabo (Cabo
  Espichel) 192
Nossa Senhora da Conceiçāo
  (Loulé) 210
Nossa Senhora da Conceição
  (Tomar) 118
Nossa Senhora da Conceição
  Velha (Lisbon) 155
Nossa Senhora da Graça
  (Evora) 222
  (Santarém) 241
Nossa Senhora de Guadelupe
  (Algarve) 207
Nossa Senhora de Lurdes (Alte)
  210
Nossa Senhora da Nazaré
  (Nazaré) 249
Nossa Senhora de Oliveira
  (Guimarães) 304
Nossa Senhora do Pópulo
  (Braga) 307
Nossa Senhora dos Remédios
  (Lamego) 118, 289
Nossa Senhora da Rocha (Rocha
  da Pena) 205
Santo Amaro (Beja) 233
Santo António dos Olivais
  (Coimbra) 260
Santo António da Sé (Lisbon) 157
Santa Clara (Santarém) 241
São Domingos cathedral (Aveiro)
  269
São Francisco (Evora) 221
São Gonçalinho chapel (Aveiro)
  270
São Gonçalo (Aveiro) 270
São Idelfonso (Porto) 279
São João de Almedina (Coimbra)
  257
São João de Alporão (Santarém)
  241
São João Baptista (Tomar)
  243–4

São João Baptista (Vila do
  Conde) 300
São João Evangelista (Evora) 220
São João Novo (Porto) 278
São João de Souto (Braga) 307
São Julião (Setúbal) 190
São Lourenço (São Lourenço)
  204
Sameiro shrine (Braga) 77
San Lucar 203
Santa Luiza (Lisbon) 159
Santa Maria (Tavira) 202
Santa Maria dos Olivais (Tomar)
  244
São Miguel (Castelo Branco)
  327–8
São Miguel do Castelo
  (Guimarães) 304
São Pedro
  (Lourosa) 326–7
  (Vila Real) 292
São Pedro de Balsemão
  (Lamego) 289
São Simão (Vila Fresca de
  Azeitão) 193
Sé (Cathedral)
  (Braga) 307
  (Evora) 220, 220–1
  (Faro) 200
  (Guarda) 323
  (Lisbon) 157–9, 158
  (Miranda do Douro) 319
  (Portalegre) 227
  (Porto) 277
  (Silves) 209, 209–10
  (Vila Real) 292
  (Viseu) 325
Sé Nova (New Cathedral)
  (Coimbra) 257–8
Sé Velha (Old Cathedral)
  (Coimbra) 258
Senhora da Paz (Vila Franca do
  Campo (Azores)) 348
Senhora da Peneda 301
Synagogue and museum (Tomar)
  243
cinemas 375
Citânia de Briteiros prehistoric site
  21, 305–6
climate 133, 217, 354
Côa Valley 291
coffee 373
Coimbra 30, 255–60
  Arco de Almedina 258
  Baixa Coimbra 259–60
  Biblioteca Joanina 255, 257
  Capela do San Miguel (St
    Michael's Chapel) 257
  Casa de Sobre-Ripas 258

Colégio de Santo Agostinho 258
crafts 258, 260
fado 255, 257
Fonte das Lágrimas 260
history 255–6
Igreja de São Bertolomeu 260
Igreja Santiago 260
Jardim Botânico 260
Jardim da Manga 259
Mosteiro Celas 260
Mosteiro Santa Clara-a-Nova
  (New Santa Clara Monastery)
  260
Mosteiro de Santa Cruz 259
Museu Machado de Castro 258
old city 256–8
Old University 257
parks 260
Pátio das Escolas 257
Porta Férrea 257
Portugal dos Pequenitos
  museum 260
Praça Dinis 256
Queima das Fitas (Burning of the
  Ribbons) celebrations 255,
  259
Quinta das Lágrimas 30, 260
Rua Olimpio Nicolau market 260
Sala dos Capelos 257
Santo António dos Olivais church
  260
Santa Clara area 260
Santa Clara-a-Velha (Old Santa
  Clara Monastery) 260
São João de Almedina church
  257
Sé Nova (New Cathedral) 257–8
Sé Vela (Old Cathedral) 258
shopping 259
Torre de Anto (Anthony's Tower)
  258
University 42, 69, 255, 256
Columbus, Christopher 91, 178,
  345, 349
Concordat 30
Conímbriga Roman site 264,
  265–6
consulates 359
Corvo island (Azores) 351
Costa, Afonso 55
Costa Cabral, António da 52–3
Costa Nova 270
Costa Verde 299–307
  see also individual place names
  beaches 299
Covadonga 23
Covilhã 325
  Penhas da Saúde ski area 325
crafts 236–7

colchas (bedspreads, Castelo Branco) 327, 328
crafts market (Barcelos) 97, 303
crafts exhibition (Barcelos) 303
Handicrafts Fair (Estoril) 177
lace-making school visits (Vila do Conde) 300
porcelain and pottery factory tours (Alcobaça) 248
pottery (Flor da Rosa) 230
potteries (Lagoa, Azores) 348
tapestry workshops (Portalegre) 227
wicker-making (Madeira) 339, 237
Crato 230
crime 70
Cromeleque do Almendres 223
crusades 25–6, 29
crusaders *26*, 34, 197
Cruz Quebrada
Cunhal, Alvaro 250
Curia 268
wineries 268

d

Dáfundo 175
Aquário Vasco da Gama 175
Delgado, Humberto 57
Dinis *28*, 30–1, 33
discos 374
driving 70, 145, 175, 181, 200, 339, 357, 361
Duarte 241
burial place (Santarém) 241
Duarte I 37, 246
burial place (Batalha) 246

e

Eanes, Gil 40, 206
earthquake, the great (1755) *49*, 49–50, 119, 120, 151
ecology 137
economy 30–1, 58, 60, 67
bankruptcy 55
cruzado 37
single European currency 60
education 43, 70
see also **universities**
Elvas 226
embassies 359
Empire 37–44, 57–8
Africa 38, 41, 57–8
Angolan uprising 57–8
Asia 40–1
Brazil *38*, 41, 49, 51
decolonisation 59–60

English Connection 34–5, 80–1, 275, 335
environment 137, 208
Esposende 300
fortress 300
Estói 210
Estoril 175–8, *177*
Autódromo do Estoril 177
beaches 176, 177
Casino 177
getting there 176
golf 177–8
Handicrafts Fair 177
Music Festival 177
Penha Longa country club 177
Port Wine Rally 177
shopping 177
Tamariz beach 176
Estremadura 241–50
see also individual place names
Estremoz *224*, 224–5
castle 224–5
crafts 225
Evora 218–23, *222*
Capela dos Ossos *221*, 222
Casa Soure 221
Convento dos Lóios 220
Cromeleque do Almendres 223
Feira de São João 223
history 219
Igreja São Francisco 222
Jardim Público 222, *223*
Jesuit University 221
Largo das Portas de Moura 222
Misericórdia church 221
Museu de Arte Sacra 221
Museu de Evora 221
Nossa Senhora da Graça 222
Palácio de Dom Manuel 222–3
Pousada dos Lóios *129*
Praça do Giraldo 218–9
São Francisco church 221
São João Evangelista church 220
Sé (Cathedral) *220*, 220–1
Temple of Diana (Templo Romano) *23*, *218*, 219–20
Zambujeiro Dolmen 223
Evoramonte 223–4
castle 224
Expo '98

f

Faial island (Azores) *345*, 350
Faro 200–1
Arco da Vila 200
beaches 201
Cabo de Santa Maria lighthouse 201

Capela dos Ossos (Chapel of Bones) 201
Igreja do Carmo *201*
Ilha de Culatra 201
Ilha de Faro 201
Museu Arqueológico 200–1
Museu Etnográfico 201
Museu Marítimo 201
Parque Natural da Ria Formosa 201
Praia de Faro 201
Sé (Cathedral) 200
Fátima shrine 77, *244*, 244–5
pilgrimage dates 244
Ferragudo 206
Fernandes, Vasco (the Great Vasco) *124*, 125, 280, 325–6
Fernando I 24, 32, 162
festivals and events 76–7, 110–11
Azeitão fair (Vila Nogueira de Azeitão) 193
Battle of Buçaco re-enactment (Serra do Buçaco) 267
beer festival (Silves) 209
Chega dos Toiros (Arrival of the Bulls) (Barroso district) 314
Dia de São João (Porto) *278*, 280
Estoril Music Festival 177
Feira de São João (Evora) 223
festival of São João (Porto) 86, 104
festivals of Terceira island (Azores) 349
Feira de São Mateus (Viseu) 326
fishermen's festival (Cabo Espichel) 192
Handicrafts Fair (Estoril) 177
Holy Week procession (Braga) *75*, 306
March Fair (Aveiro) 269
Moliceiro Regatta (Torreira) 87
New Year's Eve festivities (Funchal (Madeira)) 333
pilgrimage dates (Fátima shrine) 244
pilgrimage and festival (Lamego) 289
pilgrimage and festival (Viana do Castelo) 301
Port Wine Rally (Estoril) 177
Queima das Fitas (Burning of the Ribbons) celebrations (Coimbra) 255, *259*
religious festival (Nazaré) 249
Rio de Onor festivals 318–9
saints days 76–7
São Bento da Porta Aberta (Gerês) 78

festivals and events cont'd
São Goncalo festival (Amarante)
286
Senhora da Aparecida
procession (Lousada) 78
siege re-enactment (Monsanto)
329
Torre pilgrimage 325
Figueira da Foz 270
fishing industry 135–6, 203
"bullfight of the sea" (Faro) 201
flora 136
Flor da Rosa 230
Flores island (Azores) 351
food and drink 91–8, 198, 258, 276
see also **wine**
bacalhau 87, 93–4
caldo verde 96–7, *99*
colonial influences 92
espada (scabbard fish) 335
Nisa cheese 230
presunto (smoked ham) 315
Serra da Estréla cheese 325
Forrester, Baron Joseph James 35,
109, 290
forestry 137
cork 137, 231, *232*
eucalyptus 137
Foz Côa *see* **Vila Nova de Foz Côa**
Franco, João 55
Funchal (Madeira) 333–8
Adegas de São Francisco 338
Câmara de Lobos 335
Câmara Municipal (Town Hall)
336
Igreja de Nossa Senhora do
Monte *333*
Jardim Botânico 336
Mercado dos Lavradores *335*
Monte 333, 335
Museu de Arte Sacra 336–7
Museu de Fotografia Vicentes
336
New Year's Eve festivities 333
Praça do Município 336
Quinta das Cruzes and gardens
336
Quinta do Palheiro Ferreiro
gardens 336
Reid's Hotel 333, 335
Furnas (Azores) 348, *349*
Fuzeta 202

g

galleries
Casa de Serralves (Porto) 280
Centro de Arte Moderna (Lisbon)
127, 168

Fundaçao Calouste Gulbenkian
(Lisbon) *126*, 127, 168
Museu de Arte Contemporânea
(Porto) 280
Museu de Arte Popular (Lisbon)
166
Museu d'Arte Sacra
(Braga) 307
(Evora) 221
(Funchal, Madeira) 336–7
(Lisbon) 162
Museu Escola de Artes
Decorativas (Museum of
Decorative Art) (Lisbon) 159
Museu Grão Vasco (Viseu) 325–6
Museu Municipal (Amarante) 287
Museu Nacional de Arte Antiga
(Museum of Ancient Art)
(Lisbon) 163
Museu Nacional de Arte
Contemporânea (Lisbon) 127
Núcleo Islâmico (Museum of
Islamic Art) (Mértola) 235
Quinta das Cruzes (Funchal,
Madeira) 336
Gama, Vasco da 40, 45, 85, 91,
166
birthplace (Sines) 231
Garrett, Almeida 53
geography 21, 134–5, 354
Geraldo Geraldes 26
Gerês 78
Gonçalves, Nuno 123, 163
The Adoration of St Vincent 123
government 354
Graciosa island (Azores) 350
Caldeira do Enxofre cavern and
lake 350
Santa Cruz 350
Grão Vasco *see* **Fernandes, Vasco**
Guarda 323–4
Guerreiro, Cândido 210
Guimarães 304–6
Castelo 33, 304
Citânia de Briteiros prehistoric
site *21*, 305–6
Convento de Santa Clara (Town
Hall) 304
Igreja São Domingos 305
Igreja São Francicso 305
Largo do Toural 305
linen industry 304
Nossa Senhora de Oliveira
church 304
Paço dos Duques 304
Santa Marinha da Costa
monastery *pousada* 305
São Miguel do Castelo church
304

Gulbenkian, Calouste Sarkis 168
Guterres, Antonio 19, *60*

h

health 356, 360
Henry the Navigator, Prince 35,
37, 38–9, 91, 207, 246, 275,
325, 345
birthplace (Porto) 275, 278
burial place (Batalha) 246
School of Navigation (Sagres)
39, 207
Herculano, Alexandre 53
history 21–61, 152–3, 197, 203,
217, 288, 325
Age of Discoveries 37, 39, 153
Bragança dynasty 48–53, 55,
217, 225–6, 317
empire 37–44, 47–8
Enlightenment, Age of 49
Hundred Years' War 32
independence from Spain 24,
30, 48
liberal revolution 51, *52*
Miguelist Wars 52
Moors 23, 34, 197, 219
prehistoric culture 21
Reconquista 23–4, 26, 29–30
republic *54*, 55
Restauradores 156
Roman era 21–3
Spanish Civil War 56
Spanish Rule 44, 47–8
Suevi 22–3
Visigoths 23
World War I 56
World War II 57, 176
hospitals 360
hotels 362–9

i

Idanha-a-Velha 328
Ilha da Armona 190
Ilha da Culatra 189
Ilhas Desertas *see* **Porto Santo**
Ilhas Selvagens (Madeira) 340
industry 68–9
fishing 135–6
forestry *137*
Inquisition, The 42, *44*, 52, 243
insurance 356

j

Jews 42, 243
João I 32, 34–5, 37, 183, 246
burial place (Batalha) *34*, 246

João II 37–8, 42
João III *43*, 44
João IV 48
João V 49
João VI 50, 51
Joaquina, Carlotta 52
John of Gaunt 32, 34
José 49, 50

k

Knights of Caltrava 29
Knights of St John (Hospitallers)
    25, 26, 29
Knights of Santiago 29
Knights Templar 25, 26, 29, 243
    disbanding of 31

l

Lagoa 205
Lagos *206*, 206–7
    Igreja de Santo António 206
    Ponta da Piedade 207
    Praça da República 206
    Praia Dona Ana 206, *209*
Lamego 288–9
    castle 33, 289
    pilgrimage and festival 289
language 378–80
Lindoso 302
Lines of Torres Vedras 35, 51
Lisbon 151–69
    Alfama *118*, 151, *157*
    Amoreiras Shopping Centre *162*
    Aqueduto dos Aguas Livres
        (Aqueduct of Free Waters)
        160, 161, 162
    archaeological museum at the
        Convento do Carmo 162
    Arco Rua Augusta 155
    Arquivo Nacional da Torre do
        Tombo 169
    Avenida da Liberdade 167–8
    Bairro Alto 151, 161–3
    Baixa 151, 153, 155–6
    Basílica da Estréla *163*
    Belém *57*, 151, 166–7
    bullfights 169
    Cais do Sodré railway station
        155
    Câmara Municipal (Town Hall)
        155
    Campo Grande 169
    Campo Pequeno 169
    Campo de Santa Clara 160
    Casa dos Bicos 155
    Castelo de São Jorge 151, 157,
        159, 159–60

Cemitério dos Ingleses (English
    Cemetery) 163
Centro de Arte Moderna 127,
    168
Centro Cultural de Belém 166
Chafariz d'el Rei fountain 155
Chiado district *161*, 161–2
churches
    Igreja de Madalena 157
    Igreja de Nossa Senhora da
        Graça 160
    Igreja de Nossa Senhora do
        Monte 160
    Igreja de Santa Engrácia 119,
        160
    Igreja de São Roque 119, 162
    Igreja de São Vicente de Fora
        160
Convento do Carmo 162
Convento da Madre de Deus 161
earthquake of 1755 49–50,
    119, 120, 151
Elevador de Santa Justa 162
Expo '98 60, 120, 161
Feira da Ladra (Thieves Market)
    160
Feira Popular (amusement park)
    169
Fundaçao Calouste Gulbenkian
    126, 127, 168
hotels 363–4
getting around 153, 161, 362
getting there 151
Gulbenkian Foundation *126*,
    127, 168
history 152–3
Houses of Parliament *see*
    Palácio de São Bento
Jardim Botânico 162
Jardim da Estréla 163
Jardim Zoológico 168
Largo das Portas do Sol 159
Mercado da Ribeira 155
Miradouro de Santa Luiza 159
Mosteiro dos Jerónimos *117*,
    166
museums (*museu*)
    Antóniano 157
    da Agua (Water) 160–1
    de Arte Popular (Popular Art)
        166
    de Arte Sacra (Sacred Art) 162
    da Cidade (City) 169
    Escola de Artes Decorativas
        (Decorative Art) 159
    da Marinha (Maritime) 166
    Militar 160
    Nacional de Arqueologia
        (Archaeology) 166

Nacional de Arte Antiga
    (Ancient Art) 163
Nacional de Arte
    Contemporânea 127
Nacional do Azulejo (Tile) 161
Nacional dos Coshes (Coach)
    167
do Teatro (Theatre) 169
do Traje (Costume) 169
nightlife 151
Nossa Senhora da Conceição
    Velha 155
Ocean Pavilion 161
Paço dos Condes de Almada
    (Palace of the Counts of
    Almada) 156
Padrão dos Descobrimentos
    (Discoveries Monument) *39*,
    150, 166
Palácio de Ajuda 167
Palácio de Belém 166
Palácio Foz 156
Palácio de Marquéses de
    Fronteira 169
Palácio de São Bento 163
parks (*Parques*)
    Eduardo VII *167*
    Florestal de Monsanto 169
    das Laranjeiras 168–9
    dos Mações 161
    Mayer 168
    do Monteiro-Mór 169
Planetário Calouste Gulbenkian
    (Planetarium) 166
Ponte 25 de Abril *151*, 166
Praça
    de Espanha 168
    da Figueira (Figtree Square)
        156
    do Comércio *153*, 155
    Dom Pedro IV *see* Rossio
    Marquês de Pombal *see*
        Rotunda
    do Municipio 155
    dos Restauradores 156
Rossio 155, *156*
    station *155*, 156
Rotunda 167
St Anthony 157, 159
    festival 111
Santa Apolónia station 160
Santo António da Sé 157
Santa Luiza church 159
Santa Maria de Belém *see*
    Mosteiro dos Jerónimos
Sé (Cathedral) 157–9, *158*
shopping 161–2
Solar do Instituto do Vinho do
    Porto (Port Wine Institute) 162

Lisbon cont'd
　Teatro Nacional 156
　Teatro de São Carlos 162
　theatre 156, 162, 168
　Torre de Belém 166, *167*
　Turismo (tourist information) 156
　University 169
literature 53
　see also individual writers'
　　names
　censorship 56, 57
　Moorish poetry 209
　troubadour culture 30
Lopes, Gregório 125
lost property 360
Loulé 199, 210
　Almedina quarter 210
　crafts 199, 210
　Igreja da Misericordia 210
　Nossa Senhora da Conceição
　　210
Lourosa 326
Lousada 78
Luipi/Lupi, Miguel 126–7
　Sousa Martins' Mother 126–7
Luís I 53
Luso 267
Luz 207
Luz de Tavira 202
　Ilha de Tavira 202
　train journey to Barril 202

m

Macaulay, Rose 276
　They Went to Portugal 276
Machico (Madeira) 339–40
Madeira 39, 91, 207, 333–40
　see also individual place names
　beaches 339, 340
　Boca da Encumeada 339
　bordados (embroidery) 335
　Cabo Girão 339
　Curral das Freiras (Corral of the
　　Nuns) 339, *340*
　discovery 333
　Parque das Queimadas 339
　Paúl da Serra 339
　Ponta de São Lourenço 340
　wicker industry 335
Mafra 185
　Mafra Palace *185*
Magalhães, Fernão de *see*
　Magellan, Ferdinand
Magellan, Ferdinand 40, 291–2
　birthplace (Sabrosa) 291
Manuel I 42, 43, 116–7, 243
Manuel II 55
Maria, Crown Princess 50

Maria II 52–3
Martinlongo 203
　Museu Minas Antigas (copper
　　mine) 203
Marvão *228*
Mateus 292
　palace and gardens 292
　wine 292
Medóbriga Roman ruins 228
Melgaço 301
Melville, Herman 351
　Moby Dick 351
Mértola 135, 234–5
　blankets 236
Mesão Frio 287–8
metro (Lisbon) 362
Mickle, William 34, 80
Miguel 52
Minho, The 76, 299–302
　Ponte da Barca 76
Miranda do Douro 319
Mogadouro 319
moliceiros see boats
　Moliceiro regatta 87
monasteries and convents
　Alcobaça 26, 30, *116*, 2478
　Batalha *32, 80, 114*, 116, *245,*
　　246
　Carmelite Convent (Aveiro) 269
　Convento do Carmo (Lisbon) 162
　Convento da Conceição (Beja)
　　233
　Convento do Cristo (Tomar) *30,*
　　117, 118, 242, *243*
　Convento de Flor da Rosa (Flor
　　da Rosa) 230
　Convento de Jesus (Aveiro) 269
　Convento dos Lóios *pousada*
　　(Evora) 220
　Convento da Madre de Deus
　　(Lisbon) 161
　Convento de Santo António
　　(Ponte de Lima) 303
　Convento de Santa Clara (Vila do
　　Conde) 300
　Convento de São Gonçalo
　　(Amarante) 286
　Mosteiro Celas (Coimbra) 260
　Mosteiro dos Jerónimos (Lisbon)
　　117, 166
　Mosteiro Refójos (Cabeceiras de
　　Basto) 313
　Mosteiro Santa Clara-a-Nova
　　(New Santa Clara Monastery)
　　(Coimbra) 260
　Mosteiro de Santa Cruz
　　(Coimbra) 259
　Mosteiro de Santa Maria da
　　Vitória *see* Batalha

　Santa Clara-a-Velha (Old Santa
　　Clara Monastery) (Coimbra)
　　260
Monção 301
Monchique *116*, 208
　Caldas de Monchique spa 208
money 355
Mondim de Basto 312–3
Monforte 316
　castle 316
Monsanto 328–9
　castle *329*
　folk music 329
　siege re-enactment 329
Monsaraz 226, *227*
Montalegre 313
　castle 313
Monte Gordo 203
Montemor-o-Novo 218
Montemor-o-Velho 270
Morais, Cristovão de
　King Sebastian 125
Mosteiro de Santa Maria da Vitória
　see **Batalha**
motoring *see* **driving**
mountains 133–4, 301
　Arrábida 191
　Cidadela 316–7
　Cruz Alta 184
　Estrela 133, 134, *322*, 325
　Fóia (Algarve) 208
　Larouco (Tras-os-Montes) 313
　Monchique (Algarve) *208*
　Monte Santa Luzia (Viana do
　　Castelo) 301
　Nervosa 134
　Ossa (Alentejo) 215
　Pico (Azores) 347
　Pico do Arieiro (Madeira) 338
　Pico Ruivo (Madeira) 338
　Picota (Algarve) 208
　São Mamede (Alentejo) 215, 227
　São Salvador do Mundo (Douro
　　Valley) 290
　Sintra 181–2
　Torre 134, 325
music and dance 373–5
　adufe (tambourine) 329
　of Alentejo 218
　in the Duoro valley *66*
　fado 151, 255, 257, 373–4
　gaiteiro (bagpipe) 318
　Manuel Barbosa du Bocage 190
　Monsanto area 329
　Rio de Onor 318
　troubadour culture 30
Muxagata 291
mythology
　Atlantis 345

Barcelos cockerel 303
Lethe, River of Forgetfulness 22, 135, 302
Wamba, legend of 304, 328

n

Napoleon 46, 51, 267
Nasoni, Nicolau 119
national parks and nature reserves
Ilha Berlenga bird sanctuary (Peniche) 250
Ilhas Desertas nature reserve (Madeira) 340
Parque Nacional Peneda-Gerês 128, 134, 299, 302, 375
Parque Natural de Montesinho (Tras-os-Montes) 316, 375
Parque das Queimadas (Madeira) 339
Parque Natural da Ria Formosa (Faro) 201
Parque Natural das Serras de Aire e Candeeiros 135, 245
Parque Natural Serra da Arrábida 375
Parque Natural Serra da Estréla 375
Reserva Natural do Sapal (Castro Marim) 203
National Republican Guard (GNR) 70
Nazaré 248, 248–9, 251
beach 248
bullfights 249
Nossa Senhora da Nazaré 249
religious festival 249
Negreiros, José Almada 84, 127
Fernando Pessoa 127
newspapers 358
nightlife 373–5
Nisa 230

o

Obidos 128, 240, 250
Igreja de Santa Maria 250
Pousada do Castelo 128, 129, 250
Odeceixe 207–8
Odemira 232
Oeiras 175
Ofir 300
Olhão 201
Olhos d'Agua 204
Oliveira do Hospital 326
Order of Our Lord Jesus Christ 31, 203, 243
Ourém 244

Ourique 232–3
Atalaia Bronze-Age site 232
Battle of Ourique 232–3

p

Palmela 189
castle 189
Panóias prehistoric site 292
parks and gardens
Alameda da Resistência ao Fascismo (Guimarães) 305
Aqueduto de São Sebastião (Coimbra) 260
botanical park (Furnas, Azores) 348
parks in Coimbra 260
Jardim Botânico (Funchal, Madeira) 336
Jardim Botânico (Coimbra) 260
Jardim da Manga (Coimbra) 259
Jardim do Palácio de Cristal (Porto) 280
Jardim Público (Evora) 222, 223
Palácio dos Condes de Carvalhal gardens (Estói) 210
Palácio Episcopal garden (Castelo Branco) 327
Parque Dom Infante Pedro (Aveiro) 269
Parque Eduardo VII (Lisbon) 167
Quinta da Bacalhoa gardens (Vila Nogueira de Azeitão) 193
Quinta das Cruzes gardens (Funchal (Madeira)) 336
Quinta do Palheiro Ferreiro gardens (Funchal, Madeira) 336
see also under **Lisbon**
passports 355
Pedro I 32
burial place 31
Pedro II 48
Pedro IV 52
Pedro V 53
Pedro and Inés 30, 247, 260
burial place (Alcobaça) 124, 247
Quintas das Lágrimas (Coimbra) 260
Pegões 218
Peneda-Gerês National Park see national Parks and reserves
Peniche 250
Peninsular War 35, 50–1, 286
Congress of Sintra 81
people 67–70, 313–4
Pessoa, Fernando 56, 67
Mensagem 56
Phelps, Elizabeth 335

Philip I (II of Spain) 44, 47, 190
Philip II (III of Spain) 47–8
Philip III (IV of Spain) 47–8
Philippa, Queen 34–5, 183, 246
burial place (Batalha) 34, 246
Pico island (Azores) 351
Museu dos Baleeiros (whaling museum) 351
Pinhão 285, 290
Pinheiro, Rafael Bordalo 127
Pires, Tomé 43
Suma Oriental 43
plant life 136, 203, 350
politics 31–2, 51–3, 55–61, 217
Armed Forces Movement (MFA) 59
Chartists 52
communism 217
constitution 51–2, 60
corruption 55
coup (1974) 59
European Community membership 60
liberal revolution 276
National Salvation 59
National Union 56
"New State" 56
PIDE 56
Portuguese Socialist Party (PSP) 60
Progressistas 53
Regeneração 53
republicanism 55
Septembrists 52
Social Democratic Central Party 60
socialism 53, 55
Socialist Party 60
pollution 67, 177, 250
Pombal, Marquês de 49, 50, 119, 120, 153, 203, 276, 285
Ponta Delgada (Azores) 347, 348
Ponte da Barca 302
Ponte de Lima 302–3, 303
Pope John XXI 185
Porches 205
Praia da Marinha beach 205
port see wine
Portalegre 227–8
history 227
José Régio museum 228
Sé (Cathedral) 227
tapestry workshops 227
Yellow Palace (Paço Amarelo) 228
Portimão 205
Porto 78, 85, 275–80
Cais da Ribeira 279
Câmara Municipal (Town Hall) 277
Casa do Infante 278

Porto cont'd
  Casa Museu Guerra Junqueiro
    277
  Casa de Serralves art gallery 280
  Dia de São João festival *278*,
    280
  Estação São Bento (station) 277
  excursions 285–6
  Feitoria Inglesa 278
  Foz district 78
  Igreja Santa Clara 277
  Igreja São Francisco 278
  Igreja São Lourenço 278
  Instituto do Vinho do Porto (Port
    Wine Institute) 278
  Jardim do Palácio de Cristal 280
  museums
    de Arte Contemporânea 280
    de Etnografia e História 279
    Nacional Soares dos Reis 280
    Romântico 280
  Palacio do Bispo (Bishop's
    Palace) 277
  Palácio de Bolsa (Stock
    Exchange) 278
  Palácio dos Carrancas 280
  Palácio de São João Novo 279
  Pena Ventosa 277
  Ponte Dom Luís I 280
  Ponte de Dona Maria Pia 280
  port wine tasting 280
  Praça
    da Batalha 279
    da Liberdade 277
  Quinta da Macieirinha 280
  Rua Santa Catarina *279, 280*
  São Idelfonso church 279
  São João Bridge 280
  São João Novo church 278
  Sé (Cathedral) 277
  shopping 279
  Solar do Vinho do Porto 280
  Torre dos Clérigos 279, *281*
  University 279
  Vila Nova de Gaia 85, 280
  wine lodges 104
Porto Covo 231
Porto Moniz (Madeira) 339
Porto de Mós 245
Porto Santo island (Madeira) 340
  Ilhas Desertas nature reserve
    340
  Vila Baleira 340
postal services 358
pousadas 128–9, 362
Póvoa de Varzim 300
Praia de Mira 270
Prester John 38
public holidays 355

q

Queiroz, José Maria Eça de 234
Queluz 181
  Noites de Queluz 181
  Palácio (Palace) *53*, 118, 181
Quillinan, Dorothy 80

r

radio 358
Ramalhoa 80
Rego, Paula 127
Régua 288
Reguengos 226
  prehistoric stones 226
  rug-making 226
religion 69, 75–8
  Catholic Church 32, 55, 69
  Christianity 22–3, 75
  Counter-Reformation 43
  cults 78
  Espírito Santo cult 347
  "Great Schism" 32
  Inquisition, The 42, 44
  Islam 23–4, 69
  Jesuits 49, 50
  Judaism 42, 69
  Marranos 69
  Midnight Baptisms 76
  "New Christians" 42, 44, 50
  patron saints 767, 159
  Pope John XXI 185
  Sufism 23
  superstition 75
Renaissance, The 43
restaurants 370–73
  A Brasileira (Lisbon) *98*, 161
  Café Brasileira (Braga) *307*
  Café Nicola (Lisbon) 155
  Cozinha Velha (Queluz) 181
  Faustino's (Chaves) 315
Restoration Day (1 December) 48
Ribatejo 241–50
  see also individual place names
Ribeira Brava (Madeira) 339
Ribeiro Frio (Madeira) 339
Ribeira Grande (Azores) 348
  spa 348
Rio de Onor 318–9
  festivals 318–9
rivers 135
  Angueira 319
  Corgo 292
  Douro 35, 85–6, 135, *274, 277*,
    275–92
  Gilão *135*, 202
  Guadiana 135, *202*, 203, 215,
    234

  Lima 22, 135, 302
  Maças 319
  Minho 76, 299–302
  Mira 232
  Mondego 135
  Oeiras 234
  Olo 312
  Sequa 202
  Tâmega 286, 312, 315
  Tejo (Tagus) 33, 135, 155, 175,
    189, 327
  Vez 302
  Zêzere 327
Rocha da Pena 205
  Nossa Senhora da Rocha 205

s

Sabrosa 291
Sagres 207
São Filipe 189–90
Santa Joana Princesa 269
São João da Pasqueira 290, 291
São Jorge island (Azores) 350
  Velas 350
São Lourenço 204
  São Lourenço church 204
Sanlucar de Guadiana 203
Santa Luzia 202
Santa Maria island (Azores) 349,
  350
  Anjos 349
  Vila do Porto 349
São Martinho do Porto 249–50
São Miguel island (Azores) 347–8
  see also individual place names
São Pedro de Sintra 181
  craft fair 181–2
São Pedro do Sul 326
  hot springs 326
São Vicente (Madeira) 339
St Vincent 207
Salazar, António de Oliveira *56*,
  56–9, 61
Saldanha, Duke of 53
Salema 207
Sampaio, Jorge 60
Sancho II 29, 30, 197
Santana (Madeira) *338, 339*
Santar 326
Santarém 241
Santiago do Cacém 230–1
  castle 230
  Miróbriga Iron-Age/Roman site
    230–1
Sarmento, Francicso Martins 305
Sebastião 44
security and crime 359
Senhora da Peneda 301

Sequeira, Domingos António 126
Serpa 234
Serra da Sintra 163
Serra do Buçaco (Buçaco Forest) 267–8
    military museum 267
    Palace Hotel 107–8, *267*
Sesimbra 192
Setúbal 190–1
    beaches 191
    Cetóbriga Roman remains 191
    golf 191
    Igreja de Jesus *190*
    Museu de Cidade 190
    Museu Etnográfico 191
    Praça do Bocage 190
    Tróia peninsula *191*
shopping 377
Silva, Aníbal Cavaco 60
Silva, Cristino da 126
Silves 209–10
    beer festival 209
    castle 209
    Sé (Cathedral) *209*, 209–10
Sines 231
Sintra 80, 81, 181–5
    Adega Regional (winery) 184
    Casa Museu Anjos Teixeira 183
    Castelo dos Mouros 184
    Convention of Sintra 184
    Convento dos Capuchos 184
    Estefânia district 183
    Museu de Arte Contemporânea 127
    Museu de Arte Moderno 183
    Museu de Brinquedo (Toy Museum) 183
    Museu Ferreira de Castro 182
    Museu Regional (Municipal Art Gallery) 182
    Paço Real *see* Palácio Nacional
    Palácio Nacional 117, *180, 182*, 182–3
    Palácio da Pena 120 *121, 183*, 183–4
    Palácio de Seteais *184*
    Parque da Pena 184
    Quinta de Monserrate and gardens 184
    Quinta da Regalaria 184
    Sintra Vila 182
    Town Hall 183
    transport 183
Soajo 301
Soares, Mário *59*, 60
Sortelha 324
Southey, Robert 80, 192
Souza-Cardoso, Amadeo 127
Spínola, António de 59

sports and activities 376
    bullfights 169, 179, 249, 314, 377
    canoeing 260, 327
    Cruz Quebrada soccer stadium 175
    fishing 327, 347
    football 376
    golf 176, 177, 178, 204, 250, 339, 347, 376
    hiking and walking 346, 347
    horse riding 179
    motor racing 177
    scuba diving 191, 347, 348
    skiing 376
    tennis 347, 376
    watersports 232, 327, 376
    whale-watching 347, 351
    wild boar hunting 217
    windsurfing 179, 376

t

Tavira 202
taxis 362
telephone 358
Teles, Queen Leonor 32, 258
Teles, Maria 258
television 358
Terceira island (Azores) 349
    festivals 349
tipping 358
Tomar 242–4
    Convento do Cristo *30*, 117, 118, 242, *243*
    Nossa Senhora da Conceição 118
    São João Baptista church 243–4
    Santa Maria dos Olivais church 244
    Synagogue and museum 243
Torralva, Diogo de 118
Torre 325
    pilgrimage 325
Torreira 87
    Moliceiro regatta 87
tourism 69, 199–200, 203, 204
tourist offices
    overseas 356
    in Portugal 359
Trafaria 189
    Cristo Rei (Christ the King) monument 189
trains 357, 361
transport *356, 357, 361*
    Corgo railway *316*
    in Lisbon 153, 362
    in Sintra 183
    train journey to Barril (Luz de Tavira) 202

Trás-os-Montes 67, 311–9
    see also individual place names
    agriculture 311
    Barragem do Alto Rabagão lake 313
    Barroso district 313
    climate 311
    geography 311
    getting there 312
    Serra de Alvão 312
    Serra da Padrela 312
Treaty
    of Alcañices 29, 30, 33
    of Lisbon 48
    of Methuen 48–9, 276
    of Tordesillas 40
    of Windsor 32
    of Zamora 25

u

UNESCO World Heritage Sites 355
    Alcobaça 26, 116, 247
    Angra do Heroismo (Azores) 349
    Batalha *32, 80, 114*, 116, *245, 246*
    Cais da Ribeira (Porto) 279
    Parque Arqueológico do Vale Côa (Douro) 291
    Convento do Cristo (Tomar) 242
    Evora 218
    Mosteiro dos Jerónimos *117, 166*
    Sintra 181–5
universities
    (Lisbon) 169
    (Coimbra) *42, 69*, 255, 256
    (Porto) 279

v

Valença do Minho 128, *301*
    Pousada de São Teotónio 128, 301
    railway museum 301
Vasco, Grão *see* Fernandes, Vasco
Vendas Novas 218
Viana do Castelo 300–301
    Misericórdia hospital 301
    Monte Santa Luzia 301
    Nossa Senhora da Agonia church 301
    Palácio dos Távoras 300–1
    pilgrimage and festival 301
    Praça da República 301
Vieira, Domingos 126
Vieira, Francisco ("Vieira Portuense") 126
Vila do Conde *299*, 299–300
Vila Franca do Campo (Azores) 348

Vila Franco do Lima 110
Vila Fresca de Azeitão 193
Vila Nogueira de Azeitão 192–3
  Azeitão fair 193
  José Maria da Fonseca winery
    and museum 193
  Palácio Távora 192–3
  Quinta da Bacalhoa gardens 193
Vila Nova de Foz Côa 291
Vila Nova de Milfontes 231–2
Vila Nova de Gaia 85, 280
Vila Real (Douro) 292
Vila Real de Santo António 203
Vila Verde 302
Vila Viçosa *225*, 225–6
  archeological museum 225
  castle 225
  Paço Ducal (Ducal Palace of the
    Braganças) 225
  Porta do Nó (Knot Gate) *226*
Vinhais 316
  Parque Natural de Montesinho
    316
Viriathus 22
Viseu 325–6
  Feira de São Mateus 326
  Igreja da Misericórdia 325
  Museu Grão Vasco 325–6

Sé (Cathedral) 325
Vista Alegre 270
  porcelain factory 270
Vouzela 326

W

Waugh, Evelyn 80
**Wellesley, Sir Arthur, Duke of
  Wellington** 35, *51*, 81, 267
wildlife *136*, 136–7, 203
wine 35, 49, 103–8, 198, 267,
  289, *290*, 299
  Alentejo 235
  Alto Douro Wine Company 276
  Barraida wine country 268
  Caves Aliança winery (Curia) 268
  Caves Borlido winery (Curia) 268
  Caves Império winery (Curia) 268
  José Maria da Fonseca winery
    and museum (Vila Nogueira de
    Azeitão) 193
  Madeira 103, *336*, 337–8
  phylloxera disease 108
  port 35, 69, 85, 103–6, 109,
    275–6, 280, 285, 287–8,
    294–5
  Port Wine Rally (Estoril) 177

Quinta da Aveleda winery tour
  (Amarante) 287
regions 107–8
Solar do Instituto do Vinho do
  Porto (Port Wine Institute)
  (Lisbon) 162
tasting 104, 105, 268, 280,
  287, 337–8
vinhos mortos (wine of the dead)
  (Boticas) 315
vinhos verdes 103, 106–7, 286,
  287
wine lodges *284*
wineries *see individual entries
  under* **wine**
women 68
  Feminism 68
  in the Armed Forces 70

Z

Zacuto, Abraham 42
  Almanach Perpetuum 42
Zambujeira do Mar 232
zoos, wildlife parks and aquariums
  Aquário Vasco da Gama
    (Dáfundo) 175
  Jardim Zoológico (Lisbon) 168

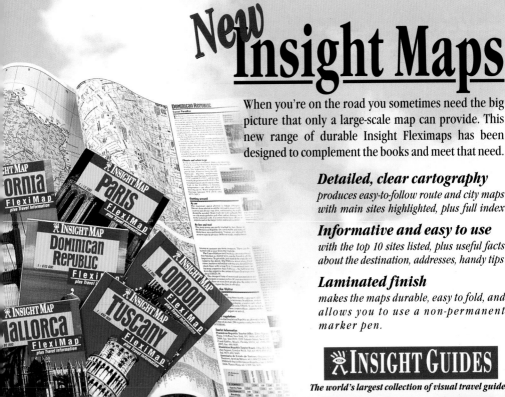